PITCAIRN

Children of the Bounty

PITCAIRN

Children of the Bounty

IAN M. BALL

VICTOR GOLLANCZ LTD   LONDON   1973

PRINTED IN GREAT BRITAIN BY
LOWE AND BRYDONE (PRINTERS) LTD, THETFORD, NORFOLK

For Lele and our small trio,
who unmutinously made this trip with me . . .

INTRODUCTION

F OR MORE THAN one and three-quarter centuries — seven generations — Pitcairn, a hump of somber basaltic rock just below the Tropic of Capricorn in the South Pacific, has been the setting for one of the most curious social experiments the world has seen. That experiment may now be drawing to a close.

The pages ahead reassess the H.M.S. *Bounty*–William Bligh–Fletcher Christian story, review Pitcairn's extraordinary and at times bizarre history, and examine the present condition of its eighty-five inhabitants, descendants for the most part of the *Bounty* mutineers and the Tahitian women they took with them as willing concubines in their search for an island of refuge. In studying both past and present, the book has two separate explorations, but the reader, I trust, will find that they mesh fairly easily and satisfactorily.

The main thrust of my historical review is a vindication of William Bligh. It is long overdue. Of the tens of millions of words that have been written this century and last about Bligh and the mutiny, a staggeringly high proportion is pure, easily detectable fiction. Yet the subject is one of the greatest adventures of the sea in our literary treasure house. If for only that reason, it deserves to rest on a historical foundation that is as honest and accurate as we can make it. It was, in many ways, the classic revolt. The high drama of it lasted long beyond Fletcher Christian's insurrectionary stroke. It set in train a fascinating progression of events that pointed up both human good and human evil. The facts themselves needed no writer's varnish.

Why, then, has each generation turned to a fictional account in its retelling of the story? Is it because we wanted the story told a certain way and no other, with the role of monster allotted to one of the protagonists, the role of romantic underdog to the other? Did it all fit so beautifully into our ideas about the South Seas and escapism that no one wanted to tamper with the tale as it had been passed down to us? Whatever the reason, Bligh's character, reputation, and the manner in which he commanded his doughty little square-rigger have been subjected to grotesque distortions over the years. Interest in the whole *Bounty* tale seems to have undergone periodic revivals this century and last. And as each new writer or scenarist has picked up the story, the tendency has been to paint Bligh a shade blacker, to toss in a few more demonic touches. Poor Bligh! If we study the portraits and engravings of him in various British museums, we are confronted with a picture of a sensible and rather benign-looking individual — a bit on the prim side, perhaps, but a person one would certainly like to spend some time getting to know. Granted, these portraits were commissioned works and the artists had a vested interest in achieving the most flattering effect. But these contemporary studies of Bligh could hardly have provided honest inspiration to the Metro-Goldwyn-Mayer publicity man who, in launching the studio's first *Mutiny on the Bounty* film in 1935, wrote that Bligh was "a sea-going disaster, begotten in a galley, and born under a gun! His hair was rope, his teeth were marlin spikes . . ."

The reader will find conjectural passages in my thesis, although not, I hope, on the level of flamboyance attained by the MGM man. I have endeavored to identify conjecture and speculation where I felt this was necessary. So far as possible, however, I have drawn my information from actual records made at the time the events were taking place. They have been available in the archives all these years; and while they have been consulted constantly, many who studied them used the material simply as a framework for fanciful literary embellishment. Unfortunately, incontrovertible facts about every aspect of the mutiny and the behavior of the principal actors are impossible to produce at this remove. In any

event, truth, like beauty, is to some extent in the eye of the be-
holder. Keats has spoken of the occasional value of "truth of imagination." And Mailer suggests that facts are hardly facts without
their nuances. Their points are well made. But in this defense of
Bligh, I attempt to show that distortion rather than honest interpretation has been the rule in the historical and literary treatment
of the mutiny. There has been, with few exceptions, imagination
in place of authenticity, "nuances" aplenty that turned the very
facts inside out.

My research was carried out over a period of fifteen months
using material from the British archives and various libraries, predominantly the New York Public Library, which has a rich and
comprehensive file on the whole *Bounty* story and on the little
community that came into being in the South Pacific as a direct
result of the mutiny. Certain handsomely published facsimile editions of rare eighteenth-century volumes in the Mitchell Library
in Sydney were also of considerable value.

To round out my research, I went to Pitcairn. It took almost
a year of planning to overcome logistical and bureaucratic hurdles.
The Pitcairn Islanders and the British government, both of whom
have had experience in the past with persons searching for a place
in which to eat the lotus, have drawn up a policy under which
any individual wishing to remain longer than twenty-four hours
on the island must first receive the unanimous approval of the
islanders. And this approval in turn must be endorsed by the
protectorate's Governor in far-off Auckland. The forms warn you
that permission is granted only in "rare" circumstances. If you
qualify, the Commissioner for Pitcairn issues a license to land
which, in the fine print, sets out certain rules for behavior on
the island, lays down a strict prohibition against ardent spirits,
and warns of instant deportation if there is any breach of Pitcairn
law. (By what means of transportation, it does not specify.)

My wife and three children, then aged from four to nine, New
Yorkers by life-style and Australian-Americans by nationality, traveled with me to the island. We undertook this 17,000-mile expedition as a family venture, partly because we are that sort of
family, and partly because I felt it would be a rewarding experience
for us all, and might, in the bargain, provide some diversion for a

community of twenty-two families living in conditions approaching total isolation from the world. We were the first family in a considerable length of time to be granted permission to reside on the island in a nonofficial capacity.

Pitcairn's physical isolation may be truly appreciated only by those who set out to reach Bounty Bay. There are other microdots on the inviting blue of a Pacific map that are not only accessible nowadays but are energetically promoted by the travel industry. Easter Island has twice-a-week jet service from Santiago. One alights from a comfortable plane today to inspect Charles Darwin's Galápagos Islands.

Pitcairn Island remains to the travel men a "special case" and probably will stay that way for as long as a settlement exists there. There is no harbor, not even a basin where the smallest yacht could find shelter, and foolish millions would have to be spent to create a safe anchorage. There are no plans, or even thoughts, of an airstrip. Even in the days when steamship lines were more adventurous, their accountants less concerned with computerized printouts of fuel-oil costs and schedules, a passage to Pitcairn was an uncertain business. The ticket was always furnished on a conditional basis. Many have set out aboard liners and freighters from Panama or Auckland with Pitcairn as their destination, only to find themselves carried past the island and on to the opposite side of the Pacific. If the captain decided that seas off Bounty Bay were too rough to warrant the time, effort, and risk in transferring passengers to the Pitcairn longboats, he would sound his siren to that effect and steam on.

One after another, the New York and London offices of shipping companies whose vessels ply the South Pacific and make an occasional mail or cargo drop off Pitcairn refused even to entertain the prospect of carrying passengers there. A veteran New York travel agent accepted the challenge of my travel requirements, tried gamely for a few weeks to find even a tramp steamer willing to take us, but was forced to give up. The last company to provide even sporadic passenger service to Pitcairn discontinued the call in 1968. A British or New Zealand Navy supply ship is usually employed to carry the occasional official who visits the island, but this course is not open to a private expedition of seven, including female members.

Had I been prepared to wait uncertain months, bags packed, ready to leave at short notice, it might have been possible to pick up a passage of opportunity aboard a small cargo vessel following the Southern Great Circle route across the Pacific, which lies a few hundred miles south of the island. This is the course the islanders have to follow when they wish to leave Pitcairn for the world, or return home. But this solution would have left me stranded on Pitcairn with no guaranteed means of departing.

The only answer was a private yacht charter which proved to be both expensive and complicated. The complications arose be- . cause I was anxious to cut down as far as possible the amount of open-ocean sailing to reach Pitcairn, partly because we were traveling with children and partly because I could not afford to spend a month tossing about on the Pacific under sail. The round-trip distance to Pitcairn from Tahiti, the only feasible chartering point, is the equivalent of a transatlantic crossing. I explored the possibility of chartering a flying boat or large seaplane. I drew a blank. The seas off Pitcairn are invariably too rough for a landing, and in any event it would require a huge craft to do the distance without refueling. The Pitcairners can look after boats but hardly planes.

In the end, I turned to the French Air Force, which I knew had plenty of aircraft in the region because of their nuclear test establishment. I found myself dealing with an organization whose full name, Centre d'Expérimentations du Pacifique, has such an awesome, Stanley Kubrickian ring to it that the local French and Polynesians try to refer to it only by its initials, CEP. The matter was referred to Paris, and somewhat to my surprise, the French authorities said we *could* venture with camera equipment and notebooks and *enfants* into the region where they detonate thermonuclear weapons, the French Eniwetok.

The French Air Force flew our party from Papeete, Tahiti, to Hao, an atoll airstrip which is the prime base for the test program, and then on to Totégégie, another atoll strip built for support functions in the Gambiers. A French naval launch was waiting there to take us, cameras sealed, across to Rikitéa, a delightful little village, the only settlement left in the Gambiers, where a remnant of a once-important Polynesian hierarchical society clings to survival in these nuclear days. Our ketch was moored in Rikitéa, a rare nonmilitary visitor to the island. The *Maylis* had sailed from Papeete for Rikitéa twelve days earlier, the day we had set out from New York. We would be using the yacht for a total of only six days but were obliged to charter it for more than six weeks.

All these islands and atolls are part of a restricted military area, carefully patrolled by the French Army, Navy, Air Force, Marines, the Gendarmerie Nationale, even the Foreign Legion. A large American schooner I had hoped at one point to charter from Tahiti was flatly refused permission to put into the Gambiers. To enter the area requires French military clearance — even, I discovered, for our four-year-old Duncan. The authorities at CEP insisted we spend ten days in Tahiti before flying to Hao and the Gambiers, a period they referred to ominously as the requisite amount of time for "file-building purposes."

With evidently clean dossiers, we headed for the antique simplicity of Pitcairn by way of some of the warts of today's society, the grim outposts of twentieth-century nuclear technology.

We lived with the Pitcairners for just short of a month, a period we would have extended for both professional and personal reasons had not the ketch been standing by for us, 350 miles away in the Tuamotu Archipelago, the fee mounting at a rate of $130 a day. With a two-member camera team, our party represented an 8.2 percent increase in the numbers on Pitcairn, an instant population explosion with which the gentle islanders coped with grace, kindness, and a good deal of hard work to make us comfortable.

In some respects, our stay on the island was a time-machine journey back to the nineteenth century, even, fleetingly, to the late eighteenth century. But we also found a community engaged in a flirtation of sorts with the things of the twentieth century, a desperate attempt to bring a little of the modern world to what is probably our planet's most remote inhabited island. (Even Eskimo outposts and small communities in mid-ocean nowadays have regular air links; heavy transport planes land at the South Pole Station. Pitcairn has never had an air service, of course, and does not envisage one.) This flirtation may represent the island's final fling. It is taking place at a time when a once self-sufficient island finds its dependence on the outside world growing slowly but inexorably, while both its human numbers and its sea links with that world decline perilously. The young, the middle-aged, all but the very old, are deserting their tax-free native island, the crumb of land Fletcher Christian thought — wrongly as it developed — he could turn into a utopian haven. His descendants no longer wish to live as the curios of the South Seas.

The present Pitcairners have seen their numbers decline from a population of 233 in 1937 to little more than one third that figure today. They now talk of the possibility that the island might have to be evacuated in the foreseeable future and wonder what will happen to their homes, their boats, their school, their church, if that becomes necessary. Will hippies from California or Australia try to take it over and make a fresh start at building a paradise in isolation? It is one of their fears.

We found on Pitcairn a handful of people both stoic and good. They exhibited some, certainly not all, of the natural imperfections in man's character. Whether from deep conscience or from the fear that many isolated people have of the spiritual unknown, the majority applied themselves diligently to the business of worshiping their Maker. Ranged against the drab picture of contemporary human greed, the eighty-five Pitcairners shine in their unselfishness and their spirit of cooperation. Yet most are as mesmerized as the rest of us by the tools of easy living and, with obvious disadvantages, preoccupied with how they might be won. "It's hard to build a Garden of Eden in this old world," said Tom Christian. "There are those who are godly and those who are careless."

The little Pitcairn society that survives is a living laboratory for those wishing to investigate such things as the social *mores* of a closed society, the laws of heredity, the economic structure, the interrelationships, the family life, the systems of law and government, and so on. The second part of my book does not set out in any way to be a work of social or physical anthropology. In those areas I have only the qualifications of an educated layman. Rather it is the result of an intensive study within a small group by someone with the credentials and experience accumulated over twenty-six years as a working journalist and correspondent in most of the countries of the world. I have tried to give the reader the flavor and feel of this remarkable community as well as its essential facts and statistical outline.

If there are areas of their life examined here and passages in this book which the Pitcairners would prefer not to be treated in public print, I hope my friends there will read them with understanding and accept that they have been set down on paper solely in the interests of an honest investigation.

I trust the reader will embark on Part I, the Improbable Past, with sympathy and understanding for the dead William Bligh, and on Part II, the Improbable Present, with those same charitable qualities for the living Pitcairners.

I.M.B.

New York City,
March, 1972

CONTENTS

PART ONE

IMPROBABLE PAST

CHAPTER ONE

A VOLCANIC AFTERTHOUGHT

I T WAS SURELY — on the part of whatever preternatural force or chemical mystery that created our planet — a volcanic afterthought. It rises like a green-and-brown iceberg from the blue immensity of the South Pacific, two degrees of latitude below the Tropic of Capricorn and 1,350 miles southeast of Tahiti. It is ringed perpetually with a collar of white, foaming water and probably has worn that ruff of crashing surf since the cosmic dawn. It was born from the sea floor in that area where the vastest of all oceans runs out of islands. It qualifies as part of the South Seas, but only just. Between it and the wastes of Antarctica lies hardly a crumb of charted land. It is among the world's most remote inhabited islands, perhaps *the* most remote.

Seen from an approaching ship — and only rarely has it been inspected from the air — it is a majestic sight, imposing in a Gibraltar-like way. It has been likened by other travelers to a crouching lion, but the simile failed to register on my imagination. Viewed at closer range, its rock escarpments rising up sheer from the breakers, clouds of sea fowl wheeling high overhead, it presents a picture both awesome and eerie, one that makes the viewer realize somberly the extremes of loneliness. Once one is ashore, it offers on all sides the soft, natural beauty of the subtropics, the pastels of the hibiscus, the perfume of the jasmine, the tranquil grace of the palms. Arcady itself? A place of eternal and supreme bliss? Not quite. In fact quite a few notches below

Pitcairn . . . a lonely rock in a lonely sea . . . viewed from the northwest.

the paradisiacal upper limits. *Gothic* is one of the adjectives that came to mind when I first saw it.

It is Pitcairn Island, the setting in 1790 for the final act of one of the greatest sea dramas of all time, the mutiny aboard His Majesty's Armed Transport *Bounty* on April 28, 1789. Inch for inch, it is the repository of more history — romantic history, bloody history, bogus history — than any other island in the Pacific.

It is a compact island, measuring a bit less than one mile by two miles for a total area of 1,120 acres or 1.75 square miles. It is roughly rectangular in shape except for a promontory of a couple of hundred yards that juts out from the northeastern corner, beginning at a place named Where Freddie Fall, encompassing Ned Young's Ground and Jack's Yam, and ending at a crescent cove called Down Rope.

From its inhospitable crags and precipices, the island rises, in the space of a few hundred yards, to a height of 1,100 feet above sea level. In total area, much of which is unusable since the cliffs make up 27 percent of the land area and flat land only 8 percent, it is a shade larger than New York's Central Park and about four times the size of Hyde Park, London. In essence, it is a basalt mass representing the top of a volcano whose base is far below the sea. It came into being as a result of progressive volcanic activity. There is no coral reef and virtually no coastal shelf. Geologists say its formation is comparable with that of other Pacific islands, such as Samoa, Tahiti, or Hawaii. The significant difference is that the larger islands have rivers; Pitcairn has none. The former have been inhabited continuously by Polynesians; in Pitcairn, there was a dramatic and unexplained break in habitation, perhaps around the end of the Middle Ages.

Pitcairn was first seen by European eyes in July, 1767, by a youth whom military nepotism had carried to the South Seas. From the fore-topgallant-crosstrees of H.M.S. *Swallow*, he let out an exultant cry of "L-a-a-a-nd H-o-o!" as the *Swallow* was beating her way south through uncharted waters.

"It is so high that we saw it at a distance of more than fifteen leagues," * Captain Philip Carteret penned in the *Swallow*'s log, "and it having been discovered by a young gentleman, son to Major Pitcairn of the Marines, we called it PITCAIRN'S ISLAND." (A few years later, the same Major John Pitcairn was to play a role in the first act of a larger drama. He was in command of George III's Royal Marines at Concord when the first shot was fired in the American War of Independence. He lived to take part in the Battle of Bunker Hill, but he died of wounds on the battlefield.)

Carteret and his crew simply saw the island in outline from the weather rail of the *Swallow*. They were unable to make a landing because of the relentless surf "which at this season broke upon it with great violence." (July is, of course, midwinter in the Southern Hemisphere.) Carteret sailed away, noting only that Pitcairn's Island had lush vegetation and obviously adequate rainfall, and appeared to be uninhabited. He returned to England in 1769 after

* A league equals three nautical, or statute miles. Our trip to Pitcairn provided one of those rare and delicious moments when one can verify personally a statistic from the history books. The visibility was wretched when we approached the island but perfect when we sailed away. In a back-to-front way, we were able to check Carteret's figure. As the tip of Pitcairn was disappearing from view, the pointer on the old brass log at the stern of our ketch was registering precisely 45 nautical miles or 15 leagues.

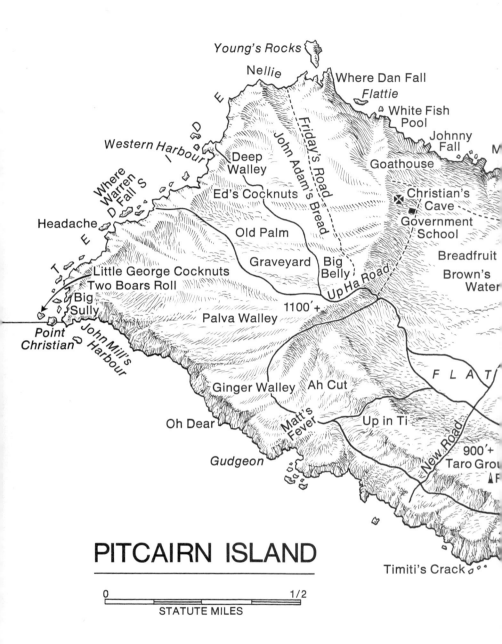

Young's Rocks

Nellie

Where Dan Fall

Flattie

White Fish Pool

Johnny Fall

E

D

Western Harbour

Friday's Road

John Adam's Bread

Deep Walley

Goathouse

M

Where Warren D Fall

Ed's Cocknuts

S

Christian's Cave

Headache

Old Palm

Government School

E

Graveyard

Big Belly

Breadfruit

T

Little George Cocknuts

Two Boars Roll

Up Ha Road

Brown's Water

Big Sully

1100'+

Palva Walley

Point Christian

John Mill's Harbour

Ginger Walley

Ah Cut

F L A T

Oh Dear

Matt's Fever

Up in Ti

Gudgeon

New Road

900'+

Taro Grou

A F

Timiti's Crack

PITCAIRN ISLAND

0   1/2

STATUTE MILES

Sam. H. Bryant

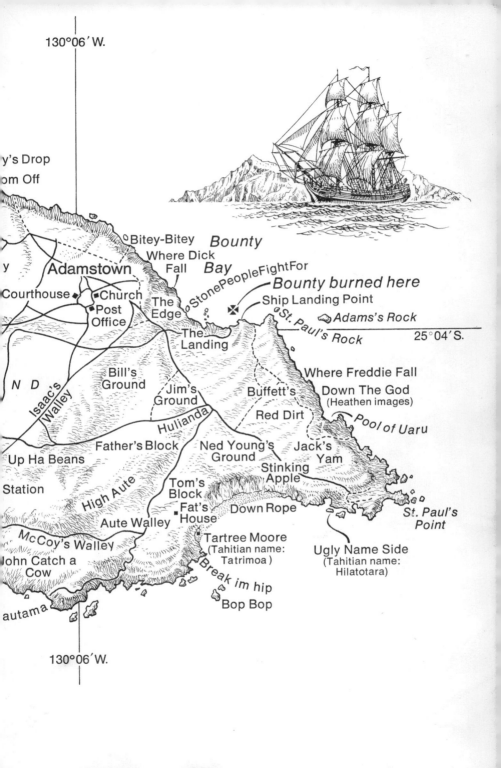

130°06′ W.

y's Drop
om Off

Bitey-Bitey   *Bounty*

Where Dick
Fall   *Bay*   StonePeopleFightFor

Adamstown   *Bounty burned here*

Courthouse   Church   Ship Landing Point

Post
Office   The
Edge   *St. Paul's Rock*   Adams's Rock

The
Landing   25°04′ S.

N D   Bill's
Ground   Where Freddie Fall

Isaac's
Walley   Jim's
Ground   Buffett's   Down The God
(Heathen images)

Hulianda   Red Dirt   Pool of Uaru

Father's Block   Ned Young's
Ground   Jack's
Yam

Up Ha Beans   Stinking
Apple

Station   High Aute   Tom's
Block   *St. Paul's
Point*

Aute Walley   Fat's
House   Down Rope

McCoy's Walley   Tartree Moore
(Tahitian name:
Tatrimoa)   Ugly Name Side
(Tahitian name:
Hilatotara)

John Catch a
Cow   Break im hip

autama   Bop Bop

130°06′ W.

circling the globe. His sketchy description and navigational fix — a few hundred miles off as it turned out, owing to a faulty timepiece — would be of only academic interest for the next twenty years until Fletcher Christian and eight of the mutineers who seized control of the *Bounty* from Lieutenant William Bligh began to comb the Pacific for an island where they could hide from both the wrath and the long arm of the British Admiralty.

Had Carteret in 1767 been able to breach the surf at Pitcairn, his landing party would have confirmed that the only mammal on the island was the Polynesian rat. But they would have made discoveries of some anthropological and archaeological significance. Scattered throughout the island, there for the picking, were literally hundreds of relics of Polynesian civilization. Crudely sculpted stone gods, related to but less ambitious than the pug-nosed tribal gods of Easter Island some 1,400 miles to the east, still guarded sacred burial rites. Human skeletons were to be dug up a quarter of a century later by the *Bounty* mutineers. Polished stone adzes, earth ovens, gouges, coconut-shell drinking vessels, and other artifacts of Polynesian craftsmanship were found abandoned. Beside one *marae*, a Tahitian-like open-air temple where simple idols were set out on a raised stone platform, rested a sun-bleached human skull. The household tools had been dropped beside the remains of dwellings built from coconut wood and tough *miro*, a darkish, handsomely grained wood native to the island.

Given the manner in which precious tools had been left behind, it is a safe assumption that the island was evacuated hurriedly by its original inhabitants. What had driven them away from their fortress island? Where did they move to? The few archaeologists who have visited Pitcairn have been unable to provide the answers. The guess is that they moved to the Gambier Islands at the base of the Tuamotus, 350 miles to the northwest, voyaging presumably in the long outrigger canoes Polynesians have used for centuries.

They paddled away from Pitcairn leaving their crude bas-relief carvings inside caves and on cliff faces. There were childish stick-men, an occasional attempt at fleshing out a human figure, awkward-looking animals and birds, crosses, starfish, and a symbol within a circle that vaguely resembles today's peace emblem. Some fine specimens survive to this day at Down Rope Cove.

If we are correct in assuming that these original Pitcairners migrated to the Gambiers and their hub, the large lagoon of Mangaréva, it presumably was a return to the land of their fathers. Some of the cliff drawings and artifacts found on Pitcairn have their rough counterparts in the handiwork of the early Mangaréva islanders. The first settlers on Pitcairn had no written language and may not have progressed much beyond the Stone Age. We do not even know what they called their island.

Three years after his discovery of tiny Pitcairn, when Carteret sailed the *Swallow* home, excitement over the "Great South Sea" was running at fever-pitch in the drawing rooms and government offices on the Continent as well as in London. The tales, sketches, and artifacts brought home by Wallis and Bougainville had triggered a sensation that diverted eighteenth-century Europe until George Washington's revolt against the Crown, and later, the French Revolution, gave it something weightier to ponder.

The Pacific, however, remained in vogue for a good many years. Rousseau, in a sense, had set the scene in 1749 when he wrote, in his *Discours sur les arts et sciences*, of the Noble Savage, the primitive man living in an earthly tropical paradise with no need of civilization's religious and social constraints. If Tahiti (or Otaheite as the white man called it until he realized he was running the Tahitian article "o" into the name), had not existed, eighteenth-century Europe would have had to invent it or some place similar. Collectors were meeting each ship that returned from the Pacific, offering dazzling prices to any seaman who would part with Tahitian idols, ornamental headdresses, drums, or even seashells and ornamental bark cloth. Landscapists, portraitists, and engravers, working from the sketches brought home by artists aboard the British and French vessels, found a ready market for their pictures, even though they were idealized and heavily Europeanized views of Tahiti and the life of the Noble Savage. The theatrical producers and writers were also busy. *Omai, or a Trip Around the World* was produced as a new Christmas pantomime at the Theatre Royal in Covent Garden in 1785. Three years later, the sensation of the Paris stage was a pantomime in four acts, *La Mort du Capitaine Cook*. Both were lavish productions with gorgeous costumes and the sort of dramatic stage effects which Radio City Music Hall indulges in today.

The accounts of the astonishingly casual approach to sex in the Great South Sea, the stories of open-air lovemaking between English tars (and the gentlemen officers) and brown nymphs under the palms of Otaheite, were adding new zest to the gossip in the coffee shops of Dr. Johnson's London. The Pacific was influencing even the divertissements being offered in the salons of eroticism which did such thriving business in London toward the close of the eighteenth century. Within months after Dr. John Hawkesworth had published in 1773 his massive official account of Captain James Cook's first voyage to the Pacific in the *Endeavour*, Charlotte Hayes, the keeper of an elegant brothel in King's Place, Pall Mall, decided to Tahitianize the proceedings in her establishment. In his *Sexual Life in England*, published in 1938, Iwan Bloch writes that Mrs. Hayes had been impressed by Hawkesworth's account of how in Tahiti "young men and girls often copulate publicly before the people, receiving good advice from the bystanders, usually women, amongst whom the most important inhabitants are to be found. Thus the girls (of 11 years) receive their information at an early age."

Mrs. Hayes decided to re-create the free love of Otaheite in a drawing room in wintry London. One day, according to Bloch, she sent the following invitation to her clients: "Mrs. Hayes commends herself respectfully to Lord —— and takes the liberty of advising him that this evening at 7 o'clock precisely 12 beautiful nymphs, spotless virgins, will carry out the famous Feast of Venus as it is celebrated in Otaheite, under the instruction and leadership of Queen Oberea (which role will be taken by Mrs. Hayes herself)."

Mrs. Hayes's clients, Bloch tells us, "were nearly all impotent debauchees who required every possible stimulation for the satisfaction of their lusts." For her Tahitian evening, twenty-three gentlemen responded to her invitation, including five members of the House of Commons. "Punctually at 7 o'clock the feast began, for which, for the men's parts, Mrs. Hayes had engaged twelve athletic youths. These youths, with the nymphs, now celebrated the

Tahiti Venus Feast before the eyes of the entranced audience; after which a sumptuous meal was taken."

Pitcairn, of course, contributed to none of this excitement. The interest in the 1770's and 1780's was in one island: Tahiti and its race of healthy, beautiful, well-adjusted people who played, made love, worked very little, and had scarcely an earthly care. (Once the first flush of excitement over Tahiti's discovery had passed, Europe would realize that the Tahitians were incestuous, strangled many of their babies at birth, made war constantly, indulged occasionally in human sacrifices, and were artful thieves. Until then, the Old World accepted almost unquestioningly the idyllic life-style of the Tahitians.)

It was against this backdrop of Pacific fever — a backdrop that has special relevance to the argument I develop in later pages — that Lieutenant William Bligh, Master's Mate Fletcher Christian, and forty-four officers and men sailed from Spithead in December, 1787, on a unique mission, the Royal Navy's first operation of a purely botanical nature. Scarcely more than half of them would ever make it back to England, ten of them doing so as prisoners in leg and wrist irons, the survivors of fourteen alleged mutineers rounded up in Tahiti and taken away in a special roundhouse prison, the infamous "Pandora's Box," built for them aboard the capture ship, H.M.S. *Pandora*.

The little *Bounty* would come to an ignominious end, cannibalized and burned to the waterline in Bounty Bay, Pitcairn, half a world away from Spithead, in an effort to cover up one of the worst crimes ever perpetrated against the Royal Navy.

The mutineers who escaped with Christian would live, not happily or ever after, but, with one exception, miserably and briefly in a strange and lonely island retreat which they managed to turn into their own special hell. They would leave scant records of their part in the *Bounty* insurrection, and in so doing spawn a controversy about heroes and villains that continues to this day.

CHAPTER TWO

THE MISSION, THE MUTINY

THE MISSION of the *Bounty* had its beginning in a simple interdepartmental memo. In the spring of 1787, a King's Messenger carried a letter from one of the Secretaries of State of William Pitt's government to the Lords Commissioners of the Admiralty. If masking in euphemistic language the fact that this was a crude official subsidy for Britain's slaveowners abroad, the bureaucrat who penned it at least came to the point:

The Merchants and Planters interested in His Majesty's West India Possessions have represented that the Introduction of the Bread Fruit Tree into the Islands in those Seas to constitute an Article of Food would be very essential Benefit to the Inhabitants, and have humbly solicited that Measures may be taken for procuring some Trees of that Description to be transplanted in the said islands. . . . I am in consequence to signify to your Lordships His Majesty's Command that you do cause a Vessel of proper Class to be stored and Victualled for this Service. . . .

The planters in Jamaica and other British colonies in the Caribbean had read eagerly the accounts of Dampier, Cook, and other early Pacific voyagers who had seen the plump breadfruit hanging like large grapefruit amidst the lacquer-shiny, serrated leaves of the bread tree. The "Indians" — the generic name Europeans were applying to all nonwhites they encountered in the Pacific — showed the intruders how to cook the breadfruit. With its rough, pimply skin left intact, the breadfruit was placed in the glowing embers of wood or coconut shells and husks and left for an hour or two. When the time was up, nature had done the work of a baker. Peel off the skin and, presto! instant bread.

At least that was the attractive theory brought home by the navigators and scientists who accompanied them. Once baked, the starchy mass inside the breadfruit* *faintly* resembled cooked dough. But there was an aftertaste, insipid enough to convince the least demanding palate that the "bread" had no connection with wheat, rye, or any other known grain. The baked breadfruit was pecked at disdainfully by the English officers and tried on the men in the forecastle with equally unenthusiastic results. But Dampier and Cook realized that it was nutritious and could keep a man alive and able to do heavy physical labor on cane and cotton plantations. It grew abundantly in tropical latitudes with little tending. It was the perfect food for black bellies. The ugly denouement of the whole *Bounty* mission was perhaps merited by the cynicism which went into its planning.

In searching for a vessel to carry out the unorthodox Royal Command, the Admiralty realized at once that it could not spare any of its big men-of-war, the imposing "seventy-fours," or the Royal Navy's "first-rates." France — or Spain or Holland — might renew hostilities at any moment, and every vessel would be needed to protect the home ports and British merchant trade.

As they had done with Cook's missions to the Pacific, the Lords Commissioners of the Admiralty looked over the merchant navy to see what was available. They found a small but sturdy vessel, a coastal trading ship, which had been built at Hull less than three years earlier. It was bought for £1,950 — the Admiralty whittled down the owner's asking price of £2,600 — and sailed to the naval dockyard at Deptford on the Thames for refitting. The modifications came to £4,456. If any cost overruns were involved, they were of the most modest dimensions. Most of the money was ap-

---

* Although it resembles a fruit when seen on the branch, it more accurately should be considered a vegetable. "Breadvegetable," however, doesn't have quite the gastronomic ring to it that "breadfruit" possesses. Not that the name mattered much to the poor blacks it was intended for.

plied in arming the vessel — not for naval encounters but for protection against hostile natives — and in sheathing her hull with
copper. The Navy decided to leave the figurehead beneath the
30-foot bowsprit — a carving of a woman dressed, for reasons
which history does not make apparent, in full riding habit.

His Majesty's Armed Transport *Bounty*, the former coastal
vessel *Bethia*, as she appeared after her conversion. (Courtesy
of the National Maritime Museum, Greenwich, England)

On the upper deck aft were mounted four four-pounders and
six swivel guns. Four other swivel guns were set on stocks forward. Even with this armament, the vessel still looked more like
a merchant ship, one of the new whalers, perhaps, than an armed
transport on the King's business. To modern eyes, she seems a tall-
rigged vessel, but compared with the Royal Navy's great vessels of
the time, she was short-masted and a bit dumpy. Her deck meas-

ured 84 feet 6 inches, and her beam was 24 feet. Her burden was 220 tons. It must have been a humbling experience for the English sailors when they arrvied in Tahitian waters and found that the high-prowed and richly decorated ceremonial and war canoes of the inferior heathens were actually five or ten feet longer than the *Bounty*.

Her hull of English oak had been wrapped in copper to lessen fouling and to protect the wood in tropical waters from the shipworm (*Teredo navalis*). The navy had pioneered the use of copper sheathing. As early as 1761, hulls had been encased in copper but with only limited success. The early experimenters had no knowledge of the phenomenon of electrolysis. They were unaware that when ferrous and nonferrous metals are immersed in the sea, a galvanic electric current is set up which soon erodes all exposed hull fittings made of iron. The problem had been solved by the time Bligh's vessel was being fitted out for the South Seas. Electrolytic erosion was prevented by making the vessel's pintles, gudgeons, nails, and other exposed underwater fittings of expensive copper or bronze. As a result, they have lasted intact to this day. In the past forty-odd years, beginning with the recovery by Parkin Christian, Fletcher's great-great-grandson, of parts of the *Bounty*'s rudder in 1933, divers in Bounty Bay, Pitcairn, have brought to the surface a small museum of metal fittings from the ship. Unhappily, as we shall see later, these scraps from Pitcairn's past have largely disappeared from the island.

In addition to arming and sheathing the vessel, the Admiralty's budget also covered the cost of turning the great cabin into a large greenhouse. A plan of the *Bounty*, drawn on November 19, 1787, and preserved in the National Maritime Museum in Greenwich, England, shows this horticultural addition dominating the entire stern section of the ship. In serried rows, the pots for the breadfruit plants extend 28 feet in from the stern and across almost the entire beam. The cabin floor had been covered entirely with lead sheeting and a guttering arrangement provided so that any of the precious fresh water dripping from the pots could be caught in two barrels on the deck below and used again. A large stove was installed in the greenhouse so that the plants would survive the journey through latitudes outside the tropics.

William Bligh, as he appeared when he was given the *Bounty* command.

Displaced by the pots from Kew Gardens, Bligh and his sailing master, John Fryer, were given two small cabins on either side of the ladderway just aft of the greenhouse. A small area of the lower deck, hard by the main hatch, was partitioned off for their mess. The turn-of-the-century immigrants who traveled, as well as they could afford, to reach America would have had only slightly less personal space than the commander of the *Bounty*.

Toward the end of the refit, the vessel was renamed the *Bounty*. Her former name, *Bethia*, was painted out and the new one inscribed on orders from London. The renaming was in recognition of George III's "bounty" to the West India planters and merchants. But for this little brainstorm on the part of some royal sycophant in the Admiralty, we would have been reading all these years about the *Mutiny on the Bethia*. Somehow it doesn't have the dash or the bravura of *Mutiny on the Bounty*. It is questionable whether Hollywood would have spent a good many millions to bring to the screen the tale of the piracy of a ship named the *Bethia*.

Bligh was thirty-three years of age when he was chosen to command the *Bethia*-turned-*Bounty*. He had been born of a good Cornish family, not the thrusting upstart some accounts have pictured him as being. His father was an Inspector of Customs, assigned to the port of Plymouth when young William came into the world on September 9, 1754. In today's terms, we would rate the Bligh family as middle class. The past lineage, at least on the male side, may have been slightly *upper* middle class. Bligh's ancestors included members of the landed gentry, a doctor, a lawyer, and one or more naval officers. His father seems to have been determined that Bligh's career should be the navy. His name was entered on the books of a man-of-war when the boy was seven, a curious and most dishonest practice followed at the time by many fathers so that their sons would have spurious years of seniority when promotions were being considered. Bligh actually had a normal, land-based education until his midteens. His school record is not documented, but the writing and navigating feats he was to perform in later life indicated that he had a good grounding at least in English and mathematics.

His naval career actually began when he was sixteen. He was

signed on as an able-bodied. His family connections, however, saw to it that he was assigned the duties and status of a midshipman. He became a midshipman proper six months later. By the time he was twenty-one, Bligh had served on three different warships. But he retained the same rank; it was peacetime, and merit promotions were rare when the Royal Navy was not involved in hostilities.

The family pull that had been strong enough to win him a midshipman's berth was not, however, aristocratic or influential enough to obtain for him early advancement to officer. Yet his talent had already been recognized. In July, 1776, when he was not yet twenty-two, he accompanied Captain Cook on his third voyage of Pacific exploration as sailing master of the *Resolution*, the larger of the two vessels Cook had been given. Without a lordly sponsor at the Admiralty, he was beginning to move up the ladder of promotion at a creditable pace.

He had yet to obtain his officer's commission — the post of sailing master, though onerous, was not a commissioned rank. In the year he attained his majority, 1775, he passed with honors the theoretical part of his officer's examinations. As was the custom in those days, the actual commission was held back until the candidate had seen rigorous service as a warrant officer. Bligh stayed at that level until 1781, felicitously the year of his marriage, when, after giving a good account of himself in a rough duel with a Dutch squadron at Dogger Bank, he was commissioned as a junior lieutenant. He saw service under Lord Howe and others on a number of vessels, notably at the relief of Gibraltar at the end of 1782. When peace was concluded a few months later, Bligh was retired from active service and put on half pay of two shillings a day.

He returned to active duty four years later when he was given command of the vessel with which his name will be forever associated. To his great disappointment, he was not made a full captain but left as a lieutenant, a lieutenant with heavy responsibilities.

A *soupçon* of nepotism was involved in his selection as commander of the *Bounty*. The wife he had taken in February, 1781 — Elizabeth Betham, a beautiful girl with reddish-brown hair, delicately raised but passionate enough to give Bligh five daughters before too many years would pass — had a wealthy uncle named Duncan Campbell. Campbell owned his own merchant ships, which carried slaves to the West Indies and brought home the sugar and rum those slaves produced on plantations owned or co-owned by Campbell. He had been one of a syndicate of plantation owners who had tried but failed to use private enterprise to obtain Pacific breadfruit for their slaves in Jamaica, St. Vincent, and elsewhere. They had offered to meet "all reasonable costs" of any merchant skipper prepared to undertake the assignment. There were no takers, so the planters and merchants turned in desperation to the Admiralty, the government, and the Throne. They were able to convince all three that this was a venture of supreme importance to Britain as a nation, that a little state subsidy was really not out of place.

Having been one of the successful lobbyists responsible for the *Bounty*'s mission, Campbell was also able to exert his influence — almost certainly through his acquaintance with Sir Joseph Banks, the president of the Royal Society — in the choice of a commander. His niece's husband, Bligh, had commanded one of Campbell's merchant ships on the West Indies run during the four-year period in which Bligh was retired from naval service. Bligh also served as Campbell's business agent in dealings with the plantation managers. He was pleased with the young Bligh's handling of things both at sea and on land, and he paid a quick call on Sir Joseph when the government announced it was putting public money behind the breadfruit expedition. In advancing Bligh's candidacy for the *Bounty* command, Campbell might have been expected to draw Sir Joseph's attention to the fact that the young man was uniquely qualified for the assignment. Not only was he an accomplished navigator. He knew both Tahiti, the breadfruit source (from his voyage with Cook in 1776), *and* the West Indies, the place to which the plants were to be delivered. Sir Joseph appears to have agreed with him, and went to the Admiralty to enter Bligh's name among those being considered for the command of the expedition.

The center of all this attention was a man quite different, both physically and in matters of temperament, from the mental picture most of us have of him. He had an aquiline nose, unusually fine nostrils, a high forehead, and, if his portraitists were honest men of their trade, an expression of some serenity. His "pale or even pallid" complexion, a contemporary description, conflicts with the popular image of him as a quarter-deck monster with cheeks the color of the red in the Union Jack flying at the stern. He had that strange combination of darkish-brown hair and bright blue eyes. The hair turned gray fairly early, hardly surprising when we consider the stress life imposed on him. By all accounts, he was a vigorous and robust man who looked after his own health and the health of those under him. He had a sense of humor, which emerges occasionally in his writing, but it was not a dominant trait. Either that, or his sense of duty compelled him to suppress any tendency toward levity in the execution of his official duties.

On only two points does the popular image of Bligh, as far as physical appearance is concerned, agree with reality: he was slightly below average height, and in his later years he had a tendency toward corpulence.

The biographical material on Fletcher Christian is disappointingly lean. Although he grew up in Cumberland, where his father was county coroner as well as a landowner, his family originated in the Isle of Man. The Christians figure prominently in Manx history. One of Fletcher's forebears, William, a little more than a century before the *Bounty* drama, had already demonstrated that rebelliousness ran in the Christian family. As head of the Manx Militia, he directed a swift and surprisingly successful revolt against the English overlords, capturing all but two of the island forts. Unlike his eighteenth-century descendant, William Christian was captured, tried, found guilty, and executed in the 1660's. (Subsequently, however, the judges who condemned William were themselves punished, perhaps to mollify the Manx peasantry.)

The Manx people are of Scandio-Celtic origin. They are apt to have light eyes and fair complexions, but their hair often is unexpectedly dark, perhaps a genetic legacy of early bride raids as far south as Spain. The typical Manxman is on the tall side and heavily built. Fletcher Christian falls neatly into this pattern, except that his skin tone, particularly after nearly a year in the tropics, was unusually dark. He possessed what a novelist might describe as "swarthy good looks."

In his "wanted men" list drawn up after the mutiny, Bligh described him as being twenty-four years of age, 5 feet 9 inches tall, "blackish or very dark brown complexion, dark brown hair, strong made, a star tatowed on his left breast, tatowed on his backside; his knees stand a little out, and he may be called rather bow-legged."

Bandy-legged or not, he was a man for the ladies, and there are at least two testimonials to show that this interest was reciprocated by the women, white as well as brown. The brown ones in Tahiti had trouble pronouncing his name and dubbed him affectionately, "Tittriano." The "tatow" on his backside? The Tahitians were very fond of decorating the buttocks with tattoos, a painful procedure carried out by perforating the skin almost to the bone with needle-sharp native instruments and then rubbing lampblack into the pattern of punctures. Fletcher, in wanting a souvenir of Polynesia, may have settled for the buttocks since a decoration there would not brand him publicly as a freak upon his return to the sub-upper-crust English society he had moved among in Cumberland and London. The star tattoo on his left breast? It is right back in fashion today, although for women rather than men. Maddeningly, no authenticated sketch, painting, or engraving of Fletcher Christian, before or after tattooing, exists. We are left to employ our imagination in seeking to decide his facial appearance. We do know that during the Tahitian stay he acquired a deep suntan that left him as brown as any Noble Savage.

There are definite, but poorly documented links between Christian's family and that of Bligh's wife. Bligh met his bride-to-be on the Isle of Man — still a haunt of the Christian family despite the move to Cumberland — and married her there in the town of Douglas. This union, as we have seen, brought Bligh to the attention of the shipowner, Uncle Duncan Campbell, gave him his first command, albeit a West Indies merchantman, the *Britannia*, and led in turn to his candidacy for the *Bounty* command being powerfully promoted. Not unnaturally, the already existing friendship between the Betham and Campbell families and the Christian clan put Bligh, through his in-laws, in touch with the young

Fletcher Christian, a social contact that led to a seagoing relationship which began on a level of professional congeniality
only to be plunged into a fatal trough of hate.

These various family interrelationships were also responsible
for young Fletcher's short-lived career in the King's Navy. He
sailed with Bligh at least three times. The first was aboard
H.M.S. *Cambridge*, which took part in the Gibraltar engagement
in the autumn of 1782. Bligh was then a lieutenant, just turned
twenty-eight; Christian was not yet eighteen, a ship's boy and
candidate for midshipman aboard the warship. It is not certain
whether the young Christian sailed aboard the *Cambridge* as a
result of some letter of reference Bligh had written or a request
he had spoken into the appropriate ear. The chances are that this
was the case, given the background of family friendships. The
Royal Navy at the time, including barges and other nonfighting
ships, counted more than five hundred vessels. If two acquaintances, an officer and a youth being considered for midshipman,
found themselves on the same man-of-war, we can assume it was
more than simple coincidence.

Fletcher became a midshipman before he was twenty-one. He
had no sooner acquired the rank than he was retired from active
service, not because he had not showed promise but because England no longer needed such a large naval fighting force. A re-
luctant landlubber again, Fletcher either drew on the family links
to renew his acquaintanceship with Bligh or was actually sought
out by Bligh, who by now was looking for capable hands, and
perhaps social company, aboard the Campbell merchantman he
was sailing to and from the West Indies. Bligh evidently was satisfied with the senior members of his crew aboard the *Britannia*
but told Fletcher he was willing to sign him on as an able-bodied
seaman, granting him, nevertheless, the status of "gentleman" member of the company. This meant that Fletcher would be called
upon to handle rope and canvas only in an emergency and could
take his meals at Bligh's table. Fletcher demanded — and here, I
believe, we have the first indication of a broad streak of conceit in
his mental makeup — that he be taken on as sailing master. Christian was then twenty-one. Hadn't Bligh held such a post under
Cook at a roughly comparable age, twenty-two? Bligh refused to

upset his ship's command structure simply to please the vanity of a family friend, and Fletcher evidently wanted the berth badly enough that he agreed to sign on as a specially privileged ordinary seaman. Their second voyage together, at least from the point of view of the human relationship, was uneventful.

But Fletcher, unknown to Bligh, revealed on this voyage another character trait which I believe is significant in the light of the trouble that lay ahead. He wrote a letter home to his brother Edward, a professor of law at Cambridge, who was later to make a somewhat sinister intervention in the train of events in England after the mutiny. Fletcher wrote to Edward — and here we have an early clue suggesting that the man who was to lead a famous mutiny possessed some delusions of grandeur — telling his brother that Bligh had appointed him "Second Mate" of the *Britannia*. All Bligh had said, in fact, was that Fletcher Christian was to be "treated as an officer."

Bligh may or may not have seen these character flaws in young Fletcher. I am inclined to believe that they *would* have escaped his attention: he was not a particularly good commander when it came to detecting human problems developing aboard his ship through no fault of his own, a defect I attribute to his utter conscientiousness, his overriding dedication to the task at hand. Wherever the truth lies here, Bligh had no hesitation in arranging for Christian's return to active service when he was given the *Bounty* command and signing him on as master's mate.

If Bligh had been disappointed at not being raised to Captain for the *Bounty* mission, he must have been delighted to see that the man on the Throne was displaying a keen interest in the whole undertaking. George III's personal involvement ensured that the conversion work on the *Bethia* at Deptford would receive top priority. Bligh and Sir Joseph Banks made frequent visits to the dockyard to supervise the project, Sir Joseph concerning himself with the greenhouse, Bligh with the vessel itself. The scientist fretted about whether the young breadfruit plants would receive enough air and warmth in the great cabin; the sailor worried about how a vessel designed for coastal sailing would fare on the mighty Atlantic and the mightier Pacific. Sir Joseph had the workmen cut ventilation holes high in the side of the great cabin; Bligh had the masts shortened slightly and insisted that the *Bounty* be provided with newer and bigger ship's boats. The Admiralty furnished him with a 16-foot jolly boat, a 20-foot cutter, and a 23-foot launch. In the largest of these, Bligh, after the mutiny, was to spend forty-one days with eighteen loyal shipmates, sailing and rowing it a distance greater than a transatlantic crossing. Many times during this nightmarish voyage he must have thought back to the day at Deptford when he decided that the *Bethia*'s original launch must be replaced by something larger and sturdier.

In September of 1787, the month after Bligh received his official appointment, the work was proceeding so well that Sir Joseph and Bligh could sit down and draw up a list of bartering items for use in Tahiti and possibly other islands of call in the Pacific. Both men knew what took the natives' fancy. They finally settled on the following:

        100   pounds of glass beads
        168   mirrors
         72   shirts, Tahitian men for the use of.
      1,000   pounds of nails
        576   cheap knives
      2,808   custom-made adzes similar in design
              to the Tahitians' stone axe-adze.
              Several boxes of saws, drills and files.

The list was sent to the Admiralty, and within a week or two this strange shopping list had been filled and the items delivered to the dockyard. The *Bounty* was almost ready for the sea, for her first and last voyage as a unit of the King's Navy. She needed only her armament and for this, on October 9, she was sailed down the Thames to an armory for the installation of her four-pounders and swivel guns. Bligh supervised this work, never dreaming that these same guns, a year and a half later, would be trained down on him.

The actual departure point was to be Spithead, Portsmouth. Storms in the Channel delayed the *Bounty*'s transfer to this point, but the gales and high seas on the short sail from the Thames

Estuary to Portsmouth gave Bligh a useful early indication of how his square-rigger, and his crew, would perform in rough weather. He was well satisfied.

After the rush to complete her outfit, their Lordships at the Admiralty displayed inexplicable tardiness in issuing the final sailing orders — the route to be taken, the alternative courses, the subsidiary aims of the expedition, and so on. The *Bounty* rode at anchor in Spithead, and Bligh arranged for Elizabeth, once more pregnant, to come down from London with their daughters to spend the final days with him at an inn.

Bligh appears to have found the wait irksome — like any expedition leader he was anxious to be under way — but he took advantage of the delay to spend unaccustomed time with his wife and daughters. So far as the ship was concerned, he had only minor crew matters to settle. He was disturbed by the discovery that the Admiralty had provided him with an alcoholic as ship's surgeon, and even more disturbed by their refusal to consider a replacement. He had to find an able-bodied seaman to replace one who had deserted before the ship was brought around from the Thames. And he was still looking for a seaman who could play a musical instrument.

His search for a suitable musician, an obsession almost, which had been apparent from the moment the crew makeup was first considered, reveals something of Bligh's character which places him more in a humanitarian class than most of the other Royal Navy commanders of his day. He had learned from Captain Cook the importance of a healthy crew on a voyage which might last two years. Bligh had decided that dancing, the folk dancing of the day that had no overtones of effeminacy, was the best form of exercise for his men, an activity that not only kept muscles in tone but also provided some relaxation and diversion from the boredom of long hauls at sea.

Bligh was determined that each day, seas permitting, there would be dancing on deck for all those not on watch between the hours of four in the afternoon and eight in the evening. He did not have in mind daily, four-hour dance marathons, but rather a period in the day's routine which the crew would look upon as time set aside for organized recreation. For this a musician was essential. At Portsmouth, he found one, although hardly the able-bodied mariner he was looking for, a man who could pull his full weight in the working of the sails as well as providing jigs for the crew. And so was added to the roll call a man who was to be the saddest participant in the tragedy that was to be mounted. With some misgivings, Bligh signed on Michael Byrne, a fiddler who was half-blind.

Throughout this preparatory period, the Admiralty's approach to the mission had one curious flaw, a fatal flaw as events were to show. Perhaps the greatest scientific mind of the time had been employed to make sure that the horticultural arrangements were perfect; the navy's best marine engineers had been given the task of modifying the ship so she would not fall apart in tropical waters; time, effort, and money had been spent on such relatively minor matters as beads, mirrors, and adzes for barter. But less official attention had been paid to the structure of the crew which would sail the *Bounty*. Bligh was at fault in accepting the manning arrangements drawn up by the Admiralty. Perhaps he was so elated over his return to active service and his winning of a major command that he hesitated to raise the issue too strongly. At the same time he must have sensed the dangers and the weaknesses inherent in the crew makeup.

He was being dispatched on a circumnavigation of the globe, vast stretches of it across waters either uncharted or mapped in the haziest of manner, and yet he was expected to direct this mission without the help of a single other commissioned officer. Among other remarkable aspects of the Admiralty's handling of the breadfruit expedition, I find this *the* most remarkable. The arrangement might have been acceptable had Bligh been assigned a security force, the squad of Royal Marines that usually accompanied an expedition of this sort, partly to protect the ship and partly to protect the captain against mutiny by acting as policemen over the crew. Why no marines? The *Bounty* was too small a vessel to allow quarters for nonworking marines. Bligh was given a *one-man* security force, a marine corporal, a crew member who, during the stay in Tahiti, turned out to be a grave liability rather than an asset when it came to keeping the hands in order.

A captain's normal paperwork burden was added to by the fact that the Admiralty did not allow for a purser. Bligh was directed to take on these duties. But more important, there were too few working hands and too many "passengers" aboard the *Bounty* for the job that lay ahead. In the "passenger" category, although their skills would become vital when the ship reached Tahiti, must be placed David Nelson, the botanist, and William Brown, the gardener from Kew Gardens. I also place in this group the dipsomaniac surgeon, Thomas Huggan, and the surgeon's mate, Thomas Ledward, whom Bligh signed on as an ordinary seaman when he guessed, accurately enough, that he might need a backup for the surgeon. The fiddler who could barely see was obviously in this category. So too were several of the five midshipmen the *Bounty* carried, six if one counts Robert Tinkler, the boy who came on board for the voyage simply because he was the brother-in-law of Bligh's sailing master, John Fryer. In the original crew structure, the *Bounty* was to carry only two midshipmen. The number climbed as well-connected parents with ambitions for their sons brought pressure on Bligh and the Admiralty to give their boys a chance at getting both a glimpse of the exciting world of the Pacific and a boost up the ladder of naval promotion.

Bligh, with misplaced confidence, may have felt he could turn young midshipmen into officer material in a single voyage, and get by successfully, without marines, with a small but enthusiastic group of seamen aboard a sound, if small vessel.

Their enthusiasm at the outset can hardly be doubted; not a single man had been press-ganged or shanghaied on board Bligh's ship, a most unusual state of affairs for any warship putting out from a British or Continental port during the period under consideration. The lure here, of course, was the Great South Sea and Tahiti, the magical land of the Noble Savage — more specifically, the complacent and lovely girls this society of Noble Savagery had to offer white visitors.

Bligh's interest in exercise has already been entered into the record. He had, too, a real concern for his crew's dietary needs that made him an unusual captain for his time. He approached the task of victualing his ship in a surprisingly scientific way, showing, as Cook, his mentor, had displayed in the previous decade, an awareness of deficiency diseases long before the discovery that the food we eat must contain certain essential vitamins for a rounded diet. Without refrigeration or proper preservatives for his larder, Bligh knew that his men would have to be fed rotting salt beef and pork, rancid cheese and butter, and weevil-laden biscuits and bread before the voyage had progressed very far. In his own writing, Bligh likes to dwell on how adequately his ship was provided with the new scurvy-preventing rations. He had prevailed upon the Admiralty to give him, in addition to the standard naval rations, six pounds of salt beef or pork a week for each man, seven pounds of biscuits, twelve ounces of cheese, six ounces of dried fish, and so on, an unusually large supply of the new "scientific" victuals. The *Bounty* set off with barrels and boxes of things which sailors might not relish but which nevertheless were *good* for them — sauerkraut, dried malt and malt essence, lemon juice, and the newest invention of English kitchen-chemists, "solid broth." Bligh liked to call this "portable soup," and the many references to it in his writings suggest that this breakthrough in preserving techniques fascinated him.

So that the ship's two cooks did not have to draw entirely on salted-down provisions, Bligh also arranged for live pigs, sheep, and chickens to be taken aboard the *Bounty* at Portsmouth. He did so at the risk of turning an area of his small ship — not much wider, remember, than an average living room — into farmyard. Whether any of the chickens were served in the men's mess is doubtful. The captain kept the delicacies for himself and the gentlemen, as was the custom of the day, but the men got both fresh mutton and fresh pork. After almost two months at sea, Bligh was to record that the galley was serving "a fresh meal five times a week" and that "We are all in good spirits and my little ship fit to go round a half-score of worlds."

It is not my intention here to treat in detail the *Bounty*'s voyage and all of the events it set in train. I do this for three reasons. First, each episode merits almost a book to itself. To deal with them in even modestly fleshed-out summaries would make this a volume of unwieldy proportions. Second, many or most of my readers will already be familiar with the chronology and characters of the whole *Bounty* tragedy. Third, so much has been written

about these matters that it would serve no useful purpose to consume space by repeating here at length Bligh's log entries, his later
writing, the court-martial transcript, and so on. The reader who
wishes to pursue the matter can choose from any number of books,
beginning with the account Bligh himself set down shortly after
he returned to England in March, 1790, just under a year after he
had lost his ship and been cast adrift by Christian. In taking on
this vast stockpile of literature — and I make my addition to it
only because I feel there are some new things to be said — the
serious student will very quickly realize that there is history and
there is *history*. The most popular books about the *Bounty* and
Bligh consistently have been the fictionalized accounts. Great reading, but hardly history. In various editions, too profuse for even
a short bibliography, and from various hands too numerous to
identify, the *factual* outline is available for the modern student
who wishes to decide for himself who was right and who was
wrong, and who *wronged*, in the tragedy. He will find also factual
gaps. And through these gaps, writers have been sailing great and
splendid clipper ships of make-believe for many years.

My plan is to draw on the contemporary record, the story left to
us through the pens of those who witnessed the events, but to deal
only with those parts of the record which throw light on the true
cause of the mutiny and also tell us something about what sort of
men Bligh and Christian were.

Bligh's ship remained in Tahiti for twenty-three weeks, October
26, 1788, to April 4, 1789. The stay began with a landfall orgy and
ended with one. In the interval, there were group and private
orgies ashore and on board the ship. The bad-Bligh theorists have
trouble reconciling his permissiveness on this score; but when it
came to unbridled sex — for his crew, that is, not himself — Bligh
seems to have been a commander about average for his time. When
the *Bounty* moved into the lagoon of Matavai Bay, she was be-
sieged by Tahitian canoes. Soon her decks were aswarm with
hundreds of native men, women, and children. The Tahitians
scrambled on board with the presents they knew, from their experience with Wallis, Cook, and Bougainville, that white sailors
appreciated most: fresh fruit, suckling pigs, and giggling wahines.

In which order the men enjoyed their presents from the shore is not exactly clear. But Bligh has conceded that his ship became a scene of complete disorder that first day in Tahiti, a confusion so great that his orders could not be heard above the happy tumult, and seamen on watch could not carry out their normal work with sails and lines. Bligh had brought his ship 27,086 nautical miles from Spithead. He had lost one man, a seaman, Valentine, a death attributed to the tipsy surgeon's determination to bleed excessively the first patient he had on the trip. The ship had averaged four and a half knots despite unusually bad weather conditions, and Bligh realized the men needed the reward they had been anticipating during ten almost unbroken months at sea. He said nothing as the *Bounty* hands, middies, and warrant officers disappeared below decks with their willing new girlfriends. It was only as the sun was going down behind Tahiti's sister island of Moorea that the skipper called the company to order. All the Tahitian men must quit the *Bounty* by sundown; the Tahitian girls so inclined would be allowed to spend the night on board. The record does not say so, but I imagine "Breadfruit Bligh" was roundly cheered when he delivered this order-of-the-night. At that moment, he hardly fitted the pattern of the ultra-authoritarian captain. Nor did he throughout the Tahiti stay. The women from shore were regularly allowed to spend the nights on board the *Bounty* in glorious Anglo-Tahitian coexistence in the fo'c'sle.

Fletcher Christian's amours were land-based. He seems to have taken his time about making a selection, a week perhaps, but when he did, she was the loveliest of the many lovelies who came to Matavai Bay. Her name was Mi'Mitti. She seems to have been as tall as Fletcher. She was of aristocratic bearing and breeding. Her father was one of the many powerful men in a society fragmented into some seven or eight rival kingdoms. Perhaps Mi'Mitti was the inspiration for the star tattooed above Fletcher's heart.

It is hard for us today to say exactly *how* lovely the Tahitian girls of the eighteenth century actually were. The pure Tahitian race has all but disappeared during two centuries of interbreeding with the white man and with most of the other races of the Pacific. To the first English visitors, they were, undeniably, feminine knockouts. When the island was first sighted by Wallis'

Dolphin, his master, George Robertson, wrote in his journal that "when our boats returned to the ship all the sailors swore they never saw handsomer made women in their lives. This piece of news made all our men madly fond of the shore, even the sick which had been on the Doctor's list . . . said a Young Girl would make an Excelent Nurse." Bligh himself took in the scene in his detached way and judged that the women were "handsome, mild and cheerful in their manners and conversations, possessed of great sensibility, and have sufficient delicacy to make themselves admired and beloved."

Fletcher took Mi'Mitti into his embrace on shore, in the comfort of a Tahitian thatch dwelling rather than in the discomfort of the cramped *Bounty.* (He contracted, alas, gonorrhea in the process, a point I take up later.) He was shore-based for the twenty-three weeks in Tahiti because Bligh had put him in charge of the bread-fruit operation. With Midshipman Peter Heywood, the botanist and gardener, and a small group of seamen, Christian had the pleasantest assignment of all — days and nights of friendly native company, delicious feasts of roast pig, lagoon fish, and luscious fruit, a stress-free time for a young man resting from the sea. And all this in a place of sumptuous beauty, a bewitching bay with a backdrop of green mountains rising to seven thousand feet, a spot where tourists from America and Australia now pay $60 a day for a vacation. The young man from Cumberland and the Isle of Man succumbed.

There were desertions by men who decided early in the stay that this was the place they wanted to remain for the rest of their lives. There was even a plot to wreck the *Bounty* so all would be obliged to stay in paradise forever, or if not forever, at least for a year or two.

On February 6, 1789, about halfway through the stay, Bligh discovered that the hemp anchor cable by which the ship was riding had been cut near the water level. Only one strand remained. Bligh at first blamed the Tahitians. He reprimanded them, and the natives took to the hills. But he had second thoughts about the incident: "It has since occurred to me that the attempt to cut the ship adrift was most probably the act of some of our own people, whose purpose of remaining at Otaheite might have been effectually answered, without danger, if the ship had been driven ashore."

This act of sabotage held a warning for Bligh. He failed to read its portents. The mission was going so well — the potting of bread-fruit shoots was proceeding at a much faster pace than he had hoped; the reprovisioning of the ship was an easy task in this land of abundance — that Bligh overlooked the fact that many members of his company did not give a damn whether the trees ever reached rich planters in the West Indies.

There is some mystery as to why Bligh remained so long in the place he has called "the finest island in the world." Within a month of the *Bounty*'s arrival, the botanist had potted more than the five hundred young trees specified in the Admiralty's orders. The popular belief is that the ship reached Tahiti at the wrong time of year. In fact, her arrival coincided with the start of Tahiti's rainy season, and there could be no better time of year to take cuttings from breadfruit or any other trees or plants on the island. (Or so I was told by present-day residents of Papeete.) Eventually they potted 1,015 young trees. My belief is that Bligh, looking back on the long haul from England and realizing how difficult it would be to repeat this mission, wanted to make absolutely sure before putting to sea again that the shoots would survive the transplant-ing, and had taken healthy root. And remembering his losing battle to round Cape Horn at the wrong time of year, he may have wanted to wait until the wind conditions in Torres Strait, between Aus-tralia and New Guinea, were to his advantage, which meant an April departure.

Whatever the reason for the prolonged stay, Bligh, at least, was a happy man when the canvas was raised and his ship put out to sea again. His crew were sun-bronzed and healthy (if we overlook the fact that a few were sailing off with Tahitian clap). The larder was bulging with salted pork. Bunches of ripening bananas hung from the yardarms. Coconuts and yams filled every available place on deck. In the pens, there were pigs and goats. "We bade farewell to Otaheite," Bligh wrote, "where for 23 weeks we were treated with the greatest kindness and fed with the best meat and finest fruit in the world."

His contentment was to last for twenty-three days. By then, the

Bounty was passing through the Tonga group. She was riding in gentle waters some thirty miles from the volcanic peak of Tofua. The breeze had dropped during the night. The moon, in its first quarter, cast a thin light on this scene of an English ship with a strange cargo waiting for fresh winds to carry her on. Bligh had retired early for the night after arranging to dine the following evening with Christian, his second-in-command having excused himself from the captain's table that night on the grounds he was feeling unwell. Bligh was to be shaken awake before dawn on the morning of April 28 to find himself the victim of what he later would describe as "one of the most atrocious acts of piracy ever committed."

Atrocious, yes. But not bloody. Considering its celebrity, the actual mutiny on the *Bounty* was rather mild. No one was injured, not even a nick from a cutlass blade. No musket was discharged. There were oaths and strong language and some roughing-up of the skipper, but that was the sum total of violence that morning.

We know from Laurence Lebogue, the sailmaker, that Christian had been drinking with the ship's carpenter, William Purcell, at midnight, even though he was to be up at four o'clock in the morning to keep his watch. His mind certainly was disturbed. He had confided to at least two members of the company that he had thought of casting adrift on a raft, making his way to Tofua, and from there, presumably, finding some means of returning to Tahiti and Mi'Mitti.

There are three basic eyewitness accounts of the mutiny. One is Bligh's *Narrative*, published in 1790. Another is the published journal of James Morrison, the boatswain's mate. The third is the transcript of evidence given at the court-martial of the mutineers captured on Tahiti. So far as the swift insurrection is concerned, the trial testimony demonstrated that Bligh had given an accurate account of the mutiny. There are points of conflict between Bligh's *Narrative* and Morrison's *Journal* but only one I consider of real significance to my argument: What were Christian's parting words to his captain as he forced him over the side and into the crowded launch?

According to Bligh, Christian, when asked why he had turned against his shipmate of three voyages, replied: "That, Captain

Bligh, that is the thing. I am *in* hell — I am *in* hell." (Italics added.) According to Morrison, what Christian said at this moment was: "It is too late, I have been in hell for this fortnight past, and I am determined to bear it no longer, and you know . . . that I have been used like a dog all the voyage."

A few historians, including those not well disposed toward Bligh, have pointed out that of the two men, only Bligh was in a position to keep an accurate record of what was said and done. He alone had writing materials at his side throughout the entire period. While Morrison presented his account as almost a diary record, it could have been put together, with the help of a London publisher, only from his recollections. In the three and a half years that elapsed between the mutiny and his appearance in the dock at the court-martial, Morrison spent many months — on the beach in Tahiti, in chains during the fearful voyage back to England — when it would have been impossible for him to keep a journal. (He was one of three defendants recommended to the King's mercy and eventually pardoned.)

In the circumstances, it is permissible to draw on Bligh's own words for an account of the seizure of his ship:

Just before sun-rising, Mr. Christian, with the Master-at-arms, gunner's mate, and Thomas Burkitt, seaman, came into my cabin while I was asleep, and seizing me, tied my hands with a cord behind my back, and threatened me with instant death, if I spoke or made the least noise. I, however, called so loud as to alarm everyone: but they had already secured the officers who were not of their party, by placing sentinels at their doors. There were three men at my cabin door, besides the four within; Christian had only a cutlass in his hand, the others had muskets and bayonets. I was hauled out of bed, and forced on deck in my shirt, suffering great pains from the tightness with which they had tied my hands. I demanded the reason for such violence, but received no other answer than threats of instant death, if I did not hold my tongue. Mr. Elphinston, master's mate, was kept in his berth; Mr. Nelson, botanist, Mr. Peckover, gunner, Mr. Ledward, surgeon, and the master, were confined to their cabins; and also the clerk, Mr. Samuel, but he soon obtained leave to come on deck. The fore hatchway was guarded by sentinels; the boatswain and the carpenter were, however, allowed to come on deck, where they saw me standing abaft the mizzen-mast, with my hands tied behind my back, under a guard, with Christian at their head.

The boatswain was now ordered to hoist the launch out, with a threat, if he did not do it instantly, to take care of himself. The boat being out, Mr. Hayward and Mr. Hallet, midshipmen, and Mr. Samuel, were ordered into it; upon which I demanded the cause of such an order, and endeavoured to persuade someone to a sense of duty; but it was to no effect.

"Hold your tongue, Sir, or you are dead this instant," was constantly repeated to me.

The master, by this time, had sent to be allowed to come on deck, which was permitted; but he was soon ordered back again to his cabin.

I continued my endeavours to turn the tide of affairs, when Christian changed the cutlass he had in his hand for a bayonet, that was brought to him, and, holding me with a strong grip by the cord that tied my hands, he, with many oaths, threatened to kill me immediately if I would not be quiet; the villains around me had their pieces cocked and bayonets fixed. Particular people were now called on to go into the boat, and were hurried over the side: whence I concluded that with these people I was to be set adrift.

I, therefore, made another effort to bring about a change, but with no other effect than to be threatened with having my brains blown out.

The boatswain and the seamen, who were to go in the boat, were allowed to collect twine, canvas, lines, sails, cordage, an eight and twenty gallon cask of water, and the carpenter to take his tool chest. Mr. Samuel got 150 pounds of bread, with a small quantity of rum and wine. He also got a quadrant and a compass into the boat; but he was forbidden, on pain of death, to touch either map, ephemeris, book of astronomical observations, sextant, time-keeper, or any other of my surveys or drawings.

The mutineers now hurried those they meant to get rid of into the boat. When most of them were in, Christian directed a dram to be served to each of his own crew. I now unhappily saw that nothing could be done to effect the recovery of the ship: there was no one to assist me, and every endeavour on my part was answered with threats of death.

The officers were called, and forced over the side into the boat, while I was kept apart from everyone, abaft the mizzen-mast; Christian, armed with a bayonet, holding me by the bandage that secured my hands. The guard around me had their pieces cocked, but, on my daring the ungrateful wretches to fire, they uncocked them.

Isaac Martin, one of the guards over me, I saw, had an inclination to assist me, and, as he fed me a shaddock (my lips being quite parched with my endeavours to bring about a change), we explained our wishes to each other by our looks; but this being observed, Martin was instantly removed from me; his inclination then was to leave the ship, for which purpose he got into the boat; but with many threats they obliged him to return.

The armourer, Joseph Coleman, and the two carpenters, McIntosh and Norman, were also kept contrary to their inclination and they begged of me, after I was astern in the boat, to remember that they declared that they had no hand in the transaction. Michael Byrne, I am told, likewise wanted to leave the ship.

It is of no moment for me to recount my endeavours to bring back the offenders to a sense of their duty: all I could do was by speaking to them in general; but my endeavours were to no avail, for I was kept securely bound, and no one but the guard was suffered to come near me.

To Mr. Samuel I am indebted for securing my journals and commission, with some material ship papers. Without these I had nothing to certify what I had done, and my honour and character might have been suspected, without my possessing a proper document to have defended them. All this he did with great resolution, though guarded and strictly watched. He attempted to save the time-keeper, and a box with all my surveys, drawings, and remarks for fifteen years past, which were very numerous, when he was hurried away with "Damn your eyes, you're well off to get what you have . . ."

Much altercation took place between the mutinous crew during the whole business; some swore, "I'll be damned if he does not find his way home, if he gets anything with him" (meaning me); others, when the carpenter's chest was carried away, "Damn my eyes, he will have a vessel built in a month." While others laughed at the helpless situation of the boat, being very deep, and so little room for those who were in her. As for Christian, he seemed meditating instant destruction on himself and everyone.

I asked for arms, but they laughed at me, and said that I was well acquainted with the people where I was going, and therefore did not want them; four cutlasses, however, were thrown into the boat, after we were veered astern.

When the officers and men, with whom I was suffered to have no communication, were put into the boat, they only waited for me, and the master-at-arms informed Christian of it; who then said, "Come,

Captain Bligh, your officers and men are now in the boat, and you must go with them; if you attempt to make the least resistance you will instantly be put to death"; and, without any further ceremony, holding me by the cord that tied my hands, with a tribe of armed ruffians about me, I was forced over the side, where they untied my hands. Being in the boat we were veered astern by a rope. A few pieces of pork were then thrown to us, and some clothes, also the cutlasses I have already mentioned; and it was now that the armourer and carpenters called out to me to remember that they had no hand in the transaction. After having undergone a great deal of ridicule, and been kept some time to make sport for these unfeeling wretches, we were at length cast adrift in the open ocean.

Notwithstanding the roughness with which I was treated, the remembrance of past kindnesses produced some signs of remorse in Christian. When they were forcing me out of the ship, I asked him if this treatment was a proper return of the many instances he had received of my friendship. He appeared disturbed at my question, and answered, with much emotion, "That, Captain Bligh, that is the thing; I am in hell — I am in hell."

That account from Bligh's hand brings out, as dispassionately as could be expected from the principal victim of the uprising, the cold-blooded way in which the mutineers committed to the open ocean eighteen of their shipmates with scant material resources for survival. It is of interest, too, to discern how far along the dawn drama had progressed before Bligh realized the full gravity of the situation, that he was actually about to lose command of his ship.

Five months later, the former company of H.M.S. *Bounty* was split into three separate groups. Christian, Midshipman Edward Young, the gardener Brown, and six seamen, John Mills, Matthew Quintal, William McCoy, Alexander Smith, John Williams, and the American-born Isaac Martin, were aboard the *Bounty*, setting out from Matavai Bay in search of the refuge that turned out to be Pitcairn's Island. With them were their native women, the six Polynesian men who realized too late they were being taken along only as *manahune*, or serfs, the wives of three of these men, and the infant native girl whom McCoy's woman, Teio, or Mary, had recently produced.

The second group was the party of loyalists, the eighteen men who made the open-boat voyage with Bligh from Tofua to the Dutch outpost of Timor, suffering on the way almost unbelievable hardship — storms, hunger, thirst, exposure, and hostile natives. Only Bligh and eleven others were to see England again. Of the seven who died, none perished in the launch at sea, an astonishing tribute to Bligh's seamanship in navigating a hideously overloaded launch, with only seven inches separating the gunwales from the waterline, a distance of 3,618 nautical miles in forty-one days.

The third group comprised the sixteen men — some guilty in the mutiny, some innocent — who parted company with Christian in Matavai Bay and elected to remain in Tahiti. By the time the Admiralty's capture ship *Pandora* reached Tahiti in March, 1791, two of these men had been murdered. The rest had taken up again with the girls they had known during the breadfruit-gathering months. Some of the Englishmen were interfering outrageously in island politics, using their muskets to establish themselves as minor chiefs or military advisers to one or another Tahitian suzerain. The *Pandora* was wrecked on the Great Barrier Reef on the voyage home. Four of the prisoners she had taken in Tahiti died in that shipwreck. The ten others, with the surviving men of the *Pandora*, made their way in small boats to Timor and eventually were returned to England and military judgment.

The court-martial of the ten men from the *Bounty* was held in Portsmouth Harbor in the great cabin of H.M.S. *Duke*, a ship-of-the-line. The president was Lord Hood, Vice Admiral of the Blue and Commander in Chief of His Majesty's ships at Portsmouth. The trial lasted from the twelfth to the eighteenth of September, 1792. While it can hardly be considered a shining beacon in the annals of English military justice — for one thing, the chief witness, Bligh, was not present, being away from England on the second breadfruit expedition, and his evidence was presented only in deposition form — the verdict was fair enough.

Four men, the fiddler, Michael Byrne, the armorer, Joseph Coleman, and the carpenters, Charles Norman and Thomas McIntosh, were acquitted. The six others were condemned to pay the price for mutiny against a lawful commander of the King's Navy, "to suffer death by being hanged by the neck" on board one of His

Majesty's ships of war. Subsequently, by King's warrant, three were pardoned: Midshipman Peter Heywood, Seamen William Muspratt, and Morrison.

The sentence was carried out on the remaining three defendants: Seamen Thomas Burkitt, John Millward, and Thomas Ellison. At about eleven-thirty on the morning of October 29, 1792, nooses of hemp rope suspended from the yardarms of H.M.S. *Brunswick* snapped the necks of these three men. Every officer and man on the vessels assembled in Portsmouth Harbor was summoned to witness the hanging. Thousands of men, women, and children from the town paid a penny or two to ride out to the ship's side in harbor craft and rowboats to observe the spectacle.

Before he went to the gallows, mutineer John Millward mounted the cathead at the *Brunswick*'s prow and delivered to the assembled ship's company, in a voice that faltered only occasionally, a remarkable speech. It was a strong and moving declaration from a man totally prepared to accept what was about to happen to him. He confessed his own errors and those of his shipmates in taking up arms against their captain, conceded that the court-martial sentences were just and deserved, and warned other members of the King's Navy to avoid even the slightest act of disobedience.

CHAPTER THREE

HERO INTO VILLAIN

E VEN TO SOME who feel they know the whole *Bounty* tale
    fairly well, it may come as a surprise to learn that William
Bligh was once an English national hero. His popular acclaim was
short-lived, perhaps five years at the most.

From that time on, history and seven generations of legend-
spinning have given his reputation a vicious keel-hauling. Few controversial figures from the past have had their characters and actions
blackened quite so thoroughly and systematically as the commander
of the *Bounty*. The perjoratives piled on his head — by his contemporaries as well as posthumously — would fill part of a the-
saurus page: tyrant, autocrat, liar, sadist, pilferer of ship's supplies,
martinet, monster, bully, oppressor, arrogant, egomaniac, snob,
glory-seeker, hypocritical, sarcastic, upstart, censorious, malevolent,
pitiless, high-handed, demon, malicious, treacherous, hateful, stone-
hearted, spiteful, bitter, venomous, torturer, persecutor, sullen, ungrateful, cold-blooded, surly, unfeeling, churlish, and just plain evil.
(In the popular histories about Bligh, I have come across all these
descriptions.)

Who would step into a rowboat with such a man to cross even
a stream, let alone spend two years circumnavigating the globe
under his lash? And why would the Royal Navy, whose efficiency
at the time was adequately attested to by sea victories and tri-
umphs of exploration, entrust a mission of national importance to
such an out-and-out demon? Desertions and mutiny plots at sea

were not unknown to the Royal Navy. In planning voyages that could cover thirty or forty thousand miles, many of them through uncharted seas, languorous climes, and seductive islands, the Lords Commissioners of the Admiralty had marked up a good record of picking commanders and sailing masters with exceptional qualities, of whom Captain Cook stands out as the gleaming example.

The end result of Lieutenant Bligh's mission was to raise substantially what accountants today would call the "cost efficiency" of Britain's sugar, coffee, and cotton plantations in the West Indies by obtaining a food source that would enable the slaveowners to feed their Negroes for literally pennies a year. A hundred breadfruit trees would provide the nutritional intake to keep fifty blacks at hard labor for twelve months of the year. With the loss of the American Colonies only a few years earlier — Bligh sailed from Spithead in December, 1787 — his mission, connected as it was with the economic yield of the West Indies, assumed added importance to British commerce. Then, too, Britain in the 1760's and 1770's was looking enviously at the phenomenal productivity France had achieved in her relatively small colony of Saint Domingue, or Haiti as it became in 1804.

Bligh, of course, had his faults, which we review in later pages. They were known to the top men of the Admiralty, who may have regarded them, given the climate of the day, as needed virtues rather than dangerous shortcomings. Before he had turned twenty-two, those virtues had carried him to a position of immense responsibility aboard one of the two vessels of Captain Cook's third voyage of Pacific discovery, the great journey that was to be Cook's last; in 1779 Cook was stabbed to death by natives in the place first known to Europe as Owhyee, then as the Sandwich Islands, and today as Hawaii. It is worth noting that the log of the revered Cook, and his private comments to fellow officers, evidently contained not the slightest element of criticism of Bligh as seafarer, navigator, and leader of men. Had this been the case, it is unlikely that Bligh ever would have been given an important command.

It is no exaggeration to say that Bligh was hand-picked for the mission to Tahiti, as carefully chosen as Cook had been nineteen years earlier. Many of the most intelligent and respected minds of the day had a hand in his selection. The key among them, as we have seen, was Sir Joseph Banks, a towering figure of late-eighteenth-century England, an imaginative scientist and an enlightened sachem of the Establishment. He was elected president of the Royal Society in 1778 and remained in that post for an astonishing term of office, forty years.

In social station, Sir Joseph ranked above Bligh. But they were reasonably close. They dined together, reminiscing, presumably, about Otaheite and the Great South Sea. Sir Joseph had visited these waters aboard the *Endeavour* on Cook's first voyage of discovery, the epic journey that established both men's reputations. The breadfruit-for-the-Indies project was a pet one of Sir Joseph's. At last, here was economic justification for the money, time, and effort expended in discovering and charting the Pacific paradise, the "New Cythera." * Sir Joseph himself had helped to unveil it and had even acquired a working knowledge of the Tahitian language.

If he had had the slightest reservations about the character of the man chosen to execute the mission, his doubts certainly would have been heeded by the Lords Commissioners of the Admiralty and the private and governmental bodies interested in exploiting to the maximum His Majesty's West India Possessions.

Some curious studies suggest that the assignment was given to Bligh because older, more prestigious officers looked upon the voyage as a demeaning one, a marathon gardening expedition to collect and transport some trees that bore a foul fruit. The facts speak otherwise. The Pacific was still high fashion, the chief distraction of the Old World trying to ride out the storms of new political thought and the shaky social conditions ensuing after the breakup of feudalism. England was at peace — France would not declare war on her until 1792 — and while vessels of war could not be spared, there were scores of Royal Navy captains and lieutenants available, in the service or serving in the merchant marine, from which a commander for the *Bounty* could have been selected.

Bligh's appointment made him the object of envy, not a target

* The name was bestowed on Tahiti by Bougainville, the French explorer who visited it in 1766. He named it after the Peloponnesian island where Aphrodite made her mythical emergence from the sea. To Bougainville, it was a veritable Eden. His contribution to Pacific exploration is immortalized in a dainty flower, Bougainvillea, and in the name of the largest settlement in the Solomon Islands.

of derision. He was bound for the most "in" place on the eighteenth-century maps, the fabled Otaheite. In the months in which the merchant ship *Bethia* was being fitted out at Deptford, the salutation Bligh received from his fellow officers would not have been, "Make the most of it, Bligh. Dig up the confounded breadfruit and come back safely," but rather, "Damn it, Bligh, but you're a lucky devil! I would give up a rank or two to be sailing to Otaheite." If one looks for a modern analogy, we may compare Bligh with one of the astronauts chosen for an Apollo shot — maybe not the epic Apollo 11, perhaps mission 14 or 15 — and liken his brother-officers, passed over for the *Bounty* command, to the astronauts who never made it to the launch pad.

After Bligh had made his way back to England from Timor, he and his men were treated as heroes, superpatriots, by the public and showered with praise by Whitehall and Admiralty. A lieutenant, soon to be a captain and finally a vice-admiral of the blue, had risked death by starvation at sea, half a world away, in the service of His Majesty. He had brought loyal members of his crew home safely after unspeakable hardship. It was leadership in the greatest traditions of the King's Navy. His almost incredible feat of sailing 3,618 nautical miles in an overcrowded and virtually unprovisioned launch was the sensation of the day. The broadsheets and journals chronicled his heroism in vivid detail. A famous print published in London in 1790, at the time that Christian was establishing his clandestine settlement on Pitcairn, mirrored the mood of the day. A proud Bligh is shown standing in the bow of the launch catching one of the four cutlasses Christian has thrown down from the windows of the *Bounty*'s great cabin. Of the castaways in the open boat, Bligh alone is drawn with eyes that betray no fear. The mutineers are portrayed as a ragtail mob, shouting invective at "Breadfruit Bligh" and training their muskets on the weaponless unfortunates in the boat below the *Bounty*'s stern.

How, then, did Bligh's reputation receive such a mauling? Why the sudden change from hero and patriot to villain and martinet? How did his very name come to be a term of English opprobrium, used by the oppressed in talking about pitiless landlords or bullying factory foremen: "He treats us like a proper *Bligh*"?

Public opinion began to change after the court-martial of the ten mutineers brought home in chains to Portsmouth after the capture ship *Pandora* picked them up in Tahiti. What brought about the change in the public's attitude toward Bligh was not the news dispatches from the court-martial being held in the great cabin of H.M.S. *Duke,* but rather the literary embroidery the whole tale would subsequently be given. Trial reporting in those days was hardly thorough and was far from instantaneous. In addition, the price of newspapers was such that they were not bought by the masses. A Londoner or a Berliner today would know far more about the proceedings of a celebrated court-martial in the United States on the very day testimony was given than the man in the street in Portsmouth in the 1790's would have known a month later about the famous trial unfolding on a man-of-war in the harbor.

By the early years of the nineteenth century, the pulp novelists and popular writers knew the way the tale should be told for their readers. Didn't the British public, and the American and European public as well, since interest in the mutiny had spread internationally, love the underdog in any adventure? Wasn't this a case of an honest, romantic, handsome, daring young acting lieutenant doing what he must to spare his men from an impossible captain?

A short time after the court-martial, the issues were clouded — perhaps unintentionally from pure feelings of fraternal concern, perhaps deliberately and with all the finesse of a trained legal mind — by Fletcher Christian's older brother, Edward, a professor of law at Cambridge. He published privately in London in 1794, and directed copies to persons in the right places, a volume entitled *Minutes of the Proceedings of the Court-Martial held at Portsmouth August 12, 1792,* * *on ten persons charged with mutiny on board His Majesty's Ship the Bounty. With an Appendix containing a full account of the Real Causes and Circumstances of that unhappy Transaction, the most material of which have hitherto been withheld from the Public.*

Edward's transcript of the trial proceedings differed in some respects from the record deposited with the Admiralty and still

---

* The book contains a curious error: August instead of September, in the date of the opening of the court-martial. The error is present, at least, in a copy I have examined of the original edition.

available to scholars today. He had obtained his minutes for a fee from the clerks who took down the proceedings aboard the *Duke*. To this transcript he added a contentious appendix, made up of depositions allegedly obtained from those *Bounty* crew members who had made their way back to England. Edward at this time had no idea what had happened to his much-loved brother. He had no way of knowing whether Fletcher was already dead, would soon surrender himself somewhere, or would be apprehended on some island by a Royal Navy vessel visiting the Pacific. His publication was intended to palliate his brother's actions, to prepare public opinion, and any future court-martial board, in such a way that Bligh's behavior would be examined critically and Christian's actions viewed in a more sympathetic light. The effect of his little book, which reached a small but influential readership, was to trigger rumors and gossip about the *Bounty*'s voyage and to lay the foundations for nasty speculation about Bligh's conduct.

Edward Christian had read the earlier accounts of the spectacular charms of the Tahitian women, of their libertine ways, and was well aware that sex had reared its jasmine-scented head during the *Bounty*'s long stay in Tahiti. Bligh, in his *Narrative*, had already described how his company had been swept off their feet by the houris who greeted them in Matavai Bay. The most remarkable part of Edward Christian's attempted defense of his brother was an effort to show that Fletcher remained aloof from the orgies, afloat and on shore, that he passed the twenty-three weeks in Tahiti in a state of total chastity.

Bligh was away from England, handling another command, when Edward published his court minutes and depositions. He moved quickly on his return to set matters straight and soon had in print a slim volume of his own, *An Answer to Certain Assertions contained in the Appendix to a Pamphlet entitled Minutes of the Proceedings of the Court-Martial etc.* This was not Bligh's own opinion. It took the form of new depositions from the very men whom Edward Christian had interviewed, and statements from other available members of the *Bounty*'s crew. The depositions effectively challenged most of the points Edward had been trying to establish and clarified others he had sought to wreathe in doubt. In particular, Bligh was able to show that Christian did have some "female connections" in Tahiti and one special girlfriend, Mi'Mitti. Bligh did not raise the matter in public print, but he possessed the sort of proof which would have convinced any inquiry board that Fletcher was hardly chaste during the Tahitian stay. All that was necessary here was the production of the *Bounty*'s pay-book record, which Bligh's clerk had managed to take off the ship as he was being put in the open boat. It contained the various "mulcts," or money docked for medical treatments — in effect fines — for having contracted clap while in the King's service. The pay book showed that Fletcher Christian was one of twelve *Bounty* men who picked up venereal disease during the otherwise happy days in Tahiti.

So much for the barrister brother's intervention. In turn, public opinion seemed to be influencing even the way the official account was being presented. In 1831, *The Eventful History of the Mutiny and Piratical Seizure of the Bounty* was published in London, anonymously at first, but it was soon public knowledge that its author was Sir John Barrow, the Secretary of the Admiralty. A year later, the same work was published in New York by Harper's Family Library. The words "piratical" and "seizure" were dropped from the title, and it was offered to the American market as *The Eventful History of the Mutiny of the Bounty*. In 1844, Harper's Family Library reissued the *same* text, but this time the title was *A Description of Pitcairn's Island and Its Inhabitants*. Fletcher Christian's little society had found its own justification in print, quite apart from the lurid story of its origins. The Pitcairners, the descendants of the mutineers, were achieving respectability in literature.

By the early years of the nineteenth century, the facts of the mutiny, the contemporary record of what had happened before and after it, were being swept aside in the interests of acceptable and saleable popular history.

In the century that followed, Hollywood was to agree wholeheartedly with this interpretation. Within a single generation, it made not one but two epic films of *Mutiny on the Bounty*. In 1935, Metro-Goldwyn-Mayer cast Charles Laughton as an insufferable Bligh, striding the quarter-deck with malevolence and snarling his orders and waspish remarks to Clark Gable as Fletcher

Hollywood's Blighs, Christians. *Above:* Charles Laughton as Bligh and Clark Gable as Christian in the 1935 version. *Below:* In the lavish remake, Trevor Howard is Bligh, Marlon Brando is Christian. (M-G-M photos)

Christian. In the lavish remake, Trevor Howard's interpretation of the *Bounty*'s skipper was slightly different. But Bligh was still the unmitigated villain. For the role of Christian the second time around, Hollywood called on Marlon Brando, thereby demonstrating afresh filmdom's fervent loyalty to the popular version.

At least the flack in MGM's publicity department in 1935 who drew up the press release when the Laughton-Gable film had its premiere sensed what the public wanted. This was the story of a monstrous little tyrant who deserved to lose his ship. "His very name," the yellowing press release informs us, "struck terror in the hearts of all his crew. A sea-going disaster, begotten in a galley, and born under a gun! His hair was rope, his teeth were marlin spikes; and the seamen who dared to disobey his mad, ruthless orders seldom lived to do it twice." Nonsense, of course, all of it. If the publicity man who composed that release is still with us, I would refer him to the contemporary portrait of William Bligh which appears on page 16. Not only would he discover that Bligh's hair and teeth were of normal human material; I think he would agree that the portrait is of an eminently sane and humane-looking individual.

But we are all, at times, ready victims for brainwashing. In 1935, the *New York Times* film critic was Andre Sennwald, a man of intelligence and perception. Yet his belief in what he saw on the screen when the first *Bounty* film was released seems to have been absolute. He agreed that Bligh was "the sadistic master of the *Bounty*, the barbarous madman who was half god and half devil . . . able but intolerably savage. . . . The spirit of revolt grew among both officers and men during the voyage as Bligh's mania for discipline increased in fury. . . . His penalties for minor offenses are the judgments of a maniac. From the swish of the lash he derives a lewd joy."

In the interests of historical accuracy and fair play, I shall take issue with what, for modern readers, we might designate the Hollywood Version of the real drama that exploded in April, 1789, in the Friendly Islands. I am not disparaging the films as entertainment — the first secured an Academy Award as best film of 1935, the second was an expensive disaster so far as the studio was concerned, although I personally felt it had enough location grandeur to justify the price of admission. But history's most fabled revolt at sea surely deserves underpinnings that are factual rather than simply theatrical, award-winning, picturesque, and humanly appealing.

CHAPTER FOUR

A MIASMA OF VILIFICATION:
THE DEFENSE

Before attempting to set straight the record on Bligh, we might pause to consider how crooked and rigged that record is. We can best do this by a glance at a few excerpts — descriptions and fictionalized Bligh quotes, well decked out with exclamation points — taken at random from the books which have been written about the mutiny. These are the "meat" of the popular version. As a professional courtesy, I shall not identify the authors; it is not all that relevant to this study. What follows is offered both as background to refresh the reader's mind and Exhibit One in the posthumous case of Bligh versus the Popular Myth:

"Kindness! Our seamen understand kindness as well as they understand Greek! Fear is what they *do* understand! Without that, mutiny and piracy would be rife on the high seas!" [Bligh to an officer.]

Bligh's face was black with rage as the man was being roped with hemp to the grating placed across the gangway. The first blow of the cat was applied . . . Bligh, having ordered the boatswain's mate to "do his duty," looked on with a thin smile of satisfaction.

"I know, I know!" said Bligh in his most offensive way. . . . He turned to Christian once more, and his manner changed to an unpleasant truculence.

"Mr. Bligh gave me a side-long glance and one of his slight, grim smiles." [A description of Bligh watching a man being flogged to his death before the *Bounty* left Spithead.]

"I'll tame you — by God, I will. Another word from you and I'll have you seized up and flogged to the bone." [Bligh to a crewman.]

"You insolent rascals!" exclaimed Bligh violently. "By God! I'll make you eat grass before I've done with you."

Bligh was a man of extremely irritable temper, of coarse habits and entertained very mistaken notions with regard to discipline. . . .

"Let [Morrison, the boatswain's mate] take care! I've my eye on him, for I can see that he spares the cat. A boatswain's mate who was not a gentleman would have had half the hide off Birkitt's back. Let him take care, I say! Let him lay on when I give the word or, by God, I'll have him seized up for a lesson from the boatswain himself!"

. . . the men resolved to bear their sufferings with patience, and neither murmured nor complained from that time. But the officers, though they dared make no open complaints, were less easily satisfied and murmured frequently among themselves of their continual state of hunger, which they thought was due to the fact that the captain and his clerk had profited from the victualling of the ship.

"You're not content! Let me tell you, by God, that you'd better make up your minds to *be* content! Everything that Mr. Samuel [the ship's clerk] does is done by my orders, do you understand? My orders! Waste no more time in complaints, for you will get no redress! I am the only judge of what is right and wrong. Damn your eyes! I'm tired of you and your complaints! The first man to complain from now on will be seized up and flogged!"

. . . I shall not speak of the flogging of Young, nor tell how Skinner's back was cut to ribbons with two dozen at the gangway. It is enough to say that Young was a different man from that day on, performing his duties sullenly and in silence, and avoiding the other midshipmen.

Reluctantly, and in angry silence, Christian unwrapped the small package to display a matched pair of pearls as large as gooseberries, and of the most perfect orient. After a moment's hesitation, Bligh spoke: "Give them to Mr. Samuel . . . Pearls are highly prized in the Friendly Islands." "Surely, sir," exclaimed Christian angrily, "you do not mean to seize these as well! They were given me for my mother!" "Deliver them to Mr. Samuel," Bligh repeated.

. . . When in one of his rages Bligh seemed insane. I had never before met a man of this kind, and my conclusion was, having observed him so often in this state, that he had little recollection, afterward, of what he had said or done. I observed that he frequently worked himself into these passions over matters for which he was really to blame. Being unwilling to admit a fault in his own conduct it seemed neces-

sary to convince himself, through anger, that the blame lay elsewhere.
. . . Bligh stamped up and down the quarter-deck, his face distorted
with passion, shaking his fists and shouting at us.

Remember that all of this, and like material, was written long
after the mutiny, by men who had never met Bligh or members of
the *Bounty* company, by authors who had no possible way of knowing how Bligh spoke, what he said to his men, and how he reacted
to specific incidents.

And so it has gone, down through the years, with Bligh getting
the worst of it even in literary footnotes. There is a choice one in
a book that appeared in Sydney in 1884 and which had a wide
readership in Britain and the United States as well as Australia. I
believe it played a part in giving the Bligh-was-a-bastard-Christian-
had-to-do-it theory enough momentum to carry over into the twentieth century.

The book was presented as a factual account. It was entitled
Mutiny in the Bounty, and it was written by Judge Alfred McFarland of a New South Wales District Court, a staunch believer in
the Popular Myth, or Hollywood Version, of Bligh and the mutiny.
At the bottom of one page, which he peppers with vilifying stuff
about Bligh, His Honor provided this footnote: "In quoting this
and other speeches of Mr. Bligh, I have purposely omitted *the
oaths* with which he garnished them."

How did Judge McFarland know what Bligh said to Christian
in the intimacy of his cabin? Christian left no account of the
voyage and his role in the revolt; the words certainly aren't drawn
from Bligh's writings. Where did the jurist-turned-author get his
quotes — precise but for the Judge's alleged laundering-out of pro-
fanities and blasphemies — of Bligh raging insanely against a midshipman or an able-bodied, or urging on the man wielding the
cat-o'-nine-tails. Who was taking a shorthand note for the Judge?
The words are not drawn from logs, diaries, eyewitness accounts,
or trial proceedings. And when no less a figure than a member of
a British bench abandons the elementary rules of evidence and
juridical fairness, Bligh's reputation is in real jeopardy.

If the Judge had been interested in drawing up a true bill of
why His Majesty's Navy lost the *Bounty*, he might have turned to

the actual documents of the day, the writings of the men who were with Bligh. A letter written by Thomas Ledward, who took over from the *Bounty*'s bibulous surgeon, Thomas Huggan, or "Old Bacchus," after he expired in Tahiti from a combination of rum and Madeira, throws a different light on Bligh's character: "The captain, though a passionate man, is, I believe, a good-hearted man and has behaved very handsomely to me." (This was after the court-martial and at a time when Bligh's historic drubbing was about to begin.) Another man, sailmaker Laurence Lebogue, who served under Bligh both on the *Bounty* and on the second vessel dispatched to Tahiti for breadfruit, the *Providence*, seconded Ledward's words: "Every person in the *Providence* would speak well of Captain Bligh — he was a father to every person. . . . Captain Bligh was not a person fond of flogging his men; and some of them deserved hanging who had only a dozen."

Bligh's detractors present a picture of a man with ineradicable meanness and hatred in his soul. If so, the company who sailed with Bligh on the second breadfruit expedition does not appear to have detected it. These men ventured forth with Bligh at a time when rumors were just beginning to spread through the navy about the man who lost tne *Bounty*. Yet the *Kentish Register* recorded on September 6, 1793, that the latest voyage, that of the *Providence*, ended with Bligh "being cheered on quitting the ship . . . and at the dock gates the men drew up and repeated the parting acclamation."

This vote of confidence in Bligh from the fo'c'sle was warmly endorsed by a fellow officer. Edward Harwood, who sailed as surgeon on the *Providence*, had a letter published in *The Times* on July 16, 1794. "Captain Bligh's general conduct during the late expedition, which was crowned with the most ample success, his affability to his officers, and humane attention to his men, gained him their high esteem and admiration," he wrote, "and must eventually dissipate any unfavourable opinion, hastily adopted in his absence." (He was referring to the subtle effect on public opinion of the book which had just been published by Fletcher Christian's brother, Edward.)

There is certainly no meanness in Bligh's own writing. In his *Narrative*, published soon after his return to London and before ten of the mutineers caught in Tahiti were returned for trial, he had these mild words for the men who had pirated his ship, subjected him to exquisite humiliation, and set him adrift with deliberately slim chances of survival; I read these as the comments of an eminently reasonable man, especially when one bears in mind what the person behind the quill had been through in the preceding months:

Christian, the chief of the mutineers, is of a respectable family in the north of England. This was the third voyage he had made with me; and, as I found it necessary to keep my ship's company at three watches, I had given him an order to take charge of the third, his abilities being thoroughly equal to the task.

Heywood is also of a respectable family in the north of England, and a young man of abilities, as well as Christian. These two had been objects of my particular regard and attention, and I had taken great pains to instruct them, having entertained hopes that, as professional men, they would have become a credit to their country.

Young was well recommended, and had the look of an able stout seaman; he, however, fell short of what his appearance promised.

Stewart was a young man of creditable parents, in the Orkneys . . . but, independent of his recommendation, he was a seaman, and had always borne a good character.

When he set down on paper his feelings at the moment he and the loyal crew members were cast adrift, the impression Bligh gives is that of a man writing with a clear conscience. After recording Christian's emotional words of farewell to him, "That is the thing; I am in hell — I am in hell," Bligh wrote:

As soon as I had time to reflect, I felt an inward satisfaction, which prevented any depression of my spirits: conscious of my integrity and anxious solicitude for the good of the service in which I had been engaged, I found my mind wonderfully supported, and I began to conceive hopes, notwithstanding so heavy a calamity, that I should one day be able to account to my King and country for the misfortune. A few hours before, my situation had been peculiarly flattering. I had a ship in the most perfect order, and well stored with every necessary both for service and health; by early attention to those particulars I had, as much as lay in my power, provided against any accident, in case I could not get through Endeavour Straits, as well as against what might befall me in them.

Bligh seems to have reacted to Christian's insurrection with genuine shock and bewilderment. He wrote in his *Narrative* that

. . . the secrecy of this mutiny is beyond all conception. Thirteen of the party, who were with me, had always lived forward among the seamen; yet neither they, nor the messmates of Christian, Stewart, Heywood and Young, had ever observed any circumstance that made them in the least suspect what was going on. To such a close-planned act of villainy, my mind being entirely free from any suspicion, it is not wonderful that I fell a sacrifice. Perhaps, if there had been marines on board, a sentinel at my cabin-door might have prevented it; for I slept with the door always open, that the officer of the watch might have access to me on all occasions, the possibility of such a conspiracy being ever the farthest from my thoughts. Had their mutiny been occasioned by any grievances, either real or imaginary, I must have discovered symptoms of their discontent, which would have put me on my guard; but the case was far otherwise. Christian, in particular, I was on the most friendly terms with: and the preceding night, he excused himself from supping with me, on pretence of being unwell; for which I felt concerned, having no suspicions of his integrity and honour.

But the *Narrative* and other writing from Bligh's hand were bogus, according to his detractors, a clever and cynical whitewash job. A comparison of Bligh's log and his subsequent journals throws down this theory. In fact, in compiling his *Narrative* and later published works, Bligh omitted certain entries from the log and his personal papers that would have shown himself in the best possible light. This is especially true on the crucial issue of his personal feelings toward corporal punishment.

The published works from Bligh's hand make rather dull reading. No wonder they have been eclipsed by the books produced later by livelier minds and imaginations. Bligh's books and journals are weighty with the minutiae of the voyage, all dutifully recorded: the Tahitians had stolen the butcher's cleaver; two men were on the Venereal List; this many breadfruit of the 1,015 taken on board were showing signs of wilting; at such-and-such a precise latitude and longitude, this minor event occurred; and so on. He records the precise number of coconuts stored in odd parts of his ship, the exact number of yams stacked behind the bitts, the full inventory of nails, knives, adzes, beads, and looking glasses given to the Indians in each exercise in bartering for food. He mentions that all chests were taken ashore on his orders to be scrubbed out with boiling water to keep the *Bounty* free of cockroaches. He was as good a housekeeper as he was a navigator.

There is really no need to refresh the reader's memory as to how well Fletcher Christian, alias Gable, alias Brando, has emerged from the Popular Myth and Hollywood Version, from the pens of nineteenth-century fictioneers and from the typewriters of twentieth-century scenarists. He is perfection unto itself. But an example or two may be in order:

— Christian was always cheerful and his example was of the greatest service in exciting his companions to labor.
— He was naturally of a happy and ingenuous disposition and won the good opinion and respect of all who served under him.
— Christian maintained the strictest discipline, but no one had cause to complain of his justice. He was a born leader of men, and knew how to rule them without the perpetual floggings and abuse which Bligh considered so essential.
— Under the influence of his appealing kindly manner I found my indignation melting away. I stood before Fletcher Christian, my friend, not the mutineer who has cast nineteen men adrift in a small boat thousands of miles from home.

Again, all these descriptions, assessments, and quotes are *fiction*, composed by inventive Englishmen, Americans, Australians, and others who lived after Bligh had gone to his grave and the bones of his ship had started to rot away on the seabed in Bounty Bay.

The bulging storehouse of anti-Bligh calumnies contains little to show that Christian until the mutiny was a grateful protégé of Bligh. In his late teens and early twenties, he learned much of his seamanship, his ability as a navigator, from the didactic skipper who was to share the stage with him in one of the greatest dramas of men at sea. No one over the years has suggested they were intimate friends in their pre-*Bounty* days, simply sailing mates in a master-and-pupil relationship.

Could there have been anything *unnatural* in that relationship? When historians set out to analyze the lives, actions, and possible aberrations of British naval personalities, the temptation is always to seek a homosexual explanation. This holds true not simply for the eighteenth century but for most other centuries — sixteenth, seventeenth, nineteenth, and twentieth. It is the special obloquy of the British Navy. Richard Hough, an English historian who has been conducting his own postmortem on the Bligh-Christian relationship, seems inclined to believe that there was not only foul mutiny on the *Bounty* but perhaps also some high-level sodomy. He has been assembling material on what he described in a newspaper interview in 1971 as "the love-hate relationship with certain homosexual overtones which existed between Bligh and Christian, two deeply passionate and deeply confused men." He theorizes that on each of their three voyages together, Bligh had either over-favored Christian or deliberately humiliated him in front of the men.

Bligh was certainly a passionate man, although hardly in the flesh sense. But confused? By no means. Bligh a bit of a gay, Christian his quarter-deck swish? Hardly. If there was anything unnatural about Bligh, it was his outright love for the navy and his infatuation with the missions it handed him. From the demands of his career, he spent little time with his wife and daughters; while he loved them deeply — his letters home are touching evidence here — he can hardly be regarded as an orthodox family man. But it was duty and the sea, not any perverted hankering for masculine company, that brought about this situation. If Bligh had chosen a shorebound career, as a solicitor, say, or a merchant, he would have been the stodgiest, most conventional husband around.

When it came to sex, Bligh's mind was as pure and straitlaced as those of the missionaries who were to follow him to the Pacific. The slightest departure from sexual norms left him quite baffled. On January 15, 1789, while the *Bounty* was at anchor off Tahiti, he wrote in his log:

On my visit to Tynah and his wife Iddeeah, I found with her a person who, although I was certain was a man, had great marks of effeminacy about him. On asking Iddeeah who he was, she told me he was a friend of hers, and also of a class common in Otaheite called *Mahoo*. That the men had frequent connections with him, and that he lived and observed the same ceremonies as the women did. The effeminacy of this person's speech induced me to think he had suffered castration, and that other unnatural and shocking things were done by him, and particularly as I had myself some idea that it was common in this Sea.

Bligh questioned Tynah, a Tahitian chief, about the *mahoos*, and from what he learned, wrote in his log that "It is strange that in so prolific a country as this, man should be led into such sensual and beastly acts of gratification, but perhaps in no other place in the world are they so common or so extraordinary as in this island."

In the very first few weeks of the stay at Matavai Bay, Bligh had picked up, over a feast with a group of island chiefs, what he called "a piece of scandal." He confided it to his log: "This was that Iddeeah, Tynah's wife, kept a gallant called Tuerree, and it was so far agreeable to both parties that both men cohabited with the wife in the same hour, and in the presence of one another. The virtue and chastity of the chief women is by no means equal to what is represented, and it certainly is not a fact that they will not grant certain favours if opportunity and convenience offers."

The man who wrote those reports, who married happily, may have been a bit on the prudish side, but there is nothing to suggest he was anything other than an archetypal heterosexual. And there is nothing in Christian's record to suggest he was anything but the most energetic womanizer, a skirt-chaser of almost fanatical dedication and considerable achievement. A sexual overachiever, in fact, in the Errol Flynn mold.

Within the cramped confines of the *Bounty*, if there had been any suggestion of a "love-hate relationship" between her skipper and master's mate, the first part of the relationship surely would have been as apparent to the crew as the second. It would certainly have been touched upon by one or more witnesses at the mutineers' court-martial. The idea, then, that the trouble on the *Bounty* was due, either directly or indirectly, to the "English vice," is one I cannot accept.

The "charges" against William Bligh, the allegations of the Popular Myth that is, may be broken down basically into six separate accusations: that he was sadistic in the use of the cat-o'-nine-tails; that he was utterly lacking in compassion for those under him; that he singled out Fletcher Christian for especially tough and unfair treatment; that he craftily shortchanged the men's rations, lining his own pockets at the expense of his crew's health and morale; that he was overthrown as a result of a popular uprising supported by a majority of the *Bounty*'s hands; and finally, that he was somehow *mutiny-prone*. I shall deal with each in turn.

Allegation No. 1: That Bligh not only considered the "cat" as essential as sails and rudder in propelling his ship but also derived unnatural pleasure in seeing the flesh being torn off men's backs.

The most spectacular and enduring allegations revolve around Bligh's use or misuse of the lash. The truth about Bligh's attitude toward corporal punishment, and his actual performance record, are preserved in black and white in various archives, in the National Maritime Museum at Greenwich, England, in the Mitchell Library in Sydney, and elsewhere. The record here must be studied in the light of what we know about attitudes toward military punishment that prevailed at the time, the standard naval operating practice of the late eighteenth century. Once the facts have been elicited, it does not require great analytical powers to reach a surprising conclusion: Bligh flogged far less than most commanders of his day, was actually guilty of being "soft" on many bad offenders, and, again judged by the standards of his day, should rightly be viewed as a liberal, at times an ultraliberal, commander when it came to meting out punishment. I shall go further and make the outrageous claim (taken up later in this chapter) that even by today's standards of military punishment, Bligh's approach to summary justice aboard his ship was one of tolerance and leniency from someone in a position of absolute authority.

From his own pen, long before the mutiny took place and there was any need for Bligh to defend or justify his actions, we have a clue as to his personal attitude toward flogging. Eight weeks after leaving Spithead, as the *Bounty* was off the coast of Brazil, she passed an English whaler, and Bligh was able to send a letter home to Duncan Campbell with the whaler's skipper. "My men are all active good fellows, and what has given me much pleasure is that I have not yet been obliged to punish any one," he wrote.

The Admiralty Articles in Bligh's time required that each and every recourse to the lash be entered in the ship's log. A captain could falsify this record only at the risk of being denounced at journey's end by one of his officers or men. A challenge from the fo'c'sle would have been considered unusual, perhaps dismissed as impertinent, but there was always the chance that a sensitive midshipman — and these were often the ones who had important social, military, or political connections — would blow the whistle on a monstrously unfair captain.

The "cat" was an integral part of naval justice. The eighteenth-century *Falconer's Marine Dictionary* states that the cat-o'-nine-tails was usually made aboard a naval vessel rather than acquired as an issue item. It consisted of nine pieces of line or cord, each about eighteen inches long, bound together in a handle of coiled rope. Each "tail" had three knots tied at intervals, the first being almost at the end of the cord to tear away at the flesh as the lash was drawn across the back. The *Bounty*'s "cat" would have been made by the boatswain or the boatswain's mate.

The facts concerning how often Bligh ordered its use have been ascertainable since the day Bligh made his way back to England. The ship's records, conscientiously recovered by Bligh's clerk, John Samuel, showed that Bligh, in the seventeen-odd months he was in command of the ship, ordered only *eleven* floggings with a total of 229 lashes. Throughout the grueling hauls across the North and South Atlantic, the Indian and Pacific Oceans to reach Tahiti, the long stay in Tahiti, and on the interrupted journey to the West Indies, the cat-o'-nine-tails had been taken from the boatswain's locker fewer than a dozen times. Other Royal Navy commanders, flogging routinely at the rate of once or twice weekly, might have decided, upon reading this record, either that Bligh was seriously losing his grip or that he had been assigned a crew of maritime angels.

In appraising Bligh's record on corporal punishment against that of one of his contemporaries, I have selected for comparison not one of the notoriously sadistic commanders of the day (for that would be a simple way of warping the record), but a man whom history has accepted as one of the greatest humanitarians of his time.

Captain James Cook wears one of the whitest hats of the eighteenth century; Bligh, of course, has been given one of the blackest. Cook's record on flogging may be studied in the Admiralty archives, and it reveals him as a far tougher man than Bligh. (The Cook-Bligh comparison, incidentally, has almost clinical precision. They undertook basically similar voyages, at a common period in British naval history, and the corporal punishment they ordered took place in the same area of the Pacific.)

On Cook's first voyage to the Pacific aboard the *Endeavour* (1768–1771), a seaman, Archibald Wolf, was brought before him on a charge of stealing nails from the storeroom while the ship was anchored in Matavai Bay. Sentence: two dozen strokes of the "cat." A little later, just before the *Endeavour* was to quit Tahiti, two marines, Clement Webb and Sam Gibson, deserted and fled to the mountains with their native mistresses. Cook had to dispatch a strong force under his second officer, and the deserters were soon recaptured. They told Cook they had fallen so deeply in love with their girls they could not bear to leave. Cook ordered two dozen lashes for each man and had them held in irons until the ship sailed.

At the same spot, some twenty years later, Bligh had to deal with a far graver act of desertion. Before dawn on January 5, 1789, the relief watch found Midshipman Thomas Hayward asleep at his post as usual and the jolly boat missing from its place amidships. Bligh was awakened, and he ordered a muster of all hands. Three of the company were missing: Marine Corporal Charles Churchill, Seaman-Assistant Cook William Muspratt, and Seaman John Millward. The deserters had got away not only with the jolly boat but also with eight muskets from the locked weapons chest. The discovery that they had taken more muskets than they might need for their personal use was of particular significance. It suggested they had probably made a secret deal with one of the warring

Tahitian chieftains, all of whom coveted the white man's guns above any other manufactured item.

In such circumstances, Cook's policy was first to seize a number of important Tahitian men and women as hostages and hold them on board his ship, or in the fort ashore, until the runaways were returned. If that did not work, he would send his marines ashore. Bligh's response was to go ashore and try to persuade some of the native leaders to help him in pursuing the men. The native grapevine quickly informed Bligh that the deserters had abandoned the jolly boat and had set out by native canoe for the coral island of Teturoa, a day's sail to the north of Tahiti.

With Fletcher Christian in charge of important work ashore, and lacking confidence in the ability of any of his midshipmen to command a pursuit mission, Bligh sought the help of two Tahitian chieftains in recapturing the men. Bad weather, however, delayed the departure of the Tahitian party for a week. In the meantime, the three deserters had slipped back to Tahiti and were in hiding further around the coast. With the help of some natives, Bligh himself set out, by boat first and then on foot, to capture the deserters. The men surrendered without any resistance, and Bligh escorted them back to the *Bounty*.

All three were guilty of crimes which undoubtedly would have led them to a naval gallows had they been brought before a court-martial at home. They were guilty of not just one but several capital offenses: desertion, entering into a conspiracy with native factions, theft of a ship's boat, theft of weapons, and interfering seriously with the work of an important Royal mission. Considering the gravity of the counts against them, Bligh's punishment was remarkably mild. Millward and Muspratt got four dozen lashes and Churchill got two dozen (the same punishment Cook gave the nail thief), the floggings to be administered over a twelve-day period. In Churchill's case, this meant two strokes of the lash per day. (Bligh did not explain why Churchill's sentence was lighter.)

I should make the point here that these strokes were the *sole* punishment carried out on the men. Bligh agreed to close the case against the men on the spot. Their desertion and other crimes would not be reported to the Admiralty, which automatically would have brought the men to trial. In effect, Bligh was sparing their lives. No wonder the three men composed and sent to their captain a letter expressing deep remorse over what they had done and gratitude for the mildness of sentence. In the case of Churchill, the light punishment was particularly surprising since the untrustworthy corporal represented Bligh's one-man security force.

Why, then, did Bligh have a mutiny on his hands after his men had tasted the delights of Tahiti, while Cook sailed home from the Pacific with an orderly ship? The major reason, I believe, is that Cook, provided with a larger vessel, had been able to take a loyal squad of twelve marines along with him; Bligh had a single marine aboard, a man not particularly well chosen for the task and one who was required to work as an ordinary seaman because of the manning problems aboard the *Bounty*.

To an overwhelming majority today, any resort to lashing is repulsive. To fully comprehend William Bligh's "restraint," we must obtain a true, if sickening, picture of the use of corporal punishment in the British military in the eighteenth and early nineteenth centuries. Our best guide here is a well-researched book, *Under the Lash*, by Scott Claver, published in Britain in 1954.* It is a standard work in a field that historians generally have ignored.

Claver's report showed that the application of *one thousand* strokes of the "cat" was not considered scandalously excessive. In Bligh's period, lashings by the hundreds were quite routine. Bligh measured the penalty strokes by the dozen — usually one or two dozen, on an occasion four dozen. In general, he seems to have kept the biblical injunction that a judge may inflict forty stripes on a prisoner but no more. Claver states that the thousand-lash punishment was routine enough to require set procedures. After the prisoner had been bound to the grating on the main deck, the ship's surgeon took his place beside the man wielding the lash. His role was to interrupt the proceedings at intervals and feel the prisoner's pulse to determine how long the flogging could be continued without killing him. If the surgeon called a halt to the flogging, the man was unshackled and taken below to have his wounds treated. After a few hundred lashes, the prisoner would

* Torchstream Books, London.

have not simply a network of intersecting wounds but one large, crimson wound extending from his shoulders to his loins. The prisoner would remain in irons until the wound had healed to the point at which the back was judged ready to take another assault from the "cat." Then he was brought up to receive the rest of his lashes. A thousand lashes might take a week or two to inflict. Often, the prisoner cheated justice by dying after one of these sessions.

The severity of these sentences, the brutality of whipping a man over the scars still tender from last week's lash strokes, were known in the highest places. With Royal intervention, an upper limit of one thousand lashes was set in January, 1807, the order being couched in terms that suggested His Majesty regarded it as a rather benevolent move. In promulgating the sentence of a private of the 54th Regiment who was awaiting *fifteen hundred* lashes for mutinous conduct, George III had this comment appended: "It appearing to His Majesty that a punishment to the extent of one thousand lashes is a sufficient example for any breach of military discipline, short of capital offence, and as even that number cannot be safely inflicted at any one period, His Majesty has been graciously pleased to express his opinion that no sentence for corporal punishment should exceed one thousand lashes." (Nevertheless, an unfortunate young Englishman in Bengal three months later was sentenced to fifteen hundred lashes; the sentence was confirmed and he received every one of them.) Claver also discovered that in the British Army in 1812, the mean number of lashes inflicted monthly for some years in a regiment in India was *seventeen thousand.*

The army flogged ruthlessly to maintain order in far-flung outposts. In the navy, the lash was used often at the whim of a captain who either took pleasure in seeing men suffer ceremonially or felt that an afternoon of terror was the most effective way of curbing a potentially mutinous or sluggish crew. Neither of these sins can be entered against Bligh's record. Compare Bligh's eleven floggings in seventeen months with Claver's account of a Marine Sergeant Lowe who set down a record of floggings he had witnessed in the service in the 1830's. He recounted that he had often seen, in a single morning, twenty men receive five hundred lashes each after being found guilty by a drumhead court-martial of slight offenses.

The navy and the marines, in fact, were so addicted to almost indiscriminate use of the "cat" during the period in question that the army had a special punishment: "Removal to the Navy." The soldier was given the choice of continuing with his severe army punishment or joining one of His Majesty's ships. The wise ones stayed away from the sea.

The Royal Navy had a broad range of punishments, some of exquisite cruelty, some invented by commanders who obviously took a perverted pleasure in sexually humiliating or even sexually mutilating the men under them. A particularly crude one was "Riding the Spanker-Boom." It was kept for the most trivial offenses and applied frequently to sailors in their teens. The offender was detrousered and forced to ride the boom sitting on a wet swab soaked with gunpowder. The itching and inflammation in the genital area took days or weeks to subside. Some of Bligh's fellow commanders ordered their carpenters to make innocent-looking wooden rocking horses. The saddle area, however, was nothing but the narrow edge of a thin, undressed plank. The offending sailor, naked, would be strapped on it and ordered to rock away his sins. Truly malevolent captains were known to have sentenced men to be shot from guns for serious offenses. Others dealt with habitual drunkenness by "blistering" — ordering boiling oil or boiling water to be poured on the backs of those who drank to excess.

There were other punishments of far greater refinement and bestiality whose descriptions are fit only for specialty works on the subject.

Bligh used none of these punishments. If he had — aboard the *Bounty* or at any time during his career — the details certainly would have emerged at the court-martial of the captured mutineers or during the campaign mounted to malign Bligh by the relatives of those mutineers still at large.

Why was Bligh's most moderate use of the "cat" not made an important prosecution theme during the court-martial? If it had been, the fiction men who came along later to sensationalize the Bligh-*Bounty* story would have found their job that much more difficult. The explanation, I believe, is twofold: first, Bligh was not present at the trial. He left a deposition for the court, of course, but at this stage no one was seriously suggesting that the mutiny was brought about by an overly harsh command. Second, the Admiralty felt absolutely no need to defend any aspect of corporal punishment aboard its ships. Not only was it part of the system, in this case, some senior officers might have considered it embarrassing to the service had it become widely known that aboard at least one British man-o-war, grave offenses against order and discipline drew no more than a dozen or two dozen lashes.

I made the claim earlier that Bligh rightly should have been judged by history as a man who used the lash relatively leniently and tolerantly, and that his ideas on fitting the punishment to the crime might surprise even present-day military commanders. To go back to the desertion in Tahiti of Churchill, Millward, and Muspratt: they confessed themselves guilty of a number of capital crimes; the price they paid, Bligh's total sentence to close the case against them, ranged from two dozen to four dozen strokes of the lash. Might not a serviceman in a modern army, having confessed to several capital crimes, prefer twenty-four or forty-eight strokes to life imprisonment or execution?

Allegation No. 2: That Lieutenant Bligh was the most authoritarian of skippers, utterly lacking in compassion for those under him, a character devoid of human feeling.

Most of us, raised from childhood on *Bounty* books and *Bounty* celluloid — even, in the 1930's, *Bounty* comics — delude ourselves into believing that we know Bligh and Christian fairly well. Didn't Bligh, simply to keep to a timetable and please his Admiralty masters, callously commit his men to a disastrous rounding of Cape Horn, driving them on long after it was clear that the ship could not battle her way against violent headwinds through the Tierra del Fuego passage? The ship's papers, however, record that he was solicitous of his men's welfare, that he kept a fire going below in dirty weather, and surrendered his own cabin during this period to the men whose own berths were awash with icy water.

On April 16, 1788, as the *Bounty* was in the nightmarish grip of a Cape Horn blow, Bligh wrote in his log that "I cannot expect my men and officers to bear it much longer," adding later: "I now ordered my cabin to be appropriated at nights to the use of those poor fellows who had wet berths, by which means it . . . rendered those happy who had not dry beds to sleep in."

Bligh's reputation as a man of irascible temper — and to a degree this is probably deserved — has obscured the evidence that he was a thoughtful and considerate man, unusually so for his day, in his dealings with nonwhites. In this, his compassion placed him several moral rungs above the great majority of his contemporary fellow countrymen, military and civilian.

One of his concerns on the eve of the *Bounty*'s arrival in Matavai Bay was to do what he could to prevent the spread of venereal disease among the Tahitians. They had contracted the disease certainly by the time Bougainville's and Cook's expeditions called at Tahiti two decades earlier. (In later years, each country's navy would lay the blame for introducing VD in paradise on the scrofulous ratings from the other side of the Channel, a tiny facet of the mounting Anglo-French hostility.) The night before he took his ship through the reef and into Matavai Bay, Bligh ordered a VD check for every member of the ship's company. Presumably it would have amounted to no more than a perfunctory examination of crew genitalia. But the good intentions certainly were there, and it was more trouble than many other commanders of his time were prepared to take in their dealings with inferior infidels.

This was how Bligh recorded the VD check in his log: "As there was a great probability that we should remain a considerable time at Otaheite, it could not be expected that the intercourse of my people should be of a very reserved nature. I therefore ordered that every person should be examined by the Surgeon, and had the satisfaction to learn from his report that they were all perfectly free from the venereal complaint." From a medical viewpoint, Bligh's log entry may have been somewhat ingenuous, particularly since he knew that the doctor inspecting the penises was probably swaying with wine or rum at the time; but it tells us something interesting about the human qualities he possessed, even when natives were involved.

Was he a sadist, the coldest of monsters? Every now and then, the log he was keeping on the *Bounty*'s voyage — and bear in mind that all these entries were made long before his character was called into question — reveals him as something of a softie. When he was called upon to take the hoary role of King Neptune for the Equator-crossing ceremony of February 9, 1788, he refused even to dunk the initiates in the water, a practice which is still observed today on some of the most civilized cruising yachts. His log for that day has this entry: "This afternoon, those who had never crossed the Line before underwent the usual ceremony except ducking, which I never would allow, for of all the customs it is the most brutal and inhuman."

In earlier pages, I have given details of Bligh's regard for his crew's welfare in matters of diet and exercise. In deciding the daily regimen for his ship, Bligh also showed consideration for his men. Instead of the customary practice, which required a man to be on duty every other four-hour period throughout the day, Bligh had decided to keep his ship's company at three watches, an arrangement that ensured a decent respite from work for every man daily. "I have always considered this a desirable regulation, when circumstances will admit of it, on many accounts; and am persuaded that unbroken rest not only contributes much to the health of the ship's company, but enables them more readily to exert themselves in cases of sudden emergency," he wrote in explaining his three-watch system.

Rest was one of the crew's basic human needs. Sex was another. And when it came to permitting the men to gratify the urgent lust in their loins, Bligh was certainly considerate. Perhaps, in view of what was to happen soon after the departure from Tahiti, overly considerate.

Allegation No. 3: That he singled out Fletcher Christian for especially tough and unfair treatment.

A captain naturally demands better performance from his officers than he does from his able-bodied seamen. His log and his subsequent writing are sprinkled with criticism of the way some of his midshipmen carried out their duties; but Christian was not a target here in the months that preceded the mutiny. He was

Bligh's protégé and was treated for the most part fairly sympathetically.

When they first shipped together on a man-o-war, Bligh is credited with having the ship's boy Fletcher Christian promoted to gunner's mate. And the *Bounty* was only a few days out from Spithead, making good headway toward the tip of Argentina and the futile attempt to take the shortcut around Cape Horn, when Bligh again demonstrated his confidence in and respect for Christian. At the risk of offending his sailing master, John Fryer, Bligh appointed Christian acting lieutenant. He was not obliged to do so, either by naval custom or by the exigencies of his ship's command structure. Had the mission gone well, and Christian returned safely to England, the commission no doubt would have been confirmed in time. It was an important assist up the ladder of naval promotion for a man in his early twenties. Bligh was raising Christian close to his own rank, a generous gesture by an officer presumably still smarting at being given a major command without the elevation to a captaincy.

There is ample evidence that Bligh regarded Christian as the most trustworthy member of his company. He placed him in overall charge of the breadfruit-potting, the primary aim of the mission. Earlier, when he had put in to Santa Cruz on Tenerife, he dispatched Christian on a courtesy visit to the Spanish Governor. Relations between Spain and England were badly strained at the time, and Bligh's choice of the envoy to send ashore would have been a careful one, particularly since he needed the fresh supplies Santa Cruz merchants had to offer.

Until well into the voyage, Bligh, at least, considered the ship's company to be a harmonious group. In his letter home to Duncan Campbell, he referred to only a single problem case: "My officers and young gentlemen are all tractable and well disposed, and we now understand each other so well that we shall remain so the whole voyage, unless I fall out with the doctor, who I have trouble from preventing being in bed fifteen hours out of the twenty-four."

Bligh and Christian had one glorious row, two days before the mutiny, as the ship was sailing between the Tongan islands of Nomuka and Tofua. This was an episode in the Stolen Coconuts

Affair. There are several versions of this affair, and the contradictions are such that it is difficult to determine who was telling the truth. At Nomuka, the ship had taken on a large supply of coconuts as well as fruit, yams, live pigs, and native souvenirs. The coconuts were especially desirable in the provisioning of the ship: they provided not only food, but also, in the sweet liquid inside, a substitute for drinking water if the *Bounty* ran into a rainless period. Bligh had supervised the stacking of hundreds of coconuts on the deck between the gun mountings, and before retiring for the night instructed those on watch to make sure that the pile was not raided by greedy crewmen. Next morning, when he was making his rounds, Bligh decided that the pile looked suspiciously smaller.

"Mr. Fryer, don't you think those coconuts are shrunk since last night?" he asked his sailing master. Fryer agreed that the pile did look smaller — it no longer extended to the ship's railing — but suggested that the men on night watches might have rearranged the nuts so they would take up less deck space. But Bligh was certain that his carefully organized larder had been raided. He apparently made a blanket accusation against all members of the company — Christian and the other gentlemen as well as the ordinary seamen. Unable to get a confession from any of them, Bligh ordered each man to produce his own private store of coconuts. The nuts were carried back from the fo'c'sle and up from the petty officers' cabins and assembled on deck. Bligh's pedantic nature now came to the fore. He questioned each individual in turn about the number of nuts he had purchased on shore and how many of these had been consumed so far. Christian and the midshipmen were included in this interrogation, a humiliating experience for men who looked upon themselves as candidates for privileged treatment, or at the very least, to be treated as a group apart from the able-bodied ranks. The case of the missing nuts was not resolved to Bligh's satisfaction. All it did was to inject a bitter note into the atmosphere aboard a ship whose company, mentally, was still back in the easy, happy days of Tahiti.

The Stolen Coconuts Affair provided a good example of what I consider to be Bligh's chief human failing, a lack of tact in his dealings with those under him. It provided also an example of his quick temper. There was aggression in this Cornishman, certainly, but it vented in short colorful tirades rather than in physical sadism. The irascible outbursts were soon over, and the morning after, Bligh would greet the object of yesterday's anger as if nothing had happened.

Allegation No. 4: That Bligh shortchanged the men's rations.

Much has been made of the suggestion that Bligh, who was required to act as his own purser, entered into a wicked partnership with his clerk, Mr. Samuel, a Jew from the East End of London. In victualing the *Bounty,* if one believes the popular version, Bligh and Samuel lined their own pockets and stomachs at the expense of the crew's well-being. No popular book on the mutiny is complete without reference to the alleged discrepancy in the ship's stores of two fifty-pound cheeses and a cask of wine. There is no proof here, one way or the other. If Bligh did, in fact, filch them and have them transported to his home before the *Bounty* sailed, he would merely have been exercising one of the privileges accorded to a ship's captain of the period. It was taken for granted in those days that a skipper of modest means, with no private income, would "liberate" a small quantity of the ship's supplies to help stock his family's larder for the year or two he would be away. It was an eighteenth-century custom, just as the modern typist who steals ball-points and stamps, or the executive who claims $90 on his expense account for entertaining a European client, when, in fact, he has taken his wife to a French restaurant and a discotheque, are adjusting their ways to contemporary *mores.*

What the ship's records bring out throughout, from the earliest days of Bligh's command when the ship was still undergoing her refit at Deptford, is the meticulousness of her captain's approach to laying in proper supplies.

Yet the Popular Myth insists that Bligh's record here was an abominable one, particularly during the months at anchorage in Tahiti. The fictionists have had great sport recounting the private customs system Bligh is said to have established at the taffrail to confiscate items his men brought back from shore or which were carried out to them by their new Tahitian friends. If the Indian *taios,* the *Bounty* men's companions on shore, paddled out canoes laden with gifts for a particular man, would not Bligh order that the pigs, fruit, coconuts, or *tapa* cloth be turned over without question to Mr. Samuel? In the midst of plenty, at the very lip of the Tahitian cornucopia, the men of the *Bounty*, if one believes the popular version, were daily deprived of the simplest pleasures of the mess table.

What happened to all these treats? No one complained at the court-martial of seeing Bligh consume a brace of suckling pigs in solitary gluttony in his cabin. Bligh was hoarding, yes, but hoarding for the long run home from Tahiti, diligently making sure that in the unknown waters ahead his ship would not run low on provisions. The voyage from Spithead to Matavai Bay had covered more than twenty-seven thousand miles and had taken the best part of a year. There were times when Bligh had no option but to put his men on short rations. On the homeward run, his prospects for revictualing stops were just as chancy. Every side of salted pork would be needed, every yam, every breadfruit, every coconut with its refreshing draft of sweet water, would be required for the ship's company. Every piece of Tahitian handicraft would be useful in trading for food with the natives of other islands. (Bligh's stock of basic trading items — nails and beads — had been sorely depleted in Tahiti for piquant reasons which we shall discuss in the following chapter.)

Bligh had learned from a virtuoso, Captain Cook himself, the art of scientifically provisioning a ship for a long voyage, of taking every advantage of land supplies when they were available. Little mention is made in the popular version of the fact that Bligh brought the *Bounty* to Tahiti through four oceans without a single death through scurvy. His French and Spanish contemporaries considered themselves lucky if they made such a voyage with the loss of only a dozen or so scurvy-afflicted sailors. Bligh's record was considerably better than that of his mentor, Captain Cook. By the time Cook returned to England in 1771 after his first voyage of discovery in the *Endeavour*, more than a third of the ninety men who had set out with him were dead of malaria and dysentery.

Bligh knew how simple English sailors would react when turned loose in the sumptuous pantry of Tahiti. They would gorge like fools and waste the very food that one day might mean survival or starvation. The men, according to all verifiable accounts of the stay in Tahiti, were far from ill treated. The crew's health blossomed. Apart from the death of "Old Bacchus" and a couple of men down with gonorrhea every week or two, the stay in Tahiti had an astonishingly restorative effect on the company. For the first time, perhaps, a ship's company of the King's Navy was truly happy, content down to the lowliest hand.

Later, after the seizure of the ship, the mutineers would appreciate fully Bligh's foresight. In the statements we have from those mutineers who surrendered in Tahiti, it is clear that Christian and company were pleasantly surprised to find the ship's storeroom so well stocked with salted pork from Tahiti.

Allegation No. 5: That this was a popular uprising, supported by a majority of the *Bounty*'s hands.

Perhaps influenced by the knowledge that the mutiny occurred in the same year as the French Revolution, some serious historians have sought to interpret the revolt as a manifestation of the class struggle that was developing on a broader scale: the mutineers were representatives of the oppressed, down-trodden ranks of English society; Bligh was the symbol of an exploiting upper class of outrageous privilege.

To some extent this is true. But it requires some contortion of the facts to consider the mutiny in its historical and social perspective and to pigeonhole it neatly under "class struggle." For one thing, the two men who became the ringleaders of the hard-core mutineers — the men who decided to strike out for an unknown future rather than risk recapture in Tahiti — were Fletcher Christian and Edward Young, both satin-breeched members of the same privileged class as Bligh.

Was it a popular revolt? The belief that it was is based on the number who remained aboard the *Bounty* — twenty-five — and the number who went with Bligh in the launch — eighteen. The truth is that Christian had a majority aboard the *Bounty* because more men could have joined Bligh only at the peril of the launch going under. Bligh actually remonstrated with Christian not to permit any more men to clamber down to the open boat, shouting up to the crowd at the *Bounty*'s high stern that he would "do you justice, lads, if ever we reach England." He meant, of course, those who were remaining aboard the *Bounty* against their will.

Nine, and perhaps as many as ten or eleven, midshipmen and crew who technically became mutineers would have thrown in their lot with Bligh had the launch been more commodious, and the prospect that its occupants were being consigned to almost certain death at sea less stark. The wonder is that eighteen members of the ship's company consented to go with Bligh on that morning in April, 1789, in a savage act of abandonment by their fellow countrymen. If we subtract nine from the number left aboard the *Bounty* when Bligh's party was cast adrift, Christian's group represented a minority, sixteen insurrectionists out of a total of forty-four aboard.

Allegation No. 6: That William Bligh was somehow *mutiny-prone.*

The accusation is based on the fact that Bligh was the victim of a second mutiny before his career was over. This was a revolt of landlubbers, the celebrated "Rum Rebellion" in Sydney in 1808.

In 1805, Bligh, four years after his heroic participation in Nelson's victory at the Battle of Copenhagen, was appointed Captain-General and Governor of the colony of New South Wales. The appointment was made at the suggestion again of Sir Joseph Banks. The British government needed someone who could bring a turbulent colonial situation under control. They dispatched Bligh as the reformer, but a reformer being sent into an impossible situation where all the might and muscle and guns were in the hands of those who had created the trouble.

He stepped ashore to assume his governorship in the wild and woolly town that was Sydney in the 1800's. Instead of sticking to their garrison roles, the army officers from England were interested almost exclusively in rackets. They had established monopolies on manufactured goods imported into the colony, were operating lucrative rum-running arrangements responsible for the nightly spectacles of drunkenness, and had formed sinister coalitions with powerful landed interests. From all these illegal operations, lieutenants, captains, and majors were amassing sizable profits which would enable them to retire in England as rich men. It was a situation in which those directing the rackets were the same men who had been sent out to put the settlement on an orderly basis.

By the time Bligh arrived, a clique of garrison officers was openly defying the authority of the Governor. Settlers were being forced to pay exorbitant prices for the goods they needed from England. Unscrupulous army officers had already made enough money to buy farms, and with free convict labor, were raising sheep and cattle for the English market. Bligh's first moves were those of a bold rackets-buster. He drew up new orders covering the distribution of foodstuffs and imported commodities, and almost overnight the army clique's illegal profits vanished.

But Bligh, just as he had been two decades before on the *Bounty*, was again an administrator without an adequate security force to see that his orders were carried out. His law enforcement agency, the army, was part of the underworld he was attempting to rout. In January, 1808, he was deposed by a mutiny headed by Major George Johnston of the 102nd Foot Regiment of the New South Wales Corps. He was held under house arrest by the mutineers until 1810 and then placed aboard a ship for England. The following year, Bligh was promoted to rear admiral. Major Johnston, meanwhile, had been subdued by a force sent out from England, brought home to a court-martial at Chelsea Hospital, and was dismissed from the service.

Of Bligh's true character and personality, some valuable shreds of evidence have survived through the miasma of vilification. There is no doubt that he had a sharp tongue and a temperament that did not suffer fools gladly or tolerate willful seamen. He was impatient with inefficiency. He was single-minded, dedicated. He had been sent with the *Bounty* to bring back breadfruit for the English planters of the West Indies, and he intended to do just that. Today we might describe him as a man "totally mission-oriented." His broader goal was to bring back from the South Seas not simply valuable trees but also a ship's company of men who were better sailors than when they had left Spithead.

For just such a mission as the *Bounty*'s, Bligh had modeled his life on the example of Captain Cook. He succeeded in emulating most of the master's qualities. He had courage, undeniably so, as the record of the trip back from Tofua demonstrated. Years later, after Copenhagen, Admiral Nelson personally would summon him to his cabin to compliment him on his gallantry under fire. He was a navigator with few equals in naval history. He lacked only one of Cook's qualities: a full measure of tact and human understanding.

CHAPTER FIVE

THAT OLD STANDBY, SEX

THE MODERN TRAVELER may walk the sparkling black sands of Matavai Bay and get a fairly authentic picture of the lure Tahiti must have exerted on the men who came aboard the *Bounty*. The last time I reconnoitered Matavai Bay, finishing up at Point Venus, the slender arrow of land on which Cook set up his scientific station to observe the transit of Venus across the sun, and near where Christian established his breadfruit nursery, I tried this mental exercise.

It was a few minutes before sundown. The westering sun was making a spectacular exit behind Tahiti's sister island of Moorea. There was an unreal quality to the whole scene, as if an experiment in superbeauty were being conducted at that moment in some supernatural laboratory for special effects. Twelve miles across the calm passage, Moorea loomed in dignified mystery. Her sculptured profile, luxuriantly green all day but for the inky shadows in her deep valleys, was now the richest aubergine tone. Above each peak was a cap of fleecy cumulus, and at higher altitudes dainty feathers of cirrus were draped across the sky. The sun's final moments that day had tinted the sky, the sea, and even the pandanus-thatched roofs along the shore in tones of peach-pink. It was a solar bonus of a warmth and intensity that bathed the whole scene in an ethereal glow. The sound effects came from the land and the sea. From a dappled palm grove behind Point Venus drifted the pealing voices of some native children singing the

Tahitian equivalent of "Ring Around a Rosy." There was a bounding happiness in those voices which rooted itself in my mind. A half mile from the shore, the ocean provided a muted accompaniment in its lethargic assault on the coral reef. Within this foamy demarcation line, the waters of the Matavai lagoon rested in plate-glass perfection. The grass that extended to the stand of volcanic sand rimming the bay was soft underfoot.

A group of young Tahitian boys had brought to the water's edge their homemade half-surfboards, the same water toys that so fascinated Cook, Bligh, and the other early European visitors to Tahiti. The boards were of no use on this gentlest of tropical nights, and the boys contented themselves with splashing and swimming. A tall and beautifully proportioned Tahitian maiden — she turned out to be a professional model in Papeete, but no matter — sauntered to the water's edge a little further along the beach for an evening dip. For a second, she toyed with the top of her *pareu* bikini as if she were about to perform a half-strip-tease (there is, in fact, a minor revival of toplessness in some parts of the island), decided against it, and plunged into the water, her brown hair streaming down an elegant back. Waiting on shore with her towel was a Frenchman in his seventies who has been happily spending his declining years in Tahiti disproving the theories about loss of sexual appetite and performance in the geriatric years.

The air was still, the temperature perfect. At this hour, at this spot, Tahiti was working all its magic.

But for a nineteenth-century lighthouse, some abstract wooden memorials to Cook, Wallis, Bougainville, and the first British missionaries, and the occasional Dole pineapple can and discarded packages of Gauloises and Chesterfields, Matavai Bay and Point Venus had not changed too drastically in two hundred years. On the far arm of the bay, a terraced tourist hotel spills down the cliff, but the architects have been respectful enough to camouflage their work, and it is not a jarring note. As they have done for centuries, the fishermen of Matavai were setting out in their outriggers for the reef that night, two men in each dugout, each knowing that the catch would be good. Movement across the still lagoon required only a lazy rhythm of shallow paddle work.

And over water, man, and shore was this incredible peach-pinkness. It was a special evening, but by no means unique. Tahiti has cast this sort of spell many thousands of evenings since Europeans first witnessed the magic. Today, sufficient of Tahiti's pristine glory remains for us to gauge the effect the island must have had on eighteenth-century seamen. The least aesthetically minded man aboard the *Bounty* could hardly have failed to make the comparison between the ugly memories of home and the sweet realities of his ship's bewitching anchorage.

In Bligh's time, a seaman's interests were blinkered toward two basic cravings — women and food. Tahiti provided both in abundance.

The *Bounty*'s arrival at Matavai had touched off a carnival of human exuberance and sex sport. The natives had already had visits from a handful of English, French, and Spanish ships, and on each occasion, to use the mildest possible cliché, a good time was had by all. For the Tahitians, the arrival of a man-of-war from Europe was like a circus visit to a remote provincial town. They knew it meant days and nights of the sort of boisterous gaiety that even this, the most fun-loving and abandoned of Polynesian societies, could not provide with its own resources. They would taste the white man's rum again and sleep off its mind-spinning effects in some shady glade. They would indulge again in the hilarious ritual of toastmaking over drafts of a spicy red liquid served in drinking containers which were miraculously transparent. They would be able to giggle again over the comic sight of paunchy men in elaborate costumes of fine wool, lace, braid, and buttons that glinted in the sun, sweating it out in the heat of a tropical afternoon. They would hear once more the terrifying boom of the white man's muskets and witness the miracle of a bird fall from the sky, or a wild pig succumb while the sailor was fifty paces distant. The guns, more so than any other of the novel items the Europeans brought to the island, convinced the Tahitians that their white visitors were at least semi-divine, if not actual gods from across the waters.

For the women (who, from all indications, genuinely relished lovemaking a couple of centuries before their civilized white sisters discovered, or acknowledged, that sex could be enjoyable), an amorous romp had also its material reward — a strange trinket of European manufacture. For the men who came on the *Bounty*, these willing creatures were the first women they had seen in many months, and friendships that began in giggling flirtation and awkward language difficulties deepened at a breathtaking pace into something far more passionate.

In every age, of course, the procurement of a bedmate on landfall has been of prime concern to all men who put to sea. The eighteenth century and the early years of the nineteenth century, however, stand as an extraordinary period in maritime history so far as unbridled sex and sexual preoccupation are concerned. In Bligh's time, "the fleet's in" was a cry that signaled far more robust activities in port than it does today. A Fellini was not there to record the orgies, but we do have a vivid description from the pens of men who witnessed them.

In August, 1821, a group of naval officers submitted to the Lords Commissioners of the Admiralty a statement they had drawn up and had privately printed in one hundred and fifty copies. It was entitled "Statement Respecting the Prevalence of Certain Immoral Practices in His Majesty's Navy." Its aim — and it appears to have achieved virtually nothing in the way of prompt reforms — was to expose the debauchery and immorality condoned by the King's Navy. Historians of the period have overlooked this document until recent years. Since it deals with practices and conditions dating back to the time of the *Bounty*, and since it offers the best evidence I have come upon to demonstrate how totally the lives of seamen of the period were ruled by basic lusts, I shall quote from it fairly fully.

"It has become an established practice in the British Navy to admit, and even to invite, on board our ships of war, immediately on their arrival in port, as many prostitutes as the men, and, in many cases, the officers may choose to entertain, to the number, in the larger ships, of several hundred at a time; all of whom remain on board, domesticated with the ship's company, men and boys, until they again put to sea," the authors said in their Statement to the Admiralty. The report continued.

The tendency of this practice is to render a ship of war, while in port, a continual scene of riot and disorder, of obscenity and blasphemy, of drunkenness, lewdness, and debauchery. During this time, the married seamen are frequently joined by their wives and families (sometimes compromising daughters from ten to fifteen years of age), who are forced to submit to the alternative of mixing with these abandoned women, whose language and behaviour are usually of the most polluting description; or of foregoing altogether the society of their husbands and parents. These all inhabit the same deck, where, whatever be their age or sex or character, they are huddled promiscuously together, eating, drinking, and sleeping, without any adequate means of separation or privacy, for the most part even without the slightest screen between their berths; and where, in the sight and hearing of all around them, they live in the unrestrained indulgence of every licentious propensity which may be supposed to actuate inmates of this description.

One naval officer of large experience asserts, that from the time he entered the Navy, about twenty-eight years ago, he had served in no ship in which, while in port, the custom of permitting women of the very worst description to come and remain on board was not tolerated, and even encouraged, by the Commanding Officer. The Lieutenants and grown Midshipmen were allowed to have women in their respective mess-rooms; where the younger Midshipmen were obliged to sit at table and associate with them, and to be witnesses of the debauchery and indecency which took place, not only there, but among the men also. It was even common for the women to employ all their arts to debauch these youths, who generally were caught in their snares, and became their prey.

It is well known [he goes on to observe] that immediately upon the arrival of a ship of war in port, crowds of boats flock off with cargoes of prostitutes. Having no money to pay for their conveyance, the waterman takes as many as his boat will hold, upon speculation, and hovers round the ship until she is secured at her anchors and the necessary work done; when he, with others, is permitted to come alongside. The men then go into the boats, and pick out each a woman (as one would choose cattle), paying a shilling or two to the boatman for her passage off. These women are examined at the gangway for liquor, which they are constantly in the habit of smuggling on board. They then descend to the lower deck with their husbands, as they call them. Hundreds come off to a large ship. The whole of the shocking, disgraceful transactions of the lower deck it is impossible to describe — the dirt, filth, and stench; the disgusting conversation; the indecent, beastly conduct, and horrible scenes; the blasphemy and swearing; the riots, quarrels, and fightings, which often take place, where hundreds of men and women are huddled together in one room, as it were; and where, in bed (each man being allowed only sixteen inches breadth for his hammock), they are squeezed between the next hammocks, and must be witnesses of each other's actions; can only be imagined by those who have not seen all this . . . Let those who have never seen a ship of war, picture to themselves a very large and low room (hardly capable of holding the men) with five hundred men, and probably three or four hundred women of the vilest description, shut up in it, and giving way to every excess of debauchery that the grossest passions of human nature can lead them to; and they see the deck of a seventy-four gun ship upon the night of her arrival in port. Add to this, that many of these poor wretches have dreadful diseases, which they communicate to the men. Let it also be imagined what must be the situation of the decent married women, who are either forced to come into the midst of such brutality, or remain still separated from their husbands, after probably a long absence.

The Statement added that some captains insisted that their men take their bought women to the assistant surgeon for vaginal examinations before permitting the couples to get down to business on the lower deck. "It must, however, be mentioned, to the honour of the assistant surgeons in the Navy, that some of them have resisted this order of the Captains, and have rather chosen to brave all consequences, than to submit to actions so degrading," the authors interjected. They alleged that some sailors frequently took two harlots on board at a time, "so that it sometimes happens that there are more women than men on board . . . giving way to every species of debauchery and abomination."

The document offered depositions from various officers who said they had served on ships of war whose captains permitted prostitutes to sail with the ship for the amusement of officers and men. One of these depositions gave these details, while concealing, in the interests of the "Old Boy" fraternity, the names of the skipper and his command:

"In 1808, Captain ——— joined us. He granted the same indulgence, and even allowed about nine women to go to sea in the ship. They were mustered on the forecastle on Sundays, and inspected by the Captain and First Lieutenant. Their conduct was so infamous, that after our arrival in the ——, two or three were turned out of the ship into a brig, for a passage to England and most of those that remained were common to the ship's company. Of one, I recollect its being stated that she admitted nineteen men to her embraces in one night. The matter was regarded with the utmost indifference, or made the occasion of obscene jests. It was common for the Midshipmen to have these women. Indeed, the Captain himself did not hesitate to take a foreign girl to live with him for some time, while we remained in those seas . . .

"I then joined another vessel. There also the Midshipmen had their women on board. The men had their women also. Some of them went to sea in the ship, and behaved in their accustomed manner, being almost continually drunk, spirits being given them by the officers, mates, and midshipmen, in payment for their occasional visits.

"At —— the scene was truly horrible, there being more women than men on board; the boys having free course among them likewise; and the midshipmen having four or five girls on board, who lived in the mess, and who, I have reason to believe, enticed the younger midshipmen on shore to their haunts.

"When the —— was lately preparing to sail for —— she was so crowded with women that the confusion and filth were intolerable. No business could be done, and the men were deserting daily. At length the First Lieutenant from mere necessity turned them all out of the ship, and sent them on shore. The Captain met them there as they landed. They addressed him, saying they were sure he was too much of a gentleman not to allow them their privileges; and he ordered them on board again. The Lieutenant, of course, received them . . ."

One of the reasons most frequently given for tolerating prostitutes aboard His Majesty's ships is: If the licence complained of herein be not given, we must lay our account with the growth of unnatural crimes.

But to this we boldly and confidently reply, that if there really exists a danger of this kind in the Navy, it arises more from the very practice which we have been reprobating than from any other cause. What can be more *unnatural*, more contrary to all the feelings of our common nature, than the open, undisguised, unblushing, promiscuous concubinage, which now takes place on board His Majesty's ships of war? Is not the person who has been tutored in this school of impurity and licentiousness, and who must there have bid adieu to those feelings which operate the most powerfully as a restraint on new modes of criminal indulgence, less likely than others to shrink from any other abomination which may be suggested to his mind?

The Statement continued with a great deal of other material — descriptions, depositions, and conclusions — in a similar vein. It presented a well-documented picture of an era which, depending upon how one views rabid sexuality, was either a horrid period in English history or the Royal Navy's finest hour. Of relevance to our study, it was Bligh's era, and the men he sailed with were the same lusty breed of English tar, and officer, as the raunchy fellows complained of in this petition to the Admiralty.

Tahiti to these men was a paradise that materialized before their sea-weary eyes, a place of undreamed-of bliss where luscious females made themselves freely available, a seafarer's heaven where single-minded young limeys could begin racking up respectable sexual scores — not in the fetid confines of the fo'c'sle but in the most idyllic surroundings imaginable. And it was not even necessary to tip the waterman a shilling or two to bring the girls out to the ship's ladder. They paddled themselves out!

It was said that while the Bounty rode at anchor in Tahitian lagoons, her company exposed for one hundred and sixty days and nights to the siren enticements of the Tahitian women, only two men remained faithful to their wives and sweethearts in England and failed to succumb. One was the dour skipper who went about his job as if Matavai was simply one more port of call. There was never any question of Elizabeth Bligh's husband slipping a "foreign girl" into his small stateroom by the mizzenmast. It has been written of Captain Cook that if Pacific natives rowed out to his vessel, bringing as gifts a voluptuous maiden and a slaughtered pig, Cook would take the pig and send back the woman. Bligh certainly would have chosen the pig, too, and rejected the maiden. But he probably also would have inspected the carcass closely to make sure it was free of bugs.

The frivolousness of the Tahitians left him aghast. There is an ingenuous note in some of his writing, particularly when he records in his Narrative what he witnessed at some of the Tahitian celebrations. Here is part of his account of one little orgy he observed ashore, a demonstration of Tahitian abandon that Bligh seems to have regarded as quite baffling and pointless:

After this the wrestling began and the place soon became a scene of riot and confusion. A party of the *Arreoys* [Tahitian priests whose chief concern seems to have been incessant sexual gratification] also began to exercise a privilege, which it seems they are allowed, of taking from the women such of their clothes as they thought worth it, so that some of them were left little better than naked.

Sex in the gentle tropics, and the promiscuity of the island society that was host to the *Bounty*, evidently were utterly perplexing matters to Bligh. Yet he was not intolerant of those who bounded ashore with trinkets to take advantage of the situation, to surrender themselves to these unbelievable nymphs with hibiscus and jasmine in their hair, gorgeous smiles of welcome, and lubricous bodies of palest copper.

So long as the ship's routine was maintained, so long as the breadfruit potting and the provisioning of the ship went ahead smoothly, Bligh allowed his men every liberty ashore — another point that does not jibe with the popular image of Bligh as a monster who regarded the occupants of the fo'c'sle as something less than human. The *Bounty*'s company seems to have had as much fun ashore in Matavai Bay as a bachelor hitting his first Club Méditerranée camp. Many of the men, the "gentlemen" as well as the A.B.'s, appear to have actually set up house in the palms behind the black sands of Matavai. Each man had a lover among the easygoing Tahitians if not an actual common-law wife.

In doing so, they were merely keeping alive a bawdy tradition of untrammeled free love between European sailors and Tahitian girls that had been inaugurated only twenty-three years earlier when Bougainville in *La Boudeuse* sailed into Matavai Bay and turned four hundred ecstatic French *matelots* loose among a few thousand ecstatic and receptive Tahitian women.

Philibert Commerson, the naturalist aboard *La Boudeuse*, wrote afterward that the Tahitians were a race who *"ne connoissent d'autre Dieu que l'amour."* But it was Bougainville himself who provided us with the quintessential reportage on the Tahitians'

Rabelaisian welcome for the early European visitors. Here is Bougainville's observations on his ship's first exposure to the recklessly flirtatious ways of the Tahitians:

The Tahitian men pressed us to choose a woman and come ashore with her; and their gestures, which were nothing less than equivocal, denoted in what manner we should form an acquaintance with her. It was very difficult in such conditions to keep at their work four hundred young French sailors who had not seen a woman for six months. In spite of all our precautions a young girl came on board and placed herself upon the quarter-deck near one of the hatchways, which was open in order to give air to those who were heaving at the capstan below it. The girl carelessly dropped a cloth which covered her, and appeared to the eyes of all beholders such as Venus showed herself to the Phrygian shepherd, having, indeed, the celestial form of that goddess. Both sailors and soldiers endeavored to come to the hatchway, and the capstan was never hove with more alacrity than on this occasion. At last our discipline succeeded in keeping these bewitched fellows in order, though it was no less difficult to keep command of ourselves. [Later] ashore, our men were invited to enter the houses where the people gave them to eat; nor did the civility of their landlords stop at a slight collation: they offered them young girls. The hut was immediately filled with a curious crowd of men and women who made a circle round the guest and the young victim of hospitality. The ground was spread with leaves and flowers, and their musicians sang a hymeneal song to the tune of their flutes. Here Venus is goddess of hospitality, her worship does not admit of any mysteries and every tribute paid to her is a feast for the whole nation. They were surprised at the confusion which our people appeared to be in as our customs do not allow of these public proceedings. However I would not answer for it that every one of our men found it impossible to conquer his repugnance and conform to the customs of the country.

Bougainville had a sea chest crammed with euphemisms. When he wrote that Venus was their goddess of hospitality, he was trying to tell us that he had sailed into the midst of a sex-mad society. They had a way of life that made constant dalliance possible and bodies that made it utterly desirable. Girls of ten and twelve were ready and willing for lovemaking. Nobody bothered about schooling because there was no point in learning anything besides cooking, weaving, fishing, surfing, hunting, dancing, and, of course, the pleasures of human coupling. Nobody had to work very hard. Wild hogs could be run to ground and clubbed with ease. Fish fell into their seines. The breadfruit, plantains, sugar cane, and coconuts flourished untended. Much of the day was spent grooming and anointing the body for lovemaking. The women bathed three times a day: early in the morning, at noon, and before sundown. They scrubbed their skin with pumice, and to round out the perfection of their bodies, plucked out their armpit hair with tweezers made from sharks' teeth. To these fragrant Lolitas, the body odor of the English and French sailors must have come as something of a shock, a price to pay for the bestowal of their favors.

To the men from the *Bounty* who had known only the grimness of the life of the lowest classes of eighteenth-century England, who had been raised in the mean, damp slums of Portsmouth, Plymouth, or Wapping, who had experienced little more than the harshness and endless toil of life at sea, it was Eden itself and much more. Here in Tahiti, the scum of the waterfront were wooed by exotic girls who ranked close to goddesses in grace and form. In the evenings when the air was balmy and none of the newcomers cared a hoot about the breadfruit, the women, as they had done for centuries for their own menfolk, dropped their shawls of glistening white *tapa* cloth and displayed their perfect Grecian breasts.

Lovemaking was thought of as casually as breathing or talking. The girls giggled in bewilderment when the men wanted to have their sexual pleasures away in a glade rather than on the open grass in full view of the village. Some of the girls set a price on their embraces, but not a very high one. Their play-for-pay price was a scrap of iron, and this accounts for the rapid disappearance of thousands of nails from the store chests aboard the *Bounty*. In the first days after the ship's arrival, the native girls asked the sailors for one nail as a token of affection for a night's companionship. Later the ante was increased to two, and finally to three nails.

All this was happening, fittingly enough perhaps, to a crew that was unusually youthful by Royal Navy standards of the day.

The youngest was seventeen, the oldest forty. Their average age was twenty-six and a half. And they took their example from a second-in-command who was an accomplished and determined sexual athlete. "A great man for the women," a sailmate in the *Britannia* had written of Christian five years earlier. "He was one of the most foolish young men I ever knew in regard to the sex."

On the quiet shores of Matavai Bay, Christian was "foolish" with one of the most entrancing specimens of Tahitian beauty the island had to offer. There is a slight possibility — a point which has never been raised in the *Bounty* legend and which I shall deal with later — that Mi'Mitti became pregnant toward the end of the *Bounty*'s Tahitian stay. (The gestatory requirement here would put the time of conception in February, 1789.) Thus there is also a slight possibility that when Bligh took the *Bounty* away from Tahiti in April for the long westward haul to Jamaica with his breadfruit, Fletcher Christian knew Mi'mitti would bear him a child after his departure and he probably would never see her again or the child he had fathered.

The details of the preceding pages are offered, not gratuitously or for the purpose of injecting some salaciousness into an otherwise unspicy review of a stern drama of men at sea, but for a very specific and cogent reason. We have come to the crux of my argument: the mutiny against Lieutenant Bligh and the loyal officers and men of His Majesty's Armed Transport *Bounty* at dawn on April 28, 1789, was caused not by the master's tyrannical regime at sea, nor by his insupportable nature, nor by his obsession with the cat-o'-nine-tails, but by that old standby, sex.

No crew of the King's Navy, no company of European sailors, had ever spent so much time ashore on any Pacific island, let alone the island which Bligh himself had called "the finest in the world." And finally they were leaving it all behind, carting off breadfruit to islands peopled only by aloof English plantation owners and sullen, cowed blacks from West Africa. With the loading of the last few breadfruit trees, the men were wrenched from an idyll that, years later, would require all the glories of Technicolor to depict. They were giving Tahitian cheek-kisses to their warm companions of the past few months, knowing almost certainly they would never see them or Otaheite again.

Some sixteen months after they had put out from Spithead, they were weighing anchor again for the long homeward voyage by way of the West Indies. They faced another tedious ocean voyage, perhaps a year of it, and a full return to navy discipline. Remembering that they were young, had come from a past of squalor and near-serfdom, had miraculously tasted the fruits of paradise, and were no doubt going home to be impressed into naval service in a new war against France, would it be surprising that most of the forty-four men aboard the *Bounty* left harboring thoughts as to how they might recapture and keep forever the ineffable bliss of Tahiti?

It was a crew *predisposed* to mutiny. The normal below-decks grievances would have swollen in men's minds into major issues. To those who had left behind pliant Polynesian women, easy living, and the soft beauty of Tahiti, firm, if rule-book direction by a captain with a mission to complete would be seen as inhuman treatment warranting desperate action if the occasion arose.

It required only a mental storm in Christian's brain to trigger what seems clearly to have been an unpremeditated insurrection, a mental storm which perhaps stemmed partly from some psychiatric defects in Christian and partly from his natural anguish at leaving Mi'Mitti, possibly a pregnant Mi'Mitti.

While it is a risky business to attempt to psychoanalyze a dead man with any real hope of precision — a task that is tackled, nevertheless, in later pages — we can guess at what these defects might have been. A psychoanalyst today might put Christian in the category of psychoneurotic. He might find traces of paranoia, perhaps delusions of grandeur.

There is a limited amount of evidence on Christian's mental state, but it is certainly worth reviewing. Bligh himself noticed something unusual about his master's mate's physical condition which may have reflected some type of emotional instability. In his "wanted men" descriptions after the mutiny, he noted that Christian was "subject to violent perspiration, particularly in the hands, so that he soils anything he handles." (Again, here is Bligh the fussy housekeeper.) The Royal Navy dress uniform in those days contained a great deal of white — breeches, white vest, white facing on the frock coats, some white lace at wrists and throats — and overly sweaty hands would leave noticeable marks on the fabric. A psychoanalyst today would be interested in any over-activity in the sweat glands of a patient. He would seek first of all to determine whether it could be attributed to a physical condition; if not, he would probably tend to regard it as a symptom of some flaw in the mental makeup.

Christian's last words to Bligh as he was ordering him into the launch to be cast adrift also have some relevance. He did not say, according to the captain's account, "Bligh, you have put me *through* hell," but rather, "I am *in* hell — I am *in* hell." (Italics added.) If he were seeking, by deposing the skipper, to remedy an intolerable situation that had existed for months, he might have been expected to allude to past injustices and utter something along the lines of the former remark. The "I am *in* hell" statement suggested he was still acting from impulses beyond his normal mental control.

In the very act of casting Bligh adrift, Christian displayed many of the dark character traits which later would be applied to Bligh's personality — callousness, arrogance, lack of pity. Setting aside Christian's personal feelings toward Bligh, all but perhaps two or three of the eighteen men he put into the small launch with Bligh had become Christian's close friends during the voyage. Yet he gave all nineteen only the slimmest chance of survival. In an area virtually uncharted but known to have hostile natives on the islands where Bligh would have to stop for food and water, Christian gave them cutlasses but refused their requests for some muskets and powder. This could hardly have been justified on the ground that Bligh and the loyal crewmen might attempt to retake the ship. The launch was wallowing in the water below the *Bounty*'s swivel guns and four-pounders. One short-range shot from any one of these would have blown it out of the water.

The *Bounty* was well stocked at that point, thanks to Bligh's foresight. Yet Christian doled out little more than starvation rations for a few days to Bligh's party: "a few pieces of pork, some water and some clothes," as the captain afterward described them.

Christian said later, to the mutineers who remained in Tahiti after he had sailed in search of his refuge, that he bore no ill will toward the men who accompanied Bligh, that he hoped every man would be returned safely to England. But he gave these innocent men, victims of his own reckless actions, a chance in a million of doing so.

He even denied Bligh's pleas for some of his maps and charts, knowing he was abandoning him in unknown seas and at least 1,200 leagues from any outpost of European civilization. (Bligh made up this lack by producing his own charts during the forty-three days at sea in the launch. In these impossible conditions, with survival, hunger, and thirst dominating every other thought, Bligh somehow managed to keep careful and valuable charts of his voyage across the Western Pacific and through the Endeavor Straits to the East Indies. Would a monster, intent only on getting home and wreaking revenge on the man who had pirated his ship, have acted so coolly in the circumstances? It would appear to reflect a notably balanced mind.)

Why didn't Christian put Bligh in irons, sail the *Bounty* home to England, and put the crew's and his accusations of subhuman treatment before an Admiralty Board of Inquiry? The explanation put forward by the adherents to the popular version is that Christian feared that Bligh, shackled wrist and ankle and confined to the brig, would manage somehow to recapture command. Yet these same authors fulsomely have depicted Christian as a "born leader of men," immensely popular with all ranks aboard the *Bounty*. If so, couldn't he have kept Bligh neutralized and out of harm's way until he got the *Bounty* back to Spithead?

If the case against Bligh had been so overwhelming, Christian and his supporters had a reasonable chance of a sympathetic hearing. It was, after all, the Age of Reason. If we accept these points, we are left to assume that they were never really interested in returning to England; whether or not they were consciously aware of it, their actions were directed only toward an early return to the Arcadian life on Tahiti, or some re-creation of it of their own devising.

Christian proved himself later to be a disastrous leader. From its earliest days, the mutineers' settlement on Pitcairn was an abysmal tale of murder, drunkenness, adultery, indecision, and cruelty to the Polynesian men and women brought from Matavai Bay. Ten years after landing on Pitcairn, only one of the mutineers, John Adams, was still alive, and all of the six Polynesian men had been killed.

Friendly assessments of Christian's character lead us to believe that he was highly strung and oversensitive to criticism. I mentioned earlier the possibility that his mental makeup harbored some delusions of grandeur. His actions immediately after the mutiny lend credence to this view.

Bligh spent the seventeen months he lived aboard the *Bounty*, not in the great cabin, the spacious stateroom over the square stern, but in a cramped, makeshift cabin that a pair of midshipmen might have considered unsuitable. He had moved out of the great cabin so it could be converted into a floating greenhouse with racks for a thousand terra cotta pots to hold the young breadfruit trees. To Bligh, interested only in the successful execution of his mission, the loss of the great cabin, a commander's ultimate status symbol afloat and the source of whatever creature comforts were available aboard a man-of-war, was not a matter of great concern. But Christian wasted no time in appropriating these grand quarters for his own use. Before the day of the mutiny was out, he had had the breadfruit trees tossed out of the mullioned stern "picture window" and was organizing the great cabin for his personal use as commander of the *Bounty*. The stateroom, which the legitimate skipper of the ship had denied himself for so long, was now eagerly requisitioned by his usurper. In the sweep of events surrounding the mutiny, it was a small incident, but not without significance.

Of the many ironies in the *Bounty* story, the greatest, perhaps, may be that we have had a convincing explanation of the mutiny before us for more than a century and three quarters, that we have overlooked it in our obsession with finding a romantic male lead who happened also, most desirably, to be the underdog.

The explanation, I believe, can be found in Bligh's own published account of the affair:

It will very naturally be asked, what could be the reason for such a revolt? in answer to which I can only conjecture, that the mutineers had flattered themselves with the hopes of a more happy life among the Otaheitians, than they could possibly enjoy in England; and this, joined to some female connexions, most probably occasioned the whole transaction.

The women at Otaheite are handsome, mild and cheerful in their manners and conversation, possessed of great sensibility, and have sufficient delicacy to make themselves admired and beloved. The chiefs were so much attached to our people, that they rather encouraged their stay among them than otherwise, and even made them promises of large possessions. Under these, and many other attendant circumstances, equally desirable, it is now perhaps not so much to be wondered at, though scarcely possible to have been foreseen, that a set of sailors, most of them void of connexions, should be led away; especially when, in addition to such powerful inducements, they imagined it in their power to fix themselves in the midst of plenty, on one of the finest islands in the world, where they need not labour, and where the allurements of dissipation are beyond anything that can be conceived. The utmost, however, that any commander could have supposed to have happened is, that some of the people would have been tempted to desert. But if it should be asserted, that a commander is to guard against an act of mutiny and piracy in his own ship, more than by the common rules of service, it is as much as to say that he must sleep locked up, and when awake, be girded with pistols.

Bligh, the major eyewitness of the whole affair, wrote and published that in London a little more than a year after the mutiny.

Was he insufferable, intolerant? It may have been that his chief fault was *over*tolerance. If he had imposed stricter discipline during the five months the *Bounty* was anchored in Tahiti, denying his men any but the occasional shore leave, the mutiny might never have occurred and the *Bounty* might have gone home uneventfully to Spithead and a hero's welcome.

CHAPTER SIX

A PSYCHOANALYTICAL POSTSCRIPT

WHILE THE EIGHTEENTH CENTURY had its allotted share of psychopaths, neurotics, and sadists, it did not have them tidily identified and catalogued for historical ready reference. The Age of Freud was to dawn a century later. Even so, the views of some sort of neutral, trained mind aboard the *Bounty* would be invaluable in attempting to assess and explain the actions of the principal actors in the drama and their mental states at the time the events were occurring. Alas, there was no such observer or recorder. The nominal candidate for the post, the ship's doctor, certainly was not the man to anticipate Freud by seeking to find out what motivated or disturbed his shipmates. In any event, he appears to have drawn hardly a sober breath from the day the *Bounty* left Portsmouth until his death a bit over a year later in Tahiti.

So we are obliged to turn to posthumous analysis, patently a tricky exercise, but of some value, I feel, in this review.

Dr. Joseph W. Owen, a prominent New York psychoanalyst, agreed to lend his medical expertise in reconstructing the personalities of Bligh and Christian. He was an ideal choice for the assignment. The literature of the mutiny appeals to him immensely, and he is a former navy man. During World War II, he was in charge of the psychiatric section of a naval hospital in the Solomons. Dr. Owen has considered my views on what caused Christian's revolt and has refreshed his memory by rereading the story of the mutiny. In general, he concurred with my hypothesis.

"I find myself in agreement with your main theme that the stay in Tahiti of five months and the sudden cessation of a pleasurable and indulgent life probably brought on the mutiny, which seemed to be a sudden, unpremeditated affair," he wrote in a report prepared for this work. "The injustices on the return trip seemed, from my reading, too few to justify a revolt. They were humiliating rather than physically cruel, but they may have been intolerable to some of the men, coming right after the flattery to their narcissism and the freedom from restraint during their stay on the island."

Dr. Owen opened his report by reviewing the three big groups of pathological characters — psychotics, psychopaths, and psychoneurotics. "For all practical purposes, the psychotics can be eliminated here except for mild forms of paranoia," he observed. "Psychotics just don't stand up under the strain of the life at sea and would break under lesser strains."

We can narrow our focus, then to psychopathic and psychoneurotic states. Dr. Owen's report continues:

The pathology of psychopaths is varied, but one outstanding characteristic is their lack of internalized conflict and internalized control. They go by external control almost entirely but usually have a fairly well developed idea of reality and what they can get away with and what they can't — except when they have too much success and develop overconfidence. The ones we may be concerned with are the less severe ones that flocked to the armed forces, and especially the Navy, in the old days.

In our day, the armed forces do not take the more extreme ones, such as criminals, considering them hopeless, but sometimes do accept inadvertently the less severe and they frequently flourish there and "welcome" the discipline. Such types for practical purposes rarely change very much. They depend on the external discipline and are very apt to explain their difficulties on the basis of the authoritative figure governing them and wrap all their troubles around him. The old man gets it.

The other great group of pathological mental states are the psychoneuroses and here one needs volumes to describe the types. However, it helps to think of them as suffering from mainly internalized conflicts (control of basic desires, oedipal conflicts, aggression, sex, perversions, etc.) The armed forces line officers do not understand these. They are bewildered by them and if their difficulties come to the surface, they are either blindly treated as psychopaths or they release them from service as ones they can't figure out or handle.

The psychoneurotics may function well in the military service though they are undependable under certain circumstances. They welcome the discipline, too, but, more than anything, welcome the direction of exactly what's to be done, since direction temporarily displaces their conflicts. Give them long periods of freedom from this routine discipline, periods of inactivity, indecision, etc., or alter their groove very much, and the internalized conflicts blossom. One form of neurosis we see a lot of is what we call the character neuroses. These have neurotic traits from way back firmly engrained in the personality. The original conflicts are lost and the neurotic traits are fixed rather solidly with little anxiety or guilt. These psychoneurotics are in a rut, but sometimes very useful ones if their area in life is well chosen.

Dr. Owen is inclined to put Christian in the psychoneurotic column but he stops short of a definite diagnosis:

Christian may have been a psychoneurotic though there isn't enough material to say definitely. Small things, however, may be suggestive: the indulgence in secondary narcissism, as revealed in his unrealistic boasting to his brother and other expansive acts; the moist hands; the rather sudden impulse to lead a mutiny, considering that he had made two previous voyages with the same skipper and returned voluntarily for this one; the possible over-sex drive; his lack of judgment in handling the men on the island (Pitcairn); his choosing a "princess" (though as an officer this might be expected in the caste system); his very poor emotional judgment in attempting to solve his difficulties; and his indication of guilt as he set the boat adrift.

Christian is a sort of relatively unknown here, but from what data we have I believe he was in great conflict regarding submission to the old man and the discipline of the sea and the desire to be something big in his own right — to get his "princess" and establish himself as an independent man, and a sexually active one, in high places. Overthrowing the old man would do it, but he couldn't bring himself to murder, except the murder that didn't seem like murder of setting him adrift, even if some of his friends perished too.

The drive now was to get to the top regardless. The top in this case might be conceived as a "normal" development urge — return to his loving Mi'Mitti, to be looked up to and favored by the people of the islands, and to escape from all the male, strict, autocratic ways of the sea. The method chosen was terrible and bespoke an immature, impulsive person — a destructive and self-destructive role revealing a severe neurosis, maybe even a temporary psychotic break.

Dr. Owen offered a general comment on the powerful attraction that home comforts — a shared bed, the absence of another male barking out orders, being rid of fear and regimentation — exert on men in the services: "In World War II, it was a well-known fact to military psychiatrists that men who developed combat neurosis and were sent home for treatment could practically never be returned to combat. Even the normal after going on home leave had a hard time returning. Women, sex, love, peace, being more or less one's own boss and respected, are strong and normal pulls."

In turning to Bligh, Dr. Owen remarked that my review of the historical documents "does not indicate marked or even mild sadism present in the captain's character. The picture emerges of a person without any degree of emotional disturbance manifested, although one may never discover more pertinent material to elucidate the total picture."

Bligh, he felt, "may have had difficulty re-establishing his authority in the early part of the voyage home. On Tahiti, he evidently stood aloof and let the 'boys' cut up sexually. But once back at sea he clamped down, and after the five months of relative freedom on the island, where they had been pampered and respected and their narcissism enhanced, the sudden change to harsh discipline, hard work and mental degradation may well have upset the balance of the unstable ones."

Finally, Dr. Owen recounted an incident from his own wartime experiences that is vaguely analogous to Christian's action against Bligh. Christian, it will be recalled, spent most of the time in Tahiti as his own boss. He was in full charge of the shore operation to obtain the breadfruit shoots, an activity that was administratively and physically separated from the running of the *Bounty*. When the ship left Tahiti, he no longer was in charge of his own show. He was back to being second-in-command, a deputy to a man who, from what we know of his character, very likely neglected to give

Christian the praise he deserved, and perhaps expected, for a job well handled.

While he was in the Solomons, Dr. Owen recalled, a marine lieutenant attempted to blow up his captain. "As I remember, there had been no outward evidence of his pathology until this episode, and he had been considered a very good officer," he continued. "The lieutenant had been temporarily placed in charge of organizing a unit, had done well, apparently had the respect and admiration of his men and took great pride in his accomplishment. The new captain took charge, apparently belittled all of his activities and humiliated him. A few weeks thereafter, the lieutenant planted a mine in the captain's tent and detonated it from the bushes."

When the *Bounty* mutiny is stripped of whatever "romance" it has been invested with over the years, we must put Christian's act in the same category of human brutality as would be assigned to that homicidal lieutenant in the bushes.

CHAPTER SEVEN

MAYHEM, SAINTLINESS, DICTATORSHIP, ORDER

H UZZA FOR OTAHEITE!" was the cry of the mutineers as the *Bounty* and the open boat carrying Bligh and his party moved apart. Matavai Bay was luring the mutineers back. At that moment of exhilaration, the deed freshly done, some of Christian's party perhaps imagined they could hide out successfully somewhere in Tahiti. Christian and Midshipman Young, however, realized this would not be feasible, and they convinced the others they would have to look elsewhere for a redoubt. Not Tahiti, but a "Tahiti" of their own making.

The *Bounty* was swung around and Christian set a course due easterly. He had selected the island of Tubuai in the Austral Group, 350 miles south of Tahiti. The ship dropped anchor there on May 25, 1789. The Tubuaians, related to the Tahitians by blood and language, were nevertheless not the hospitable Polynesians the *Bounty* men had known at Matavai Bay. For one thing, they saw no reason why they should surrender their women to white intruders. But Christian and the mutineers decided that geographically the island was ideal. It was small but fertile, and sufficiently off the beaten track to Tahiti to permit them to live out their days without real fear of discovery by the pursuit ships they knew London would dispatch if Bligh ever made it home. Tubuai lacked only two things — accommodating women and livestock. Since both were available in Tahiti, and none in his party was willing to accept a life of sexless vegetarianism, Christian decided to return to Tahiti to collect these essentials.

On June 6, the *Bounty* once more sailed through the opening in the reef and dropped anchor in Matavai Bay. Knowing that the Tahitian chiefs would wonder why Bligh was no longer aboard, Christian concocted a story that they had met "Toote," the Tahitians' name for Captain Cook (knowledge of whose death had been kept from the islanders), and that Bligh had transferred to his ship. The *Bounty* had been sent back to take on fresh provisions. The deception worked. Both Cook and Bligh were well liked by the Tahitians, and within a week, the *Bounty* had been supplied with more than three hundred pigs, almost a hundred chickens, and thirty-eight goats, as well as the bull and cow Bligh had presented to the islanders. The ship also acquired some pets — two dogs and two cats. Nine women, including Mi'Mitti, and eighteen Tahitian men and boys decided to sail with the Englishmen when the *Bounty* set off for Tubuai. The loyalists, who had been held aboard the ship, sailed with the mutineers. Christian had threatened to shoot any man who attempted to desert in Tahiti or who told the natives that Bligh had been deposed and set adrift.

This second attempt at settling on Tubuai got off to a more auspicious start. The men from Tahiti were able to act as interpreters and problem-solvers; the Tubuaians were happy to see that the white visitors now had their own women as well as an ark of strange animals. A local chief, Tamatoa, assured by the Tahitians that the white men could contribute something to the Polynesian life-style, actually became a "name brother" with Christian. The Tubuaians, the Tahitians, and the Englishmen sat down together to a splendid feast, and Tamatoa offered the newcomers a fine tract of land in his kingdom. Christian, for unknown reasons, spurned this offer and foolishly started courting a rival chief for land in his kingdom. His decision cost the would-be colonists the goodwill of most of the Tubuaians and set up frictions that were to doom the attempt at a settlement. But Christian decided to persevere. He drew up plans for an immense fort, with a perimeter of four hundred yards, high walls on which the guns from the *Bounty* were to be mounted, and a moat twenty feet across. It was to have ramparts, lookout towers, and even a drawbridge.

With boyish enthusiasm on the part of English sailors and Polynesian laborers, work was started on this crazy project to put a structure from Medieval England on a South Sea island. In the first weeks, Christian realized his plans were far too grandiose and reduced the dimensions of his castle by half. It was still far from completed when the Tubuai factions Christian had offended began making daring raids on the colonists, using their women to lure them into ambushes. The natives were angry over many things. The pigs the white men had introduced to the island were running wild and destroying the crops of the Tubuaians. The Englishmen were arrogantly trying to appropriate anything of Tubuai which took their fancy — girls, a hand of bananas, a bunch of yams. They were even stealing religious idols.

And the men in Christian's own party were also beginning to grumble. This was not the easy life they had mutinied to win. Digging ditches under a tropical sun and hauling tree trunks and rocks for a stupid fort to pamper Christian's ego was not their idea of paradise. Had the Tubuaians, particularly the women, been friendlier, the toil may have seemed worthwhile. But they weren't, and Christian soon sensed there was mutiny in the air once more. Nightly, the argument was resumed. A growing number of malcontents wanted to return to Tahiti and take their chances there. Eventually, after several of the men had challenged Christian's leadership, he agreed to put the matter to a vote. He lost decisively. Sixteen of the twenty-five Englishmen raised their hands in favor of returning immediately to Matavai Bay, where it was possible "to get women without force." Christian accepted their decision, and in doing so, according to Morrison's account, made this melodramatic appeal: "Gentlemen, I will carry you and land you where ever you please. I desire no one to stay with me, but I have one favor to request, that you will grant me the ship, tie the foresail, and give me a few gallons of water, and leave me to run before the wind, and I shall land upon the first island the ship drives me to. I have done such an act that I cannot stay at Otaheite. I will never live where I may be carried home to be a disgrace to my family."

When he had finished speaking, his closest friend, Edward Young, exclaimed: "We shall never leave you Mr. Christian, go where you will." Seven men, Williams, McCoy, Martin, Mills, Brown, Smith, and Quintal, announced then they were throwing in their lot with Christian and Young. And so was formed the party of nine mutineers which four months later would found an unhappy colony on Pitcairn. Before doing so, they had to carry out their promise to deposit the loyalists and the other *Bounty* men on Tahiti. After one more ugly skirmish with the Tubuaians, while the Englishmen were vainly trying to round up their livestock, the *Bounty* set sail again for Tahiti. On September 22, for the third time in eleven months, the ship was sailed into the lagoon at Matavai. Sixteen men who no longer regarded Christian as their leader went ashore. At dawn the next day, the *Bounty* moved quietly out through the reef on her final voyage.

Christian at that moment had no destination in mind. Presumably he had already consulted the works on Pacific exploration in the small library Bligh had been forced to leave in his cabin. He returned to this study and came up with several possibilities — the Marquesas, the Solomons, and the Santa Cruz islands. He rejected the Marquesas upon reading that their Spanish discoverer, Mendaña, had encountered ferocious cannibals ashore. He and the mutineers agreed to inspect the Solomons. They proved an elusive destination, hardly surprising in view of the fact that Mendaña's longitudinal fix was almost two thousand miles east of their true position.

Week after week, the *Bounty* cruised aimlessly across the South Pacific, stopping occasionally at islands that appeared on Admiralty charts, but only to take on fruit and water. In these discouraging weeks, Christian stumbled upon a reference to Pitcairn. In Bligh's library, he had found a leatherbound volume entitled *Hawkesworth Voyages*. A page was devoted to Captain Carteret's description of Pitcairn's Island, as it was then known, and an account of his discovery of it. It seemed to meet all his requirements — it was uninhabited, fertile, warm, and well away from the area of Polynesia which was becoming well known to the Royal Navy. The lack of an indigenous population was an important point; after the two attempts to settle on Tubuai, Christian had made up his mind that only an uninhabited island would meet their needs. The course was changed for Pitcairn. On January 15, 1790, they sighted it.

Christian sailed several times around this strange, surf-lashed rock looking for an inlet or a bay where he would anchor. As skippers who followed him would also discover, he found it a forbidding place for a landing. There was only one possibility, the little indentation which later would be raised to the status of "bay" and named after the *Bounty*. With three of the Tahitians and three Englishmen, Christian went ashore in the ship's cutter to reconnoiter. After scaling the cliffs, they reached a fertile savannah. Breadfruit, yams, and bananas were flourishing. The people who had planted them had long since departed.

This was certainly not the "Tahiti" the men had been looking for. Physically, it was inferior to Tubuai or some of the other islands they had inspected. But they had voyaged hard and long, and Pitcairn's Island met many of their requirements. Christian was for it. Reluctantly, it seems, since there was already fresh talk of returning to Tahiti, the rest of the *Bounty* men agreed to settle for this lonely fortress.

The *Bounty* was sailed on a grinding run across the rocks about a hundred yards to the east of Pitcairn's present landing ramp. The ship was tethered by a hemp line to a stout tree on shore while a stern anchor was dropped to keep her reasonably steady in the pounding surf. Working long days, the mutineers and the native men and women stripped the ship of everything of value. The hatch covers were used as rafts to ferry the material to a narrow ledge of rock and shingle. The goats, pigs, and chickens brought from Matavai were landed in this fashion. The *Bounty*'s decks, masts, and cabins were torn apart for the good oak and other timbers they had been built with. The sails, every scrap of metal, and all the stores were also carried ashore. At the end of a week, the *Bounty*, tethered to shore and seabed, resembled an ungainly barge. And on January 23, Christian gave the order to put what remained to the torch. (One version has it that Matthew Quintal, a heavy rum drinker, upset a lamp while rummaging for things in the carpenter's shop and accidentally set the ship on fire. I am inclined to believe, however, that the ship was deliberately fired, with Christian's knowledge, since it had always been part of his plan to destroy all trace of the *Bounty* as soon as he had found the island he was searching for.) The *Bounty* burned to the waterline. The surf soon completed the job of destroying what was left of her hull.

For the first few months of the Pitcairn settlement, the *Bounty* nevertheless provided the colonists with their basic human needs: food, shelter, clothing. The ship's stores were sufficient to keep them going until Brown, the gardener, could get the established plantations back in shape and organize the planting. The ship's canvas enabled the settlers to put up tentlike houses while they started the task of building permanent homes, several of two stories, with the *Bounty*'s oak and local timber. (The English influence was dominant here; the architecture borrowed little from Polynesia.) Later, as their English clothes wore out, the *Bounty*'s sails would be cut up and turned into sarongs, trousers, and jackets. When *these* wore out, the women would go back to beating bark into *tapa* cloth, a skill remembered from Tahiti.

Christian, eight shipmates, and their Tahitian *taios* were making a fresh start at society-building. They were settling in a new place, totally isolated from the rest of the world, even the Polynesian world. They had utopian dreams.

That these hopes were destined to fail should have been evident from one of Christian's first acts. After a survey of the land, he divided it into nine equal parts. Nine white men, therefore nine plots. The Tahitians, who had sacrificed a lot in joining the mutineers in this risky venture, were left landless, even though there was ample ground to give all a share.

Given the extraordinary conditions that attended the founding of the Pitcairn community, I find it curious that Christian, an educated man, did not grasp immediately that these unusual conditions invited the establishment of an unusual society. If ever a situation called for an experiment in true communal living, with communal ownership of land and produce, this surely was it. Christian might even have anticipated Marx and Engels. What he did was to implant on Pitcairn the familiar English ways of private ownership of land, crops, and dwellings. In this scheme, the brown *taios* played only the roles of servants and unpaid laborers.

Two threats hung over the community as it settled down to the business of building homes and organizing the crops and livestock. The subjection of the Tahitian men was bound eventually to trigger an explosion. And women were in precious short supply. It needed only one of the white men to lose his concubine to touch off a crisis with the Tahitian men. There were six native men, and they appear to have shared the three women available to them by dividing into three uneven households. Tararo, the most aristocratic, had his own woman, Toofaiti, whom the *Bounty* men called Nancy. Three others shared Mareva, and the remaining two lived as a *ménage a trois* with Tinafanaea.

The community was barely two years old when not one but two of the Englishmen's women died. The girl whom John Williams had selected in Tahiti plunged to her death on the rocky coastline while gathering eggs on the cliffs. Alexander Smith's woman died of some disease of the throat or lungs. Since none of their shipmates was prepared to share his woman with them, they faced the monastic prospect of ending their days on Pitcairn in celibacy. Williams even talked of building a boat and sailing off in search of a native wife on some distant island. It was fairly obvious that Williams and Smith would soon be eyeing the women living with the Tahitian men. This is exactly what happened. With the consent of the seven other mutineers, Williams forced Nancy to leave Tararo and Smith broke up the *ménage a trois* and took Tinafanaea into his house. Deprived of land, relieved of all but one of the women they had brought with them, the Tahitians, not surprisingly, drew up a plan of revenge.

The fullest account of the colony's early years is contained in a book published in London in 1831, *Narrative of a Voyage to the Pacific and Bering Strait*, by Captain F. W. Beechey, who had called at Pitcairn in 1825 aboard H.M.S. *Blossom*. He appears to have been the only visiting captain to have inspected the fragmentary diary Midshipman Young kept on the island — the diary itself has disappeared — and he based his account on Young's journal, as well as on his interviews with Alexander Smith, who by then had changed his name to John Adams and was the revered Patriarch of Pitcairn. Beechey's work is the only reliable record of the turbulent first years of the colony, and I shall draw on it here. Beechey reported that the native women sided with the mutineers after learning that the Tahitian men were plotting against their white masters:

Fortunately, the secret was imparted to the women, who ingeniously communicated it to the white men in a song, of which the words were, "Why does black man sharpen axe? to kill white man." The instant Christian became aware of the plot, he seized his gun and went in search of the blacks, but with a view only of showing them that their scheme was discovered, and thus by timely interference endeavouring to prevent the execution of it. He met one of them (Ohoo) at a little distance from the village, taxed him with the conspiracy, and in order to intimidate him, discharged his gun, which he had humanely loaded with powder only. Ohoo, however, imagining otherwise, and that the bullet had missed its object, derided his unskilfulness, and fled into the woods, followed by his accomplice Talaloo [Tararo], who had been deprived of his wife. The remaining blacks, finding their plot discovered, purchased pardon by promising to murder their accomplice, who had fled, which they afterwards performed by an act of the most odious treachery. Ohoo was betrayed and murdered by his own nephew; and Talaloo, after an ineffectual attempt made upon him by poison, fell by the hands of his friend and his wife, the very woman on whose account all the disturbance began, and whose injuries Talaloo felt he was revenging in common with his own.

Tranquillity was by these means restored, and preserved for about two years; at the expiration of which, dissatisfaction was again manifested by the blacks, in consequence of oppression and ill treatment, principally by Quintal and McCoy. Meeting with no compassion or redress from their masters, a second plan to destroy their oppressors was matured, and unfortunately, too successfully executed.

It was agreed that two of the blacks, Timoa and Nehow, should desert from their masters, provide themselves with arms, and hide in the woods, but maintain a frequent communication with the other two, Tetaheite and Menalee; and that on a certain day they should attack and put to death all the Englishmen, when at work in their plantations. Tetaheite, to strengthen the party of the blacks on this day, borrowed a gun and ammunition of his master, under the pretence of shooting hogs, which had become wild and very numerous; but instead of using it in this way, he joined his accomplices, and with them fell upon Williams and shot him. Martin, who was at no great distance, heard the report of the musket, and exclaimed, "Well done. We shall have a glorious feast today," supposing that a hog had been shot. The party proceeded from Williams' towards Christian's plantation, where Menalee, the other black, was at work with Mills and McCoy; and, in order that the suspicions of the whites might not be excited by the report they had heard, requested Mills to allow him (Menalee) to assist them in bringing home the hog they pretended to have killed. Mills agreed; and the four, being united, proceeded to Christian, who was working at his yam-plot, and shot him. Thus fell a man, who, from being the reputed ringleader of the mutiny, has obtained an unenviable celebrity, and whose crime, if anything can excuse mutiny, may perhaps be considered as in some degree palliated, by the tyranny which led to its commission.

McCoy, hearing his groans, observed to Mills, "There was surely some person dying," but Mills replied, "It's only Mainmast (Christian's wife) calling her children to dinner." The white men being yet too strong for the blacks to risk a conflict with them, it was necessary to concert a plan, in order to separate Mills and McCoy. Two of them accordingly secreted themselves in McCoy's house, and Tetaheite ran and told him that the two blacks who had deserted were stealing things out of his house. McCoy instantly hastened to detect them, and on entering was fired at; but the ball passed him. McCoy immediately communicated the alarm to Mills, and advised him to seek shelter in the woods; but Mills, being quite satisfied that one of the blacks whom he had made his friend would not suffer him to be killed, determined to remain. McCoy, less confident, ran in search of Christian, but finding him dead, joined Quintal (who was already apprised of the work of destruction, and had sent his wife to give the alarm to the others), and fled with him to the woods.

Mills had scarcely been left alone, when the two blacks fell upon him, and he became a victim to his misplaced confidence in the fidelity of his friend. Martin and Brown were next separately murdered by Menalee and Tenina; Menalee effecting with a maul what the musket had left unfinished. Tenina, it is said, wished to save the life of Brown, and fired at him with powder only, desiring him, at the same time, to fall as if killed; but, unfortunately rising too soon, the other black, Menalee, shot him.

Adams was first apprised of his danger by Quintal's wife, who, in hurrying through his plantation, asked why he was working at such a time. Not understanding the question, but seeing her alarmed, he followed her, and was almost immediately met by the blacks, whose appearance exciting suspicion, he made his escape into the woods. After remaining there three or four hours, Adams, thinking all was quiet, stole to his yam-plot for a supply of provisions; his movements, how-ever, did not escape the vigilance of the blacks, who attacked and shot him through the body, the ball entering at his right shoulder, and passing out through his throat. He fell upon his side, and was instantly assailed by one of them with the butt end of the gun; but he parried the blows at the expense of a broken finger. Tetaheite then placed his gun to his side, but it fortunately missed fire twice. Adams, recovering a little from the shock of his wound, sprang on his legs, and ran off with as much speed as he was able, and fortunately outstripped his pursuers, who seeing him likely to escape, offered him protection if he would stop. Adams, much exhausted by his wound, readily accepted their terms, and was conducted to Christian's house, where he was kindly treated. Here this day of bloodshed ended, leaving only four Englishmen alive out of nine. It was a day of emancipation to the blacks, who were now masters of the island, and of humiliation and retribution to the whites.

Young, who was a great favourite with the women, and had, during this attack, been secreted by them, was now also taken to Christian's house. The other two, McCoy and Quintal, who had always been the great oppressors of the blacks, escaped to the mountains, where they supported themselves upon the produce of the ground about them.

The party in the village lived in tolerable tranquillity for about a week; at the expiration of which, the men of colour began to quarrel about the right of choosing the women whose husbands had been killed; which ended in Menalee's shooting Timoa as he sat by the side of Young's wife, accompanying her song with his flute. Timoa not dying immediately, Menalee reloaded, and deliberately dispatched him by a second discharge. He afterwards attacked Tetaheite, who was condoling with Young's wife for the loss of her favourite black, and would have murdered him also, but for the interference of the women. Afraid to remain longer in the village, he escaped to the mountains and joined Quintal and McCoy, who, though glad of his services, at first received him with suspicion. This great acquisition to their force enabled them to bid defiance to the opposite party; and to show their strength, and that they were provided with muskets, they appeared on a ridge of mountains, within sight of the village, and fired a volley which so alarmed the others that they sent Adams to say, if they would kill the black man, Menalee, and return to the village, they would all be friends again. The terms were so far complied with that Menalee was shot; but, apprehensive of the sincerity of the remaining blacks, they refused to return while they were alive.

Adams says it was not long before the widows of the white men so deeply deplored their loss, that they determined to revenge their death, and concerted a plan to murder the only two remaining men of colour. Another account, communicated by the islanders, is that it was only part of a plot formed at the same time that Menalee was murdered, which could not be put in execution before. However this may be, it was equally fatal to the poor blacks. The arrangement was, that Susan should murder one of them, Tetaheite, while he was sleeping by the side of his favourite; and that Young should at the same instant, upon a signal being given, shoot the other, Nehow. The unsuspecting Tetaheite retired as usual, and fell by the blow of an axe; the other was looking at Young loading his gun, which he supposed was for the purpose of shooting hogs, and requested him to put in a good charge, when he received the deadly contents.

All the Tahitian men were now dead; five of the mutineers had been murdered. The two Englishmen who remained in the village, Young and Adams, advised McCoy and Quintal up in the hills that it was now safe for them to return. At first they refused. There had been so much treachery and deception on the island, they insisted on being shown the hands and heads of the slain Tahitians. Adams produced the grisly proof, and McCoy and Quintal left their hideout.

The quarreling was far from over. Friction now developed between the four surviving mutineers and the ten women. There was even bitterness over how the dead Englishmen should be buried. Young was disturbed that the Tahitian women wanted to keep the skulls of their dead "husbands" in their houses, sometimes even carrying them with them when they went on errands. "I thought that if the girls did not agree to give up the heads of the five white men in a peaceable manner, they ought to be taken by force, and buried," Young wrote in his diary.

The women must have had more serious points of difference with the surviving mutineers. Young's diary reported that "since the massacre, it has been the desire of the greater part of them to get some conveyance, to enable them to leave the island." By April, 1794, such was the squalid mess to which Christian's "Utopia" had degenerated, Jenny, one of the more determined of the native women, decided to build her own "conveyance." The desperate woman "tore up the boards of her house, and endeavoured, though without success, to persuade some others to follow her example." A vessel for the unhappy women was, however, built in the next few months. It was launched in Bounty Bay on August 15, 1794. The native women got in their escape boat but were soon back on Pitcairn again. "According to expectation," Young drily wrote in his diary of the boat's maiden voyage, "she upset."

The native women seem to have lost face as a result of the incident. The following day, they agreed to give up the skulls of their slain lovers — the Englishmen, not their own countrymen — and the mutineers buried them. In October of the same year, the whole community gathered at Quintal's house for a ghoulish feast to celebrate the murder of the Tahitian men.

Young's diary does not say what had happened to restore harmony on the island. It was a short-lived truce between the sexes. A month later, a conspiracy among the women to murder the white men in their sleep was discovered. The men forgave them after the women promised to mend their ways "and never again to give any cause even to suspect their behaviour." Young wrote in his journal: "We did not forget their conduct; and it was agreed among us, that the first female who misbehaved should be put to death; and this punishment was to be repeated on each offence until we could discover the real intentions of the women." The former midshipman acknowledged that he was "bothered and idle."

The women were now in the majority, ten against four. The *Bounty* men became alarmed at the prospect of their former concubines gaining the upper hand. Two muskets were hidden one night in the bush, "for the use of any person who might be so fortunate as to escape, in the event of an attack [by the women] being made." The expected attack came on November 30, 1794. The women were subdued and eventually returned to their households "on being once more pardoned."

This tense state of affairs lasted for another four or five years. Periodically, the women would regroup, "whenever their displeasure was excited," and hide out in unfrequented parts of the island. They had managed to seize some muskets and powder, and for a time they defied the white men from inside a barricaded retreat they had built on the high ground. "In this manner," says

Beechey, "the men were kept in continual suspense, dreading the result of each disturbance."

Much of the friction undoubtedly was due to the mean, violent nature of two of the surviving mutineers, McCoy and Quintal. In fearful ways, the latter abused all of the women he was able to get into his bed. He bit off the ear of one of the Tahitian girls.

If the women had suffered before April 20, 1798, there was worse to come after that date. On that day, McCoy, remembering what he had learned from the days when he worked in a distillery in Scotland, adapted a copper kettle from the *Bounty*, made a mash of *ti*-root, and "succeeded in producing a bottle of ardent spirit." Soon Quintal had a still of his own. Moonshine liquor had come to Pitcairn, and the four Englishmen, who had tasted nary a drop of hard stuff since the supplies of rum and Madeira from the ship had been exhausted, went on a binge which evidently produced horrific hangovers. Two of the men, at least, Adams and Young, resolved never again to touch spirits.

For McCoy, the bacchanal ended in a fit of delirium. He tied a rock around his neck and hurled himself from a cliff to his death on the rocks below Christian's Cave. Quintal, his drinking companion, went on producing fiery stuff with his still. He became meaner with each passing day. Adams and Young kept well clear of him. But when Quintal lost the woman he had been living with — another death caused by a slip on the cliffs while in search of eggs — his need of a replacement precipitated a new crisis. Although there were seven available women on the island, "nothing would satisfy him but the wife of one of his companions." Quintal was now a raving drunkard and a menace to the community. Adams and Young decided he had to be removed. They invited Quintal to Adams' house, let him get helplessly drunk on his own *ti*-whiskey, and then split his skull in two with an ax.

In an unmarked grave, beside the bodies of Christian and the other mutineers who had been murdered, Quintal was laid to rest. The island they had chosen as their Eden had given them instead a few years of misery and bloodshed and, finally, anonymous graves. Or was this so in the case of Fletcher Christian?

Throughout the nineteenth century, students of the *Bounty*

story were fond of speculating on the possibility that Christian somehow managed to make his way back to England. In the Lake District near Christian's birthplace, rumors abounded in 1808 and 1809 that the leader of the mutiny had returned to his homeland. The story was that he had been able to build himself a small craft on Pitcairn and sail it to one of the Spanish outposts in South America. There, with a sum of gold ducats the *Bounty* was carrying at the time of the mutiny, Christian, according to this theory, bought passage back to England. (The gold, incidentally, has never been accounted for; occasionally today, Pitcairn young mount a treasure hunt for Bligh's ducats.)

The theory hangs on some flimsy evidence. A person resembling Christian was seen by one of the pardoned *Bounty* men, Peter Heywood, then a captain in the Royal Navy, in Fore Street, Plymouth, about the year 1809. The stranger, hearing someone hurrying up to him, turned around, looked at Heywood, and fled. One book that picks up this point, C. S. Wilkinson's *The Wake of the Bounty*, even claims that it was Christian who inspired Coleridge to write *The Ancient Mariner*. And while interest in the mutiny was still at a high pitch, a magazine in London claimed that it had acquired Christian's own story. On September 13, 1795, *True Briton* reported that Fletcher was now in "lucrative establishment under the Spanish Government in South America," having sailed from Pitcairn to Juan Fernandez, finally making his way to Chile. *True Briton* announced it had picked up its scoop while Christian was on a visit to Cadiz.

There is no question in my mind that the article was bogus. But whichever literary hack in London concocted this fake at least put forward a truer account of the cause of the mutiny than others who were to follow him. For this reason alone, it is worth a moment's study. This 1795 story made the point that the revolt had not been caused by Bligh's conduct but was due to "the unconquerable passion which he [Christian] and the major part of his crew entertained for the enjoyments which Otaheite held out to their voluptuous imaginations." It quoted Christian as saying that "we banished the remembrance of Old England entirely from our breasts. I suffered more than words can express from the conflict of contending passions; but I had gone too far to recede: so, put-ing the best face on the business, I ordered the boat to be cut adrift, wore ship, and shaped our course back for Otaheite."

The theory about Christian's escape from Pitcairn and his mysterious second life can be demolished fairly easily. One entry in the diary kept by his closest friend, Young, makes it clear that Christian was among those murdered in the massacre carried out by the Tahitian men. In 1794, when only four mutineers, Young, Adams, McCoy, and Quintal, were left alive on Pitcairn, the diary records that the native women were carrying about with them the skulls of *five* white men. Since only nine mutineers reached Pitcairn, one of those skulls must have been Christian's.

But there *is* genuine mystery concerning when and where Fletcher obtained the first of his half-caste heirs, that fabulous character in the Pitcairn story, Thursday October Christian. In an earlier chapter, I raised the possibility that Mi'Mitti was pregnant when the *Bounty* made her first of several departures from Tahiti.

Of the birthdate of Christian's first son, we know that he was born on a Thursday in October. Christian couldn't bring himself to give the boy a native name. An English one would have brought painful memories of home. So he followed the neutral course of naming him after the day of the week and the month of the year in which he arrived in the world. But which October was it, 1789 or 1790? The standard version is that the boy was born on the island in 1790. But whenever his age was recorded by those outsiders who talked with him in later life, the year of birth that emerges is 1789, which would mean he was born on the *Bounty* as Christian was searching for his island of refuge. He would have been conceived, then, at Matavai Bay in February.

When the American skipper of the sealer *Topaz*, Mayhew Folger, discovered the Pitcairn community by chance on February 6, 1808, the young Christian gave his age as eighteen. If he had been born on the island, he would not have turned eighteen until nine months later. Similarly, when the first British warships, the *Briton* and the *Tagus*, called at Pitcairn in 1814, Thursday October gave his age as twenty-five, which would make it appear that he was born in 1789. And when a census was taken in 1831 by Captain Alexander Sandilands of H.M.S. *Comet*, Thursday October's birth year was placed even earlier than 1790. His age was given then as forty-four, but this was clearly an error.

On the day he came into the world, his father had made a simple calendar error. The boy was first christened Friday October and continued to be known by that name until the skipper of the *Topaz* came ashore in 1808 and informed the islanders that, while their chronometer from the *Bounty* was still accurate and they had kept meticulous track of the days, months, and years, Fletcher had slipped up on one basic point. After deposing Bligh, and while the mutineers were sailing back to Tahiti, Fletcher forgot to record that they had crossed the International Date Line. His first son was born on a day the Pitcairn colonists observed as Friday. Actually, east of the Date Line, it was Thursday. Friday October thanked Captain Folger for pointing out this error, and henceforth was known as Thursday October.

By the time of Folger's discovery of the community, Adams, the sole surviving mutineer, was the revered Patriarch of the little Pitcairn society that now numbered thirty-five. Although by now a deeply religious man, Adams lived with a harem of nine Tahitian women. He had fathered many of the twenty-five children on the island, but all the young looked up to him as father and accepted his word as law. As the children reached puberty, Adams refused to let them marry until the boys had shown they could care and provide for their wives. From what he could remember of the Church of England ceremony, he performed marriages in the little house of worship he had had built. A single wedding ring existed on the island, and Adams used this to unite each couple which came to his worthy, if unconsecrated altar.

By the early 1800's, under Adams' strict puritanical rule, the community was developing in a state of utter tranquillity. Those outsiders who saw the community in its pioneer years mustered every superlative they could find to describe the piety and the goodness of Adams' strange flock. From mutiny and slaughter had emerged a society that may well have been the purest and gentlest community ever to grace this earth. It had set its standards in total isolation from the world. When its cocoon was pierced, it was fortunate that the outsider was an American, not an English skipper.

John Adams, alias Alexander Smith, the mutineer who became Pitcairn's revered Patriarch.

Fletcher Christian's celebrated first son, Thursday October
Christian, in the hat with cock feathers he wore to greet
the first visitors from the outside world.

Captain Folger's *Topaz*, out of Boston, had been on a round-the-world voyage in search of sealing grounds in the Southern Hemisphere. When he came upon Pitcairn, he assumed that the British Admiralty records were correct and that the island was uninhabited. He was about to launch his boats to explore the shore for seals when he saw with his glasses a twin-hulled craft being paddled out through the surf. There were more surprises in store for Captain Folger. The three youths in the canoe hailed them — in perfect English!

One of the trio was Friday (soon to be Thursday) October Christian, a strapping six-footer wearing a straw hat with black cock's feathers stuck in it for decoration. Astonished that he could converse with them in English, Folger told the boys in the canoe that he was an American.

"Where is America?" they asked. "Is it in Ireland?"

The boys presented Folger with a gift of coconuts and invited him to visit a white man who lived on the island. Folger was further surprised when the brown youths who clambered aboard his vessel announced: "We are Englishmen."

"Where were you born?" the man from Boston asked.

"On that island which you see."

"How then are you Englishmen, if you were born of that island, which the English do not own, and never possessed."

"We are English because our father was an Englishman."

The youths then told Folger about their Patriarch and were astounded to learn that the skipper had never heard of him. And then came the final surprise for the captain of the *Topaz*.

"Well, then, did you know Captain Bligh of the *Bounty?*" the boys asked him. Folger wrote later that "the whole story immediately burst upon my mind, and produced a shock of mingled feelings, surprise, wonder, and pleasure, not to be described."

The refuge of the missing *Bounty* mutineers had been discovered more than eighteen years after the revolt. It was a moment of keen drama in a lonely corner of the world. Before the drama proceeded, there was an awkward pause. The boys extended a warm welcome to Folger to accompany them ashore and meet their Patriarch. The American hesitated. He knew the *Bounty* story and knew that the

lone member of Christian's party who survived had an appointment with a hangman's noose at Spithead. Might not Adams prove
to be a desperado who would seize any outsider who set foot on
his island and hold him captive to prevent word of his whereabouts
getting back to England? For his part, Adams was also apprehensive.
Might not the captain of the *Topaz* be acting as an agent for the
British, come to seize him and take him back to civilization in
chains, perhaps for a reward?

The result of this caution on each man's part resulted in Thursday October and his companions making three trips between the
island and the *Topaz* before Folger agreed to accept the youths'
offer. He and his men were greeted warmly by Adams and the
women and children. Folger and Adams spent most of the day in
conversation. The American was given an expurgated account of
the mutiny and the violent deaths of those who had followed
Christian to Pitcairn. Adams questioned Folger avidly about what
had been happening in the outside world. He learned about the
French Revolution, Bonaparte, and England's wars with France.
As a seafarer, Folger gave Adams a stirring account of Nelson's
victory at Trafalgar. At hearing this, some dormant pride at having
once been part of the King's Navy stirred in the Patriarch's heart.
Folger reported that Adams "rose from his seat, took off his hat,
swung it three times round his head with three cheers, threw it on
the ground sailor-like, and cried out: 'Old England forever!' "

In a strange act of furnishing his visitor with proof that he had
discovered the *Bounty* mutineers' hideout, Adams presented Folger with the ship's chronometer before the *Topaz* put to sea again
before sundown. Folger sailed on to the island of Juan Fernandez,
left the chronometer there with the Spanish Governor, and moved
on to Valparaiso. There he sought out an English naval officer and
told him he had solved the mystery of the missing *Bounty* mutineers. A report on Folger's discovery was dispatched to the English Admiral in Rio de Janeiro, who forwarded it to London. It
reached the Admiralty on May 14, 1809. Their lordships, however,
were preoccupied with the war against France. The *Bounty* mutiny
was a closed book; in any event, no ship could be spared to ap-
prehend the lone mutineer who survived.

Puzzled that his discovery had aroused so little interest in England, doubly so considering the fuss that had been made at the time the mutiny on the *Bounty* had first come to the Admiralty's attention, Folger in 1813, in a letter dated Nantucket, gave a full report to the Admiralty on his visit to Christian's retreat. Again, the Admiralty took no action. The following year, by happenstance, two majestic vessels of the King's Navy, the forty-four-gun *Briton* under Sir Thomas Staines, and the *Tagus*, approached Pitcairn unaware of the *Topaz*'s visit and assuming it was uninhabited. Sir Thomas was as surprised as Folger had been to find that the islanders hailed his ship in "very good English." He and Captain Pipon, the commander of the *Tagus*, went ashore with Thursday October, and all got thoroughly drenched in the wild run through the surf. After talking with Adams and his flock, to whom Sir Thomas refers as "the descendants of the deluded crew of the *Bounty*," both commanders agreed that it would be an inhuman act to arrest the surviving mutineer and deprive the community of his leadership. Adams had atoned for past sins. On that day in 1814 began the long association between the Royal Navy and Pitcairn, an association that was to shape its development for most of the nineteenth century. It was a sentimental link and a strange one, considering that the community had been born out of an act of defiance against the same King's Navy.

The visiting navy skippers brought them supplies, drew up Pitcairn's early laws and constitution, and once, in 1838, even had to rescue the islanders from a dictator. This dictator had the gentle name of Joshua Hill. He was in his sixties when he came ashore from a passing ship and presented letters allegedly giving him authority to act as Governor of Pitcairn. He soon altered this title to "President of the Commonwealth of Pitcairn." He was obviously deranged, but the simple islanders, impressed by his bogus credentials and his stern and lofty manner, did not realize until too late that they were dealing with a madman.

Hill arrived at the end of 1832, soon after the Pitcairners had returned from Tahiti in the first of two unhappy attempts at resettling the colony on larger islands. (I deal with these hegiras in detail in the chapter which follows.) The Tahitian experience

had had a demoralizing effect on the community, and some of the
men had brought back to Pitcairn with them the art of distilling
a crude whiskey. The community had lost its guiding hand with
the death of Patriarch Adams in 1829. The leadership had passed
into alien but kindly hands. Three English settlers had arrived in
the 1820's — John Buffett, a shipwright from Bristol, and John
Evans, a Welshman, in 1823, and George Nobbs, said to be the
illegitimate son of an English peer, who arrived to stay in 1828.
Nobbs was an educated man, and he soon took over from Buffett and
Evans the work they were doing to instruct the islanders in the
ways of God and man. All three married island girls and founded
families. But for the liquor problem and some other bad habits
picked up in Tahiti, the community was making progress. And
then arrived a puritanical busybody, the mad Joshua Hill.

He was sane enough, however, to realize that the only opposition
he faced on the island would come from the three outsiders, Nobbs,
Buffett, and Evans. He had Buffett lashed to the church entrance
and flogged for questioning his authority. He threatened to whip
women whom he suspected of gossiping about him. He wrecked
the men's stills and started a temperance society on Pitcairn. But
the islanders submitted to his will. Hill denounced Buffett, Evans,
and Nobbs as "the lousy foreigners" and insisted they leave his
"Commonwealth." Eventually, they were forced into exile, Nobbs
to Tahiti, and Buffett and Evans to the Gambiers.

Hill's despotism continued for six years while Nobbs, Buffett,
and Evans unavailingly petitioned the British government to do
something about him. Of the minor figures of history, Hill is one
of the most gorgeous lunatics I have encountered. His character is
best revealed in a long self-testimonial he wrote during his rule on
Pitcairn. Preserved in the island's archives, it makes hilarious reading. When it was first published in London in 1853, Victorian
society must have had a great chuckle over it. I shall quote from it
fairly extensively:

I am aware that pedantry and egotism become no one, and myself
perhaps less than any. But for certain reasons, the following credentials,
as a memorandum, I hope will be pardoned on the present occasion —
they are truths.

I observe, *in limine*, that I have visited the four quarters of the globe, and it has ever been my desire to maintain, as far as lay in my power, the standing of an English gentleman. I have lived a considerable while in a palace, and had my dinner parties with a princess on my right, and a General's lady upon my left. I have had a French cook, a box at the opera. I have drove my dress carriage (thought the neatest then in Paris, where I spent five or six years; as well I have known Calcutta), and the handsomest lady, Madame R——, to grace my carriage. I have drove a curricle with my two out-riders, and two saddle-horses, besides a travelling-carriage. A valet, coachman, footman, groom, and, upon extraordinary occasions, my *maitre d'hôtel*. I have (at her request) visited Madame Bonaparte, at the Tuileries, St. Cloud, and Malmaison. I might thus mention many others of note abroad.

I have frequently dined with that remarkable woman, Madame Carbanas, afterwards the Princess de C——. I have had the honour of being in company; i.e. at the same parties, with both his late Majesty George IV, then Prince Regent, and his present Majesty William IV, then H.R.H. Duke of Clarence, as well with their royal brothers. I have ridden in a royal Duke's carriage, with four horses and three footmen, more than once, and have dined at his table, and drunk the old hock of his late father, George III. I have visited and dined with some of our first families, and have been visited by a Duke, and others of the first noblemen. I have known and dined with (abroad and in England), Madames Catalini, Grassini, Georges, etc. And I have given the arm to Lady Hamilton (of Naples renown), whom the hero of the Nile has given his (one) to more than once. I have dined with a Viceroy Governor (who was a General and a Count), and with Admirals, both on board their ships and on shore. I have entertained Governors, Generals, Captains (R.N.), on board my ship, more than once. And I have commanded several ships, and went to sea at the beginning of the French Revolution. . . .

I have visited the Falls of Niagara and Montmorency, the natural bridge in Virginia, the great Reciprocating Fountain in East Tennessee, the great Temple of Elephanta at Bombay. I have dined with a prince, as well as with a princess; and with a count, a baron, an ambassador, a minister (ordinary and extraordinary), and have dined with a *Chargé d'Affaire*, and lived with consuls, etc. I have visited and conversed with "Red Jacket," the great Indian warrior. I have visited and been visited by a bishop. I have frequently partook of the delicious Hungarian wine (tokay), Prince Esterhazy's; as also of Prince Swartzerburgh's old hock, said to have been 73 years old; and I was intimate with the brother-in-law of this last German nobleman. I have dined with a principal Hong merchant at Canton. I have sat next to the beautiful Madame Recamier and Madame Carbanus, at the great dinner parties. I have written to the Prime Minister of England; and have received the late Earl of Liverpool's answer with his thanks, etc.

I was at Paris when the allies were met there. I have visited and breakfasted with the late Warren Hastings, Esq., at his seat in Gloucestershire. I have had a permission with a party of friends to hunt over his grounds. Entertained etc. two or three days at the sporting lodge of an Earl, now a Marquis. I have made a crimson silk net for a certain fashionable Marchioness, which she actually wore at her next great party of five or six hundred persons. I have danced with the Countess Bertrand; i.e., Mademoiselle Fanny Dillon, before she married the Marshal. I was at Napoleon's coronation. I have been invited to the Lord Mayor's, and to the dinner of an Alderman of London; to those also of the first merchants and bankers. . . .

I wrote and published in the London *Morning Post* (7th March, 1811), on naval power. I have seen the Vestrises, father, son and grandson, at once (the only time), dance on the stage at the opera at Paris. I have given a passage to many on board my ship, but never in my life received a farthing as passage-money from any person. I am decidedly against the use of ardent spirit (malt liquor may do for those who like it), tobacco, etc. And as for wine, that only at dinner; it even then ought to be good, if not the very best, as the Gourmet would have it. . . . I have had a fine band of music on board my ship, and my four kinds of wine on my table. (I am not sleeping on a "bed of roses" now, but in a humble hut or cabin.) After all, what does the foregoing amount to? — vanity of vanities. I will merely add, that I have had a year in the Church of Christ, and that I am a life member of the Bible Society. That I am looking with the blessed Lord's help to something of far more intrinsic worth and consideration — "the price of our high calling" — the life to come. I am now in my sixty-second year of age, and of course it is high time that I should look upon this world as nearly closed on me. I might perhaps say much more, but must stop. I am now an humble teacher upon Pitcairn's Isle for the time being.

This, and more, was rich fare indeed for the early Pitcairners. Not only a friend of kings and emperors, but a life member of the Bible Society! It made less heady reading for a captain who called

at Pitcairn in 1837 on H.M.S. *Actaeon*. The captain was interested especially in a claim by Hill that he was a "very near relative
of the Duke of Bedford, and that the Duchess seldom rode out in
her carriage without him." The captain was Lord Edward Russell,
the Duke of Bedford's eldest son, and he had never heard of Hill.
He saw immediately that the simple Pitcairners had given themselves into the hands of a fool and a scoundrel. Without orders
to remove him, Lord Edward Russell simply reported the situation
to London. The following year, the navy dispatched H.M.S.
Imogene to carry Hill off the island and land him in Valparaiso.
Quietly, he slipped off the stage of history.

The Pitcairners learned a lesson from Hill's dictatorship. They
saw that life for them could never again be as simple as it had
been in the days of Adams' patriarchate. American whalers and
British and Spanish merchantmen and men-of-war were now calling
fairly regularly at the island, and as the men came ashore, the
Pitcairners learned more and more about the harsh side of the big
world. They realized they would need an established system of
government as well as regulations governing the conduct of themselves and their visitors; and for this, the children of mutiny turned,
ironically, to the captains and admirals who themselves had learned
something from the *Bounty* revolt.

On the opposite side of the world, another irony had come to
full flourish. Bligh, as we have seen, returned to Tahiti and succeeded this time in carrying breadfruit trees to the West Indies.
They did well in a climate similar to that of Polynesia. By the
early years of the nineteenth century, lush breadfruit trees were
growing on every slaveholder's plantation. The fruit was cooked
and served in the slaves' messhalls. They found its taste objection-
able and contemptuously spat out the new miracle food acquired
at a cost of mutiny, bloodshed, shipwreck, suffering, and exile. The
planters were obliged to resume their expensive imports of wheat
and corn to keep the slaves alive. It had all been in vain.

CHAPTER EIGHT

・ GUILT AND RIGHTEOUSNESS

Throughout the nineteenth and into the twentieth century, religion nourished the Pitcairners as much as their stewed goat meat, baked fish, sweet potatoes, bananas, mangoes, and pies. Survival challenged their limbs as the fiercest taskmaster to rule over any community. But the stimulus to their minds was limited almost exclusively to scripture and theology. And it was the gentlest of stimuli, both in the period when John Adams struggled to translate the biblical intricacies into simple stories for his clan and later when the descendants embraced the Seventh-Day Adventism of an America that was inventing new religious cults of its own. They replaced their fundamental interpretation of English religion with an even more fundamental one, an exchange that had its roots in the simple trust the islanders placed in the words and religious tracts conveyed to them by men who set out in sailing ships from San Francisco to convert the Pacific. Religion and righteousness — and a curious Pitcairn sense of guilt and shame — are worthy of separate, full-length treatment. I shall review them here in summary and return to the subject in my study of the contemporary society. Upsetting the chronology, the review begins with the period when the islanders changed their religion, as I believe that this shift revealed significant things about the islanders' spiritual and temporal ways in an even earlier period.

Two Seventh-Day Adventist Elders, J. N. Loughborough and James White, paved the way for the islanders' conversion with something of the technique used by an astute salesman in plotting the conversion of a target client from Brand X to his own product. In 1876, the Adventists sent to Pitcairn a trunk of literature outlining the tenets of Adventism. While there was no immediate follow-up visit, the initiative of the Adventists was regarded by church leaders in England and by some on the island as the cheekiest of missionary acts. Since the island had turned from bloodletting in the late 1790's, Pitcairn had been a cherished outpost of the Church of England. It was to develop a special affection for Queen Victoria, an unquestioning belief in her role as Defender of the Faith, and a touching trust in and love for England as the Mother Country. One of Pitcairn's earliest chroniclers, the Reverend Thomas Boyles Murray, wrote admiringly in 1853 of the islanders' adherence "to the teaching of the Church of England, those good principles with which the very name of Pitcairn has been so long and so happily associated."

True to Mr. Murray's faith in them, the Pitcairners at first perused the Adventist literature with distaste and distrust. Among other things, the literature spoke of the imminence of the Second Coming and implicitly rebuked the islanders for observing the wrong Sabbath, Sunday instead of Saturday, the seventh day of the week and, theoretically, of earthly creation as set down in Genesis. To the trenchermen and trencherwomen of Pitcairn, Seventh-Day Adventism, with its strict adherence to Mosaic dietary laws, would have denied them many of the island's delicacies, the culinary legacy from their Polynesian half-ancestry: roast suckling pig done in ground ovens in the Tahitian manner, crayfish, shellfish, raw, marinated flesh from scaleless fish, and so on.

But on an island deprived of diversion and novelty, desperately short of reading material, that trunk of literature furnished by the Adventists held out an irresistible temptation. The tracts were distributed, and gradually the islanders began perusing them with the interest that any isolated, church-minded society might be expected to take in the beliefs of a new sect which had troubled to make contact with them. Their interest at first was totally academic. But over the years it deepened to the point where the word of Adventism was being discussed as much as the familiar Anglican teachings. The Seventh-Day Adventists made no further overtures to the island until 1886, ten years after the dispatch of the box of religious tracts. In October of that year, John L. Tay, an Adventist missionary, arrived in Bounty Bay. He soon discovered that he had landed, for proselytizing endeavors, on the most fertile of shores.

He spent little more than six weeks on Pitcairn, living with those families which were most attracted to the new beliefs. By the end of his stay, he had managed to persuade a majority of the islanders to adopt the articles of Adventism.

To the dismay of the captains and chaplains of visiting British naval vessels, an exotic American cult had established more than simply a bridgehead on this remote yet curiously *British* island. Almost overnight, it had become the majority church. And from that position of strength, it soon became the sole island religion. In London, those who had nurtured the Pitcairners' faith, raised sums to bring the pastors to England for training, and seen to it that the island's first native pastor, George Nobbs, had an audience with none less than Queen Victoria and Prince Albert before sailing back to the island, felt that their wards in the South Seas had betrayed them. The Reverend Mr. Murray's Society for Promoting Christian Knowledge spoke of a "religious debauch" in their own little bailiwick in Polynesia.

The attraction Seventh-Day Adventism held for the little colony had, as I interpret the archive material, a threefold explanation.

First, and most significant, the islanders were flattered by the attention paid to their little flock by urbane and scholarly men from California and the East Coast of America. The whalers that had arrived so regularly in the middle years of the nineteenth century — almost one vessel a *week* in the years 1846 and 1850 — were no longer calling at Bounty Bay. Pitcairn was returning to the isolation it had known in its earliest years. In these circumstances, anyone who showed a genuine interest in their welfare and their souls was assured of the islanders' respect.

Second, Adventism held out for the islanders a heightened form of spiritual *excitement* in its root belief that the Second Coming of Christ, a *visible* return of the Savior, was near at hand. Here was divine drama, or rather the prospect of divine drama, that the Church of England, with its lofty and mystical theology, could never provide. To people living flat, unchanging lives, far removed from a world inventing ingenious new machines and social forms, this promise of the Savior's return for a Millennium of divine guidance and judgment must surely have been regarded as the only dazzlingly high plateau the future earthly landscape presented. It is significant here that Seventh-Day Adventism always has had its strongest appeal among those living in rural areas or in isolated communities, which is not mentioned in any sense as a denigration of the moral improvement it has achieved among its converts.

And third, Adventism held out a special attraction to the women of the community. With its religious, rather than purely social or legal, prohibitions against the use of alcohol and stimulants in general, it offered the women a unique way of keeping their menfolk under more orderly control. The older Pitcairn women had lived through two or three fearful episodes of unrestricted moonshining. They had seen how the strong liquor obtained from the *ti* root in backyard stills could turn their husbands and sons from creatures of pious contentment into rampaging maniacs who acted either violently and incestuously toward their own women or predatorily toward the wives and daughters of others. They championed Adventism for some of the reasons that the women of America were later to vote for prohibition.

It was not so much a case of an idea whose time has come. Here was a belief with an almost tailormade appeal to an island commune.

The manner in which Seventh-Day Adventism moved from being the majority religion to the island's sole belief is a tribute to the Pitcairners' feeling of unity. To maintain unanimity in their church life, the minority, which had clung to the Church of England, eventually agreed to adopt the new faith.

In 1890, the one-hundredth anniversary of Fletcher Christian's landing on Pitcairn, the entire community was baptized in a mass ceremony. And to remove the temptation to eat the now-forbidden pork flesh, all the hogs on the island, wild and domesticated, were disposed of in a mass execution. One tale I heard on the island is that they were slaughtered and the carcasses thrown into the sea from a cliff, a rather bad act of marine pollution by a community which is not otherwise an offender on this score. (The livestock that died on that day when pig meat ceased to be a part of the Pitcairn diet were not just *ordinary* pigs. They were the descendants of the pigs which had come on the *Bounty* from Matavai Bay, Tahiti; their porcine ancestors had made the vessel's historic last voyage.)

By now, the Mother Church of the Seventh-Day Adventists had named a missionary ship the *Pitcairn*. She arrived toward the end of the centenary year, on November 25, bearing the most persuasive of missionaries, John Tay, Mrs. Tay, and a party of Adventist elders. There were several weeks of intense religious activities, and when the visit was over, three islanders left aboard the *Pitcairn* for that land which had sent them visitors both kindly and wicked, America.

Two and a half years later, the *Pitcairn* was back, and this time it deposited on the island a particularly energetic couple of American Adventists, Elder Gates and his wife. While Elder Gates cared for their souls, Mrs. Gates looked after both the minds of the very young and the career potential of the teen-agers. Having established the island's first kindergarten and nursery, she set out to teach shorthand and secretarial methods to the older children. Predictably, since the island had no need of secretaries or court reporters, as indeed is the case today, the experiment with the teen-agers was a fiasco, the Adventists' first and only real setback on Pitcairn.

In both the Anglican and Adventist periods, the Pitcairners, despite the charming picture they usually have presented of mildness, piety, and honesty, have also displayed distinct traces of a fundamental guilt, a collective shame. It survives to this day, and the contemporary evidence will be considered in Part II. From the time when the first schoolhouse was erected on the island, the mutiny, the event that led directly to the formation of the community, has never been taught on Pitcairn. Seven generations of schoolchildren have grown up knowing only that their forebears, long, long ago, did something wrong on an English man-of-war. As the children reached maturity, some read the *Bounty* literature, but with no desire to probe the record to discover whether their ancestors were out-and-out villains or had some redeeming qualities.

There is a sense of collective guilt also in the hymns composed by the Pitcairners of another era, hymns which are still sung in the island Church. Study these verses from the special hymn composed by an anonymous member of the community to celebrate the island's centenary in 1890:

> To this fair land our fathers sought
>> To flee their doom their sins had brought,
> In vain — nor peace nor rest was found,
>> For strife possessed th' unhallowed ground.
>
> Darkness around their path was spread:
>> Their crimes deserved a vengeance dread;
> When, lo! a beam of hope was given
>> To guide their erring feet to heaven.
>
> The holy word, a beacon light,
>> Had pierced the shade of sin's dark night,
> And poured a flood of radiance where
>> Had reigned the gloom of dull despair.
>
> We own the depths of sin and shame,
>> Of guilt and crime from which we came;
> Thy hand upheld us from despair,
>> Else we had sunk in darkness there.

The closing verse of this hymn of thanks to God reminds the Almighty that, "Thou know'st the depths from whence we sprung."

The fountainhead of whatever guilt is innate in the Pitcairn psyche was, without question, the troubled mind of one man, John Adams, mutineer-turned-patriarch. Gentle hero and remarkable man though he became in the closing half of his life, Adams carried to his grave a crushing burden of guilt — guilt over the mutiny, of course; guilt that he alone among the Englishmen survived the first ten terrible years on Pitcairn; guilt that his vote had contributed to the decision to transplant twelve Tahitian women, six of their men, and an infant Tahitian girl from the tranquil Polynesian life they had known to the servitude, and finally, the carnage, that Pitcairn brought; guilt that, from his sailor's lust and the lust of his *Bounty* companions, there had been established on an obscure rock in the ocean a strange community of half-castes, a wild experiment in miscegenation whose future prospects for survival were uncertain to say the least. Adams, remember, came from the simplest of eighteenth-century English stock, Thames-side slum stock at that, a member of a class which, while not averse to finding sexual gratification in the arms of a woman of dark skin, nevertheless looked upon Negroes and "Indians" as creatures to be treated little better than animals.

There is clear evidence of guilt in Adams' decision to change his name — from Alexander Smith as he was entered on the *Bounty*'s rolls — at some unknown time after the party of mutineers established themselves on Pitcairn. Adams was his actual family name. What earlier shame had caused him to conceal his true identity when he signed on Bligh's ship? The record on Adams' English past is hazy, and we shall never learn the details. The second name change, the one on Pitcairn, was done perhaps only partly in the hope that it might one day help him to dodge the arm of justice. Even when he remained as the sole Englishman among the colony of Tahitians and half-castes, he must have realized that it would be next to impossible for him to conceal that he was a human relic of the *Bounty* uprising. His very body incriminated him here. He had Tahitian tattoos over a great part of his torso, souvenirs of the wild times at Matavai Bay, and thanks to Bligh's thoroughness, the Royal Navy knew this identification detail. In drawing up his list of the missing mutineers, Bligh had written of Adams, in addition to his height and other physical characteristics, that he was "much tatowed." In deciding he wanted to be called Adams and not Smith, was the Patriarch attempting to dissociate himself from what "Smith" had done on the *Bounty*? I am inclined to believe that he was.

And if further proof of his guilt were needed, we have it in the well-documented record of the two horrific visions Adams had in the early 1800's when he was the sole white man left on the island with some twenty-five Tahitian women and Anglo-Tahitian offspring. In both these dreams, Adams recounted, he was given a preview of hell and his past transgressions were shown in vivid detail. Satan himself had come at Adams, brandishing a spear and warning the simple sailor of the intensity of the netherworld's furnaces. Even today, the story of John Adams' visions, minus, of course, the speculation that he might have been under the influence of *ti*-whiskey at the time he had them, is trotted out for the edification of the young. It is one of the few father-to-son folktales to survive.

In his laborious way, Adams had already begun to read to his flock from the Bible which had come off the *Bounty* together with a copy of the Book of Common Prayer. The books had come ashore in Fletcher Christian's sea chest; the Bible, "God's Book" as it was called by the very first Pitcairn religionists, is still there to be inspected today in the island Church. Adams' tutor in reading had been the well-educated midshipman Edward Young. Until Young's death from asthma in 1800 robbed him of his sole English companion, Adams had had a few months, perhaps a year, of instruction from this "gentleman" mutineer in reading and writing. Like most ordinary seamen of his time, Adams was barely literate when he joined the navy. Young succeeded in giving him adequate, if rather spindly and uncertain, handwriting. We may examine a specimen of it below the engraving of the Patriarch which appears on page 115.

But for those few months of tutelage in the arts of communication, the first generation of Pitcairners almost certainly would have grown to manhood and womanhood at the same level of literacy as that of the Tahitian half of their ancestry. From a remarkable exercise in self-improvement, Adams, the son of a Thames lighterman, the Cockney orphan, had managed to give the education of his English betters to his flock. He also produced on the island an atmosphere of hyper-religiosity which, with two or three interruptions, has prevailed until the present day.

With Adams as their teacher and figurehead, the children of the mutineers grew up with minds directed into only two avenues of thought: survival and Christian rectitude, the stomach and the soul.

Deeply religious men though they were, the ship's captains and officers who saw Pitcairn in its years following the colony's discovery, and conveniently set down on paper what they witnessed, were astonished by the devotional regimen Adams had instituted. The day began and ended with family-prayer services. At the table, they said grace, not once but twice. The custom had already begun to go into decline in England; but in Adams' community, meal-times took on a religious fervor. Until one of his visitors from the outside world advised him that it was not really necessary, the Patriarch had decreed that there should be *three* meatless days each week — Friday and Wednesday as well as the Sunday Sabbath. Adams had taken with him to the island some vague recollection of Good Friday and Ash Wednesday being meatless days in England. He could not remember the implications of these religious bans, so to be on the safe side, he decided to make *every* Friday and Wednesday a meatless day in addition to directing his children to abstain from meat-eating on the Sabbath itself. Food, Adams struggled to recollect for the food-loving Polynesians he lived with, was necessary, of course, for Christian stomachs, but there was also something somewhere in the Scriptures about eating being one of the sins of the flesh, like copulation and boozing.

An early visitor to Pitcairn, Captain W. Waldegrave of H.M.S. *Seringapatam*, later the Earl Waldegrave, gave this account of the grace ceremony: "Before they began a meal, all joined hands in the attitude of prayer, with eyes raised to heaven, and one recited a simple grace, grateful for the present food, but beseeching spiritual nourishment. Each answered, Amen, and after a pause, the meal began. At the conclusion, another grace was offered up. Should anyone arrive during the repast, all ceased to eat. The new guest said grace, to which each repeated, Amen, and then the meal continued."

Occasionally, of course, the younger children forgot the rules. If, out of hunger or eagerness, a child gulped down something before grace had been said, Adams insisted that it be regurgitated and the offender make a fresh and proper start in offering thanks to his Maker. The procedure instilled a respectful discipline among the children; it could hardly have had a salutary effect on the appetites of Adams' distinguished visitors. (I am happy to report that the custom of making a forgetful child empty his stomach has been abandoned on Pitcairn; while grace-before-meal is still the island rule, the odd, meal-before-grace slipup is excused without any fuss.)

The Sabbath in Adams' time was set aside entirely for devotions, meditation, and religious instruction. There were no fewer than five church services, and all but the infant young attended each one. No work of any kind was permitted on Sundays. No boat was allowed to be taken out to sea. The food to be eaten on the Sabbath had been prepared the previous day. We saw the evidence of Adams' legacy on the Pitcairn of 1972. Observance of the Sabbath remains a basic aspect of island life, and most of the old rules still apply.

The best early account of the intensity of Sabbath observances on the island has been provided by Captain F. W. Beechey of H.M.S. *Blossom*, which called at Pitcairn in 1825, four years before the Patriarch's death. In his description of the services he attended in Adams' little church, he emphasized that not only were there services throughout the day but that each service was an elaborate exercise in worshipful repetitiousness. Adams had belatedly "got religion," and he was determined that the women and children left in his charge would do likewise.

"The prayers were read by Adams," Captain Beechey reported,

and the lessons by [John] Buffett, the service being preceded by hymns. The greatest devotion was apparent in every individual, and in the children there was a seriousness unknown in the younger part of our communities at home. In the course of the Litany they prayed for their Sovereign and all the Royal Family with much apparent loyalty and sincerity. Some family prayers which were thought appropriate to their particular case, were added to the usual service, and Adams, fearful of leaving out any essential part, read in addition those prayers which are intended only as substitutes for others. A sermon followed, which was very well delivered by Buffet; and lest any part of it should be forgotten, or escape attention, it was read three times. The whole concluded with hymns, which were first sung by the grown people, and afterwards by the children. The service thus performed was very long; but the neat and cleanly appearance of the congregation, the devotion that animated every countenance, and the innocence and simplicity of the little children, prevented the attendance from becoming wearisome. In about half an hour afterwards we again assembled to prayers. They may be said to have church five times on a Sunday.

Beechey also observed, and reported in a book he published in London in 1831, *Narrative of a Voyage to the Pacific and Bering Strait*, an important and most relevant aspect of the character of the first Pitcairners — an almost total inability to indulge in fun or frivolous diversion. "During the whole time I was with them," he wrote, "I never heard them indulge in a joke, or other levity; and the practice of it is apt to give offence. They are so accustomed to take what is said in its literal meaning, that irony was always considered a falsehood in spite of explanation. They could not see the propriety of uttering what was not strictly true for any purpose whatever." (They remain today a stoic race, but their sense of humor is considerably better than it evidently was in Beechey's day.)

Adams permitted them to dance on only one day of the year, Queen Victoria's birthday, an occasion which an early chronicler described as Pitcairn's "grand day; it is kept up with feasting and dancing . . . and all sorts of merriment. Among the first questions everybody asks is, How is her Majesty the Queen?" The double irony here might be pointed out. These were children whose half-ancestry was a brown race which built much of its life around dancing. Here they could dance only once every 365 days — and then on the birthday of the ruler sitting on an English throne their fathers had turned against in mutiny!

This preoccupation with religion, the seriousness, the joylessness (between Victoria's birthdays, that is) that developed in young minds nurtured on a dozen or more sermons each Sunday were surely further reflections of Adams' guilt. This is not to suggest that the old man's Christianity was anything but utterly sincere. It was a piety, belated piety, of the most naïve kind. When Adams briefly was a guest of Captain Beechey aboard the *Blossom*, sharing Beechey's cabin, the Captain tells us that the Patriarch unselfconsciously fell on his knees in a corner of the stateroom to say his prayers before retiring. The next morning, Beechey would be awakened by Adams, again on his knees in the corner, offering in his rough Cockney, prayers for the new day. John Adams had come a long way from "Alexander Smith," the mutineer with musket and cutlass.

As the colony settled down, as the mixed-breed children of the mutineers began to raise more intricately mixed breed children of their own, the guilt of one man was translated into a communal guilt. The perpetuation of this island guilt is difficult to understand. But the transmittal of it can be comprehended more easily. In the community's formative years, Adams had been the sole voice of authority, the only real force in shaping the little society's ways and establishing a life-style for all to follow.

They developed no folk culture of their own. Admittedly, it was a scrap of a community, and it would be unreasonable to expect too much from it in the way of unique creative accomplishment. But its ancestry was a union of two races each rich in folk history and culture. Some of the English came through, and steadily cemented itself in place as the dominant influence, a very little of the Tahitian, apart from such basics of living as cooking, cloth-making from *tapa* bark, and shelter. In language and church, Adams imposed an Englishness on the community but an Englishness that lacked the gusto of the home country in his century. The children and grandchildren grew up proud of their godliness, intensely so, proud of their ability to survive, but with virtually no pride in their origin.

As the ships began to call, the islanders greeted the visitors almost in the roles of supplicants and penitents. Only one among them — Adams — bore any guilt in the *Bounty* mutiny or in the killings that had occurred in Pitcairn's first years. Yet all in the community seemed to be awaiting the smite of censure from the outside world. Perhaps to becloud the issue, Adams deliberately gave conflicting accounts of what had happened on the island to the first three captains to interrogate him. He also, at first, lied about his participation in the mutiny, claiming that he had been forced to join the insurrectionists, had been, in fact, asleep when Bligh was taken captive, and while still rubbing crumbs of sleep from his eyes, had found himself holding a musket in his hands, a loaded gun thrust on him by one of Christian's men. These discrepancies were reported back to London, where they seem to have been attributed to the failing memory of a man who had been through many horrors. He was described as "venerable" by some of his early visitors even though, at the time of the community's discovery in 1808 by Captain Mayhew Folger, he was only forty-four years of age. He died on March 5, 1829, at the age of sixty-five.

The piety of those he raised verged on sanctimoniousness, even among the very young. Adams told an early visitor of an occasion when he assigned two boys to make a mattock from iron recovered from the *Bounty*. They worked hard in the island smithy, fashioning a splendid tool on the anvil which had been carried off the ship. Adams had promised them, as compensation, a small amount of gunpowder from the dwindling supply so the youths could go hunting with a musket from the *Bounty*'s armory. When they presented the mattock to Adams, they basked in his praise for a moment and then told him they would not take the gunpowder. They said they would prefer as their reward that the Patriarch give them a few extra lessons from "God's Book."

Some years later, during Captain Waldegrave's visit in 1830, the islanders were overjoyed when the ship's chaplain came ashore to lead them in prayer. An exchange that took place on the edge of Bounty Bay that day was recorded by Waldegrave and was to be repeated by preachers — in America as well as in Britain — in countless Victorian sermons.

"God bless you, God bless you," one Pitcairn woman told Waldegrave with much fervor when he announced that the chaplain, the religious professional, was coming ashore. "Will he stay with us?" Captain Waldegrave had to disappoint her.

"You bad man, why not?" she asked.

"I cannot spare him, he is the clergyman of my ship. I have brought you clothes, which King George sends you," said the captain in an effort to mollify the woman.

"We rather want food for our souls," was the reply.

A collective guilt was present on Pitcairn even before Adams' patriarchate began, present perhaps from that morning in January, 1790, when the *Bounty* was stripped and burned.

The very lack of documentation and records from the hands of Christian and his fellow mutineers might be taken as evidence of their deep, unsettling awareness of the outrage they had perpe-

Christian's Cave (darker area in upper-central part of photograph), to which the mutiny leader would retire for long periods to reflect on what he had done. (Courtesy of Tom Christian)

trated. All but Adams went to their graves without knowing whether, in addition to the slaughter of trusting Tahitian *taios*, they also had on their consciences the deaths of Bligh and the eighteen other fellow countrymen they had abandoned at sea in a small, overloaded boat, with scant provisions and in a part of the world where cannibalism was still practiced by many of the races closest to the point of abandonment. The eight white men who had joined Christian had dreamed of creating an earthly paradise of self-indulgence, had seen it degenerate into violence and tormented loneliness, and must have realized in the process that it had all been utterly reprehensible, a conspiracy of mindless bloodletting and cruelty,

Is it any wonder that Christian spent much of his time on the island in brooding meditation, alone in the cave that looks out to sea from the gray rock that looms up over the settlement? Adams left no doubt in his chats with visiting sea captains that Fletcher Christian was a most unhappy man on Pitcairn. The charm and personality attributed to him by those who knew him before the mutiny were not qualities much in evidence on Pitcairn. The point was well elucidated in a book that was very popular in mid-Victorian England, *Pitcairn: The Island, the People, and the Pastor,* by the Reverend Thomas Boyles Murray. In a passage about Christian's Cave, he wrote a fitting postscript to Fletcher's life:

On the top of a high rock, is a spot which he [Christian] called his "look-out." Whilst many hearts, thousands of miles off, were wounded, if not broken, by suspense and uncertainty respecting the fate of himself and his companions, he was either employed in surveying the ocean around him, under the apprehension of the approach of the officers of justice, or in endeavouring to control the turbulent community, among whom he had irrevocably cast his lot.

It may be observed, that punishment in this life often bears a startling likeness to the sin which has been committed, and which not only thus finds the offender out, but shows him that it has done so. Within the narrow limits of the island, as in the confines of a ship, Christian had enemies at hand, who harassed, and at length took away his life; and it is a remarkable fact, that he who had raised his hand in a criminal manner against his superior in command, should have suffered death from those whom he looked upon as men under his authority.

We have assessments aplenty about the mutiny from other minds but none from those who led it. Christian and his closest friend, Midshipman Young, had each received polished educations in England and must be regarded as men of learning and urbanity. One of Christian's younger fellow pupils in Cumberland, incidentally, was the poet William Wordsworth. Young came from a fairly aristocratic family — an uncle was a baronet — and had grown up in a refined atmosphere of good schools and private tutors.

On Pitcairn, they had both the writing materials (from the *Bounty*) and the time — certainly they had the time! — to compose a message to their families, to the world, a farewell if not a *mea culpa*. Yet neither man attempted to set down on paper his side of the seizure of the *Bounty*. The explanation, I think, is shiningly clear — unless, of course, and this is a tiny "if," such writing existed only to be burned by Adams before 1808. The silence of Christian and Young I place among the strongest clues to the guilt they took with them to their grave.

If we jump ahead in Pitcairn's history to the periods of two mass migrations from the island, in 1831 and 1856, the reasons for these evacuations may also be studied in the light of the island's communal guilt. Declining rainfall and the thought that Malthusian theories about overpopulation might have classical relevance for Pitcairn were given at the time as the reasons for these migrations — the tragic experiment in transplanting the colony to Tahiti and the later, better organized mass movement to Norfolk Island off the eastern coast of Australia.

But the contemporary records do not indicate that the droughts and crop damage were of such severity to warrant abandoning the island. Crops were declining to some extent, probably because the land had been planted and replanted without any enrichment from fertilizer. (Later, they were to collect seaweed for use as fertilizer.) But famine was not in prospect at any time. There were staple foodstuffs from the flat ground, pigs and goats in the highlands, and an ocean teeming with fish. In short, a variety of food sources sufficient to sustain easily the swiftly expanding island population. To take one item of foodstuff alone: pigs were being slaughtered at a rate to provide every man, woman, and child on the island with an average of fifty pounds of pork a year, a fairly high consumption of one type of meat in a community which had as varied a diet as that of their contemporaries in America and Europe.

And the island was no longer developing in total isolation from the outside world. The *Register of Pitcairn's Island* records that more than 330 vessels touched at Pitcairn between 1808 and 1853. If supplies of water and food were to peter out with dramatic suddenness, rescue was near at hand. One or two naval vessels or whalers could have evacuated the two dozen families with ease if the situation threatened to become perilous or the population pressures built up alarmingly.

Nothing I have found in the archives suggests that either of these specters was present on Pitcairn before the two hegiras. In fact, in the 1930's, the island's 1.75 square miles was comfortably supporting without any scientific agricultural innovations, far more inhabitants than in the first half of the nineteenth century.

It was in this earliest period of the colony's development that British and American visitors reported, with only one or two exceptions, that the Pitcairn community presented a glimpse into the Golden Age, an earthly society which had achieved an unearthly harmony and virtue in its daily life, a peaceable kingdom of togetherness. Yet the second- and third-generation Pitcairners displayed a definite anxiety to quit, to leave what seemed to others to be a tranquil and idyllic island home. If "rat race" had been a voguish phrase at the time of the Industrial Revolution, Britons, Europeans, and Americans would have regarded Pitcairn as a community blissfully out of the running. But the Pitcairners wanted to abandon it all. Not a single family stayed behind when the British transport barque *Lucy Anne* sailed for Tahiti on March 7, 1831. When the evacuation was repeated in April, 1856, with the *Morayshire* setting out on a thirty-six-day voyage to Norfolk Island, the decision to quit the island was similarly unanimous.

Why these migrations? A convincing answer has never been provided by the Pitcairners themselves. Even today they are not at ease attempting an explanation. Although the British government went along with each decision to abandon the island, subsequent Royal Navy studies discredited the Pitcairners' fears that they might soon be running desperately short of food, water, and space. I find each of these migrations a deeply fascinating episode in the island's past; my belief is that the true reason for them was not stated, or even apparent, at the periods in question, either to the islanders or to the British government.

Did they occur because the islanders looked upon Pitcairn as an accursed rock in the ocean, a place founded in killing and misery by men who already had committed at sea an act of ruthless criminality? In the secret regions of their consciousness, did the good people descended from these founders nurture a belief that the community would never find real contentment on the soil of a constricting island which had been well wet with blood, the blood of ancestors wantonly put to death and in terrible fashion?

The answer to each of these questions, I feel, is Yes. It is conjecture on my part — a conjecture I trust the contemporary Pitcairners will accept with understanding — since the early islanders never put any such feelings into words, either for themselves or for outsiders. But shame, disesteem, guilt are among man's most effective silencers. In the hymns the community wrote, though, there are allusions to these communal feelings of unease about their island home: the mention of Pitcairn as "th' unhallowed ground," the emphasis on "the depths from whence we sprang," the "sin and shame . . . guilt and crime from which we come," the "darkness" and "despair" of the colony's origins.

Perhaps it is not surprising that these simple, God-fearing people welcomed the chance to make a fresh start somewhere else and felt in their innocence that they could make a go of it together. It was not to be that way.

Neither of the hegiras was undertaken because the islanders had been dazzled by the glimpses they had had through their contacts with visiting ships of life in the world beyond. They were *not* seeking the burgeoning cities of America or the bustle of imperial London. In both of the evacuations, their terms were that the colony should be permitted to continue to live in much the same isolation as existed on Pitcairn. For their first new home, Queen Pomare had offered these stepsons and stepdaughters of Tahiti a rich tract of land where the colony could settle and retain its cohesive community life, well apart from the rapidly changing Tahitian society.

The move to Tahiti began auspiciously. During the sixteen-day voyage of the *Lucy Anne*, a baby girl was born to the son and daughter-in-law of mutineer Matthew Quintal. She was named — what else? — Lucy Anne. This birth, which brought the colony numbers up to eighty-eight, was perhaps the only joyous event in the whole Tahitian hegira.

Reared in isolation, the Pitcairners had no natural immunity to the new diseases the world had brought to what was now the bustling hub of Polynesia. Some of the men — the old as well as the spirited young bloods — succumbed in other ways. The records tell of a descent into debauchery, without, alas, providing much detail. Tahiti, of course, had changed considerably since the mutineers picked their concubines from among the island beauties and sailed off into limbo. The missionaries had come with the gospel and Mother Hubbards in place of the guns and gonorrhea the first white men had brought to the Tahitians. While there were far fewer Tahitians around, there were far more white faces. The first real settlers had arrived in 1797 aboard the London Missionary Society's vessel, the *Duff*. She put ashore in Matavai Bay a remarkable band of thirty men and women who diligently set about converting the heathens. The destruction of the open-air temples with their triangular stone altars was begun. The intruders from the *Duff* built English-style churches and homes and schools. They taught the Tahitians that their wall-less houses were totally immodest. Before too many years had passed, other missionary vessels from London had arrived with the looms to establish small factories and a printing press to spread the word of the Lord.

But while there was less promiscuity and less of a Rabelaisian approach to life than in Cook's or Bligh's time, Tahiti was still a far racier place to live than Pitcairn. It was also more than two hundred times as big. With a flock which had been confined through all its existence to barely a thousand acres of rock in a deserted sea, the Pitcairn elders understandably had their troubles in confining the colonists to the land Queen Pomare had set aside for them. Whether or not the libertine fire of their Tahitian ancestry was rekindled, the men certainly reacquired the taste their mutineer forebears had had for strong drink.

But Tahiti was to inflict far more on the transplanted islanders than simply drunkenness. The Pitcairners began falling to disease within days of their arrival. Within a month, Thursday October Christian was dead. Almost every week brought a new funeral. The toll eventually reached sixteen. Pitcairn's "survival" scheme was threatening to wipe out the colony.

A month and a day after reaching Tahiti, part of Christian's family, some Youngs and Quintals, and John Buffett and family decided they must return to Pitcairn. They acquired a small schooner and set sail from Matavai. They were soon blown hopelessly off course — the seamanship which permitted them to conquer the hazards of Bounty Bay was not of that much value in dealing with the open ocean — and the party had to take shelter on Lord Hood Island. The families remained there until a French vessel rescued the party and carried them on to Pitcairn. They stepped ashore on their native island on June 27, 1831, sixteen disastrous weeks after they had left it.

Those who had remained on Tahiti, meanwhile, were still burying dead, nursing the sick, and observing with horror how easily the more impressionable members of the community were sliding into turpitude. The decision was taken to go home. In August, the *Charles Dogget*, a brigantine out of Salem, Massachusetts, arrived in Tahiti, and the remaining Pitcairn leaders chartered it for the return journey. The skipper had set a price of $500. As pathetic part-payment, to induce the captain to remain in Tahitian waters until the full sum could be raised, the Pitcairners gave up the copper and bronze bolts from the *Bounty* which were among the items they had brought with them to Tahiti. They also sold the blankets they had carried with them in the *Lucy Anne*, blankets which weren't really necessary in Tahiti but which were necessary in fall and winter months on subtropical Pitcairn.

By September 2, 1831, the colony was reunited on Pitcairn, their numbers sadly reduced, their moral fortitude badly cracked by this first mass exposure to life beyond their rock fortress.

Two years later, a British naval skipper, Captain Fremantle, went ashore at Pitcairn from H.M.S. *Challenger* and found the community still suffering badly from the aftereffects of the Tahitian misadventure. "The islanders," he reported to London, "are not improved by their visit to Otaheite, but on the contrary much altered for the worse, having, since their return, indulged in intemperance to a great degree, distilling a spirit from the tee root, which grows in great quantities on the island." Those in London concerned about the islanders' spiritual well-being, learned that "their health suffered in the new climate, and the licentious habits of the place proved distasteful to a well-ordered Christian community. . . . Some had yielded to the temptations to intemperance."

The sober ones on the island told Captain Fremantle that it would never happen again. Yet it did — less than twenty-five years later.

Again worried, supposedly, about their ability to feed themselves and the prospect that a dry spell might be prolonged, the islanders petitioned the British government to find a new home for them. They were offered Norfolk Island, which Britain had abandoned as a penal colony in 1855. It had ready-made shelter in the solid, stone barracks the soldiers had used and the compounds built for the convicts. In addition, there were a couple of churches, a government house, and individual homes built for the officers. The Pitcairners, now numbering 187, accepted the offer, and a large British transport was sent to carry them to their new home.

The rock of Pitcairn was returned to the ghosts of an anonymous Polynesian civilization and to whatever new phantasma had been introduced as a result of its selection by Fletcher Christian as a place for nine men to hide.

Pitcairn's abandonment was short-lived. Some two years after the community had been settled on Norfolk Island, two homesick families, a total of sixteen adults and children, decided to return. They got home, in January, 1859, just in the nick of time. Paris had heard that Pitcairn had been abandoned as an informal colony by Britain. It was a period when France was anxious to extend her influence in the South Seas, and a military vessel was dispatched to raise the Tricolor in Bounty Bay. The French war-

ship arrived — days? weeks? the island records are not exact —
but very soon after Pitcairn had been resettled.

The first sixteen to return, and the thirty-one others who followed them back from Norfolk Island in 1863, found their homes
in ruins — man-made ruins rather than an act of nature reclaiming
for herself a lonely scrap of the planet. Sailors from some shipwrecked vessel had made their way up the cliffs, camped briefly in
the deserted homes, and decided evidently that death at sea was
preferable to life on Pitcairn. We do not know the name of their
vessel or their country of origin. Whoever these intruders were,
they had no scruples about ripping apart the little cottages of
Adamstown to build a craft to carry them away from Pitcairn
and on to some staging point toward home. Some of the dwellings
they wrecked had been built originally from planks, nails, and
bolts from the *Bounty*. So in this strangest of ways, scraps of
Bligh's ship were re-employed in carrying men across the Pacific.
Whether these anonymous visitors to Pitcairn ever reached their
destination, any destination, remains a mystery.

We do know that the Anglo-Tahitian colony, the forty-seven-
strong flock of the children of the children of mutiny, was successful in restarting the Pitcairn society in the 1860's. They began
breeding, less prolifically than they had in the early years; they
were delighted to find that the island once more was producing
abundant crops; they rebuilt their village, their church, and their
school. Before another generation had died, they were to adopt a
new religion, as we have seen earlier in this chapter. They entered the twentieth century as godly as they had embarked on the
nineteenth, and with the material resources for survival only
slightly superior to those they possessed in the earlier period. At
intervals, the world would forget them. The two big wars that
world would fight were to become especially isolated periods for
Pitcairn.

Periods of isolation. Periods of minor world acclaim, pulpit
acclaim at least. Times of bloodshed and saintliness, drunkenness
and reform, turbulence and peace, abandonment and resettlement,
immorality and puritan ways. An era of dictatorship thrown in for
good measure. Years that are meticulously chronicled and years
that remain enigmas. It is all in this island's improbable past. As

Part II carries on the story to the island's improbable present, I shall close the historical section with a reflection on the periods I consider the *most* enigmatic in the island's past, the migrations.

With high hopes, the Pitcairners had fled from their island on two occasions. But twice they had returned gratefully to their home rock. I think the fairest interpretation we can place on these departures and homecomings is that there existed between the early Pitcairners and their own little island a most curious love-hate relationship.

I believe that in the Pitcairn society of 1972, those same feelings are still manifested. A third migration? If it occurs, it almost certainly will be the final chapter in the Pitcairn saga.

PART TWO

IMPROBABLE PRESENT

CHAPTER NINE

PASSAGE TO PITCAIRN

I T WAS AT FIRST a fog-colored smudge on the horizon. It en-
larged gradually into the rich greens and chocolaty brown of
the Pitcairn rock. Smudge-into-rock, it was no less welcome a
sight to us on the storm-strewn deck of the Tahitian ketch *Maylis*
than must have been presented one hundred and eighty-two years
ago to another group, Fletcher Christian, his eight companions
in mutiny, and their Tahitian company assembled expectantly
along the weather rail of H.M.S. *Bounty*. They had spent eight
and a half months sailing their stolen square-rigger erratically
about the South Pacific in search of this redoubt. We had pitched,
humped, corkscrewed a path southeast to our destination through
a tropical storm that closed in as we set out from the little jetty
at Rikitéa within the atoll lagoon of Mangaréva in the French
Gambier Islands, the southernmost point of the Tuamotus. The
name Pitcairn will lodge forever in our memories as a synonym
for haven. Had the island not been inhabited by the most hospitable people on this planet, that might still have been the case.

Pitcairn normally can be seen from a distance of from forty
to forty-five miles at sea. Because of the storm haze, we picked it
up at about twenty miles, and for some five hours, from ten in the
morning until three in the afternoon, were beating a track slowly
toward it across pounding seas. The silhouette of the island was
familiar to me from the engravings in old books about Pitcairn in
my library and from the sepia and color photographs taken by

more recent visitors. But they had not prepared me for the totally un-Polynesian appearance of the island. It is simply a crumpled rock that looms from the sea. That it has a good deal of vegetation is obvious at a distance, but the coconut palms are not visible until close in to shore. It has an aspect of compact might and durability but none of the drama, the theatrical beauty, of the larger volcanic islands of the Pacific. There is no fringe of white sand here, no coralline barrier out from the shore enclosing a lagoon of placid, aquamarine water several shades lighter than the ocean itself. There is simply the Pitcairn rock and the sea, and where they meet, a furious encounter of spray and foam. It is the sort of landfall one expects to find sailing in the Outer Hebrides, the Orkneys, or the Faeroes, not here just below Capricorn.

Our first view was of the northwestern and northern coasts of the island. From this aspect, it looks totally uninhabited, disturbingly deserted for a place that is journey's end. There was no sign of a man-made shelter, no track, no plantation. By finding some reference points on a map laid out on the *Maylis* deck, we could make out a few of the physical features named by the mutineers. Straight ahead were Young's Rocks, named after Midshipman Young of the *Bounty*. To the starboard was Christian's Point; to port, McCoy's Drop, the cliff where home-brewed spirits did in one of the rebels. There was the escarpment the mutineers named simply Headache, the rock they called Flattie, the "walley" they named after the wretched breadfruit, the eerie cave high on a rock face they called after their leader who spent much of his time there, brooding and waiting, "half in hope, half in fear," for the sighting of a sail.

It was not until we were almost abeam of Bounty Bay that we could pick out the first houses of Adamstown, tucked away discreetly in the vegetation on some relatively flat ground above the cliffs. In physical appearance, the settlement seemed a shy little community. The mutineers had built their houses in depressions in the land and behind great, dense banyan groves or high trees, so that no sign of human construction was visible from the sea approaches. The present-day Pitcairners have no reason to hide from anyone, but the appearance of their village still has a reticence about it, a vague feeling of withdrawal. Perhaps it is simply because they have continued to build homes on roughly the same sites selected by the mutineers.

A couple of miles from the shore, we could make out the landing slip and the cluster of boathouses behind it where the islanders lodge their dories and smaller craft from the elements. Through binoculars, we strained for a sign of activity at the slip and in the boathouses.

"It's Saturday," I said to Gildas Le Guen, the young Breton skipper of the *Maylis*. "Pitcairn Sabbath. Perhaps they intend to leave us out here until the morning." Gildas, who had called briefly at Pitcairn a year previously aboard a French yacht sailing from Panama to Tahiti and had been deeply impressed by the kindness of the islanders, suggested we wait for a while before moving on in search of sheltered water along the southern coast. "Pitcairners know as well as anyone what it's like to be out in seas like this," he said.

In my last radio-telephone talk with the island from New York, over the facilities of the Seventh-Day Adventist radio station in Glendale, California, I had promised Tom Christian, the island radio officer, that we would arrive on any day but a Saturday. "We would come out in an emergency," Tom told me, "but none of the men likes to launch the boats on Sabbath day." But for the storm and a delay in Mangaréva, we would have arrived on the Friday.

Gildas' hunch was right. Soon, through the binoculars, we saw men hurrying down the talus to the landing slip. Others were man-handling a white longboat out of its shed. We learned later that we had interrupted the Pitcairners at their Sabbath service. When the old village bell was sounded five times to announce that a sail had been sighted, the men had had to go home and change out of their clean shirts and Saturday-best trousers into dungarees, working shirts, and oilskins.

Suddenly, the longboat was alongside our ketch, above us one moment on the breast of a swell, below us the next when the sea ran from under them. I was anxious to get moving; nevertheless, I remember feeling disappointed that the islanders had not come out to get us in a longboat under oar power, the traditional Pitcairn fourteen-oared whaler. This boat's design was the same, island-built along the lines of a whaler Queen Victoria had presented to them, but it moved under one of the diesel units they had acquired a few years ago when the island's manpower resources began to dwindle alarmingly. This boat was named *Rosalind* after the late island poet Rosalind Amelia Young, the only Pitcairner to establish any sort of reputation in the arts. It was crowded with men and boys, twenty-five perhaps, almost the entire roll call of able-bodied Pitcairn males.

The tallest man in the boat was a dominating figure in neat khaki shirt and khaki pants that emphasized his height by having the cuff line at midcalf. He was managing effortlessly to stand upright on one of the thwarts despite the violent movement of the boat. I recognized him from photographs as Pervis Young, the Island Magistrate.

"Welcome to Peet-carn Island," he called across the water. "I'm Perwis. You must be Mister Ball and family from New York, with the film chaps. We were expecting your sail yesterday."

I apologized for arriving on their Sabbath. "O-ah, did you think we'd let you sit out here in this?" Pervis answered. "Church don't forbid it — coming out on the Sabbath to help people," shouted another voice. They all seemed to be relishing this bit of excitement on the Sabbath.

Pervis was in booming conversation with Gildas: "We can't do anything about moving the folks off in this. Follow us round to the lee o' the land and you can drop your hook there. We can get the folks and the children and their things off dry there."

Gildas was prepared to follow the longboat but had no intention of risking an anchor. He had brought up from the hold the cheapest anchor the ketch was carrying, an expendable piece of equipment he intended to use, however, only in extreme emergency. He knew that the first time the *Maylis* had called at Pitcairn, a charter ten years earlier with a party from the Smithsonian Institution, the crew had lost all three of its anchors in quick succession when it tried to tether the boat in the tricky swell off the island.*

---

* That visit is still recalled on the island with uproarious anecdotes. The ketch, with a thirsty captain at the wheel and an all-Tahitian crew, set out from Mangaréva and managed to miss the island by three hundred miles, a navigational error equal to the total length of the voyage! A course back to Mangaréva was being steered when accidentally the yacht raised Pitcairn. The crew

With the Pitcairn boat plunging through the swell ahead of us, we moved out of Bounty Bay and down toward the southeastern tip of the island in search of lesser seas. We sailed past the spot named Where Freddie Fall, past a cliff the mutineers' descendants called Down the God because it was there they found carved idols of a lost Polynesian society, and down toward St. Paul's Point and Ugly Name Side, the last so called because the Tahitians who sailed with the mutineers had first named it Hilatotara and the Englishmen had found the word distastefully unpronounceable. Finally, we were in comparatively manageable water.

"Drop ah hook — it will find bottom somewhere here," the men in the longboat shouted. Gildas shook his red-bearded head in furious opposition.

The Pitcairners threw us their lines, and the two vessels were warped closer together, riding uneasily in tandem. Pervis sprang across to the ketch to carry out one of his duties as Island Magistrate — ensuring that no one aboard was down with the smallpox or some other source of serious contagion. "We are all just over the flu," he informed us. "It came in with a cargo boat from New Zealand, and suddenly three quarters of the people were in bed with a high fever. It hits us real bad."

Half the men from the longboat were soon aboard the ketch, giving us and the Frenchmen powerful handshakes and gentle smiles of welcome. Husky brown arms began moving our score of crates and bags over the rail of the *Maylis* and into the well of the longboat, the men handling the cargo as easily as if they were passing boxes of cornflakes to one another. It was odd to think that these men with huge, hairy chests and stevedores' muscles had, because of their isolation, far less resistance to worldly viruses than a skinny kid from a ghetto.

Pervis himself lifted us into the longboat. The boat was broad enough to allow our whole family to huddle together on one of the thwarts. Ominously for the ride ahead, the islanders were spreading tarpaulins with great care over our boxes and bags. Solicitous hands were draping across our shoulders an oily black tarp. The

---

at first thought they were back where they started. The Pitcairners discovered that the skipper had with him only the navigational tables for latitude. They lent him the longitudinal book and prayerfully sent him on his way.

children all but disappeared within its folds. "We'll do our best to get you in without taking a green one," said one of the Pitcairners. "Let's turn 'er and go in," shouted Pervis.

The *Maylis* hands had been hoping that the ketch might be able to stand off the island, permitting the six of them to go ashore in relays. In these seas, it was obviously not feasible. Gildas decided that he had to head back, immediately, for Mangaréva. He shouted assurances to us that he would be back the following month to pick us up, and, auxiliary thumping, swung the ketch around into the northwester headwind. In our crowded open boat, we were bound for that magical name on the log of seafarers' destinations — Bounty Bay!

We shipped some seas moving toward the land, but we were concerned less with the discomfort than with using this first opportunity to study the island men. Some three or four had obvious Polynesian origins. With a couple of unusually fair-complexioned exceptions, there was a trace of this in every face, particularly in the broadening of the noses. But if one were looking for an even genetic balance of Anglo-Saxon and Polynesian, the evidence of a white sailorman from the Thames siring heirs by a brown concubine from the South Seas, there was disappointment. On the whole, the men looked uncannily like the more celebrated half of their ancestry, eighteenth-century English seamen transported to the South Pacific. They had ruddy faces from the ocean and the sun, and immense, knobby paws of hands roughened from a lifetime of hard work with the rope of the sea and the tools of the land. All were barefoot, with the heavy callousing and splayed toes of feet that have seldom worn shoes. (Later, I was to envy the men's natural shodding as I struggled in desert boots up the cliff track to the settlement. Our children were to abandon shoes for the duration, even falling into the island pattern and attending classes in the little schoolhouse barefoot.)

The men's dress was more ordinary than a romanticist might have wished — an assortment of tattered and stained jeans, torn old shirts, some with the collars and sleeves ripped off for comfort, tweed jackets from a lost day of men's fashion, and a few sea jackets with "Property of the Australian Government" stamped across the backs. Some of the boys sported white T-shirts emblazoned with the words *"Commandant Riviere,"* souvenirs from a French warship that had called at Pitcairn a few months earlier during France's latest nuclear tests on nearby Mururoa. In his matching khaki, a uniform of sorts befitting his official position on the island, Pervis was the sartorial prizewinner.

To us, the Pitcairners had spoken a slurred English, slightly singsong in the West Indian manner, with occasionally a trace of the nasalization that so bothers the British when they talk with Australians or New Zealanders. Among themselves in the boat, they used Pitcairnese, the dialect that is part invented, part pidgin English, and part a melange of the English of George III's time and the Tahitian of King Pomare's. "Illy-illy," they said of the swell. Although the adjective had a strange ring to it and a needless duplication, it was not hard to guess it came from the English word "hilly," adapted by and for native tongues. "Foh yu whant dah?" they said when someone asked for something in the boat. I realized fully for the first time that the Pitcairners are actually a bilingual people.

The conversation among the men died down as we neared Bounty Bay again. We could now study it. It is simply a rock-bound dent in the coastline; nowhere else would it rate as a "bay." We were running close in to shore now, perilously near, I thought, to the craggy, coal-black rocks that spilled out from the base of the escarpments, repelling the rollers in a frenzy of white water. The longboat steered a fine course between the coastal rocks and a little sentinel island, Adam's Rock, on the summit of which a single coconut palm had found improbable rooting.

Facing the rock was a weird natural formation in the cliff face, a vast slab of gray-black stone suspended above the waves and etched with what looked like the hieroglyphics of a race of giants. My senses were reacting, of course, to the excitement of the run in; but there was a secondary feeling that none of the many books and articles about Pitcairn had prepared me for. There is a spectral mood about the place, a quality of eeriness and brooding in the landscape that obviously is intensified at night but is there, too, in midafternoon. The Pitcairners certainly sense the haunting aspect of their island. My stay there was to convince me that it has played over the years a crucial role in forming the Pitcairn character, shaping their attitudes toward religion, life, and death, and coloring the innermost, unspoken feelings about their home turf.

Warren Christian brought my thoughts back to the moment at hand. "Landing's coming in sight," he bellowed to prepare us for the climax of the ride. We were passing two small but treacherous-looking rocks jutting up from the expanse of surging foam that covered the bay almost from one arm to the other. They are key reference points for navigating the home run into the "harbor." The Pitcairners endearingly have given the rocks the names Mummy and Daddy.

Finally we were poised for the final swoop into Bounty Bay, this hazardous landing that outsiders have been describing since 1808 when the American sealing skipper discovered the mutineers' hideout.

The diesel was thrown to idle. We were pausing for the right wave. There was a certain added tension in the longboat. It was quite apparent on the part of the newcomers, only just perceptible among the men and boys who had come out to fetch them. Duncan, our smallest child, who was squeezed in between Lele and me, made a soft protest: "Mummy, why are you holding me so tight?"

"Lift ah tillah!" said someone. The heavy rudder, which could be wrenched off if the longboat were to be carried by the breakers over one of the rocks hiding just below the surface, was hoisted.

"Pass ah steering oar!" said the helmsman, and a stout, broadbladed oar was handed back over our heads.

Again we paused. The sea below, a few frigate birds above, provided the only sounds.

One half of the men had their eyes trained seaward, gauging the force of each successive wave that threw the vessel up for a moment and then let us drop into a depression. Occasionally, their eyes like electronic sensors, they would squint to left or right, instantly recording where we rested in relation to the Mummy and Daddy rocks on the one side and the western flank of the bay on the other. The other men in the boat, those aft of the enginehousing, had set themselves the assignment of surveying the route ahead to the landing slip, studying the final shore-surge of the swells passing beneath us.

Perhaps to take my mind off the minutes that lay ahead, I passed the time by studying the inner hull construction of the *Rosalind*. It was not very reassuring. There were, in fact, some touches of gimcrack shipwrighting. *Rosalind*'s outer skin had looked sound enough. For her innards, the hull lining, the men had slapped in place bits and pieces of dunnage and wood from packing crates.*

We were under way again. "Yes, now! Now!" yelled Pervis to his son at the diesel. "Straight ahead!"

"Pull ahead!" came the voice of an old-timer who evidently was still back in the very recent past when the Pitcairn boats had only oars against the ocean.

We shot in like an overpowered skiff, keeping nimbly ahead of the big swell the men had chosen, taking full advantage of the additional clearance the roller would give us as we passed over the rocks in the bay. We skittered through the narrowest of channels, rocks visible below the foam just off each beam. The passageway seemed to be no broader than ten yards.

And then came the moment of madness!

Not only were we using a whaler with thirty-odd people aboard as a surfboard in powerful seas and over dangerous rocks. We were about to attempt a sharp turn to port!

Somehow they did it, they accomplished the feat without swamping us all and tearing *Rosalind* to pieces. There had not been a single spoken command. The boat had a formal skipper, but each Pitcairner in it could have taken over the role, even the youths. They were simply putting a vessel through a dangerous maneuver they had learned in boyhood and had practiced to perfection ever since. It was a lot harder on the boat than the men. A longboat normally has to be scrapped when it is eight or nine years old.

That turn was the last bit of excitement until the longboat shud-

* On June 23, 1972, the longboat failed the islanders. Caught by a large wave in violent seas in Bounty Bay, the crew were tossed out and the whaler was smashed to pieces on the rocks. Half of the able-bodied men on the island sustained injuries. Among the more critically injured was Tom Christian, whose leg was broken.

dered to a halt against the foot of the slip. The strong arms that had lifted us into the longboat now hoisted us out and onto dry land.

We stood at last on the little lip of rock and shingle that had been Fletcher Christian's first landfall on Pitcairn.

Physically, Bounty Bay has changed little since the pirated *Bounty* was rammed through the narrow channel, grounded, stripped, and burned. Nature has made one dramatic subtraction, a vast landslide of earth and rocks that has shorn the western arm of the bay of vegetation and given it a desolate appearance. Man the Builder, a lethargic and handicapped builder here, has made additions and subtractions as best he could.

A few of the anthracite-black rocks have been winched or blasted out of the way to make the channel slightly safer. Their removal has meant that the final sweep to the landing ramp can be made with just a shade less navigational precision and just a shade less apprehensiveness on the part of new arrivals. The long boathouses at the Landing, which the earliest Pitcairners built of coconut trunks and which still had pandanus thatch roofs as late as the mid-1960's, are now somewhat more permanent, stormproof installations with corrugated iron roofs. In front of them, on the small jetty of rock and cement, stands a primitive derrick to ease the job of unloading cargo from the longboats. Overhead, its hawser curving up in a weary sag over a lush scene of banana palms, frangipani bushes, and a score of different trees and shrubs sprouting from the red earth, is the old "flying fox," which New Zealand engineers installed during World War II during the building of a radio station on the island, and which the islanders use to haul cargo up to The Edge, three hundred feet above the water.

The strand of gray shingle and grayish sand, which probably gave the mutineers the first clue that here was a relatively safe landing spot, has disappeared in recent years. With makeshift dredging, performed by swinging the derrick out over the water and scooping up drums of seabed material, the sand and shingle have been sucked away by the sea and now rest at the bottom of the bay. The loss of that scrap of "beach" is the price the islanders have paid for the modest improvements that have been made to their gateway to the sea and the world. In the process, Pitcairn's young lost a bit of the rationed pleasure of growing up on the island.

We had met the male descendants of the mutineers. We left them now hauling the whaler up out of the water and into its shed. We were about to meet the women and the few children growing up on the island.

Before that meeting, we faced the Hill of Difficulty, the adequately expressive name the pioneer Pitcairners gave to the grueling slog up the rough track sliced out of the cliff face. It leads one, panting and sweating, up to the first glimpse of level ground, The Edge, three hundred feet above the landing point. It is the assembly point for the women, the children, and those in their dotage whenever someone new arrives — a schoolteacher, a pastor, a writer; once, with jokes and pomp, Prince Philip, Duke of Edinburgh — or when someone from their midst is departing for the world. The wait for the longboat drama to be decided in the surf far below is usually a long one. Benches have been placed under a large shade tree at The Edge so they will have some place to rest.

The women were in clean print dresses, but barefoot like their menfolk and with the same thick callousing. There was something about the female Pitcairners that immediately nudged a tired mind, and it was only after a few minutes of studying them that it registered fully. While the men generally could pass for rural or seafaring English types, most of the women were strongly Polynesian in appearance. By what genetic freak, what gametic chance, had the Tahitian blood prevailed only in the female line? Before the Pitcairn numbers dwindle any further, before the island blood is mingled through marriage with more polyglot strains in New Zealand, Australia, Britain, or the United States, there is surely a challenge here for a geneticist to attempt an answer.

The old ones, Melville and Mima and Theo and one or two others, took our hands with feeble, shaking fingers. We might be the last new arrivals from the "Outside" they would meet. The youngsters shyly introduced themselves to our children and were

soon off leading them into Robinson Crusoe adventures in the banana palms, the breadfruit trees — yes, breadfruit, of course! — and the lush undergrowth. The women had brought baskets of pineapples, bananas, passion fruit, and some of the first crop of watermelons. As we ate, I caught a glimpse of the *Maylis* bucking her way through the haze toward a lonely gray horizon. For the first time in a life of travel that has taken me deep into Siberia, to both Poles, and across every continent and ocean, I felt totally isolated from the world.

The view from Ship Landing Point of Bounty Bay — a cross marks the spot where the *Bounty* was rammed against the rocks and burned — The Edge, and the tin roofs of Adamstown, nestled on the relatively flat land above the cliffs.

CHAPTER TEN

TWENTY-FOUR HOURS

THAT THEY LIVE, most of them, in shanties was the initial shock. Surely a tightly united community that is sober, hard-working, and honest could have done better than this with the materials at hand. They labor, hard and diligently for the most part, on the beauty and order of their souls; they are content to pass their mortal days in unlovely, ramshackle homes and in an environment that contains great blots of unnecessary squalor. I found myself comparing them with another simple society, the Pennsylvania Amish, a people who live in withdrawal from the world, spurning its glut of luxuries, yet a community which manages to keep its homes and farms tidy and pleasing enough that tourists drive distances to inspect them.

Whether from apathy innate, from the church's teaching that earthly days are but time passed in a wretched waiting room, or from a sad lack of faith in their island's future, the Pitcairners have done little to bring beauty to their homes and into their lives. Or is the outsider at fault in envisioning this community always within the context of remembered pages from history books, the accounts that painted a veritable picture of the Golden Age that came to Pitcairn after the first terrible years were over?

Certainly the sea captains who visited the island in its earliest years and wrote rapturously of Adamstown's neat little cottages grouped around a village green would not find much charm or grace in the present-day architecture and community style. There are exceptions, of course. Anderson's garden is a feast of flowers, an oasis of botanical uplift. Agnes' and Vi's homes have a spotlessness that homebodies anywhere would approve. But other island houses are on a par with the tumble-downs of Appalachia, the shacks of Mississippi.

The decay, the sloppiness, are by no means a recent development. Dr. Harry L. Shapiro, the distinguished anthropologist of the American Museum of Natural History, whose study* of the islanders will be referred to in a later chapter, came away from a ten-day visit in 1934 with this impression: "There is perhaps too much of a suggestion of shanty white about these islanders — the not quite neatly built houses, the cast-off clothing, the necessarily makeshift furniture, the air of utilizing the junk shop — which makes them too close to our seamy side to be truly romantic. . . . The fault lies with civilization. We have taken away their fresh, crackling *tapa* and offer only discarded clothing in its stead, we have shown them the uses of tin and destroyed the beauty of thatch, we have sent them our broken-down furniture and displaced their simple benches."

The higgledy-piggledyness of the place makes the deepest impression as I take my first walk over the muddy track that runs on an undulating course of about half a mile from The Edge, through the village, and peters out after an uphill climb to the white schoolhouse. Labyrinthine dirt paths lead off the arterial track to rickety, tottering dwellings half submerged in the dense foliage of trees and vines. A few of the houses are so close to the road that a passerby has a clear view into bedrooms, living rooms, and smoke-blackened kitchens. Privacy is one of the many things Adamstown lacks. It is of little concern to its inhabitants.

The houses are uniformly unpainted. The wood that has been used for the sides — dunnage from the sea, island timber cut roughly into clapboards with a pit saw, and plywood from tea chests — has acquired in places thick coatings of gray-green moss that only partly conceal the rot that is eating away the walls. Termites are close to claiming total victory over some of the

---

* *The Pitcairn Islanders,* formerly *The Heritage of the Bounty,* New York: Simon and Schuster, 1936.

structures they have attacked. Walls sag perilously in places where casual foundations — logs laid over small boulders resting on the ground — are beginning to decay. In some cases it is difficult to distinguish inhabited dwellings from derelict ones. The roofs are of corrugated iron, patched and rusting. Windows are rough examples of island carpentry. Without cords or weights, they have an assortment of homemade devices — sticks, wedges, bottles — for keeping the lower panes raised. The housewives have gone to scant trouble with the curtainings, possibly because they are never drawn, possibly because of the difficulties in acquiring the fabric. Most of the rooms on show have the rich disorder of old attics.

Where the houses have porches, the clutter extends outdoors: homemade beds with grass-stuffed mattresses for afternoon naps, dusty old rocking chairs, a litter of children's playthings, many of them hand-carved, stacks of empty jars, bottles, and drums, odd scraps of timber kept for the day when they might be needed for patching, lengths of rope, bits of derelict machinery, and so on. Every house has a strip of iron set in low wooden uprights by the front door for scraping the gooey Pitcairn mud off the soles and sides of bare feet.

In contrast, the public buildings — courthouse, post office, church, and a small dispensary, grouped around three sides of the Square cut out of sloping ground "upside" the main path and at about the midway point in its meander through the village — are neatly built and freshly painted white. Tithe money, and the subsidy funds which Britain provides out of the annual profit from the sale of Pitcairn postage stamps to collectors, are invested in the lumber and paint the homes need so desperately.

Here in the Square are the only two pieces of *Bounty*ana on public display on the island. Mounted on a concrete plinth beside the courthouse is the *Bounty*'s twelve-foot stern anchor, one of at least five anchors the ship was carrying. It was recovered in 1957 in fifty feet of water just outside Bounty Bay by Aqualung divers from Irving Johnson's magnificent old brigantine *Yankee*, a veteran of Pacific cruising and, until her sad loss seven years later, a fairly regular caller at Pitcairn. It was this anchor which Fletcher Christian dropped at the entrance to the bay and then paid out hemp cable to control the *Bounty*'s fatal, grinding run on to the rocky shore of the inlet. The anchor has the straight-V flukes which distinguish Royal Navy anchors in use until 1800– 1810; rounded flukes came into use after that period. Pitcairn children today use Bligh's anchor like a playground fixture, and through lack of parental and grandparental interest in keeping the past alive, have no real sense of the part it played in their heritage.

The other piece of *Bounty*ana is in the church across the Square from the courthouse. In a glass-topped wooden case with a lock that can be turned only by using two keys entrusted separately to two island officials, rests the *"Bounty* Bible." Actually it was not the ship's Bible, but one Christian's mother gave to him when he first went to sea; he found it some time after the landing on Pitcairn while he was rummaging through his sea chest.

The islanders today revere the frayed and worn Bible where their ancestors in 1839 were quite willing to part with it in exchange for a mass-produced Bible of larger print. It was given to Levi Hayden, mate of a whaling ship from New Bedford, Massachusetts, who talked to the islanders of how beautifully it could be rebound in America. It eventually came into the hands of the Historical Society of Connecticut. When the Pitcairners, a century later, learned where it was, they asked for it back. It arrived back on the island in 1950 after being inspected in London by the King and Queen, rebound there by a rare-book specialist, and given its present case by native cabinetmakers in Fiji. The Bible is used occasionally in special religious services, but its small print and faded type tax even the keenest eyes. It is the one *Bounty* relic the Pitcairners are determined will not leave the island again so long as a settlement survives there. (They have given away or sold most of the other memorabilia.) Today, with touching contemporary impartiality, this precious Bible of Fletcher Christian's shares company in the display case with a record of the marriage of his celebrated adversary. Dropped casually alongside the Good Book Mrs. Christian gave young Midshipman Fletcher, as if it were the most natural thing in the world that these two items should rest together for eternity, lies a facsimile of the February 10, 1781, page of the Register of the Onchan Parish Church, Isle of Man, stating

The Pitcairn Cooperative, the only store and open only two hours a week.
(Courtesy of Tom Christian)

that "Mr. William Bligh and Miss Elizabeth Betham of the Town of Douglas were married in this Church by licence."

There are two other naval touches in the Square — the ship's bell from H.M.S. *Dainty*, which Prince Philip presented to the islanders during the Royal Yacht *Britannia*'s call there in February, 1971, and which the island men have provided with an undainty mounting; and a framed picture, with ship's pennant, of a square-rigger under sail, the *Esmeralda*, used by the Chilean Navy for training. The picture was presented to the islanders many years ago during a visit by the ship; the Island Council, feeling that the Square could use some more reminders of their heritage of sail, put it up on the courthouse wall.

Across the Square and a short distance up the main track is the only visible evidence that any commerce is transacted in this community. Pitcairn has no shops, but a couple of years ago the islanders, after much delay and debate, formed the Pitcairn Cooperative. They housed it in an unimposing little structure, with windows on either side of the entrance to make it look like a real shop and a Wild West-style porch in front where the men and women shoppers could gather to discuss the prices and availability of the limited selection on the shelves inside. There are about as many male as female customers since, having grown up without shops, there is no traditional assignment to feminine hands of the marketing chores. The shop is open for an hour on Monday afternoons and for another hour on Thursday afternoons, which makes organizing the week's shopping expeditions a relatively straightforward business.

When I passed the Coop on that first day, there was a sign in each window. One announced: "Disinfectant, 40¢ a pint. Please bring an empty bottle." The other stated: "22 pounds of butter left." It remained thus for three weeks.

In a rack on one wall are the account books of the Coop customers with their given names or nicknames printed along the spines. "We only use first names on Pitcairn," was one of the first pieces of advice I had been given that day. "Mavis," "Noggie," "Maynard," "Christy," "Irma," "Thelma," "Lila," "Pervis," "Nola" are all that are required for identification purposes in this one-big-family community. Under the heading "Visitors," the first-name rule is abandoned. The Pastor's book is inscribed "Missionary," a quaint anachronism in a community that has been thoroughly Christianized, in more ways than one, since 1800 and totally Adventist since 1890. The schoolteacher's account ledger is marked "Education Officer." The opposite wall is given over to a large poster calendar from the Pretoria government which urges the Pitcairners, in English and Afrikaans, to spend their vacations in the Republic of South Africa.

The shelves along the wall facing the entrance hold a skimpy array of goods. The community cupboard is almost bare; there has not been a supply ship for many weeks. But there is a fair assortment of canned meat — ox tongue, savory casserole, bully beef, sausages with vegetables. Adventist friends had told me that the Pitcairners came close to the Church's ideal of vegetarianism. I was to learn that, in fact, most are ravenous meat-eaters. Many of the other canned goods on the shelves seem unnecessary imports from distant farms to an island with the richest possible volcanic soil and a gentle subtropical climate. The stocks that day included some cans of mixed vegetables, peas, beans, sliced peaches, even tomatoes, which I had already seen ripening in profuse supply in the gardens. The Coop's best sellers, always bought out immediately after a supply ship is unloaded and regarded as "luxuries," are bags of potato chips, "lollies," condensed milk, and canned spaghetti.

The Coop, I learn from Vi McCoy, who helps keep the accounts straight, takes in about $800 in an average month.* Having been through periods of shortages, most recently a stretch without supply ships in 1970 which the islanders refer to as the "Five-Month Starve," there is an understandable hoarding streak in their mentality. The takings in a single hour's trading on the day the crates from a supply ship are unpacked can run as high $500. The Coop accepts most of the currency in use in the Pacific — the American, Canadian, Australian, or New Zealand dollars, the pounds and Polynesian francs the islanders gather by trading aboard ships. The yen, kroners, marks, and pesos they also pick up from time to time are donated to the Church, and the Pastor is left to convert them. To build up a purchasing kitty, the Coop adds 17 percent to the cost of the goods in New Zealand. The freight costs are donated by the shipping companies as their contribution to Pitcairn's survival. In the first two months of operation, the Coop cleared a profit of $340, and the islanders suddenly became aware that after all those years without a store, one of their number could have made a livelihood by becoming a shopkeeper.

It hardly needs a shopkeeper's inventory to realize that there is a good deal more food growing or littering the ground around the Coop than there is on its shelves. Children are amusing themselves

* The dollar amounts given in this and later chapters are in New Zealand dollars, the most common currency on the island. A New Zealand dollar is worth slightly more than a United States dollar. At the time of our visit one U.S. dollar was exchanged for 89 cents N.Z.

by pelting each other with just-ripened mangoes. Custard apples hang heavy on the trees. Perfect grapefruit are found squashed along the dirt road. Oranges, limes, and lemons may be picked at will from roadside trees. Where the track passes through a little gully, there are banana palms with leaves as big as a man and untouched bunches of fruit.

Some of the wasted fruit in the road has been flattened by treaded wheels. On an island where, until the mid-1960's, virtually the only application in transport of the principle of the wheel was to be found in the traditional low-slung wheelbarrows made from cabbage-tree wood, there are now thirty Japanese-made motorcycles. These noisy little machines, in vivid red, orange, or yellow lacquer that contrasts sharply with the absence of color in all other man-made things, represent a late injection of twentieth-century ways. A single Honda arrived in 1966, and the bikes quickly became a fad. By raiding their savings, most of the families found they could afford a motorbike and a gallon or so of gasoline a week. *Bounty* heirs astride two-strokes, the powerful brown thighs of their women gripping the pillions! One should have been prepared for it, aware how far-reaching is the spread of the internal-combustion engine these days. It was a shock, nonetheless.

The Pitcairners still seem entranced with their powered wheels. Young Dave will take his out for a trip of less than fifty yards. Noggie, on his newish bike, throttles down to a halt beside me for a chat on Main Street, and I notice it has more than ten thousand miles on the clock. On an island where the longest round-trip journey is about four or five miles, this represents enormous and constant usage.

I arrive, by pillion, at the house of Warren and Millie Christian, where it has been decided we should board. The Island Council has set a rate: $10 per person per week. Warren, at fifty-seven the oldest on the island to invest in a motorcycle, has fetched the bags in the trailer he built to haul behind the Honda. Lele and the children have been whisked from The Edge by old Christy Warren and given an afternoon tea that turns into a banquet of several courses on a table crammed with jars of preserves and spreads, baskets of fruit and vegetables and plates of cookies and doorstep slices of Mima's homemade bread. Only the spicy pickled onions which are Christy's pride have gone uneaten.

Warren and Millie's house is much like those I have already glimpsed. It has a rough porch across the front with a length of rope tacked along the rail for a nautical touch. By the single step up to the porch is an old stone well with an uncertain arrangement of improvised and rusting downpipes leading into it for rain catchment from the roof. Right beside the cistern is a hand basin and a white Victorian pitcher so that the person arriving may scoop up some well water and wash off the mud and dust of Pitcairn at the very moment of entering the house. It is also possible to brush one's teeth at the threshold. A rack, fashioned from wood, holds a clump of old toothbrushes.

The sides of the house are a blend of weathered, moss-covered old timbers and rusting iron. Part of it was built by Warren's father, part by Warren after his marriage. The splendor of the few flowering trees in a careless garden — frangipani, hibiscus, a delicate little *tiare Tahiti* tree carried to Pitcairn from its native island and being raised in a tub — is in vivid counterpoint to the drab, paintless state of the house itself. Five bunches of bananas in various stages of ripeness hang on a low branch of a peach tree by the porch. Purple grapes on a vine behind the well are a third ingredient in this fruit-salad greeting for the arriving visitor.

Close by one side of the house is a roughly enclosed chicken run where the "chooks," as Millie calls them, are pecking away desultorily at bananas and the skins of mangoes, pineapples, and avocados tossed to them over the fence. Across the dirt track that leads up to the house, is the start of an immense grove of banyans, the very same banyans that were described in the accounts of Pitcairn published in the 1820's. Today they are well over sixty feet high, forming, with the aerial roots that have grown down in search of fresh soil to sustain the "walking" growth peculiar to banyans, a succession of vast arches, a natural cathedral that has both an eeriness and a delicate beauty. Warren and Millie's house is built alongside the site of John Adams' original house, and the appearance of the banyan grove tallies with the descriptions given by the first English and American visitors who interviewed the old

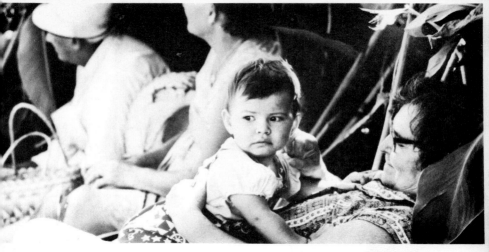

Millie Christian, with granddaughter Jacqueline, at a communal picnic.

Patriarch in his home. The aesthetics of the scene today, however, are almost totally sabotaged by a jumble of old drums, wood, and assorted junk at ground level.

The disorder of the out-of-doors finds its match on the porch. It would not be possible to give a full accounting of the things dropped, lying, stored, or placed there. The most prominent, and unexpected, are two large, ancient wall telephones. One, measuring three feet from top to bottom, with a big, dovetailed cabinetry belly for the works and the batteries, an ornate French handpiece, and a row of five large silvered terminals across the curlicued top, is simply gathering dust. It had been made by Ericsson of Sweden in 1912. Its companion, an English Ericsson, vintage 1917, slightly less baroque, is also gathering dust but is, at least, connected, with a pair of wires casually strung across the porch. They are part of a shipment of hand-me-down crank telephones the island bought many years ago and rigged up to give the community a multiparty telephone service that sometimes works and sometimes, particularly after a rainstorm, doesn't. (A merchant seaman, seeing these antique beauties in every house, offered £10 apiece recently for the ones not in service. He carried a few away and was able, I was told, to make a fivefold return on his investment from a London antique dealer.)

Millie promises she will instruct me the following day in the mysteries of the working Ericsson and give me the various rings, the shorts and longs, for people I might have to call. To an older generation, "shorts" are "iddies," "longs" are "umpties." I was to persevere with that instrument throughout our stay but succeeded in completing only two calls.

There are four bedrooms, including the small sleeping cubicle which Warren, only the previous day, had finished building for our daughter on one end of the porch. They open off a sitting room which is never used for that purpose but which has a motley collection of furniture — two of a total of six old seamen's chests I counted in the house; a table heaped high with papers, bric-a-brac, spectacle cases, a big chiming clock, sewing, and unfinished handicraft work; across from it a homemade couch piled with clean and dirty laundry; and at the far end of the room, two cabinets, one curtained and filled with old clothes and vintage copies of the *National Geographic* magazine, the other glass-fronted and containing nothing but twenty-one spare glass chimneys for the oil lamps. The only decorations in this room are a calendar from a publishing firm in Takoma Park, Washington, D.C., specializing in "religious, health and educational literature"; two identical reproductions of the old Adventist mission ship *Pitcairn*; a plaque "To Mother" which somebody had sent from the Empire State Building; a colored print of the Savior, dust-laden and drooping from the wall; and a small, dingy picture of the British Royal Family.

Beyond the sitting room and across a sagging wooden breezeway of sorts that runs from the outdoor bathhouse to a second stone well is the large dining room. The walls are left unlined so that the interior decor is the ancient wood of the uprights and the rusting metal of the corrugated iron siding. There are two homemade tables, each about nine feet in length and covered with old oilcloth. One, which is used for eating, is flanked by hard benches. The other table is the repository of a vast collection of jars, bottles, tins, baskets, and packages, some containing foodstuffs, most of them empty and abandoned there for some not easily perceived reason. There is a tall cupboard that Warren has built from scraps to house a rich assortment of crockery, much of it obtained from passing ships and some bearing the crests of forgotten liners. In one corner is an old wire-mesh-sided safe, its original green paint all but obscured by the marks of use. Its legs sit in four rusty cans that once contained English plum pudding and whose function now is to keep the ants at bay. In another corner is a battered old American refrigerator, a flue at the back carrying off the fumes from the kerosene unit. It, too, has been given a rough paint job in green, careless necklaces of surplus paint running down the door and sides, but like the safe, the color is almost lost beneath the workaday grime of hands that have opened it. Millie tells me the fridge fell into the ocean when it was being slung from a cargo ship off Bounty Bay. It was fished out, brought in by longboat, and has been working perfectly for the past twenty-two years.

On boxes and old chairs not required for sitting, there are enough fresh fruit and vegetables to stock the produce shelves of a small store. Left in the palm-frond shoulder baskets Warren has used to carry them down from his garden "up ah hill" are at least two dozen pineapples. There are bowls filled with glorious grapefruit, large, wrinkled-skin lemons, and oranges which our young boys inspect dubiously because there are no blue-printed messages on the skin in the interests of brand recall. There are also tubs of tomatoes, beans, and cucumbers. Each receptacle has its halo of fruit flies, dispersed every once in a while by a sweep of Millie's strong hands.

Under a grimy window is an old Singer treadle sewing machine on which those same hands work at dressmaking or stitching the delicate floral adornments she puts on pandanus baskets for trading aboard ships. It still functions despite the fact that its wooden parts are almost eaten away by termites. Beside another window is a spare wood-burning stove covered with copies of the New Zealand *Herald* dating back to 1959. On a small sideboard is a tray with a hundred pieces of mixed cutlery. Everywhere, in corners, in tea chests, on unused benches, are scraps and snippings of the brightly dyed or sun-bleached pandanus leaf strips which Millie uses to weave into intricate baskets with a tiny diamond design incorporating the words "Pitcairn Island." Three days' work on each, asking price $3; but the tourists often manage to beat her, and the other women, down to a dollar.

The floor of the dining room, as most of those in the rest of the house, are broad boards cut on the island pit saw and roughly dressed. Coin spots of sunlight, shining through old nail holes in the reused roofing metal, shift in fascinating patterns across the flooring boards. The room's only wall ornaments, hanging on nails on either side of a door, are what look like spare lavatory seats. They are used, I discovered later, as forms for weaving straw hats.

The dining room opens onto a large kitchen. Some effort has been made here with blue paint and lining plywood to make Millie's other working quarters attractive. A bucket from the stone well is the only source of water, however. A window over a sink is always left open so Millie can throw scraps of fruit or bread out into the yard for the "chooks." There is a large American wood-burning stove of the type one might still see in a farmhouse kitchen in the Middle West, and beside it a six-foot-high sack of roots and lengths of rose apple tree wood for the fires.

Some of the other items in the kitchen are minor museum pieces, Tahitian-inspired implements which have been in use on the island since the mutineers' women taught the Englishmen how to make them. There is a low wooden stool with a neck at one end that holds a piece of iron that has been beaten and filed to give it a comb of sharp teeth. Millie calls it her *ana* and sits astride the stool to grate coconut. Beside it is a *yolo*, a large slab of black stone that has had diagonal furrows cut into it to give it a rasplike surface. It is used for grating — or more accurately, mashing — green bananas, *kumara*, and *taro*.

Beyond Millie's kitchen, as in all the Pitcairn homes, is a second kitchen. Housed in a shed apart from the dwelling proper, it contains an open-hearth fire built on a sandbox and used to heat a large, blackened kettle or to cook things in heavy old saucepans. To the right of the fireplace is a Polynesian-inspired stone oven made from slabs of soft volcanic stone that can be shaped with an ax and chisel. The chamber, which measures almost a yard in each direction, is closed by propping a sheet of old iron across the front opening. The floor in this second kitchen is pounded-down dirt. Along one side of the shed is a good supply of firewood — rose apple logs and dried coconut husks. The outdoor cooking arrangement is called, for reasons which no contemporary Pitcairner seems able to recall, "the bolt." Through ingrained habit, the women, young, middle-aged, and old, go on using "the bolt" even though their cast-iron stoves imported from the outside world are a shade more convenient.

Beyond this second kitchen are a couple of tin sheds in sad states of disrepair. They house mountains and landslides of useless and useful items — broken musical instruments, cases of bottles, six galvanized washtubs in addition to the ones Millie has in daily use, a vast collection of empty, one-gallon cooking oil containers, discarded boxes and cartons, derelict stoves, old bedsteads, and so on. Millie and Warren are savers. All Pitcairners are; they acquire the habit in childhood.

A "chook"-infested track past these junksheds leads down to the two-holer privy erected over a twenty-foot-deep pit at the end of their land. Black spiders, five inches in diameter, inhabit its corners. "We call it ah 'dunkun,' " says our hostess. "Don't ask me why." Only toward the end of my stay did one of the older islanders come up with the explanation that the Pitcairnese word was probably based on the old-English word "dunikin" or "dunnekin." It presumably was the name given to the very first Pitcairn one- or two-holer, or something far less grand, by the men from the *Bounty*.

Millie has told us that we are invited to a birthday party at a neighbor's after the Sabbath sun has gone down, and we set to bathing away the salt and grime of the day as quickly as the facilities will allow. In Adamstown, the nightly bath is good for muscular tone as well as bodily hygiene. Water has to be heated during the afternoon with a wood fire beneath a forty-four-gallon drum known as the "copper" because it is lined with that metal. The water is then moved by bucket from the outdoor copper to the outdoor bathhouse and tipped into the ancient tub that came from England. To cool the water down to the right temperature requires several more journeys with bucketloads of water drawn from the well which happens to lie in the opposite direction. Since the bucket-hauling takes place over stretches of ground that are mud traps in wet weather and are carpeted with red dust during dry spells, one is in need of a bath at the end of the water-ferrying procedures even if that had not been so at the outset.

The birthday party is the first of about a dozen such feasts we shall be invited to on the island. For some, their guest list embraces every man, women, and child on Pitcairn. Other party-givers are only marginally more selective, inviting some fifty or sixty of their neighbors, those members of the branches closest to theirs in a genealogical thicket of intertwined family trees. The social life revolves around one thing: food. The dining room where the party is being held, indeed the house itself, is not unlike Warren and Millie's. The food is on two long, homemade tables covered with floral oilcloth. There are benches for those who elect to limit their access to the comestibles by remaining seated part of the time or are just too frail to enter the scrimmage.

By my count, there are forty-two different dishes on the table, perhaps half of the food brought along under cloth covers by the guests themselves. There is goat meat and chicken in the pots they were cooked in, and bully beef and tongue, cold and in the squat cans they were imported in from New Zealand. A big favorite is canned spaghetti. The islanders like to eat it cold from the can, and the hostess does not trouble to do anything more to it than rip off the top with an opener and set it out, label and all, on her buffet table. She had bought a prudent supply when it last appeared on the shelves of the Coop. There is pickfish, an island invention which is made by picking apart into tiny pieces the meat of any white-fleshed fish and then frying it with almost an equal quantity of chopped scallions. Alongside the local fish are cans of sardines from Portugal. There are steaming platters of Irish potatoes and sweet potatoes; bowls of string beans cooked in coconut milk; peas, cold and left in the can, as with the spaghetti; jars of pickled onions; stewed tomatoes; boiled carrots, bananas, and cabbage; baked pumpkin and baked beans. There are cans of butter set out between the dishes, boxes of chewy cabin-bread crackers and home-baked bread and biscuits from a dozen different stone ovens. The salads are in great variety — tomatoes, cucumbers, cabbage, a little lettuce. The same dressing has been used on each, salted coconut milk. Less appetizing are the mysterious slabs of the local staple, *pillhai*, a starchy dish made by baking mashed green bananas or *kumara* in envelopes of banana leaves.

The desserts are placed on the table along with the first courses. There are several fruit gelatins, pumpkin pies in square pans made by the menfolk from flattened-out tin containers, sliced peaches in cans, and a superabundance of cakes, buns, and cookies. Fresh fruit is missing from the display, presumably because the islanders see so much of it in their daily lives. Another item one would expect in this sort of buffet display — cheese — is also absent. The Pitcairners have no taste for it, and in fact, use no dairy products apart from butter, condensed milk, and occasionally, powdered milk for the babies. The local goats are eaten, never milked. In any event, they are wild livestock.

The drinks are all freshly homemade — peach and pineapple juice and powerfully sweet lemonade. The women are ferrying in the pitchers from "the bolt." Although the temperatures during the day have been in the eighties, the fruit drinks are served hot.

The guests range in age from eleven months to eighty years. The islanders, all but a few senile ones well scrubbed from their baths and changed into unpretentious but neat clothes, are chatting away excitedly with cousin-neighbors with whom they have already spent most of the day. The talk among these communards revolves around food — what is on the table and what is growing on the high ground. We are kept busy dealing with questions about how we like Pitcairn and whether we could end our days here. There is seemingly no interest in querying new arrivals from the outside world about what is happening in that world, what life is like there. We are asked about the meals we eat at home and invited to draw a comparison with what is on the Pitcairn table before us.

The noise level — shouted instructions by the women about the food arrangement, guests exuberantly greeting late arrivals, children playing disorganizedly — is rising to perilous decibel heights when the host calls for silence.

"Grace, if you would." The hearty voice which has instantly quieted the gathering, now, in a solemn moment with his Maker, delivers the offering in a recalcitrant-schoolboy mumble:

> *Lord bless this food which now we take*
> *To do us good, for Jesus' sake.*

Everyone in the room joins in the "Amen," and then the host yells, "Now get tah it!" "Make sure yawley get enough!" the hostess advises the guests.

Once the table is picked clean, there is a chorus of "Happy Birthday." A few, derided good-naturedly as "heathens" by the more conscientious followers of the Adventist faith, ask for, and are given, cups of tea. Some of the teen-agers and the children drift off from their elders into bedrooms to sing to Tom's guitar. The favorites are wonderfully square withdrawals from the museum shelves of popular music: "She'll Be Coming 'Round the Mountain When She Comes," "On Top of Old Smoky," and so on. The voices that have a reticent and deprecatory quality in conversation with outsiders are lusty and unrestrained when it comes to singing. Even the rough-looking boys sing well, and surviving through the power of their voices, there is a clear, curiously ringing quality that is characteristic of Pitcairn singing.

The party breaks up early, about ten o'clock. The food seems to have been the main event. With Millie and Warren leading the way with flashlights, we pick our way home through the maze of narrow paths winding up and down gullies. We still have electric light when we reach the house. The little community generator installed three years earlier provides a ration of about four and a half hours of electricity — until eleven o'clock most nights but an hour earlier on Friday nights to get everybody in bed earlier on Sabbath eve. Since the kettle is still hot on the stove, Warren suggests tea.

He is an inveterate tea-drinker, a habit that Millie, a conspicuously more devout person, does not seem to be entirely happy about. She drinks nothing stronger than rainwater, "God's water from the well." Occasionally, she takes it boiled, with a spoonful of Golden Syrup (a refined molasses) dissolved in it. Her favorite meal, it develops, is a bowl of canteloupe and avocado, chopped and mixed with hot baked beans. She washes it down with a steaming cup of the Golden Syrup dilute. Warren will drink cup after cup of strong tea from his chromium-plated teapot but will not touch coffee.

Our hostess, Millie Floria Christian, is sixty-four, the daughter of a sailmaker from Nantucket, Philip Coffin, who was shipwrecked in 1881 on Henderson, an uninhabited island a day's sail from Bounty Bay. Rescued by the Pitcairners, Coffin found a bride as well as a haven on the island. She likes to refer to herself as an *American* Pitcairner. She has a gentle, round face and a soft, round body to match. Yet her great, leg-of-mutton arms have the strength of a man's. She is unusual among the women in that she has no Polynesian traces in her features. Moved from a barefoot island existence and her daily regimen of cooking in stone ovens and weaving strips of palm fronds into baskets, Millie could be a stand-in for any plump, solicitous grandmother from rural America. Among her distinctions in the Pitcairn society, I discover, is the fact that she wears the first set of dentures made on the island, a workable unit of false teeth put together by a neighbor, Hilda Young, in 1954 after she returned from New Zealand having "picked up a little of dentistry" there.

Warren Clive Christian is seven years younger than his wife; female seniority in married couples is relatively common on the island. In thirty years of marriage, they have not had the children each wanted but they have an adopted daughter, Betty, Tom Christian's wife. Warren is of average height and strongly built. He is a shy man, and like many other Pitcairn men has a soft and diffident smile that hardly matches his powerful physical frame.

He is the sixth-generation descendant of Fletcher Christian and Mi'Mitti. By the glow of the oil lamp on the dining room table — it is now past eleven o'clock and the generator has been shut down — he recites a pedigree, rubbing his brow occasionally when the name of a link in the Christian line escapes him momentarily:

"Fletcher get Friday October, who we later called Thursday, and Friday/Thursday get Thursday October the Second, and *that* Thursday . . . let's think who that Thursday get . . . yes, *that* Thursday get Francis, and Francis get Edgar, and Edgar get my father." He pauses for more tea. "I've got that right now. It's even difficult at times for us Christians."

Warren's skin still carries a residue of Mi'Mitti's color, the *café-au-lait* Polynesian brown of the girl who was the genearch's mistress. He is proud of his Tahitian blood and reminisces happily about the two visits he has made to Tahiti, once in 1938 aboard a trading schooner to work with four other Pitcairners for ten months on an out-of-the-way pineapple plantation, another time a few years ago when an American survey ship gave a party of island men a free ride to and from Papeete. "This is a Polynesian man — almost — who is pouring the tea," he tells us. "But oooh-ah, it doesn't stop me from getting sunburned when I spend a whole day in the sun, particularly up here where's it's balding. I burn real bad."

Warren's dark yet sun-susceptible features are in the mold of a fairly characteristic Pitcairn male face I had noticed first in the longboat — curved nose ending in a broadening at the nostrils, hazel eyes under prominent brows, and a forehead that slants back sharply. The forehead I found particularly interesting. It is not a common feature in either the English or the Tahitian face.

When it comes time to retire, we discover that Millie and Warren have given up their bedroom to us so we shall be more comfortable, and also have a glimpse of the Pacific on arising. They have shifted to a cramped little room on the other side of the house. The last time they relinquished their master bedroom was eleven months previously when their adopted daughter moved into it for the delivery of her first baby.

After toothbrushing by the well and a lamplit trip to the "dunkun," the big, homemade bed, spread with Millie's best embroidered sheets, is a welcome sight at the end of our day. There are mosquitoes and a breed of dive-bombing cockroach in the air. Termite dust is dropping onto two piles accumulating on the floor beside the bed. Two or more ants are busy demolishing parts of the ceiling; the different colored piles accumulating on the floor beside me, one cream sawdust, the other medium-brown, indicate that they are working on different types of island wood. A little gecko lizard, poised and ready to pounce on any bug that moves near his beat on the ceiling, is trying gamely to reduce the insect population in the room. A rat or a mouse is scurrying in the rafters somewhere above us. We blow out the oil lamp. Despite the many little companions sharing the room with us, seen and unseen, buzzing and silent, airborne and creeping, we are quickly lost in undreaming sleep.

Soon after five the next morning, the "bolt" fire is going and Warren has tea on the table for the sort of breakfast that is served in this house only very rarely when strangers visit.

"I start ah day with just glass of water usually," says Millie. "On

Pitcairn we eat just two meals — a meal we *call* breakfast but which we have around eleven or in middle of ah day and ah supper when ah work is done at end of ah day. If I call you at midday and say, 'Breakfast is on table,' don't think my head is not right. It's Pitcairn way. Would your children like eggs now? We have no bacon on island because Bible forbids pork."

For this unorthodox early meal, Millie produces a pot with a dozen white and brown-speckled soft-boiled eggs. We eat these and a pineapple apiece. "We call 'em just 'apples' here 'cos no ordinary apples grow on Pitcairn," says Millie. With just a cup of rainwater for sustenance, Millie is plunged into a Sunday morning of prodigious labor and productivity. She has all the qualities we associate with the pioneer women of the West. With this bent for hard work, it is not surprising that a colony has managed to survive so many years on this little mound of rock and earth in mid-ocean. By 11 A.M., Millie has done *our* breakfast, baked eight loaves of bread in the outdoor oven, finished a pandanus basket for the schoolteacher's wife, dyed more pandanus leaves she has been bleaching in the sun to make more baskets, cleaned — in a fashion — the rooms of the house, done the dishes, prepared the *proper* breakfast for serving when Warren comes down the hill from his gardening and wood-gathering, and still found time to chat and answer our questions.

After Warren has raced through the grace — a halfhearted preliminary in which only the word "Jesus" is distinguishable — we start on a lunch-breakfast of chicken soup with rice and noodles, a platter of French fries, and more of the delicious pineapples. Warren's side dish with his chicken soup is Millie's bread, thickly sliced and coated generously with peach jam. Our hostess excuses herself with the dishes. She also has a pile of laundry. "Sunday is washday on Pitcairn," she explains, "has been, I suppose, since we changed ah Sabbath day."

CHAPTER ELEVEN

POPULATION: 85

A SPECIAL FRAME of reference is required in considering a community as small as Pitcairn's. There are villages and settlements around the world, of course, that have fewer than eighty-five inhabitants; but invariably these outposts have land links with larger, parent communities, or ready access to them by sea or air. Pitcairn is a unit to itself, a self-contained society, isolated by a stretch of empty sea equivalent to half the width of the Atlantic from the nearest touchstone of the modern world. That this link-place is Tahiti, itself an outpost and one of the most exotic we have, does not lessen the sense of isolation.

If things go awry on Pitcairn, if the business of living raises special problems and hazards, there is no one a person may turn to instantly for the remedy other than those who share the island with him or her. For this reason, perhaps, while they crave many of the things the outside world offers, the Pitcairners are quite unintrigued by the setbacks the big world suffers and the advances it rings up. They have lived over generations with isolation and a unique society has evolved to cope with it.

A collection of eighty-five people is hardly greater than the number of passengers who can be squeezed into a city bus at rush hour. The most threadbare imagination could grasp what it must be like to live, grow old, and die in a society bound by such numerical limit. At the very outset of our journey to the island we were presented with a handy analogy. Aboard a Douglas stretch-jet from

New York to Mexico City, the captain apologized for a crowded flight. All but one of the two hundred and eight seats were occupied. In this aluminum tube rushing through the air there were well over twice as many people as the total human resources of Pitcairn. The island schoolteacher worked out for his pupils one day that the population of India increases itself every three and a half minutes by a figure equal to the entire population of Pitcairn. In the time it takes to boil an egg, as many Indian babies have come into the world as the total number living on Pitcairn and keeping its minisociety functioning.

Adamstown is surely the easiest place in the world for the job of census-taking. Within the space of two minutes one Sabbath afternoon as the community was gathered in the Square, I was able to make an accurate head count of the islanders. It came to eighty-one. There were four absentees. Only a simple check with an islander was required to establish the reason for the discrepancy — two senile couples had not ventured from their houses.

In considering the island numbers, I am confining myself to actual Pitcairners. At the time of our stay, seven non-Pitcairners were in temporary residence, each there for two-year terms. They were the Adventist Pastor and his wife, both Australians, and the New Zealand schoolteacher, his wife, and their three young children. The visiting schoolteacher is required from time to time, whenever the absentee Commissioner for Pitcairn deems it necessary, to make an official count. The teacher has access to the full file of island birth certificates, so his census has a completeness and an accuracy that the science of people-counting in far more sophisticated societies can never hope to match. Using his report as an unassailable foundation, I was able to build some modest demographic studies of my own.

The present population has a preponderance of males — 46 to 39. Unexpectedly, males are in the *majority* in the upper-age brackets, in the *minority* in the school-age years and in the conventional child-bearing period. This is the exact reverse of the situation census-takers in most countries expect to find when they break down their figures by sex and age. It is also a reversal of the sex-ratio situation that was recorded on Pitcairn little more than a generation ago.

In his 1934 study, Dr. Shapiro found that while there were more males than females in the total population, 101 to 98, the women were in the majority in the over-sixty-five bracket. There were nine female senior citizens and only three male. This was nicely in keeping with an almost universal pattern that demonstrates women are able to outdistance men in life's race. "There appears to be no escape from the conclusion that man is the weaker vessel," Dr. Shapiro commented at the time.

The visiting anthropologist discovered, as he probably expected from experience with statistical records of other societies, that in the figures for infants and the young age brackets, the Pitcairn sex ratio was decidedly in the favor of males. In the under-eighteen group, there were 36 males and 27 females; in the eighteen-to-forty-four bracket, 44 males and 38 females. By the middle period of life, the higher male mortality rate that is found elsewhere had taken its toll on the island. There were 24 women aged between forty-five and sixty-four but only 18 men.

The Shapiro study established that the sex ratio at birth among the pre-1934 Pitcairners was weighted in favor of male children to an unusual degree. From 1865 to 1933, there had been 165 male to 139 female births, or 118.7 males to 100 females. From 1841 to 1916 in England and Wales, the origin of that half of the Pitcairn ancestry for which accurate statistics exist, the sex ratio at birth varied from 103.5 to 105.2 males to 100 females.

In my breakdown of the population into age groupings, I have arbitrarily taken the years between sixteen and forty as the child-bearing period. This has been done to give the reader a clearer understanding of the social situation on the island, particularly as it affects the younger ones attempting to build a future there. The upper limit may have been placed unnecessarily high on the age scale. In practice, the contemporary Pitcairn women cease having children at a comparatively early age, certainly far earlier than was the case in the nineteenth century and in the early part of this century. With the exception of three who were teen-age mothers, the women on the island have borne during their twenties what few children the present population includes, and then, it seems, closed the door on further parturition. Or perhaps, in view of the evidence suggesting a startling decline in fertility on the island, the door has been closed for them.

In recent years, births to island women in their thirties or forties have not occurred, whereas the earlier Pitcairn women went on having children right up to the onset of menopause. In calculating the women's *average* age at final parturition, the Shapiro study came up with the astonishing figure of forty-five years for the first-generation Pitcairners and forty-two years, five months for the second-generation mothers. They not only began child-bearing at a far earlier age, but the period of fecundity was of unusually long duration. Fletcher Christian's granddaughter Mariah, born in 1815, was married at the age of fourteen to the first of three husbands she was to survive and produced by them twenty-five children. In those days, the average age at first marriage was fifteen in the colony; today it is in the twenties.

The composition of the population living on Pitcairn at the beginning of 1972 was as follows:

	MALES	FEMALES
Preschoolers (−5)	3	3
School age (5–15)	7	9
"Child-bearing" (16–40)	8	9
Middle age (41–65)	16	11
Old age (66–84)	12	7
	46	39

The table, minuscule though its entries are in their numerical sweep, will contain surprises for demographers, sociologists, and anthropologists.

Male and female births for the very recent years are at level pegging, although the numbers involved are too small to have any real meaning. In the geriatric years, the men have a clear majority, 12 to 7, that is decidedly unexpected in a world which now takes for granted the phenomenon of superior feminine longevity. Three of the four octogenarians are men, as are eight of the fourteen septuagenarians. The oldest islanders are Norris Young and Theodore Young, both born in the second half of 1887.

It would be absurd, of course, for me or anyone else to draw any thundering biological conclusions from these figures. The human sample is too small. The distortions caused by movement away from the island by family groups and single men and women are important enough to make any such conclusions both pointless and suspect.

But the social implications for a society that has infrequent contact with outsiders are clear and powerful. Consider just two basic areas — a young person's selection of a mate, the problems confronting a society which has men living to ripe age with far fewer women to care for them — and the stark Pitcairn statistics take on fuller meaning.

The numbers continue to dwindle. The steady growth until the late 1930's and the steady decline since then are recorded in this table:

	TOTAL	MALES	FEMALES
1790	28	15	13
1808	35		
1825	66	36	30
1842	112	53	59
1849	155	76	79
1855	187	92	95
1936	200	110	90
1954	136	66	70
1961	126	59	67
1966	96	50	46
1972	85	46	39

No breakdown by sex is available in any records for the year 1808, the time the colony was discovered by the outside world. The Americans who solved the mystery of where Fletcher Christian and the mutineers had disappeared to were evidently too exhilarated to attend to the fine points of census-taking. They simply counted the heads. With the arrival of the Royal Navy, the place was put on a sounder statistical basis.

There is a gap in this table between 1855 and 1936, not because figures for those years do not exist, but because the removal of the entire colony of 194 to Norfolk Island in 1856, and the subsequent return of only a few families, result in a major, unnatural dip in the growth curve. Some eight years after the evacuation was carried out, 45 Pitcairners had returned to restart the colony. By 1873, the population was up to 76, by 1894 it stood at 115, and by 1924 183. The present Pitcairners trace their basic descent from the 45 who had repatriated themselves from Norfolk Island by 1864.

Similarly, the peak population year, 1937, when 233 were in residence, is not included in this table because I regard it as an unnaturally high figure. The 1936 census showed only 200; in a single year there could hardly have been a net gain of 33. The explanation, the islanders told me, was that a number of Pitcairners in voluntary exile in New Zealand or Australia, seeing the war clouds gathering on the international scene, did what Fletcher had done before them and took off, for somewhat different motives, for a refuge in the South Pacific.

The decline in numbers accelerated in the 1960's. The decade began with a resident population of 144 and ended with 90. The most significant point about all these statistics is that Pitcairn today, from a population standpoint, is at precisely the same stage it had reached by the beginning of 1831, forty-one years after the little party of pioneers had clambered ashore from the foundering *Bounty*.

There are twenty-two "households" on the island today, including the widowed and bachelors living alone. Only thirteen of these households include children, in five cases the number of offspring being limited to one. The school-age population, in fact, is dropping close to the point where the expense and problems of hiring a professional teacher from New Zealand may cease to be justified. The islanders would then have to go back to the old system of delegating the teaching of the young to those in their midst with the time and the education to handle it.

There are now only six family names on the island. Three of them perpetuate the surnames of mutineers who sired children on Pitcairn — Christian, Young, McCoy. The Pitcairn pedigrees started by three other mutineers, John Adams, Matthew Quintal, and John Mills, have died out so far as island nomenclature is concerned, although their descendants are still found in the daughter-colony started on Norfolk Island. McCoy has no male heirs on the island today, and his name will survive only for the lifetime of the widowed Violet McCoy. The other three mutineers, William Brown, the gardener taken on to care for the breadfruit trees, John Williams, and the American-born Isaac Martin, did not leave their seed on the island. Whether this was because the men were sterile, a condition reflected perhaps in the many entries on Bligh's "Venereal List," or because they were killed before there was due time for them to start families, history does not enlighten us. Brown's name is to be found on the island but only coincidentally. The present bearers of the name trace their origin to a forebear who migrated from New Zealand.

Fletcher Christian's seed has been by far the most tenacious. A total of thirty-one of the eighty-five Pitcairners carry his name. There are many other descendants, probably upwards of one hundred and fifty, living in New Zealand, Australia, the United States, or elsewhere. There are twenty-three islanders today who bear the surname of Midshipman Young. The present community has sixteen Warrens, descendants of Samuel Warren, a Providence, Rhode Island, seaman who gave up the life of a whalerman in the 1850's to marry Agnes Christian. There are nine Browns and five Clarks, a family line that was introduced when an American, Lincoln Clark, who first saw Pitcairn in his cabin-boy days as a shipwreck survivor, decided to return with his son some years after his repatriation to California.

Nine of the present Pitcairn inhabitants were born off the island — five children in New Zealand, two men in the United States, one woman in Australia, and another on the island of Mururoa, where France now explodes her hydrogen bombs. The American-born Pitcairners are Roy Clark, seventy-eight, the son of Lincoln Clark, and Charles Christian, whose parents were in San Francisco when he came into the world forty-one years ago.

The injection of this new blood — English, American, and a drop more Polynesian — may not have been the island's salvation, but it has certainly helped, numerically at least, if not in more subtle ways that refreshed the genetic reservoir. This last point is taken up in the next chapter. But it is obvious to today's observer, and has been to perceptive outsiders over the years, that most of the finest Pitcairners — judged by physical stature, native intelligence, and moral character — are those with the purest island heredity, the men and women who trace their descent directly from the doubtful original mix of English outlaw and Polynesian common-law wife. Among today's generation of Christians and Youngs are some impressive specimens, Tom, Ben, Pervis, Warren, Ivan, and others, who can respond to almost superhuman island challenges with resourceful minds and well-tested limbs. The late Parkin and Fred Christian, both of whom died during 1971 three years short of ninety, were men of self-assurance, dignity and breeding. They lived active lives well past the accepted span, and without such stalwarts the Pitcairn society would have perished long since.

The old-timers who were around when the dirt lanes of Adamstown were "positively crowded" with people — "Oooh, imagine, there was once more than two hundred Peet-carners here" — now talk of the danger level in island manpower. It is generally considered to be around thirty able-bodied men and youths. The island population at the start of 1972 was almost precisely at that danger level. Island Magistrate Pervis made the count thirty-one, or thirty-three if two men who are excused from "public work" because of their age and health are included. Even so, the "able-bodied" list includes some in their late sixties or early seventies.

From this meager labor reserve, the men in charge of the longboats must be able to call on a minimum of twenty-seven "working men and boys." A roster is drawn up, and nine men are allocated to each of three boats, the only means by which the islanders can make contact with passing ships. Nine is the absolute minimum number of hands required to launch a boat, control it at the side of a ship ,and get it safely back on shore. The boat captains like to have at least a dozen aboard to make the job safer and easier. Two longboats usually are sent out to each caller from the world beyond.

In theory, each boat crew "works" twenty ships — a ship can be a liner, a freighter, a warship, or a yacht — and then is spelled for the next ten ships that call. The system dates from the days when

A longboat puts out from Bounty Bay against the strong surf. It was designed to be handled by fourteen oarsmen. With dwindling manpower, the boats sometimes must be taken out with shorthanded crews. (Courtesy of Tom Christian)

ship arrivals were far more frequent than today. It was drawn up so that, in rotation, one crew at a time would be free to devote themselves to trading aboard ten ships for a period known well in advance. In practice, owing to sickness and temporary absences from the island, the five-bell summons to the Landing often has to be answered by almost every man and teen-age boy able to move. And there have been times recently when the manpower situation, even with every longboat crewman reporting for every ship, has deteriorated to desperate levels at which desperate procedures become necessary.

In 1968, the island population had fallen to seventy-six as a result of several families having taken up temporary residence in New Zealand. The island was left with only twenty-nine men, aged from sixteen to eighty-three. The "able-bodied" list, of course, was well below twenty-nine.

The short-handed crews found they could get two longboats out to the ships off Bounty Bay, but there weren't enough hands to bring both in safely. The men's solution was to swim!

What happened was that a full crew would be mustered at sea to bring one boat back to shore while a skeleton crew was left behind to look after the one remaining beyond the breakers. *Dumpy*, say, a longboat that acquired her name because of her unladylike movement across even light seas, would be brought in first, while four or five men stayed behind with *Boxhead*, so named because she attacked the waves with all the bow-action finesse of a freight car being rammed through an ocean swell. Once *Dumpy* had been hauled up the slip, her crew would strip to shorts, dive off the rocks into fearsome seas, and swim out to help the party left aboard *Boxhead* bring the boat home. A swim of at least half a mile, sometimes more, was involved. The men, incidentally, have withstood this sort of punishing improvisation better than the vessels. *Dumpy* broke apart in heavy seas two years ago and went under with no human loss.

Today, the Pitcairn society gives desultory consideration to the possibility that its salvation may lay in limited and very selective immigration. It wonders, at times, whether the Adventist Church in America or Australia might select and sponsor young settlers eager to be rid both of urban overcrowding and societies turning to crime, eroticism, and drugs. Aren't many of the young in the big world, who see crises of meaning in their lives, existential discontent, boredom, alienation, looking for just such a haven? Some believe they have found the answers to loneliness and the self-search for purpose in the communes they have formed in remote rural areas. Isn't faraway Pitcairn, unadulterated and unpolluted by the big world, the ultimate commune?

But those on the island who are old enough to recall it are aware that the last experiment in accepting migrants ended in disaster and bad debts. A nineteen-year-old Australian youth pestered the Island Council with such persuasive letters that it was decided to let him sail to Pitcairn and settle. His mother arrived a bit later to see how the lotus-eating was going. Mother and son stood it for a few months and then borrowed passage money home. They were not heard from again.

So if Pitcairn is to survive, the islanders will either have to lure home those who have left or themselves breed in sufficient numbers to keep the economy functioning. Neither of these remedies seems likely to come about.

Warren Christian talks of the relatives he and other islanders have in New Zealand: "If all the people in New Zealand came back, we'd be stacked for people here. But they're not so stupid to come back. What would they come back *for*?"

Christy Warren, a buoyant fellow of seventy-three who has the heartiness and build of a Liffey docker, agrees that the exiles would be "crazy to come home." He adjusts to a more comfortable position on his overalls the leather belt required only to hold the seamen's knife on his hip, and talks of his New Zealand relatives. If just his grandchildren were to return, they would raise the island population by more than a third.

"They *breed* over in New Zealand," says Christy. "For some reason the Pitcairn young don't *breed* on Pitcairn, but they breed like rabbits in New Zealand. I have thirty grandchildren there now. Christy's children, growing up as little Kiwis! Why, they're a-populatin' New Zealand they are, and a good life they have, too. They won't come back."

Although Christy himself is a happy man, waiting now both

exuberantly and confidently for a meeting with his Maker, he would not think of urging his absent progeny to return to find earthly contentment on Pitcairn. He and his second island wife, Mima, who has never gone beyond the perimeter of Pitcairn in her eighty-two years, live in one of the more comfortable and pleasant island homes. They have ample food from their garden and good friends to pass the time with. But Christy is not an island booster so far as his grandchildren are concerned. He realizes that the Pitcairn society is too fragile and vulnerable a community within which the young should be counseled to build a future. Eighty-five souls. Becoming fewer as Christy's years grow more.

Christy talks of the bleak years of his island youth, of the time when Pitcairners lacked even clothes: "I went about in just a guernsey sweater, that's all. I had nothing to put under it. We kept tugging the guernsey down, tugging it down so's we'd be decent in the community. Fifteen years of age, and I got my *first* pair of pants. The girls had scraps of dresses but nothing underneath, like us in our guernseys, nothing underneath. We would go out picking oranges and the mischief in us made us send the girls up the tree first . . . Just guernseys and scraps of dresses. No other clothes for so many years. And all of us in the same boat, all poor and struggling." He jumps from the petty problem of juvenile Peeping Toms to the fundamental one of his blood relatives turning away in manhood from their native island: "The men were leaving the island then. They went away to support their women and children because there was no money on Pitcairn. Who blames them for leaving? The world forgets about us every now and then, and when the war came along [World War I], we really lived underground for those years. There were no provisions coming in. You couldn't go out to a ship with pineapples and oranges and call on the chief steward and hear him say, 'Here, take this piece of beef,' or 'Where's your bag for the Irish potatoes,' or 'There's the sugar bin, dip into it.' We had no flour for the bread, no grease for the cooking, and we tried to make do with biscuits made from the manioc. The food tasted tough as the devil. It was just like animals living underground."

I heard from many of Christy's generation similar accounts of the years when life on Pitcairn was immeasurably tougher than it is today. Some, like Christy, recalled the past with a garrulous zest; others spoke of it with the listless voices of men who remember things with pain. Most had tasted the life of the outside world — if only, as in Christy's case, a job in an Auckland foundry making farm tools — and had returned, not because they had not found the life good and exciting, but because parents were dying at home and were in need of a son's or daughter's solace.

Much as they now need at their side the sons and daughters of those who failed to return, the islanders feel it would be selfish, and a bit dishonest, to urge them to rejoin the ranks. They are prepared to struggle on by themselves a while longer with the ration of help they get from London and Auckland. And the more glimpses they have of what lies beyond the horizon, the more samples they acquire from a world of consumerism, the lonelier and harder that struggle somehow seems to become.

I sought an assessment from a man who had spent three years on the island, Russell Henry, the schoolteacher who was packing to go home to New Zealand when we arrived. He had become an integral part of the community, knew all its strengths and weaknesses, and had thought deeply about its problems and resources.

"For fifteen or twenty years now, people have been predicting that in five years' time there will be no one left on Pitcairn," he told me one day as we chatted in a schoolhouse that, while small, sorely needs more pupils. "I came with an open mind on that point. My period here coincided with a time when we couldn't count on regular shipping. There were times when we went for four or five months without supply ships, when we often waited two and a half months for mail to come. There were times when there simply wasn't enough food on the island for us, at least food suitable for our three children. You'd get into a ridiculous situation where you have plenty of money in the bank and yet you have to sit there and watch your children with food on their plates that they found unpalatable. They actually gagged on it. If you had a thousand pounds to spend, it wouldn't make any difference. That's the great leveler here. In those times when there are no ships, money means nothing." (He was talking here, of course, as an outsider with an outsider's tastes, and of a particularly lean period, the "Five-Month Starve," in the recent past. His remarks made me aware of something I had not really considered while attending all those Adamstown feasts: how dependent these seven dozen people were becoming on food supplies from the outside.)

The schoolteacher had discussed with his pupils' parents, even with the pupils themselves, how new life might be brought to the society, but the discussions were always circuitous explorations that brought them back to a starting point: "When we have talked about finding an economy for the island, it always comes back to certain things — the lack of regular shipping, the smallness of the labor force, the things the Church wants to see happen and doesn't want to see happen. There have been ideas for a fishing industry, and you'd have no trouble getting the men to go out for the tuna. There are plenty in the sea. I've seen them come back with thirteen or fourteen big tuna from a few hours' fishing. It would also give the women a job in canning the fish on the island, and the brighter young ones could learn how to do the accounts. But nothing is done about it, and probably won't. If we could get another source of revenue, and get the islanders interested in it, then Pitcairn may change.

"There is talk about tourism on a small scale — the climate is wonderful — but it would mean that the islanders would become servants and waiters and cooks, and I wouldn't like to see that. It could bring in many of the bad things of civilization, and the Church wouldn't like that. There is the idea of a citrus industry — in the season, there are so many oranges here they are all over the ground — but it comes back to the old problems of shipping and a labor force. They need finance, of course, but it's also a question of how to provide jobs for these people. There are more Pitcairners in Wellington than there are on Pitcairn. If you could persuade them to come back, the island would have something to work with."

A pause here in which the schoolteacher mused on the ingenious salesmanship that would be required to lure Fletcher Christian's great-great-great-great-grandchildren home. He shook his head in sorrow over what the future held for this island he had grown to love.

"Unless something can be done soon," he said, "I'll be one of those people who predict that, before too many years are past, this place will have to be evacuated."

By the end of the stay I had formed the same opinion. When the lure of the big world is even faintly visible, when there is just enough "affluence" and outside help to give at least some of the young the intellectual stimulus of higher education, eighty-five people living in a community apart are no longer, it seems, an economically viable and socially feasible unit. As the numbers drop, the problems that confront a little society on a far-off island mount geometrically, not arithmetically. In 1856, when the decision was made to transport the entire community to Norfolk Island, one hundred and ninety-four inhabitants were considered too many for Pitcairn's 1,120 acres. In 1972, eighty-five Pitcairners are too few.

CHAPTER TWELVE

WHEN COUSINS MARRY

GENETICALLY, THIS SOCIETY is in a class by itself. It was launched with a textbook case of *out*breeding, a cross between the totally unrelated strains of eighteenth-century Polynesians on the female side and, with a single Celtic exception, McCoy, Anglo-Saxons on the male side. It has perpetuated itself through a textbook case of *in*breeding, among the most remarkable the contemporary world has seen. The dynastic Egyptian rulers mated with their sisters or brothers because they considered it their divine duty. The Pitcairners have married first cousins out of sheer necessity. For investigators of the laws of heredity, the island is a human laboratory *sans pareil*. Only its remoteness has saved it from becoming a haunt of international medical detectives, specialists in human biology in semipermanent residence.

It began with a gene pool provided by six white men and fewer than a dozen native women. We do not know precisely how many of the *Bounty* men's brides and appropriated women bore children. The six Tahitian men who were taken along by the mutineers in servant roles fathered no children on Pitcairn, even though three of them took their women with them when they left their home island. That the native men died without leaving progeny is surely testimony to the condition of total serfdom the mutineers imposed on healthy, young Tahitian studs. Scientifically, however, it was a decided advantage for any future investigators in that it kept the mating elements in the original biological mix in neat sex compartments — exclusively white fathers, exclusively brown mothers.

That initial pool of inheritable characteristics and traits has served the Pitcairners fairly well. Ironically, they began siring children by cousins at the very time that the civilized world was formulating its rough theories, not much more valid, really, than old midwives' tales, about the dread consequences of cousin marriage. A closed, inbred society, the Victorians postulated, was bound to result in steady, possibly spectacular, mental and physical enfeeblement.

So far as Pitcairn was concerned, these Victorian fears were not realized. On the contrary, on the far side of the planet, the Pitcairners were proving the exact reverse. A new breed was establishing itself that was certainly taller than representative specimens of the English and Tahitian races, and was also healthier, more vigorous, and for a time at least, more fertile.

From old Admiralty records and from Bligh's descriptions of the mutineers at large, we know the individual heights of the six *Bounty* men who became fathers on the island. Their average height was 5 feet 7 inches. (Christian, at 5 feet 9 inches, had the superior stature desirable in a leader of men.) In height, the mutineers were representative of Englishmen generally of their day. Compared with the mutineer fathers, the representative Tahitian of the day had a height advantage of about one half of an inch.

But the Anglo-Tahitians that resulted on Pitcairn loomed inches above most of their first American and English visitors. None failed to record the fact that Fletcher's son, Thursday October Christian, stood well over six feet tall. Captain Beechey, who arrived in 1825 in H.M.S. *Blossom,* sent his surgeon ashore to measure the island men. The shortest was just over 5 feet 9 inches. The average was 5 feet 10 inches. It is unlikely that the tallest Victorian Englishmen, the well-nourished upper classes, could have boasted such height averages.

Over the years, the mean height on Pitcairn has fallen slightly, but physically, they remain an impressive breed. The Pitcairners were — and are — men and women of immense strength. In one of the earliest published descriptions of the islanders, there is a vivid account based on the experiences of a Lieutenant Wood, who went ashore from H.M.S. *Pandora* in 1849: "A young woman, eighteen years of age, had been accustomed to carry on her shoulders a hundred pounds weight of yams over hills and precipitous places, and for a considerable distance, where one unaccustomed to such exercise would scarcely be able to scramble. A man, sixty years old, with ease carried the surgeon of the *Pandora* up a steep ascent from the landing-place, which he had himself in vain attempted to mount, the ground being very slippery from recent rains; and the officer being a large man, six feet high, rendered it the more surprising. Indeed, Lieut. Wood said he was himself borne aloft in the arms of a damsel, and carried up the hill with the utmost facility." (Having done that same climb many times, I can vouch for the physical exertion that is required simply in propelling one's own body up the hill, let alone doing it at the age of sixty with a six-footer as burden.)

In those days, the islanders would often furnish visiting ships with water and fresh supplies by swimming out through the heavy surf with casks. Today, the Pitcairners will concede that a softening-up process has begun. Nevertheless, I have seen one of the men move a two-hundred-pound burden up a steep hill in his wheelbarrow and arrive at the top showing no signs of fatigue.

For a society that exists without a doctor, and has done so throughout its history, the island has had an exceptional health record. In a place where daily life poses unusual hazards — the records over the past century show that roughly one in every five Pitcairners has died accidentally, at sea, in falls from cliffs, or in shooting mishaps — the life expectancy certainly appears no worse than that for the United States or Britain and is perhaps better. (This is based on a medical reading of recent census figures. Accurate figures are not available since life-expectancy studies have not been conducted.)

There are no obviously apparent degenerative conditions and no diseases endemic to the island. A typhus plague claimed twelve lives in 1893 after the islanders went to the rescue of a foundering vessel and took into their midst lice-ridden survivors. Commonsense hygiene corrected that situation, and since then, tuberculosis has been virtually the only infectious disease to make any fatal inroads. Pitcairners nowadays, if they have survived the perils of land and sea in their most active years, confidently expect to die of old age. Asthma, influenza, colds, sprains, and infected cuts are the chief concern of the resident Pastor's wife who administers the small dispensary. (It has become the sensible practice of the Adventist Church to appoint to Pitcairn only Pastors whose wives happen to be trained nurses.) High blood pressure, which laymen tend to associate with the tensions of urban life but which medical investigators are not surprised to find when they study the inhabitants of isolated communities, is a condition that troubles a few Pitcairners.

Only unofficial infant mortality statistics have been attempted from time to time. What records exist compare fairly favorably with those for societies with ready access to obstetric and pediatric skills. A recent estimate of infant mortality under one year put it at about fifty-six per thousand births. The island mothers have no doctor to turn to for pre and post-natal care and guidance, yet their babies and young children are robust and alert. Their aptitude for learning, however, is below that of schoolchildren in, say, New Zealand or the United States; environmental factors, however, must be taken into account here.

Once, while studying the islanders' family records, I came across a frank parenthetical comment, "halfwit," beside a name. Today, one man, a bachelor in his sixties, meets the description of village idiot; the islanders, while their nickname for him is a bit unkind, generously allow him to drift into their homes and join them for "hot drink" or a chat. A couple of the grown-ups, and one boy in a school roll of sixteen, might be considered mentally slow. I did not find this incidence of below-average intelligence particularly surprising. Some hamlets in the European Alps have *two* village idiots.

In summary, then, today's Pitcairners, after seven generations of intense inbreeding, are basically healthy, strong, and alert individuals. (They have terrible teeth, granted, but so, too, do peers of the English realm who provided one-half of their ancestors.)

So we turn back to examine that initial supply of genes which the *Bounty* brought to Pitcairn in the loins of six men and fewer than a dozen Polynesian women. A reasonable supposition is that Pitcairn was fortunate in acquiring initial breeding stock which, despite a record of criminality on the male side and of promiscuity on the female, was remarkably free of transferable genetic defects. Dr. Shapiro points out that the old fear of inbreeding is not completely irrational, adding: "Numerous enough instances of cousin marriages which have led to disastrous results suggest that such a prohibition is more than an empty taboo. Inbreeding will increase very considerably the chances of the appearance of a latent defect — if there is a defect latent in the stock. But if the genetic line is sound, there should theoretically be no unpleasant consequence from cousin marriage. In fact, mice and other laboratory animals have been brother-sister mated for generations without producing an unnatural number of defectives. . . . And in many primitive societies, where cousin marriage has been a general and ancient custom, it has not inevitably led to degeneration."

Far from bringing about *degeneration*, the early Pitcairners, in their enforced choice of cousin-spouses, were actually *improving* the species, at least for the span of a few generations. What was occurring (and the practitioners of inexact Victorian medicine were as ignorant of this as the islanders themselves) was the phenomenon of hybrid vigor. Dissimilar genetic lines had been crossed, and each had served to invigorate the other.

In our time, plant biologists would discover the application of the principle of hybrid vigor in the development of new strains of corn and other grains. But these same crop doctors also learned that hybridization has its limitations. For one thing, the forces generated by mixing different strains may show signs of exhaustion after the passage of time. This could be the case with the human mix on Pitcairn, at least in the area of fertility.

A marked decline in fertility is the most significant medical fact about the current generation of Pitcairners. The year 1971 saw three deaths and only two births. No new Pitcairners were detectably on the way at the time of our stay.

In a world of exploding population, the islanders are not even reproducing at a rate to maintain the existing population. An adult (over-eighteen) population of 61 lives on the island with 24 children. This, of course, is not a true picture of procreation there since some of the offspring have moved away upon reaching manhood or womanhood. But the statistics over the years present a gloomy picture of a birthrate falling at a steady and alarming pace.

In those early years when the sons of the *Bounty* men were doing stirring things at sea during the day, and also, quite evidently, on land after sundown, each of the daughters produced by the original mix of mutineer and Tahitian women gave birth in turn to an average of more than ten children. By the middle of the nineteenth century, the average number of children per female had dropped to 6.8. By the beginning of this century, it was down to 2.4. Today, the average is dramatically lower, as the simple population breakdown above — 61 adults, 24 children — and census figures in the preceding chapter will attest.

For the years between 1864 and 1933, the population increased by an average of 27 per decade. For the decade ended in 1953, the increase was 2. Today, the population figures are moving into the minus columns. As old Christy says: "For some reason the Pitcairn young don't *breed* on Pitcairn."

The sharply declining birthrate is not attributable to any significant degree to the use of modern methods of contraception. Certainly condoms and pessaries were unknown on the island seventy years ago when each female descendant of a once remarkably fertile society was bearing an average of only 2.4 children. The Pill has not been responsible for the continuing decline.

Inbreeding presumably has played a role here, perhaps a major one. As the hybrid strength acquired in the 1790's has genetically ebbed away after serving so well the earlier inbred generations, the Pitcairn descendants have become less and less fertile.

A conclusion that inbreeding is the sole culprit would be a reckless one, of course. Sterility has many causes, and among the more common in both sexes is untreated gonorrhea. At this late stage in the life of a community which has existed without a doctor from the very beginning, there is no way of knowing or even estimating how prevalent venereal disease may have been on Pitcairn down through the generations. Had the nineteenth-century Pitcairners kept such medical records, they were the sort of people who would have concealed the community stain from outside eyes.

Certainly, the gonorrheal microorganism arrived on Pitcairn with the *Bounty*. Fletcher Christian was one of at least twelve *Bounty* men who contracted clap in Tahiti. It is a safe assumption that some of the women the mutineers took with them were infected. It is also a reasonable, if somewhat unpleasant, supposition that the disease was brought ashore in the early years by sailors and whalermen who managed — occasionally — to seduce or overwhelm the innocent maidens of Adamstown. Venereal disease at that time was one of the factors that were bringing about a precipitous decline in the population of Tahiti, from about forty thousand when the English and French first visited it to about a quarter that total only two generations later. The ravages of the disease were also being felt in the little offshoot colony that set its moral sights far higher. And while doctors came to Papeete to try to remedy the situation, Pitcairn was left to its own devices.

How inbred are the Pitcairners? A few of the families have kept fairly accurate genealogical tables, and I was able to study some of these. One Christian family pedigree I examined was a record penciled in a copperplate hand on a chart that had been made by pasting together ten sheets of foolscap. When carefully unfolded, road-map style, it covered a card table and hung over the edges. Pencil had been used rather than pen because corrections and expansions were made from time to time when the family tree was compared with others on the island. In showing it to me, the owner imposed a condition: "It's all right to mention some of the very early illegitimates but don't go writing about the recent ones."

It began, of course, with the mutiny leader and the tall beauty he chose at Matavai Bay. Her name has been presented in so many variations — Mi'Mitti (the version I have adopted because it is the one her living descendants seem to favor), Maimiti, Mauatua, Isabella, among others — that it sometimes seems Fletcher Christian took with him a veritable harem. This family tree did nothing to clear up the confusion:

"*Fletcher Christian — wife Maimite, Isobel, also called Mainmast (because of her height) or Memas (Tahitian way of pronouncing Mainmast).*"

Their children:

"*Thursday (Friday) October, Charles ('Hupper' meaning sickly), Mary, and possibly a fourth son (illegitimate).*"

The trunk and lower limbs were in place. The tree here began a luxuriant branching-out:

"*Thursday (Friday) married Sussanah (also called Tiopite and Doubit) who was first wife of Edward Young and the youngest girl that came on the* Bounty. *Children — Charles ('Big Charles'), Joseph (halfwit), Polly (Nuni), Peggy, Mary, Thursday October (the second).*

"*Charles ('Hupper') married Sarah (Sully) McCoy (daughter of Will McCoy). Children — Charles, Fletcher, Mary, Margaret, Isaac, Mariah, Edward.*

"*Thursday October (the second) married Mary Young. Children — Albert, Elias, Agnes, Alphonzo, Julie, Hayward, Daniel, Francis, William, Harriet, Sadley, Charles.*"

And so, removed from the world, a curious little society begun by a band of fugitives was coming into existence.

Christians in the earliest days married Youngs or McCoys or Adamses. There was evidently some extramarital or premarital coupling: "Moses Young, illegitimate son of Polly." Or, "Not of Nancy, mother unknown, illegitimate child." Or, "Della, daughter of Spanish father." The reference to the bastard Nancy was raising was puzzling. It might be expected that the identity of the father would be unknown to the recordkeepers or deliberately concealed by them. But here there was uncertainty over an illegitimate child's *mother*.

As time passed, Christians married Christians and Youngs married Youngs. The marriage columns of the old *Book of Records of Pitcairn Island* and its predecessor, the *Pitcairn Island Register*, are dotted with entries in which the bride and groom have the same family name.

In his study of the islanders, Dr. Shapiro applied an index of inbreeding and calculated the averages for each decade from 1850, by which time a little new blood had been added, to 1919. Under this system of measurement, a brother-sister mating in a family previously "outbred" would give an index of 50 percent, a first-cousin marriage an index of 75 percent. In such cases, the index would be lower if previous inbreeding had occurred. For the decade beginning in 1850, he obtained an average index of inbreeding of 84.38 percent. By 1900, the index stood at 61.96. By 1910, it had dropped to the astonishing figure of 51.53. For one decade, 1860–1869, it had shot up temporarily, to 91.07 percent, and this was explained by the arrival of an outsider, Samuel Warren, the whalerman from Providence, Rhode Island. Four of the children born in this period were his.

"These figures," comments the compiler of the study, "indicate a very rapid increase in inbreeding to the point where the index is practically the same as that for the offspring of a brother-sister marriage. It should, however, be noted that an index of 51.53, such as is found for the youngest subjects, is not really equivalent to an index of 50.00 for brother-sister marriage. In the former, part of the reduction comes from the doubling of ancestors five, six or seven generations removed, while the latter reaches back only two generations."

One subject, normal both physically and mentally, was found to have an inbreeding index of 25.56! He was a true child of mutiny. In his pedigree, Fletcher Christian appeared seven times, Edward Young six times, John Mills three times, William McCoy three times, Matthew Quintal three times, John Adams once, and John Buffett once.

Anyone who examines the Pitcairn genealogies and genetic inheritance will come upon any number of individuals with ancestries that rate close to this man's on an inbreeding scale. The investigator will also encounter one major area of doubt and one major mystery.

The doubt surrounds precisely how much new blood has been added to the population over the years, how many and what type of "foreign" chromosomes were acquired through regular and irregular matings. So far as the present community is concerned, there have been about a dozen identifiable additions since the original cross. There were the Englishmen George Nobbs, John Evans, and John Buffett who arrived in the very early days; the Americans Samuel Warren, Philip Coffin, and Lincoln Clark, the last two shipwreck survivors; Peter Butler, another who was saved from a foundering vessel and decided to make the island his home; and some more recent additions, two from Polynesia but with mixed ancestry, and the others from New Zealand.

It may have been that these injections of new genetic strains occurred at just the right time and were of a type that was precisely what was needed to refresh the bloodline and correct any undesirable breeding tendencies that might have been developing.

The unidentifiable additions are, of course, those visitors from the sea who sired illegitimate children by island women. In time, the young became solid Pitcairn citizens and raised families of their own, thereby injecting into the record of island breeding and inbreeding various unknown and unknowable ancestors. In studying the genealogical trees I would occasionally come across instances where the arrival of a fatherless child had been duly recorded with the appropriate question marks. "Father — American?" or "Father — possibly a whaleman?" In the 1840's alone, 224 ships, mostly American whalers from New England, called at the island. They carried rough crews, and while most respected the islanders' virtue, there were ugly exceptions. Lady Belcher, who in 1870 published a book about the Pitcairners, wrote of one whaler's "ruffian crew" who spent two weeks on the island, "during which time they offered every insult to the inhabitants and threatened to violate any woman whose protectors they could not overcome by force." So some of whatever amount of new stock was introduced through irregular unions may have been acquired through simple cases of rape.

The mystery I have mentioned is something for geneticists to ponder. Why, after seven generations, do the Pitcairn women display more of the physical features of their Tahitian ancestresses than their Anglo-Saxon ancestors, while the exact opposite is true in the case of the men? In any large gathering of islanders, it is at once apparent that the women are darker-skinned and darker-eyed than the men. The hair color of the women is predominantly black. Hazel eyes, however, are not uncommon among the men. Their hair color ranges from black to light brown, and there is even a blond youth and another with a touch of reddishness. The men tend to be lean and muscular, while many of the women are fine exemplars of Polynesian plumpness, weighing up to 250 pounds.

In their physical appearance at least, the Pitcairners would be of special interest in any examination of the theory of sex-linked inheritance which holds that the hereditary characteristics of pro-

OVERLEAF: The men tend to be lean and muscular (the man here is Warren Christian) . . . The women generally have a Polynesian plumpness.

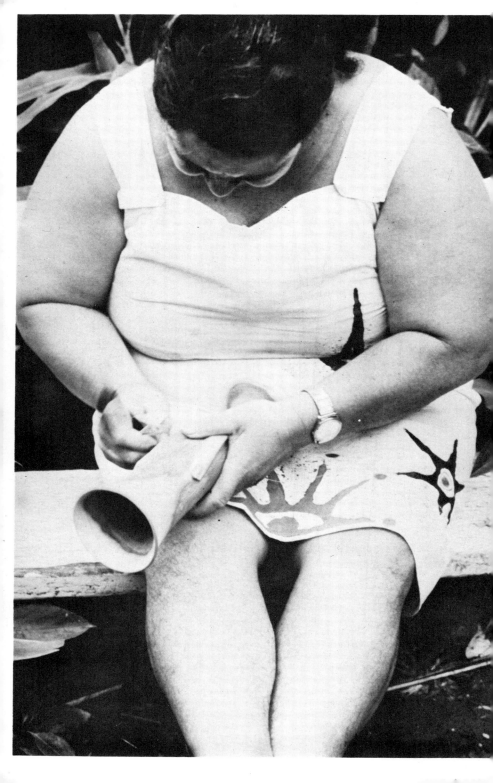

genitors, male or female, are slightly more likely to be carried on by those descendants of the respective progenitor's own sex. The additions to the original stock present no complications here; almost all have been both male and white, following, quite accidentally, the pattern of the founding generation.

Whatever else might be involved when cousins marry, it at least makes possible a simplified marriage announcement. In Millie's house one day, I came across a souvenir of her adopted daughter's marriage six years previously. It was one of the homemade invitations they had extended to all on the island:

WARREN & MILLIE CHRISTIAN
Extend an invitation
to

---

to attend
The Wedding of their daughter
BETTY *to* THOMAS

Light refreshments (drinks, cakes etc.) will
be served in the square 4.30 P.M. approx.
Please bring own plate, spoon and cup.

It would have been pedantic of Millie to have specified that Tom was also a member of the Christian family. Betty, like many other island girls, bore the same surname going to and coming from the marriage altar.

CHAPTER THIRTEEN

MANNERS, MORALS, MINDS:
THE CONFLICT OF CULTURES

A SOCIETY AS SMALL, as closely knit as Pitcairn's theoretically should present a straightforward assignment for an outsider who travels there to study it. To a degree, this is true. In my stay there I talked with, or at least greeted, every individual in the community, from seven-month-old Dean-Hugh Christian to eighty-four-year-old Norris Young. I dandled the babies on my knee, I went to sea with the islanders on fair days and foul, and I joined them at the worship pew and the feast table. But familiarization and observation are only the first plateaus on the slope up to understanding. The outside observer will soon come to realize that the very *simplicity* of the Pitcairners is a complicating element in any such study. Their simplicity is of their own special kind and quality, quite unlike that found in other unsophisticated societies which have developed apart from the mainstreams of European or non-European civilization.

In its evolution, the island's stark isolation and its small numbers are obviously the more important factors. But their remarkable origins, the hangover of communal guilt, the fundamentalist religion they inherited from Victorian forebears, the fact that they are all so totally interbred, the difficulties they have surmounted in the past, and the decisions they reluctantly face now about their future have all played a part in its development.

The outsider's first and strongest impression is the one-big-family one. That a family, a true, blood-meshed family, can number eighty-five, dwell in houses encompassing no more than a few thousand square yards in total area, and live and work in reasonable harmony is not all that difficult to accept and comprehend. Pitcairn, after all, is a commune. The one-big-family impression remained valid throughout the stay; and if the hackneyed phrase turns up periodically in these pages it is because of that validity. But if a nuclear family of, say, eight, can have factions and secrets, so can our cousin-family of eighty-five. The secrets will be ones exclusive to these internal factions as well as those kept communally from the eyes and ears of outsiders. Again as with the smaller family, the members of a faction will rally at times to score points off a target group. But the point-scoring will be dropped the moment the cousin-family's real group interests are at stake. That this is invariably the case in the Adamstown "family," yet frequently is not so with an orthodox family, rebounds tremendously to Pitcairn's credit.

Many forces have been at work in shaping the "simple" Pitcairn character, and it is this multiplicity of influences that makes a study of the islanders difficult and even a trifle hazardous. One can undertake an in-depth study of a far larger community, the Aleuts, say, or the Kurds, confident in the knowledge that there has been a uniformity in their past, an evenness in their development that has prevailed over many centuries. The Pitcairners are the result of a classic revolt that led to a classic collision of cultures. It would be hard to conceive of two more disparate societies than those of eighteenth-century England and a Polynesia whose centuries-old cocoon of isolation had been newly punctured by the white man.

While few, if any, give it a conscious thought, the present-day Pitcairners are still trying to resolve this cultural conflict. It is, after all, of relatively recent origin.

When the womenfolk wrap their foods in banana tree leaves for the stone oven, or sit cross-legged on the ground weaving pandanus leaves, they present a picture of Polynesians garbed in the fancy dress of the white world. When the men talk engagingly of their "muskets," or put to sea in dirty weather, grim-faced in their hooded black oilskins, they are a remnant of a lost era of Eng-

Mavis Warren stokes the fire in her Polynesian-style stone oven. Later the coals will be raked out, her bread dough in the homemade tins will be placed on racks inside, and the opening covered with a sheet of tin. (Courtesy of Tom Christian)

lishmen, the descendants of sailors who wore pigtails and conquered the world. At services on the Sabbath, the community strains to be impeccably *Anglo*. At a feast in a neighbor's home on Saturday night, once the sun has set on the Sabbath, they are unmistakably Polynesian in their gargantuan appetites and their uninhibited assault on the table's burden. In their passionate love of fishing, they remain close to their Tahitian ancestry. In their sentimental affection for the Royal Family, they display an Englishness that has long since gone out of popular style in the home country. (In the homes I visited, the standard living room decoration, without exception, was a set of portraits of the Queen, Prince Philip, and the Prince of Wales. Vi McCoy has no fewer than twelve, probably a record for the island. In only one home was there any sign of *lèse majesté*. The Queen's front teeth had been inked out to give her a Halloween expression. When Prince Philip came ashore from the Royal Yacht on a visit in 1971, the islanders were horrified that he noticed it. The Queen's husband looked grave for a moment and then told his hosts: "I had no idea my wife had lost that many teeth." It got over a bad moment.)

The Pitcairners use can openers but also cling to native implements that are going out of style in other parts of the South Pacific. They can accept a bikini in Bounty Bay (the Polynesian passion for bodily freedom), yet be censorious about a girdle advertisement in an Australian magazine (a reflex acquired from those outsiders who have tutored them in the ways of a puritanical religion.) In their deep aversion to even short-term planning, they embrace the Polynesian way of living for the single day ahead of them. Yet they are preoccupied with the concept of an afterlife and heavenly rewards to a degree I have rarely encountered in other societies.

In each compartment of human activity, there is a detectable interaction between an *Anglo* life-style, which now must be broadened to include influences from the United States, New Zealand, and Australia as well as Britain, and the enduring Polynesian ways. Each cultural force over the years has shaped or tempered its rival one. In most areas, the victor has been the *Anglo* side. Yet in that most dominant of human interests and activities — sex — the Polynesian ways would appear to have won the day, or at least to have exerted the greater influence.

That is not to say that the girls swim barebreasted in secluded coves, bathe nude under the one small spring, or that there is fleshy cavorting after dark in the shanties of Adamstown. Far from it. But if we accept a society's attitude toward premarital sex as a key indicator of its general sexual standards, then the inhabitants of the *Bounty* isle today are closer to their Tahitian past than their English one. The phrase "sleeping around" is not used on Pitcairn, but that is how many of the young pass their evening leisure hours. The front bedroom of the home of one of the community's most sincerely religious families was used regularly as a love nest by a courting couple, neither of whom belonged to that family. It was set aside exclusively for their use with the full knowledge of the head of the family. No attempt was made to shield the arrangement from the rest of the village, let alone cloak it from the eyes of prying outsiders. It is a practical way to resolve an obvious problem. In a community without shops, dance halls, movie houses, clubs, or organized sporting or cultural activities, what else is there for young people to do? Not only is there nothing *serious* to occupy their minds after dark, there is virtually nothing *frivolous* for them to do. Perhaps in a small, isolated, and underprivileged community such as Pitcairn's, there is inevitably more temptation, even pressure, in the direction of sexual experimentation than there is for young people elsewhere. A Pitcairn girl will return in the dawn light from an overnight date without a thought as to what parental reaction might be. And bear in mind that we are studying here a religious society and one which basically must be considered in the context of "white" rather than "native" manners and norms.

When I explored the situation with one of the island men, the answer I got was pithy enough: "When it comes to sex, and young people are involved, we are Polynesian first and whatever else second." But he qualified this by suggesting that if a Kinsey examination were made of the married Pitcairners, it would reveal a level of sexual activity well below that found in other societies. His theory was that sex blooms young on Pitcairn, is allowed without hindrance to come to full flower, but withers on a still-robust vine. When I asked why he felt this was so, his guess was that it was a reflection of the hard work survival on Pitcairn demands of the adults and the lack of any real leisure time. I suggested that it might also have something to do with the dearth of outside stimulation, the almost total absence of the type of books, magazines, and movies that are concocted for the titillation of Western society. He took this point under advisement.

It is worth recording here that the only specimens of eroticism or commercial sex I saw on the island were three gatefolds of Mr. Hugh Hefner's Playmates for 1971. The rosy-breasted ladies had been tacked up on the walls of a prefabricated hut which had been left behind by an American survey party. The hut, on Pitcairn's dirt main road, is used by the young as a teen-age hangout. It is their privileged retreat, the source of raucous Country-Western music that blares late into the night. Late, that is, by Adamstown standards — 10:30 to 10:45. Grown-ups are not invited there and seldom venture inside. This little outpost of youthful decadence is less than thirty yards from the prim little church. Whether the Pastor has ever permitted himself a peek at the decor, I cannot say.

Copies of *Playboy* are one of the items the young men eagerly accept when gifts are offered by crew members of the freighters that stop occasionally off Bounty Bay. The cargo ships are also their source of condoms, the only type of contraceptive that appears to be employed on the island. The women told my wife that the Pill had not been tried yet on Pitcairn. The problems of ensuring an uninterrupted supply are obvious.

Influenced or not by such innovations, the sexual climate has changed vastly since those days when the islanders presented a united front to outsiders in concealing any of their lapses from chastity. In 1830, when Captain Waldegrave called at Pitcairn, he had unexpected difficulty in taking an accurate census. When he inquired about their total number, the islanders replied eighty-one. But when he and his officers compiled a list of names, the tally invariably came to seventy-nine. Eventually, a member of the community, taking pity on the statistically bewildered Englishmen, came forward and whispered to Captain Waldegrave the first names of two Pitcairners previously withheld. The parents, however, were not identified. "It would be wrong to tell my neighbors' shame," Waldegrave's informant explained.

Illegitimacy since those times has become a fact of life on the island, and the attitude toward "neighbors' shame" has undergone some changes. In 1934, when he spent ten days on Pitcairn to prepare his study of the islanders, Dr. Shapiro estimated that "practically 25 percent of births at present are illegitimate and a considerable number of the permanent unions are not legitimatized, even though they have produced large broods of children." Today, the percentage may be higher. In casual conversation, without wishing to apply any real reportorial zeal in probing an embarrassing area of the community's affairs, I was able to establish that at least five of the present crop of Pitcairn young came from illegitimate unions. There almost certainly are other cases of illegitimacy. In a community with few young and a school roll of only sixteen, this is a substantial number being raised out of wedlock.

Some, the majority perhaps, have been fathered by nonislanders. (The island boys, at least, use the condoms they get from the cargo ships.) One unwed island girl, trying bravely to raise two sturdy boys, has produced her babies exactly a gestation period after the conclusion of successive French nuclear tests on the atoll of Mururoa, 530 miles away. The surprise new additions to the Pitcairn stock are the amorous legacy of British or American monitors stationed on Pitcairn during each French test season to record fallout and blast effect. One of the boys, I was told, "is ah spittin' image of that nice RAF fellow who was here." He even carries the given name of the long-since-departed father. No attempt was made by the family, among the poorer members of the community, to extract child-support money from the men responsible. The boys are being raised as his own sons by their forty-one-year-old grandfather, and a more endearing "father-son" relationship would be hard to find anywhere. Wayward mothers and their illegitimate offspring are accepted by the community as a whole with little, if any stigma attached.

I had the rather uncharitable impression that the Pitcairners of all age groups welcomed any new additions to the colony, regardless of how and by whom the seed was planted. In a community of eighty-five, the birth of a baby, even in irregular circumstances, is an event of resounding importance, emotionally as well as socially and economically. "It is good new stock for the island," several said when the post-test-season babies arrived.

When I discussed with the Pastor the morals of his small flock, he hazarded the guess that the island illegitimacy rate was "5 percent or so, not much more." He recalled with horror reading a recent account that put the current proportion of illegitimate births in New Zealand at one in three. Either the Pastor is not aware of what goes on in his community or is concerned with shielding its defects from the outside world.

He and other leaders of the community are able, however, to shield the Pitcairners from much of the outside world's meretricious offerings. Few movies reach Pitcairn, but those that do are censored twice, first abroad and again when they reach the island. As film-makers crank out increasingly spicier material, the result is that the list of films acceptable to the island entertainment com-

mittee has been shrinking at a fast pace. I joined the islanders for
a Saturday-night picture show in the courthouse, which is an all-
purpose building for public meetings and is used perhaps once or
twice a year, if that, for its nominal purpose.

The two-ring tolling of the community bell, signifying "public
gathering," had given the community thirty minutes advance notice
of the movies. Admission was twenty cents for adults, children half
price. For that, we got a program that was rich in variety but a bit
lean when it came to entertainment. It began with a black-and-
white NASA film on the 1969 Apollo 11 mission, the early *preparations* for it, not the glorious completion. Then we swung into a
film about the operations of Auckland's jet airport that had about
it the heavy hand of a PR film-maker. This was followed by some
celluloid uplift, *Miracle on Pitcairn*, a film made on the island in
1963 by the Seventh-Day Adventist Church. This, the evening's
only color offering, provoked shrieks of laughter and heckling from
the teen-agers as they saw themselves as docile primary-graders.
The evening closed with a look at kangaroo hunting in Australia.

The night at the picture show was not uninstructive. In addition
to picking up a few pointers about air-traffic control in Auckland
and kangaroo tracking in Queensland, I learned for the first time —
it was at the very start of our stay — that Pitcairners *do* use swear
words. It came as a surprise, since every published account I have
read of the Pitcairn society has underscored the point that their
language is as clean as their air. Church publications have also held
up the Pitcairners as a community that abstains from profanity of
any kind. But when the film in the 16 mm. projector snagged and
ripped for the first of innumerable interruptions, the projectionist
at the back of the hall exploded with the first of several "s——'s"
that were to punctuate the evening. From outside the hall came a
response of "f—— ——."

Having been exposed until then only to the gentleness of the islanders, those first few expletives had the effect of an ice-cold
douche. I was to hear plenty of other explosions of four and more
letters during the rest of the stay, although that is not to say that
swearing is anywhere near as common on the island as it is in most
other communities. In general, the young men swear much more
easily and confidently than their fathers. The habit, quite clearly,

has been picked up outside the older male society of the home. Presumably it is a reflection of their contacts with crews of passing ships, a contagion that the Church apparently is no longer able to counteract. The swearing I heard from the lips of older men was reserved for moments of extreme, personal stress. In group actions, however, even during the moments of backbreaking toil involved in manhandling the longboats into and out of the water, the air was unsullied by bad language.

But even the limited amount of swearing to be heard on the island today marks the passing of one more Pitcairn tradition. From the community's earliest days, the word *please* has been used in a special way. At necessary moments, it was barked out either as a term of reproach or for its shock value. It was an *ersatz* cuss word that gave *please* a force and a meaning not found in any dictionary. An older generation still employs the power-packed *please*, but it is a speech refinement the young have spurned.

Those other household-name vices of society at large — nicotine, alcohol, hard and soft drugs — are known on Pitcairn only inasmuch as their traces are introduced occasionally by outsiders. One or two of the island men take a beer when they are offered one in the bar of a visiting liner. Some have acquired the taste for whiskey in trips abroad but have promptly dropped it on their return. The community is one of teetotalers, by law and by popular wish, and a group discipline exists to see that it stays that way. Still, it is faintly disconcerting to see husky Pitcairn men, six-footers with powerful, sea-weathered faces, gathered in a group at a social function quaffing glass after glass of homemade peach or strawberry drink.

The schoolteacher is granted a special license to import a limited amount of beer and liquor, but he is forbidden to offer a drink to an islander, and in practice, none badgers him for a nip. The only liquor I saw in a Pitcairn home was the heel of a bottle of Johnnie Walker Red Label which Christy Warren keeps for medical emergencies. He asked me if I would like a "cocktail," but the level in the bottle was perilously low for me to take him up on his offer. He said he was one of the few on the island to believe in the restorative properties, when wisely used, of Scotch whiskey, and proceeded to tell me the tale of how he had come by this discovery: "I was working over in New Zealand in a foundry for nine months and one day I started coughing up blood. Big Christy down with the pneumonia! My daughter had a bottle of Scotland whiskey in the house, and Christy took a full measure in the bottle cap each morning and night. I kept on going to work with the pneumonia — working hard, mind you, bending the metal into hoes and spades we were making, not spending half an hour in the toilet for a smoke like the other men — and soon I stopped feeling the pneumonia. Then one night my daughter showed me the bottle, almost gone the whiskey was, and said, 'Christy, what happened to this?' I told her what good it had done me when I was down with the pneumonia. That whiskey cut away the pneumonia. It tore right through it until I was no longer spitting up blood. I could feel the whiskey *warming* my chest, *lightening* it as I swallowed the capful before going to work. . . . I give credit to that whiskey. It was *medicine*."

Occasionally, an islander will surreptitiously bring off a visiting ship a few bottles of duty-free Scotch he has taken in exchange for a carving or a collection of Pitcairn stamps. But the liquor is acquired purely for trading purposes. It is kept, untapped, in a seaman's chest, against the day when a yacht will call after a long sail from Panama or Tahiti and the captain will be in a mood to barter frozen meat or chocolate or some other luxury.

Only one Pitcairner, bachelor Morris, sixty-five, smokes, and his source of supply is a mystery to his fellow communards. From the battered tin in which he carries his smokes will come a luxury-length American mentholated one minute and the next an English Virginian with the maker's royal "By Appointment" coat of arms in gold on the paper. By buttonholing the chief stewards of each passing ship, Morris seems able to ensure that he will pass his days without experiencing the ordeal of nicotine withdrawal. Pastor Webster, and the more serious religionists among his flock, have not tried to cure Morris of his ways. He lives alone, is not the brightest of souls, and is hardly the one to set a bad example for the young. But the Pastor was peeved to discover that in the new schoolteacher dispatched from New Zealand, the island had acquired a strong personality who also happened to be a chain-smoker. The children soon dubbed him "Smoke Man." It was a purely descriptive nickname, with no derogatory connotations.

So far as I could determine, the youth drug culture has impinged on the island only twice. A few years ago, a young volunteer from New Zealand, who had arrived to spend a few months helping the islanders in farm husbandry methods, was caught conducting his own irregular bit of horticulture. He had planted marijuana seed on a hillside, and the first crop of Pitcairn Gold was coming along nicely. On one inspection trip, however, he failed to notice that the wife of a church leader had trailed him up the hill. She knew what the plant was and the threat it posed to one of the smallest and most vulnerable groups of young people to be found anywhere. "Burn it!" she demanded. The New Zealand youth hesitated. "Burn it, or I'll report you at once to the Island Magistrate!" The pot farmer pulled up his crop, stacked the leaves, and set fire to them.

A short time later, nineteen pounds of harvested, joint-ready marijuana were landed on Pitcairn and remained there for a few weeks, unwrapped, unrolled, unsmoked. The package of pot was being taken home from Australia by an American youth traveling aboard a freighter that stopped off at Pitcairn. Perhaps it was the simplicity he encountered among the Pitcairners; perhaps he saw here the makings for the cruelest of practical jokes; perhaps it was simply the imminence of confronting a U.S. Customs officer. Whatever the reason, the American traded his nineteen pounds of marijuana for a turtle carved from *miro* wood. The Pitcairn youth who acquired the drug knew his market. He kept it until a French cruising yacht called at Bounty Bay and sold the marijuana for, he claims, $250.

There is, of course, no prostitution in Adamstown — although one notorious Pitcairn girl who migrated to New Zealand was earning a good living as a hooker on the streets of Auckland a few months after landing — and only occasional instances of adultery. Oddly enough, in this society where individual and family privacy scarcely exists, where neighbors drop in uninvited and join a meal already in progress, a spouse has been known to cheat on his or her partner for years and not be detected. One woman, almost every day for two years, undertook mysterious treks into the interior of the island. It was some months after the expeditions had ceased that the islanders learned the reason for the trips, a tryst with a married man. The affair by then had cooled. The juiciest bit of scandal Pitcairn had produced for some time had been wasted on the birds and bees of Aute Walley.

In many areas, there are tight constraints on what young people may do and how they should behave. Dancing, under an Adventist ruling that is reinforced by the Island Government, is strictly forbidden. The Pastor occasionally may lead the schoolchildren and the teen-agers in a tepid square dance, but that is all. Denied dancing in public, the young people obediently refrain from it when they get together in one of their hangouts to listen to records. Dancing for them seems to be invested with mystical taboos. They simply *listen* to the music. There is not even the toe-tapping or syncopated finger-snapping one would expect to see at such gatherings of young people. They know the lyrics of the Rolling Stones or the Beatles, but they lack any rhythmic feel for the music.

I discussed with the Pastor the Church's fear of what dancing might do to these young minds and bodies. He had an answer at the ready, and I suspect he has had to provide the explanation more than once before in cozy chats with young members of his congregation. He was quite satisfied that the ban on dancing was warranted, particularly in a small, remote community that had Polynesian blood moving through its veins.

"It goes back, I suppose, to the first migration from Pitcairn in 1831," he said. "The islanders went back to Tahiti with all hopes of rejoining their ancestry on that side. Instead, they saw the moral degeneration of the Tahitians. They couldn't get out and home fast enough. They saw the *dancing* on Tahiti and saw what we know today, that most of the demoralizing orgies of the South Pacific are associated with *dancing*. It starts with the *dancing* and ends up in other things, other activities. The Pitcairners have been very wary of dancing ever since. A lot of the old people wouldn't know what you meant by dancing."

The Pastor was clearly determined that there would be no dance-inspired teen-age orgies — he pronounced it distastefully and with a hard "g" — during this, his second two-year posting to Pitcairn.

He felt that the record players, which the younger set have acquired in recent years and which shatter the evening calm of Adamstown, were "an invasion of the island," but he wasn't quite sure where it was all leading. "It activates their feet," he allowed. "What they do with them, I don't know. But it doesn't form itself up into mixed dancing as I see it."

If they lack both the ability and the license to dance, the young people of the island have qualities not found in their peer groups in the world beyond. A burly eighteen-year-old boy will spend an afternoon amusing a neighbor's toddler and not consider it either unusual or a waste of time. The teen-age girls care for their cousins' children with all the tenderness and solicitude of the natural mothers. At parties or community gatherings, babies are fed, cuddled, amused, and held by a teen-ager one minute, a grandmother the next, then perhaps by an uncle or a cousin, and sometimes even the actual parents get a turn. This happens, of course, in other communities but certainly not with the naturalness and warmth one finds here. From its earliest moments of consciousness, a baby on Pitcairn acquires the one-family spirit. If the first three or four years of life are the most crucial ones in shaping human character and building up an individual's inner strength, then the infants here are handed security blankets that should serve them for the rest of their lives. Each has not one or two major figures to love and be loved by but, in everyday contacts, as many as a dozen such figures.

Baby-sitters, of course, are unnecessary. When my wife asked two girls in their midteens whether they could look after our children for an afternoon, the girls were noticeably shocked by the offer of payment for their services. Faithfully each morning at 7:15, sixteen-year-old Dave would arrive by the porch of our house to give our six-year-old a lift to school on the pillion of his Honda.

Whatever else it may have done to them, isolation has engendered in the Pitcairners a true sense of caring for another individual, whether he be eight months or eighty. Each human life is precious on this remote rock. The spirit of cooperation that has enabled the community to survive is based only partly on practical considerations. It is rooted as much in the heart as in the mind.

What little each family might have is there for all to share if need be, a Pitcairn attitude that long ago was institutionalized into the "Share Out." Whenever a ship calling at Pitcairn makes the islanders a gift of food, the cargo is carried up the hill, deposited in the Square, and divided into twenty-four equal lots — one for each of the twenty-two households and one each for the Pastor and the schoolteacher. Frequently, the lots are pathetically small — tiny piles of three or four potatoes, a dozen or so crackers taken from a large box, a single tin of sardines, an odd-lot of flour, and so on. A "household" is considered to be any individual or group living under a separate roof. By a puzzling Pitcairn logic, bachelor Morris, living alone, is entitled to the same size lot as Len, who heads a household of seven.

Four bells are sounded on the old ship's bell in the Square to announce the start of the Share Out, and the families gather there with baskets and empty cans. The Share-Out ceremony is conducted in a manner devised around the middle of the nineteenth century to avoid the slightest hint of favoritism in the distribution. Once the piles have been set up on the ground or on trestle tables, the Island Magistrate starts a most formal divvying process. He selects a pile, walks toward it, and announces: "Who gets this lot?" A clerk, with his back to the proceedings, so he has no way of seeing which particular pile the Magistrate has paused beside, reads off at random from a list the name of a household. The family then steps forward with their containers to collect it. (This same procedure, even the words, "Who gets this lot?" was used by eighteenth-century English seamen whenever food or goods were being shared, either some treat that had come the ship's way, or in times when there was hardship and scarcity. Bligh himself used it during his open-boat voyage to Timor whenever the loyalist party had been able to catch a noddy bird. Bligh's phrase was a little daintier. After the pigeon-sized noddy had been dissected into eighteen pieces, he would hold up the pieces and start asking: "Who shall have this?")

Occasionally, there are bonanza days. Recently, a New Zealand freighter stopped at Bounty Bay and the captain asked the islanders whether they could use 1,800 pounds of frozen prime rump steak. The meat had been part of a consignment from New Zealand to the United States. Through an import quota mixup, only part of it could be offloaded. The 1,800 pounds left on board were carried back to New Zealand, where the shipper found that the meat, once exported, could not be placed on the domestic market. The cases of rump steak remained in the freezer when the freighter sailed for Panama. The captain's instructions were to dispose of them as he wished. He had called at Pitcairn before and knew of the islanders' craving for meat that had survived all the years of Adventist preaching on the dietary and religious benefits of vegetarianism. The meat was accepted, of course, and each household carried home from this glorious Share Out 75 pounds of rump steak. They gorged on steak for a week and salted down the remainder in earthernware jars for later use in stews and soups.

The Share Out mentality has had a subtle effect on some of the outsiders who have lived on Pitcairn for any length of time. Russell Henry, the schoolteacher from New Zealand, told me that when he began his tour of duty there, his attitude was that it would be wrong for him, the recipient of a princely salary by island standards, to participate in Share Outs. "But after a while I felt that I was in the same boat as the islanders and, as such, I wanted to get my share," he added. "The same applied to the Pastor. I have watched my children become real Pitcairners. When there is a Share Out, they make sure they get their bit of what's going."

The experience on Pitcairn changed Henry in other ways that are reflective of the Pitcairn character. It has cured him and his family of the wasteful habits of a consumer society. "I am going home a far thriftier and resourceful man than I was when I arrived," he said. "One of the captains of a ship that stopped by the other day called out to Pervis [Island Magistrate Pervis Young], 'Do you take hessian?' Pervis shouted back, 'We take anything!' I've found that I've got into this habit. I collect and save things. I never throw anything away anymore. If I take a screw out of a piece of wood, I put it carefully in a jar. Perhaps that's why I'm leaving with twenty-three crates when we arrived here with seven or eight! And I've also become a more resourceful man, a jack of all trades. I fix things now that I'd never dream of tackling in New Zealand — 16 mm. projectors, typewriters, electric razors." The schoolteacher also surprised himself and his family by building a motorboat from materials and designs shipped out from New Zealand.

The schoolteacher said that in general, he found the children were one, two, or more years behind their New Zealand counterparts, a not unexpected degree of backwardness. In secondary grades, which Henry was not obliged to teach but did so as an accommodation to the island young, the difference in educational performance was more pronounced. There were many things he liked about teaching school on Pitcairn — he stayed a year beyond his two-year term — and some things which irritated him.

"They are without doubt the most obedient children I have ever taught," he said. "But you wonder sometimes what you are educating them *for*. They don't read, and I found it impossible to get them to develop an interest in reading. All the children are interested in are the ships out there. Even the books that could be of use to them, the 'How to Do This,' the 'How to Do That' books, they either can't manage or aren't interested in. When they reach sixty here, and when their work in the gardens is over each day, they simply vegetate. The young who have gone abroad look back on this as a dead-end society, and I suppose they are right."

In a world that is perhaps overly supplied with mental stimulation, Pitcairn has virtually nothing to challenge the intellect or churn up the mind. The situation is remediable, of course, but the society does nothing to change things. Not *once* did I see a Pitcairner engrossed in a book other than the Bible. They weren't watching television sets, because they don't exist here and probably never will. They do have a tiny public library which is open for thirty minutes two evenings a week. Book borrowing is rare. The shelves offer mild fiction but virtually nothing about the islanders' own history. Current affairs is another void. Many of the homes have short-wave radios, but they are rarely turned on. We lived on Pitcairn in almost total ignorance of what was going on in the world at large, in a news vacuum in which many members of the community are content to spend the rest of their lives. The only item of news that was brought to our attention — two days after the event — was President Nixon's devaluation of the dollar.

This development was one of the very few things occurring in the world that could have an impact on their society. A cheapened dollar would have to be taken into account in trading aboard passing ships. They have no interest in discussing, say, the horrors of Bangladesh or the changes in China and no real desire to become informed about the political cataclysms of our time. A minor earthquake in New Zealand, where most of the islanders have relatives, is of far more interest to them than a major war in the Middle East.

Though of comparatively recent origin, their own language holds mysteries for most of them, mysteries that apply even to words the islanders have coined in this century.

That two tongues came to Pitcairn when it was settled is immediately apparent. The derivation of perhaps half of the words can be guessed at with reasonable accuracy once one becomes used to the intonation, the way simple English words have been adapted, and the pattern of syntactical distortion. In island dialect, "good-bye" is *toby*. It is pronounced to-*bai*. It is a good example of the pidgin-English element in Pitcairnese. A toddler will often say something like "to-*bai*" when he makes his first attempts at pronouncing "good-bye." It is not hard to imagine the *Bounty* men, as they struggled to teach their Tahitian companions English rather than accept the native tongue, the majority language brought to the island, giving their pupils the word "good-bye" and hearing it come back as "to-*bai*." "How are you?" became W*ut a way you?* *Humuch* developed as an all-purpose phrase for "how often" and "how many" as well as "how much." *Humuch shep corl ya?* — "How often do ships call?" *Humuch cocknuts?* — "How many coconuts?" (The islanders say *cocknuts* because that is the way the word was pronounced by eighteenth-century Englishmen.) *I'sa dona* ("I have finished") is clearly pidgin. When there is a duplication of a word, one must search for a Polynesian origin. *Mono-mono* means "excellent." In Tahitian, *mona* means pleasant or sweet.

I came across many words, however, that some of the best brains on the island could not explain. *Fa'hilo* was one. It means toilet paper, either rolls or cut-up newspaper. It was a puzzling word because there is no apparent connection with either Tahitian or English. I asked questions about its derivation but to no avail. On our final morning, an old-timer came down to The Edge specifically to enlighten me on this word. "The first real paper for the *dunkuns* we saw on the island came from Hilo on the big island of Hawaii," he said. "We used to call Hilo 'far Hilo' from the days when sailing vessels used to come down here from the Hawaiian Islands. And that's the name we gave the toilet paper that came from Hilo, the rolls from far Hilo — *fa'hilo*." In such ways as this, the Pitcairners have added to the unique language that came into being when a few Englishmen, thrown together with a few Polynesians, evolved a common working tongue that has been spoken over the years by a total of little more than a thousand people.

A common early impression of outsiders who have spent some time on the island is of a colony of unusually creative people. They do meticulous carving, basketwork, and other souvenirs. One soon comes to realize, however, that the items represent workmanship alone, with just the merest flick of creativity. Every turtle, every gull, every flying fish, every shark the men carve is a replica of the one that was completed yesterday. The carvings are often done from templates, sometimes patterns handed down from father to son, and most still hew fairly faithfully to the designs originally developed by an Austrian named Laeffler. This man, the father of Pitcairn carving, spent some time on the island in the early part of the century and is responsible for the curio industry that has developed. And today, as the men carve, they are thinking of only one thing: the cash return it will bring when a ship calls. Still, it is probably unfair to expect more from the Pitcairn carvers than what they are producing by whittling and sanding and waxing bits of *miro* every second they can devote to it. The curios are virtually their sole source of private income. They make what will sell. Yet many times I found myself wishing that one man, just one Pitcairner, would attempt something ambitious, would apply his undoubted carving ability to a genuine work of art. It has never happened and probably never will.

When a ship arrives, they offer their carvings for three, five, or ten dollars, and the tourists or crew members try to knock the price down to half what was asked. Trading in these circumstances often can be a demeaning experience. A man who has spent two or three days carving and polishing to perfection a glorious leaping fish will hear the ship's departure siren sound and may be forced to sacrifice the labor of his hands for a couple of devalued dollars. Some of the men and women have a zest for trading. Christy and Anderson Warren are natural salesmen who would have prospered in the most competitive of societies. But most of the men and women find the hawking of curios a humiliating experience, conscious always that they themselves are being examined by the tourists as human curios. It is certainly one of the factors that have contributed to the collective inferiority complex one finds on the island. They assume automatically that outsiders will know more than they do, even on subjects intimately linked with their own existence.

They have a singular reluctance to commit themselves to any course of action. The Pastor one day was trying to extract an expression of opinion from his congregation on whether the two church Elders to be elected for the following year should have equal status or whether they should continue the practice of having a senior and a junior Elder. The Pastor and the committee had recommended the change be made. It was explained to the sixty-odd people in the hall in the simplest possible terms. But when Pastor asked those in favor to raise their hands, there was not a single affirmative vote. "Those against?" Again not a hand was raised. "Then you all abstain?" Pastor asked, not, presumably, intending any pun. Nobody signified that he wished to abstain. Pastor explained the proposition again, and this time when he called for "yea's" there were three hands raised. "Then it is carried," he announced, a note of slight desperation in his voice.

They are a diffident people and markedly superstitious. Fear of the dark exists in this society that lives without crime. There are no muggers, but it is easy to imagine some nameless threat lurking in the night among those dark, still dirt lanes with the weird, twisted "walking banyans" looming overhead. And always in view from Adamstown, by the starlight of the clear constellations if there is no moon, is the ghostly gray cave to which Fletcher Christian retired to think about what he had done. In some lights, it looks uncannily like an abstract skull sculpture. No human threat exists . . . but might not there be something else, perhaps something worse? One man even makes a fetish of it. Even by day he can be seen with three flashlights in the hip pockets of his jeans. About half an hour before each sundown, he tests each to make sure it is working, to check that batteries, which are among the luxury items on Pitcairn, have not gone dead in unison. Pastor has noticed the superstitiousness and mentions it. I had asked him, for some reason which I now forget, why the outhouses were always two-holers. His belief was that the arrangement enabled a husband or wife, if he or she wished, to have a *known* companion on the trip to the privy if one were necessary in the depths of the night.

Among their other distinctions is their attitude toward food. When you go through the parting formalities after one of their parties, the dining room and kitchen a disaster area of emptied dishes and plates, the host's good-bye is always: "So long as you get enough." The Pitcairner's life, as the reader may have guessed, is oriented toward the acquisition and the consumption of food to what may be a unique degree. Six days a week, the Sabbath being the exception, Warren's and Millie's entire waking days are applied to activities that are somehow connected with food. The day will have started with Warren building the open fire in "the bolt." Millie will spend the morning preparing beans or *pillhai* or a stew of chicken. Warren will be weeding or harvesting in his garden on the high ground. The noon hour will be spent eating and cleaning up after the "breakfast." Millie's afternoon will be devoted to more preparation of food, bread baking, Warren's big "tea," perhaps a cake or a special dessert for her son-in-law's house. Warren will be off to the high ground again, either working in his garden or gathering firewood for the stove and oven where the vegetables eventually will be cooked. If there are spare moments during the day or at night, they will be applied to the production of curios — Warren's carving and Millie's weaving of baskets, hats, and pandanus fans. The dollars obtained when they are sold will be used exclusively to buy flour or imported canned food.

The routine is broken only on the Saturday Sabbath. The fires

At the end of an island feast, Tom Christian samples his host's watermelon.

are lit for "hot drink," but all of the food for consumption on the Sabbath will have been cooked on the Friday which Pitcairners call "Preparation Day."

An island etiquette has developed around the subject of food. It can be witnessed not in the arena of table manners, which tend to be sloppy, but in the outdoor life. The tradition has always been that an islander may raid someone else's coconut tree for the water in the nuts if he becomes thirsty while trekking across the island. If he becomes hungry away from his house, he may help himself to the pineapples, oranges, or mangoes of others. The stipulation, however, is that the fruit must be eaten on the spot. Then, it is merely relieving a stomach pang; to carry it home would be stealing. The islanders' appetites may have provided the inspiration for this rule of etiquette. One day, while resting on the ground after a walk, my Pitcairn companion put away four sun-warm pineapples and then used the seamen's knife that all men carry at all times on their belts to slice up a small watermelon. And this was simply a snack between "breakfast" and "tea." Fortunately, we were resting in his own orchard patch.

The food intake, heavy though it may be on starchy vegetables, is certainly not unhealthy. A Texas physician, Dr. David Gibson of Grand Prairie, who arrived aboard the brigantine *Romance* a month after I had left and spent some time examining the population, gave them a glowing health report: "It would be difficult to find a comparable population anywhere in the world as healthy, robust and physically fit as these people. I am amazed to see fifty- and sixty-year-olds trotting up and down the steep paths of this little island. And it is nothing to see Pitcairn men of more than seventy scrambling up rope ladders to the decks of ships like only twenty-year-olds elsewhere might do. Apart from some minor surgical procedures, there really isn't much to do."

The Pitcairners have mental traits which seem to be attributable either to their origins or to the special conditions of island life. Both men and women have a phenomenal memory when anything dealing with ships and the sea is involved. On other topics — local history, dates, events, local origins of words or customs — they seem to be curiously forgetful. But the visits of liners, warships, freighters, and yachts remain stamped indelibly in their minds long after the event. At one social evening, the maritime traffic of ten, twenty, even thirty years in the past was being recalled by a group of islanders. As each ship's name was mentioned, those in the room remembered exactly who had disembarked or taken passage on her, what major cargo had been offloaded, the sea conditions at the time, what dunnage the captains had put over the side for them to use as lumber, the moods of the captains, and so on: "We slept in ah longboats all night in ah lee o' ah land for that 'un to come." "That was ah time we lost *Dumpy* [a longboat]." "Remember that captain from Denmark? He was in a right temper. Kept 'er running ahead all ah while we was offloading — threatened a' one point to tek off wi' all ah menfolk aboard and carry us on to Panama. 'What, wi' Christians and Youngs on board!' we told him. Oooh, what ah mutiny *he* would've had if he'd set off for Panama wi' us aboard."

As parents, these people can be exceedingly indulgent with their children. Once he has completed his island schooling, a youth is not required by his father or mother to meet any set regimen of duties around the house or on the family's fruit and vegetable garden. Instead, he follows a rather aimless — at least by outside standards — routine of drifting about the village, fishing or swimming, or doing some casual carving. The real work — the planting, weeding, and harvesting, the gathering of firewood for the kitchens, the essential repairs to homes that constantly need further improvisation, the stockpiling of curios for trading when the ships arrive — is done by the parents. It reflects, perhaps, a real fear on the part of the parents that if life is made too hard for the young generation they will all leave for the easier city life of Australia or New Zealand.

In a part of the world where dogs sometimes turn up cooked on the tables of humans — on a few atolls in French Polynesia, mongrels are still raised as the only source of meat — the Pitcairners cherish pets. The English blood seems to have prevailed

In matters of tidiness, they compare unfavorably with many other small communities of Polynesia. A litter of things acquired from the Outside and carelessly discarded becomes a play area for the children.

here. The island mutts are big, black lumbering hounds that may have had some Labrador in their past. One sire, with the appropriate name of "Super," has fathered all sixteen of the dogs now on the island. There are only two bitches to keep him company in his waning years, and one of these, the islanders told me, appeared to be some sort of canine hermaphrodite. The pet owners always bring a doggy bag along for scraps when they attend a party.

In their human dealings, the islanders are astonishingly generous, embarrassingly hospitable and honest to a cent. They are not, however, uninterested in money. They are as anxious to amass it as any ma-and-pa storeowners in Brooklyn, and as anxious, too, to find out exactly how much their cousin-families are amassing. In our last days on the island, perhaps a quarter of the community came individually to me and asked, courteously but point-blank, how much we were paying the young man whom we had hired as grip to move the documentary film equipment. In a society which exhibits few, if any, outward signs of human greed, their intense curiosity surprised me. There were rumors that Noggie was getting $100 a month, $35 for a single chore, and so on. (In fact we paid him $10 a week; over a month, it meant that a casual film grip was receiving more than the $37 stipend of the Pitcairn chief executive, Island Magistrate Pervis.)

Racial prejudice exists to a degree. It is apparent when a ship calls with Chinese, Indian, or Negro crewmen. It is present in the nickname "Nigger" the teen-agers have applied to one of the boys whose skin is considerably darker than the Pitcairn norm. Yet on occasions they boast of their Polynesian blood. What animus exists seems to be directed at non-Polynesian color. It is traceable to Pitcairn's earliest years. When Fletcher Christian's half-caste son, Thursday October Christian, went on board one of the first Royal Navy ships to call at Pitcairn after the colony's discovery, a contemporary account records that he became agitated over the presence of a West Indian steward in the captain's cabin. "I am leaving now," said young Christian. "I don't like the look of that black man."

And somehow, the nineteenth- and twentieth-century hates of a Europe half a world away have managed to spread a seed or two to this little rock in the ocean. Several times I heard the word "Jew" used as a verb meaning to cheat or defraud. "He tried to *Jew* me," said a Pitcairner of a crewman he had been trading with. In this usage, a remote colony was accepting and perpetuating the prejudice of a distant world. (The Jews are not a seagoing people; how many Jewish traders would have made contact with the Pitcairners over the years?)

The community's lack of aesthetic appreciation I found a depressing feature of island life. With few exceptions, the Pitcairners have done very little to bring any touches of charm to their homes or their community environment. They are content to live, as I saw on my very first day, amidst indescribable litter. The walls of their houses are generally bare of decorative touches. When the men make a bed or a bench or a table, it is slapped together in the simplest style and without the adornments of carving or painted design which are added by craftsmen in many peasant societies. Clothes that may or may not be worn again someday are heaped in odd corners of their houses. I doubt whether windows are ever cleaned. The corrugated metal roofs and sides of houses rust away without knowing the lick of a paintbrush. There is money in many of these households for a few gallons of paint; but I imagine that the solitary can I saw on the shelves of the Coop store — the shade was Placid Green — will remain there for months to come. Only in the homes of those Pitcairners who have lived abroad for any length of time does one encounter any decorative touches, any evidence of proper housekeeping.

In matters of tidiness and aestheticism, the Pitcairn colony, I regret to say, compares unfavorably with communities of pure Polynesian stock. The home of a Tahitian of equivalent education is far tidier and more attractive. In Mangaréva, a distant outpost of French Polynesia and Pitcairn's closest neighbor, a tiny Polynesian community, with no more resources than the Anglo-Polynesians of Adamstown, has managed to create a village that is trim and charming. There are bright *pareu* curtains at the windows, the grass is clipped around the houses, the rooms are neat, the floors are washed. The Mangarévans, like Polynesians across the Pacific, use their sumptuous flora to make crowns for their hair and garlands for visitors. The Pitcairners may appreciate the lush flowers their home island produces, but they have lost the art of using them for personal decoration or to bring a splash of beauty into their homes. On a couple of occasions when I saw a Pitcairn woman place a white frangipani blossom behind an ear, it was done with such self-consciousness that the gesture lost all of its natural charm.

Who and what have robbed these half-Polynesians of such traits as this? Is it the strength of the English admixture? The Church? The historic isolation?

A bit of each perhaps, compounded by the very impermanence of the Pitcairn society. In a community which regularly reviews the prospect that the island might have to be evacuated one, five, ten

years from now, there is understandably little incentive to raise
shanties to the level of homes. And each Sabbath day they are
solemnly reminded of the home they will have someday for eternity,
the heavenly mansion Jesus is preparing for their use.

CHAPTER FOURTEEN

COMMUNAL WORK, COMMUNAL PLAY

THE ARRIVAL of an Ecuadorian banana boat from Guayaquil provoked no less interest on Pitcairn than a call by a majestic cruise liner. "A ship is a ship," they say on the island. No matter what size, what nationality, the arrival of a ship brings the outside world to Pitcairn's doorstep, the same world their ancestors long ago were fleeing.

The previous night, only three men had attended the seven o'clock Tuesday Prayer Meeting. "It must be the ship," said the Pastor. "It's due at three or four in the morning." The ship, the *AE*, had been the chief topic of conversation for several days. Every ship is a "sail" to the Pitcairners, even a liner or an oil tanker, and there had been no "sail" sighted since our ketch had paused briefly in stormy seas off Bounty Bay to deposit our party. Even though the *AE* was less than three thousand tons, was arriving with no passengers, and had only three Dutch officers and a small crew from Guayaquil, the women had been weaving with redoubled energy and the men were rushing carvings to completion or assembling their display sheets of Pitcairn stamps. The potential market was ridiculously small. But at least it was a *market*. The islanders began dropping by the house of Tom, the radio officer, to find out whether he had heard a definite time of arrival.

The retiring schoolteacher, his wife, and three young children were going home to New Zealand on the banana boat, and most

of the available manpower on the island had been needed a day
ahead of the ship's arrival to move his personal belongings down
to the Landing. We had had torrential rain, almost without in-
terruption, for three days and the tracks of Adamstown had become
obstacle courses of gluey, sloshing red mud. In these conditions,
the little tractor could not negotiate the steep pathway cut into
the cliffs rising above Bounty Bay. The crates were moved down
to the Landing on the telpher, the old cable hoist the islanders
call the "flying fox," but the motorboat the schoolteacher had
built on the island, and some of the other bulky items, had to be
manhandled down the steep incline in pounding rain. It was one
of those moments on Pitcairn when the few machines the island
possesses are rendered useless by the elements, and the demands
on men's muscles are the same as in the eighteenth or nineteenth
centuries.

Our host, Warren, retired for the evening unusually early,
around nine o'clock, having dispensed with his customary prebed
ritual of three cups of strong tea, consumed while carving a wooden
vase or sanding and waxing some model Pitcairn wheelbarrows for
trading. He had laid out his sou'wester and assembled in a well-
used plastic bag the few items he planned to offer on the AE. He
promised to call me at two thirty in the morning so we would have
time to light the fire and get some hot tea inside us before going
out to the banana boat.

We were already awake and dressed, then, when the community
alarm bell was rung around three in the morning. Five bells, repeated at intervals for a bit over a minute, the signal to the
islanders that a "sail" had been sighted. The Pitcairners have used
the ship's bell in the village square as their basic means of communication throughout most of the island's history. One of the
earliest lessons taught to children is that they must never, never
in play sound the main bell or the relay bell about a hundred yards
down the track from the Square. The relay bell today has a deep
hole dug beneath it, the remedy the islanders adopted when one
toddler could not be cured of reaching for the rope, clanging the
bell a confusing number of times, and putting the community on
false alert. Over the years, the bell code has remained the same:

Five bells: "Sail Ho!"
Four bells: Public Share Out of goods received from passing ships
Three bells: Public work, in lieu of income tax, for all able-bodied
    men between fifteen and sixty-five.
Two bells: Village meeting.
One bell: Religious services.

Some of the young men had spent the night on the cliffs, straining their eyes across the dark Pacific for the first pinpoint of light from the masthead of the visitor from Guayaquil. When they saw it, they had raced down to the Square to ring the bell, letting out exuberant whoops of "Sail H-o-o!" as they went. It was a brooding, moonless night. There was something excitingly Conradian about the shouts and the bell ringing in the midst of a sleeping community of seafarers, the sort of excitement one rarely experiences when the events, even the role-players, of a lost era have sudden and authentic rebirth before one's eyes and ears. The bells started the black mongrels of Adamstown barking and wailing, as if they, too, felt they had a part to play in alerting the village to the imminent arrival of people from the "Outside."

We stumbled and slipped by flashlight along the quagmired track through the village and gingerly began the descent down the cliff track to the Landing. The heavy rain had loosed landslides down the final stretch of the Hill of Difficulty, and a day of public work would be needed to put it back in shape. Pervis and a half-dozen men were already at work in the large boathouse, starting the routine of moving two cumbersome longboats out of their shelter and onto the slip in preparation for launching. More men and youths were arriving every few minutes. Some carried coconut-frond baskets packed with pineapples, grapefruit, mangoes, and watermelons to barter with the *AE*'s crew. One man, forgetting presumably that we were meeting a banana boat, had in his load a bunch of the delicious little Pitcairn "apple-bananas." All the men had carvings at the bottoms of their baskets. Since women are not allowed to trade on cargo ships, the men had brought with them samples of the hats and shopping baskets their wives and daughters had woven from dyed pandanus strips.

The first longboat moved fairly easily down the slipway and was tethered beside the rough little concrete-and-stone jetty for loading. Even at the lip of the slipway, the assault of the surf can be brutal. Two men were posted in the longboat to watch the ropes and see that the flank timbers of the hull were not splintered against the dock. The rest of the men turned to the second of the thirty-seven-foot-long whalers, and this launching proved far more difficult. In the darkness, the scarred white longboat shuddered a few yards down the slip and then sat stubbornly on the seaweed-slimed ramp. Two dozen men put their shoulders to the sides·of this sturdy vessel they had built with their own hands. Bare, calloused feet strained to get a grip on the ramp.

"Wun, ta-a, three-ee," signaled Pervis. "Move ah shi-i-i-p."

It took about a quarter of an hour before the longboat joined its twin in seas that were surging with undiminished fury right up to the little rim of shingle at the Landing. I was in the second boat to leave, and I watched a bit dubiously as the first tackled the nearest high, curving threat of breakers some twenty yards from the slip.

With fifteen men aboard, Pervis gripping the stern with one powerful arm and using the other to work the long, battered steering oar, the longboat reared up violently against the sea at an angle of fully forty-five degrees. It hung on the breaker for a moment, long enough for us on shore to see the scars and gouges of sea ravage on the underside, and then plunged back into the water. Progress ahead was painfully slow, and to accomplish what little headway they made, the men in the boat were taking the sort of pounding and drenching one might expect to get far out at sea but hardly within hailing distance of a "harbor."

The waters of Bounty Bay that morning were boiling with the commotion of an ocean that had not felt the resistance of land since its great roll from the East had washed against Easter Island, 1,400 miles distant. In the inner reaches of the bay there was hardly a patch of blue water. In the predawn half-light, it was the color of oyster stew, the specks of black rock jutting up through the foaming surface like ground pepper from a giant's mill.

The men in our boat, still moored heavily to the jetty, instinctively kept their eyes trained on the whaler that had gone ahead. They had seen this sight hundreds of times in their lifetime, yet it held as much fascination for them as it did for me. Partly,

of course, there was concern that sons or fathers, uncles and cousins, would move out unscathed through the slams of the ocean. But they relished it, too, as an *event*, a rare injection of drama and excitement into the Pitcairn existence.

Once the first boat had negotiated the surf and was bobbing about in the ocean swell, the Lister diesel in our longboat was started up and we set out to form a little convoy with her. I had no oilskins with me so Warren thoughtfully draped a tarpaulin around my shoulders. It provided little protection. I was soon soaked to the skin. I remember thinking bitterly at the time whether a passing banana boat could possibly be worth all this effort and bone-pounding discomfort.

The sun by now had risen fiercely red behind the tall, jagged outcrop of rock that Pitcairners call Ship Landing Point. The banana boat, her white hull bathed in the warm pink of a Pacific sunrise, was hove to about two miles from the island. When the longboat twins tossingly came alongside, we discovered that the islanders had got her name wrong. She was not the *AE* but the *EA*. The Dutch captain later told us that she had been built to carry expensive refrigerated cargoes to the sheikdoms of the Persian Gulf, but had been demoted to banana boat when a Japanese concern gave the sheiks a much better charter deal. The name she bore was that of a pre-Mohammedan Arabian goddess, the one charged with controlling the oceans, lakes, and rivers, and the destinies of the men who sailed them. On this particular day, she wasn't performing at her best, so far as we were concerned.

From her rail high above us, the *EA*'s Ecuadorian crew stared down in bafflement at the odd gaggle of men in our boats, men who looked like sailors, but obviously weren't, who weren't white men, weren't natives either, but something in between.

There was a delay while Pervis convinced the captain by shouts and signals that the water was too rough for boarding or cargo handling. "Better in the lee o' the land," the Island Magistrate bellowed up to the bridge. The longboats led the way around to the sheltered side of the island, and the *EA* dropped her Jacob's ladder down to us. To the Pitcairners' keen disappointment, the *EA* kept her derricks in their nests. Once they had boarded the ship, the islanders would have to drop ropes to the longboats and hand-

Dirty weather in Bounty Bay. One longboat is safely in the water, the second is about to be manhandled down the slip. It was the morning the *EA* called.

haul up the side of the vessel the departing schoolteacher's motor-boat and all twenty-three of his heavy crates. "But this captain isn't too bad, really," one of the islanders informed me. "Some of the cargo boat skippers keep their engines running ahead all the time we are alongside, as if they were *deliberately* testing our seamanship."

About a third of the Pitcairn men stayed in the longboats or at the freighter's rail to handle the freight and four bags of mail going aboard the ship. The *EA* was carrying no cargo for Pitcairn because, like many other steamship companies today, her Dutch owners were not willing to delay a vessel off Pitcairn for more than an hour or two to take care of the island's modest needs.

The human freight she was taking aboard went up the side with dispatch. The black-bearded schoolteacher looped a rope in turn under the armpits of his three young children, and a Pitcairner on the deck hauled them up from the bucking longboat. It was a wild departure for the teacher's family but only an experience to match their arrival. The Russell Henrys had come by freighter three years earlier, arriving off Pitcairn in thunderous seas in the middle of the night. The captain refused to hang around until sunrise, and the Henrys, with a twelve-month-old baby boy and two girls under four, had to make a midnight transfer into the longboats. The children were put in rucksacks and lowered down ropes from the ship's side. The surf in Bounty Bay at the time was too stormy to attempt an entry by night, so the longboat captains decided to ride out the darkness on the lee side of the island. The children and their parents spent the night in one of the open boats, huddling under tarpaulins with the Pitcairn crew. "The price of education," the schoolteacher remarked philosophically.

The men had just under an hour of trading aboard the *EA*. In general, they are most reticent about discussing their personal trading profits, almost as if the specter of income tax had arrived on Pitcairn and an Internal Revenue spy were eavesdropping on their sales activities. But I was present in the captain's stateroom when Pervis and a friend clinched a $75 sale for four carved fish and an assortment of birds and turtles. The captain also bought, for a dollar apiece, five copies of a booklet, the official Pitcairn *Guide*. He had intended to buy only a couple, one each for his two sons, but he fell victim to a classic example of Pitcairn soft-sell. "You might as well take all five. They're all I have left," said the seller with a hang-dog expression. The captain couldn't resist.

In calling on the captain, Pervis, in addition to doing some personal trading, was also performing one of the Island Magistrate's unwritten duties — to keep a visiting skipper engaged in conversation for as long as possible so that the men have more time for selling their wares. Some of the Island Magistrates have developed whole repertoires of anecdotes so they can entertain the captains with Pitcairn exotica long beyond the time the ships had allotted for their calls.

As do most ships, the EA permitted the Pitcairners to wander at liberty about the decks. Captains and crews know the islanders' reputation for scrupulous honesty and know there is no risk in leaving cabins unlocked. When the Royal Yacht *Britannia* called at Pitcairn in February, 1971, her captain, for the first time in the ship's history, permitted shore visitors to roam freely about the ship and even, forfend! to hawk their goods aboard.

The islanders' trading aboard the EA gave them an unknown amount of dollars, about twenty pounds of fresh meat, a real luxury, and a few cases of Coca-Cola. The appeal that Coke had for both the young and old men I found both fascinating and a bit distressing. Here were people from an island that produced the most delicious fruit juices imaginable — orange, pineapple, lime, grapefruit, strawberry — and in quantities to quench the thirst of an army. Yet they craved the artificial pop from a distant factory. For a small case of it, they would surrender a carving they had worked at, off and on, for a week or two.

The commerce aboard the banana boat must have been reasonably good as the island treated the EA's crew to the traditional hymns and songs of farewell. "If the folk on a boat haven't bought, we often pull back to shore in silence," a Pitcairner enlightened me. "It's *bad* of us to do it, but it's what happens."

Those aboard ships which give the island carvers and weavers a disappointing commercial return are the losers here, for the chorusing from the longboats is a moving and memorable experience. With gray-haired Christy Warren leading the singing with his booming voice, the clear tones of some thirty naturally gifted

singers wafting across the howl of the ocean, they sang "Cling to the Bible, My Boy," "Shall We Gather By the River, That Flows By the Throne of God," and last, the "Good-bye Song," composed and written on Pitcairn last century by the only poet and composer . the island can boast, Rosalind Amelia Young:

> Now one last song we'll sing — Good-bye, Good-bye;
>   Time moves on rapid wings — Good-bye;
> And this short year will soon be past,
>   Will soon be numbered with the last,
> But as we part to all we'll say —
>   Good-bye, Good-bye, Good-bye,
> But as we part to all we'll say,
>   Good-bye, Good-bye, Good-bye.

The Dutchmen on the *EA*'s bridge answered with some blasts on the siren, the longboat men shouted "Godspeeds" to a well-liked schoolteacher waving from the stern rail, and it was time for this mighty (it seemed) banana boat to continue plowing on across the ocean, returning Pitcairn once more to her isolation.

We shipped more seas on the rough ride back in through the surf, but at least we dodged those vicious black rocks again. We clambered ashore sea-soaked, glad to see that the womenfolk had troubled to make the long climb down from the cliffs with steaming pots of tea and mugs and lemon slices.

On Monday, the Pitcairn men had been seafarers. On Tuesday, they went back to being tillers of the soil. On Wednesday, they gathered soon after dawn at the sugar press, a ramshackle piece of equipment in a ramshackle shed by the cliffside burying ground.

Charles Christian had four barrowloads of sugar cane to be crushed. Most of the men and some of the women came along to lend him a hand. There was also a good turnout of children, even the toddlers being aware that cane-crushing day offers a bonus, a sort of candy porridge. The confection has no name, and the islanders claim it was invented on Pitcairn.

Their cane crusher was shipped to them from the West Indies after seeing service there for most of the nineteenth century. A museum piece, blackened by the cane juice of a hundred island

The longboats are safely back at the Landing. Packed in pandanus baskets, the fresh meat and other items the islanders acquired on the *EA* are hauled up to The Edge on the "flying fox," or telpher.

The day they crushed Charles Christian's sugarcane. His daughter Carol feeds the lengths of cane into the old crusher while the men and youths man the spokes of the creaking capstan.

harvests, it is held together now by baling wire. The press uses the principle of a ship's capstan. Half a dozen men were assigned to each spar of the capstan, some pushing the nine-foot-long arms made from tree trunks, others tugging at them with ropes. Charles's daughter, Carol, fed the cane, a stalk at a time, into the jaws of the press, dodging down each time the heavy spars passed over her. Meanwhile, in a little shed adjoining the press, his wife, Charlotte, and some women friends had built a furious fire of roots and coconut husks in a stone pit. On this, they laid a vast rectangular pan that was perhaps twice the dimensions of one of the plots in the nearby graveyard. As the clear cane juice trickled from the spout of the crusher, it was caught in tubs and the women ferried the syrupy yield to the pan where it was boiled and converted into amber molasses. The refining process was not carried beyond this first stage. The molasses — Charles that day obtained four large pitchers of it — is used for drinks, to make cakes, and for pouring over sweet-dumpling desserts.

Before the sugar-crushing bee was over, the children made sure that some of the bubbling cane juice was set aside in a large basin for their treat. Charlotte had brought along a sack of arrowroot. While the sugar syrup was still hot, she beat this thickening ingredient into the children's molasses. The still-warm mixture was served on pieces of banana palm leaves. So the children could spoon it up, the men used their seamen's knives to carve little scoops for them from lengths of uncrushed sugar cane.

Working the crusher had not been easy, but the island men turned it into an occasion of joviality. In the old days, occasionally even today, one man was detached from the group to squat on the hub of the spars and sing sea shanties to the kinsmen around the capstan, the men on the spars joining in for the choruses and suggesting new stanzas. Once, when the Hondas were a novelty, the men hooked up a motorcycle to the capstan, and it went like a bat out of — well, like a bat out of Hector, as the nonswearing members of the community would put it.

As often happens in this community, a day of work — public work or helping out a neighbor — had been turned into a minor social occasion. For the *major* ones, the entire cousin-family plunges into the preparations once the entertainment committee has decided on the game plan. The committee members are usually hardpressed to find ways of injecting some variety into island social life. There are, however, certain perennials. The island launches each new year with an outdoor feast of some sort, combined with an afternoon of sports. The New Year's Day feast this year was a Maori *hangi* in which a great variety of meat, fish, and vegetables is cooked in an underground oven with heated stones. It was the schoolteacher's idea and it was not an unqualified social success, some of the older ladies mumbling, as we heaped food from a dirt oven and piled it on "plates" sliced from banana palm leaves, that it gave the impression the Pitcairners were reverting to nativism.

The games they enjoy are those which were played on village greens in nineteenth-century England — rounders, cricket, sack races, tug-o'-war, and so on. The tug-o'-war is given a Pitcairn twist — it is staged as an annual Battle of the Sexes. Almost invariably, the women win; the Polynesian plumpness ensures that the ladies' team has not one but a whole succession of formidable anchors. How formidable? I would guess that the four largest together would tip the scales at almost half a ton.

If tug-o'-war falls within the ladies' domain, another recreational legacy from their English half-ancestry is decidedly in male hands.

Anglo-Tahitian cricket is a Pitcairn offshoot, or more correctly an aberration, of one of man's oldest, most stylized, and most meticulous sports. Purists of the game will be relieved to learn that it has found a natural quarantine on this isolated speck in the South Pacific, too remote from any other outpost of British culture for the contamination to spread. We played the Pitcairn version of the game one broiling hot afternoon in Aute Walley on a wicket that had been sliced out of the rich, chocolaty soil and undergrowth by the little bulldozer blade on the tractor. The axis of the wicket was lined up between Up Ha Beans inland and Break Im Hip on the coast. On one far flank of the field was Tom's Block and Fat's House, and on the other the spot known as John Catch a Cow.

The men had not played a "proper" game of cricket for almost eight years, a measure of the social and recreational malaise that has crept over the island with the decline in the number of able-bodied men. In former years, cricket had been an intensely popular pastime. Encouragingly, when a match was suggested during our stay, interest in the game was dramatically rekindled. Cricket fever gripped Adamstown for almost a week, longer even than had the social side of Christmas. Early in the preparations, the islanders made the discovery that almost all of the equipment sent out from Britain or New Zealand — the bats, wickets, pads, wicketkeeper's gloves, and so on — had been lost or broken. I assumed the match would be scrubbed. But one day, passing the workshop where Pervis and Len often do their carving work together, I noticed that there were new wooden shapes on their chip-littered benches and across their knees. The men had set aside the fish, vases, and walking sticks they had been fashioning and were carving cricket bats. Warren, meanwhile, had cut six strong saplings and was working on the wickets. Altogether, eight men were carving bats out of *pulau* and various island woods. Some were decorated with flags and palm trees. One had a female figure, roughly in the Statue of

Liberty pose, drawn down the flat side of the bat. Another had a crude notation printed on the face of the bat of one of the local rules: "Lorse ball — six runs." Charles had painted his bat gleaming white, as if he were expecting the game to extend late into the dusk and was sportingly anxious to give the bowler every opportunity of hitting it. Fortunately, five well-used, red-leather cricket balls had survived. Four were to burst open during the game, one exploding spectacularly in midair, showering down its innards on players and spectators like a Roman candle.

With the homemade equipment, picnic baskets, and thatch mats for the spectators to spread on the spiky grass, the village trudged or rode up the steep track to Aute Walley. Some of them also took along their "muskets" as a goat hunt was to be held after the cricket.

The spot in Aute Walley had been chosen for cricket because it is one of the very few areas of the island that offers relatively level terrain. The wicket, however, was pitched unavoidably at a slope, rising toward Up Ha Beans at an angle between ten and fifteen degrees. Among the other imperfections were the thick, chest-high undergrowth that extended to within ten yards of the wicket, and the large flowering trees and banana palms growing at strategic places on the "field." High above the scene, along the ridges of the Walley, a few tenuous coconut palms moved easily in the breeze. On the Walley slopes, some of the old people, with no time for cricket, worked on their sweet potato patches during the afternoon. One seventy-year-old collapsed from the heat and had to be carried down the hill.

The spectators — all the island women and the children and babies — took up positions perilously close to the wicket. The only shaded spots that offered a close-up view of the action, a large old pandanus palm and an umbrella-shaped frangipani tree, were sited in the positions known on a cricket field as short slips. The "muskets," the spare bats, and the shoulder baskets of pineapples, sandwiches, and containers of fruit juice and water were stacked around these trees. The womenfolk and the young lounged about waiting for something to happen. (It was as if a large family had arrived at Shea Stadium and had picked a spot for their picnic some ten yards behind the home plate.) Near the wicket, children were delightedly finding the heads, bodies, and tails of rats that had been taken by surprise by the bulldozer blade and executed. Garth Harraway, the newly arrived schoolteacher, attempted to give the players a refresher course in the rules of cricket:

"Do you play six balls to an over?"

"What's an over?"

"Where is the boundary when a 'six' is hit?"

"Oh, we run 'six' always. There's no *boundary*."

He soon saw he would have to abide by Pitcairn rules. The rule-book stroking he displayed at bat during the match seemed ludicrously out of place. Unexpectedly, he was bowled for a "duck" (zero runs) the first time at bat. There is always the element of surprise in cricket played on a foreign turf.

The captains were Pervis and Len. In dress, the islanders' approach deviated from the cricketing ideal of white "longs" and white shirts and tended toward the football world of contrasting uniforms. A notice tacked up in the Square had said that Len's side should turn out in blue shirts with white shorts or long trousers, while Pervis' team was urged to come in all white. Pervis arrived in ballooning gray slacks with suspenders over his white shirt. Others played in T-shirts imprinted with the names of French warships which had visited the island recently during the French nuclear tests. Most of the shirts came off as the afternoon grew hotter and the men played in bare chests, something one is *not* supposed to do in cricket. All took to the field with the seamen's knives they carry on their belts. One player fielded with his machete to help find lost balls in the undergrowth of lantana grass.

When the players took the field, it turned out that Pervis' team had fifteen players — four more than the customary eleven — and Len's side was short one at a muster of ten. It was decided, nevertheless, to proceed on this basis, even though Pervis' inflated team contained many of the strongest players, a decision which says much about the Pitcairners' approach to sport and their general lack of competitiveness.

The imbalance in the teams was only the first of many irregularities. The most noticeable was the Pitcairn practice of having player-umpires, a custom born of necessity in view of the limited number of men available for a match. I could accept *that*, but not the arrangement under which both umpires were drawn from the same side, the larger one at that. Pervis combined the functions of captain, player, coach, and umpire. The other ump was Pastor Webster, who had been assigned to the Island Magistrate's squad. He had read the notices about the preferred uniforms but chose to turn out in neutral hues, mustard-colored shirt and brown slacks. I could only reason that the umpires had been selected because of their respective status in the community. Pervis represented the colony's temporal leadership and Pastor was the spiritual head.

When they were not batting or bowling, both umpires took up unorthodox positions. Pervis stood at a spot where he could bellow partial encouragement to batsmen from his own side as they were running between wickets: "Move it there, Reynold!" "Run, Pastor! Come Pastor!"

No two hand-carved bats were the same. Some splayed illegally into bell bottoms to give added batting surface. Pervis had pasted coarse black emery paper across the entire surface of his bat in the hope that this would ensure securer contact with the ball. His family picnic basket held two spare lengths of emery paper in case the modification worked well and replacements became necessary. Another player had evidently set out to make a jumbo baseball bat and had then sliced it in half to provide the flat hitting surface required in a cricket bat.

There were endless "lorse balls." When the bat connected with a ball, it was lofted high into the distant scrub and hillocks. If there had been a boundary, these shots automatically would have given the hitter six runs apiece. But they ran each long hit with gusto and with cackles of glee from their womenfolk in the hazardous vantage points at short slips. Miraculously, the balls were found each time. "Hit's in ah palm there," the batsman would shout helpfully to the party of fielders who had raced off to the general area to retrieve it. The batsman by that time would be safely home after making his six runs.

If the ball were lost for an inordinate length of time, the women would appropriate the pitch for some underarm-bowled cricket. Young Brenda, in bikini bottoms, a sleeveless top open at the back and showing her Maidenform bra, and with a sailor's knife strapped to one brown thigh, took a few exuberant swipes off a weak bowler handicapped by floppy hat and long dress. The young children, meanwhile, were playing a secondary match off in the flattened-down grass. A kerosene can was their wicket, and they played with half-sized bats which the men thoughtfully had carved while making their own. Again, it was a picture of a community en-joying its leisure time as one large family. It was the simplest, roughest kind of pleasure, banal at times and corny in the extreme, but very endearing.

Each time the men succeeded in finding the lost ball, the women were shooed off the pitch with male-chauvinist arrogance and dis-dain of a high order. The women said they would set up their own match the following Sunday and the men could sit on the sidelines.

The males this day were monopolizing the field and were intent on playing until sundown. Their stamina I found quite astonish-ing, since they had already put in six hours of grueling work with the longboats in a raging sea before going up the hill to start the cricket. (It was the day the banana boat, the *AE* that turned out to be the *EA*, had called. Every man and youth on the field had been summoned at three that morning to the Landing to do their duty in Bounty Bay.)

Instead of the regulation two innings for each side, the men were talking of four and five innings apiece, possibly more. When the schoolteacher had produced an old cricket scorebook with twelve pages unused — a page for each inning — Marie Christ-ian, the scorer, had asked: "But what do we do when we get through six innings a team?"

By late afternoon, the batsmen were just getting into their full swing. In one disastrous period for the blue-shirts, Reynold hit five "sixes" in succession. (The baseball equivalent would be five home runs by a single batter from consecutive pitches.) To deal with this hitting-machine, Steve secreted a reserve ball in his shirt and dashed with it each time one of Reynold's hits took off on a high trajectory into the scrub. Steve would pretend to have found the ball and hurl his reserve one to the bowler or wicketkeeper in an attempt to run out one of the batsmen. The trick was soon un-masked. With true Pitcairn honesty, the fieldsmen would persevere in their hunt for the ball actually in use. When it was found, the "run-out" batsman would be restored to the batting crease. (He would go back to bat.)

The match ended with the white-shirts claiming 195 runs, and the blue-shirts, 140.

The largest communal social event of our stay had, for us, both familiar and unfamiliar aspects. By local decree of Church and State, Christmas Day was observed on December 26 as the twenty-fifth fell on a Saturday, the Adventist Sabbath. To the little group of outsiders on the island, it seemed odd that the religious observances could not have been combined with the social trappings of Christmas. To the Pitcairners, it was unthinkable. "Sabbath is Sabbath and Christmas Day is Christmas Day," I was told.

Christmas on Pitcairn brought home to us just how totally our own concept of Christmas is molded, directed, and almost controlled by the media and by the immense apparatus of merchandising. Until Christmas "Eve" — Christmas Day itself for us — no one among the islanders had talked, or apparently thought much, about Christmas. In shopless, TV-less, newspaperless, Santa-Claus-less Pitcairn, none of the strident reminders were there. When I told Millie that Christmas decorations appear along Fifth Avenue by the end of October and that the shopping frenzy is beginning to fray parental nerves by the early weeks of December, she raised her eyes to the perilously sagging ceiling of her dining room and withheld comment, as if this were the only way to excuse the madness of the outside world.

There were no announcements about Christmas on the church board or on the notice boards by the courthouse and at the junction of two strategic tracks in Adamstown. The only notices dealt with the imminent elections for chairman of the Internal Committee and the two councilors. The balloting customarily is held on Christmas Day, Voting on the Sabbath, of course, was out of the question, so the election was put off until the twenty-seventh, a Monday.

There was not, in this most religious and Jesus-adoring community, a single Christmas decoration in any of the homes I visited, at the school or on the three public buildings around the Square.

Blessedly, there was not one Styrofoam Santa, plastic holly wreath, or piece of dime-store junk in sight. No lights, no trees, no cotton-wool mangers, no stenciled snow on the panes. Landing the necessities of life on Pitcairn is work enough without bringing in the disposable seasonal frills. By the twenty-fourth, the austereness of Christmas week was beginning to unnerve our nine-year-old daughter. With a few balloons we had brought with us, some scraps of colored paper, and palm leaves and flowers, she made a desperate effort to decorate her five-foot-by-six-foot bedroom, the spare little cubicle formed by partitioning off one end of the front porch with scraps of plywood. Her newfound island friends thought the embellishments were nice enough, but they couldn't really see the point of them. The start of the schoolchildren's Christmas break came at the very end of Christmas week, the afternoon of the twenty-fourth.

We saw the first tangible signs of Pitcairn Christmas on that same afternoon. To avoid having to cook on the Sabbath, Millie was rushing her preparations at the "bolt," the outdoor kitchen. Warren had collected perhaps fifty dried coconut husks to heat up the Polynesian stone oven. The husks blazed, disintegrated into fiery embers which heated the stones to furnace intensity, and two hours later were raked out. Millie was baking an unusually large quantity of her delicious loaves, some this day of whole wheat as a Christmas offering for relatives or friends who preferred it over her snowy-white bread. When the stones had cooled to the right temperature, the tins of dough were placed in racks in the cavernous interior of the oven.

Millie then turned to the goat meat which would be part of the Christmas dinner we would have the following evening, after Sabbath sundown, at her son-in-law's house, just across the dirt trail by the big banyan tree. She was stewing the ragged-cut pieces of goat in water and oil. A big pinch of salt went into the pan but no pepper or herbs of any kind. "Goat meat used to be our traditional Christmas dinner," she told us. "Now there's chicken and t'other things. There are so few goats left t'hunt, and those who have 'em as pets don't like ah kill 'em. But we have a little goat for you." The next night we were to see what the "t'other things" amounted to.

Warren, meanwhile, had divided the day between his garden a mile away on the high ground and his favorite outdoor carving place, a rough bench made from oil drums and planks, and placed in the shade of the banyan across from the house. From his garden he carried home pandanus baskets bulging with perfect specimens of grapefruit, small pineapples, oranges, passion fruit, carrots, tomatoes, cucumbers, cabbages, and a few bunches of bananas. From his al fresco workshop, the white paint just dry in time for Christmas, came two splendid models of the Pitcairn longboats for our boys. With the letter punch he ordered from Montgomery Ward so many years ago he has forgotten when, he stamped on the hulls his name and "Pitcairn Island."

Christmas Day was a subdued day set aside largely for worship. People wished each other Merry Christmas, but there were no presents in sight, nor were they mentioned. At nine thirty in the morning, Morris, the toothless island reprobate, a cigarette butt dangling from his lips, his shirt pocket crammed with a dozen carefully sharpened pencils to cloak his illiteracy, began pounding the bell in the Square to announce Sabbath school. He was still ringing it long after all the island children and most of the grown-ups had arrived at the Square. Ringing the bell is Morris' favorite assignment. It was taken away from him for a time as punishment for some infraction of the island mores, but he is now back in Pastor's good graces. To re-establish himself as bell-ringer, he even offered to go to church regularly. He regained his job, but his pew usually remains empty.

Including the children and babies, sixty-three of the eighty-five islanders came to Christmas Sabbath service. It was a normal attendance. The church was undecorated apart from a vase of fresh flowers on the table in front of the pulpit. Sabbath school lasted until eleven, and then everyone, the squalling babies, the octogenarians, the bare-footed youths in American printed T-shirts, the women in homemade print dresses, the men in clean white shirts and jeans, mostly tieless but some wearing unaccustomed leather or canvas on their feet, moved into the church for Sabbath service itself.

In Sabbath school they had sung four verses of "Silent Night," but at the main church meeting it was worship-as-usual with a curious lack of emphasis on the anniversary of Christ's birth. There were three hymns but none with a Christmas message or flavor. I asked one of the old-timers about this, and her reply was: "Christmas is in our hearts and our souls. There ain't need for it t'be on the hymn board."

But Brother Pervis, at six feet four inches the tallest man on the island and fittingly its elected leader, did his best to inject a Christmasy note, even at the risk of some historical error. Pastor had invited him to deliver the sermon that day as the Island Magistrate was retiring as Church Elder and this was his last Sabbath in that post. Hunched toweringly over the green baize of the pulpit, Pervis gravely adjusted his glasses and reminded the congregation of "our Jesus who was hanged on that tree in Calvary, that Christmas tree in Calvary."

After Pastor had blessed his flock, including those who had sat through the service on the bench in the church entrance hall and whose participation had been offhand in the extreme, we ambled outside into the hot sun. It was a muggy eighty degrees, weather that underscored the inappropriateness for the Southern Hemisphere of so many of the northern Christmas traditions and carols. The day had started with a sudden downpour that turned the roads into slippery red mud. We were on the far fringe of a tropical depression, and Millie had predicted at daybreak that day: "We may have a bit of gray-way at Christmas." (Heavy rain is known in the island slang as "gray-way." Millie pronounced it almost like "gravy.") But it had cleared up by noon, and the banana palms across from the church were beginning to steam when we left the service.

With their devotions attended to, the islanders were in no hurry to go home. They had eaten their combination breakfast-lunch early, before going to the Sabbath service, and there would be no other meal until the sun had set and preparations for the Christmas dinner would begin. The Christians, the Youngs, the Warrens, and the Browns moved to their time-honored places along the rickety benches in the shade of old trees along one edge of the Square. They would spend the next hour or two there, chatting and watching the passing parade. "Passing" is perhaps too strong an adjective here. What movement there was seemed to be taking place

in slow motion. On bench seats they had drifted to all their lives
after Sabbath worship, perhaps the same resting places that had
been appropriated by their families for two or more generations,
these gentle heirs of mutineers were content to spend the Christmas Sabbath afternoon in reverie or hushed talk.

Slowly, some Christmas touches were materializing. Tom Christian had tacked to the main notice board the first of five messages
of seasonal greeting he had received on the radio from Pitcairners
in self-exile. One had come from Port Angeles, Washington State,
addressed simply to "The People of Pitcairn."

By midafternoon, the trails through Adamstown were even more
deserted than usual. Some of the older islanders were preparing for
Christmas dinner by taking a snooze on cots on the porch. The
middle-aged men were busy finishing their Christmas carving, or
building up their stocks of curios for trading on the next vessel. A
Christian youth had taken his Honda "topside" to pick a dozen
winy-sweet pineapples from his patch as a Christmas present for
his sweetheart, a first cousin. Other men were sorting through their
dwindling stocks of *miro* wood to find a good block for carving,
which could be a Yule offering to a friend the next day. *Miro*
wood, we learned from these men who depend on carving it for
all their "luxuries," is in critical supply. The tree has been cut so
heavily on Pitcairn that the island men have to make occasional
longboat trips to uninhabited Henderson Island, 110 miles away,
where the tree grows abundantly. One man had set aside a good
piece of lead which he proposed giving to a neighbor as the raw
material for fishing sinkers.

Our hosts for Christmas dinner were Tom and Betty Christian.
There were fourteen of us, and we sat on benches on either side of
a table about twelve feet long in Betty's roomy, if cluttered kitchen.
The table was covered with floral plastic oilcloth and set with
floral-patterned china and shiny new stainless cutlery. We waited
for Tom to say grace and surveyed the smorgasbord of Pitcairn and
imported goodies that filled every inch of space between the rows
of plates. Millie's goat-meat stew was just the beginning. There
were platters of chicken pieces baked with tomatoes, corned beef,
fried goat liver, baked pumpkin, sweet corn, beets, roast potatoes,
sweet potatoes, cold canned peas, bowls of imported butter, home-

baked bread, cabbage, tomato, and cucumber salads with the coconut-milk dressing, and two kinds of *pillhai*, the Pitcairn staple that visitors find soapy and almost inedible. For drinks, we had home-made apricot juice, sour-orange-lemonade, and the juice extracted by boiling wild strawberries. Each was served in half-gallon pitchers. There were two desserts. Betty brought first from the stove the sort of basketball-size plum pudding they ate in England in Disraeli's time. There was a pot of custard to pour over it.

"The servings might be a bit on the heavy side," said Tom. He was not criticizing Betty's cooking but warning us that coins had been buried in the pudding. The children collected a nice haul of American nickels and New Zealand ten-, two- and one-cent pieces.

The dinner had begun with polite passing of platters. Seconds were obtained with darting application of the boardinghouse reach. In honor of the occasion, and out of respect for the trouble Betty had gone to, the men were trying determinedly to suppress belches by the time she brought the final dish to the littered table — a huge bowl of tiny wild strawberries and a deep-freezer dish of ice cream made with powdered milk. There was no coffee or tea. Although Tom is not the vegetarian the Church would like him to be, he is among those two or three dozen Pitcairn Adventists who otherwise obediently adhere to their Church's dietary rules — no pork, no shellfish, no scaleless fish, no alcohol, no stimulating non-alcoholic drinks that might be habit-forming. As a result, Pitcairn is probably the only place in the South Pacific where suckling *pua'a*, usually served roasted and arranged on banana tree leaves, is not the *pièce de résistance* of a feast day. Also, of course, the one place in Polynesia where there are no drinks, at Christmas parties or anytime. The only hot drinks served in Tom's house are mugs of Ovaltine or Milo, which are not considered to have any stimulating effect and are usually prepared before retiring.

After Christmas dinner we inspected Tom's pumpkin patch in the twilight, saw the Rhode Island Reds and Black Orphingtons he was trying to raise beneath the coconut palms from fertilized eggs brought in from Auckland, and moved down to where his garden ends on the rim of the sheer cliffs. Tom pointed to a black escarpment a few hundred yards along the jagged coastline and told me it was at that spot that Will McCoy, one hundred

and seventy-three Christmases ago, threw himself to his death on
the rocks at the waterline in a fit of the home-brewed D.T.'s. He
had tied a rock around his neck to make sure the job would be
finished. McCoy's Drop, they called the spot. He chose a place that
had the right somberness for the job at hand. Yet there was also
to this shoreline a wild, melancholy beauty, a nice change for the
eyes from the Polynesian setpiece of arching palm, untracked white
sand, and outrigger riding in tame surf. Here there were no trees,
no sand; just black rocks and stormy white water.

For the island children that night, the last act before an unusually late bedtime was to hang pandanus baskets on the front
porches. Pitcairn has never had a Christmas-stocking tradition,
partly because there are no living room fireplaces and partly because in the earliest days of the colony, stockings were simply an
exotic memory of eighteenth-century London and Portsmouth.
Once the young were in bed, the Christmas spirit belatedly seized
the island. The festive mood prevailed for the next twenty-four
hours, until almost midnight on the twenty-sixth, when it ceased as
suddenly as it had begun.

With baskets heavy with candies, fresh-baked cookies, pineapples and other fruits, balloons and trinkets, the grown-ups set out
on foot to tour the houses of Adamstown, tiptoeing up to the
front porches to drop a few treats into each child's basket. By some
unspoken rule, the Hondas were left under their galvanized-iron
lean-tos that night. A few of the Pitcairn Santas made their rounds
ringing ancient hand bells, a nice Dickensian echo in the still South
Pacific night. By both bloodlines and social necessity, these eighty-
five people are members of a single family, and this was never more
apparent to us than on this Christmas night as the islanders made
their rounds in the milky moonlight.

After we had done our tour with the supermarket candies and
things we had brought from New York, we climbed the hill to our
temporary home and our flashlight picked out Millie filling the
three baskets our children had hung along the sad porch. In each
she had placed a grapefruit, shiny yellow, blemish-free, and measuring perhaps eight inches in diameter, and a pineapple. "Just to
make their little hearts happy," she murmured. She had also added
some of her cupcakes, but she rescued them and transferred them

to the safe in the dining room when three columns of ants began moving toward the three baskets. In the beam of the flashlight, we inspected the treats each child had been given. Each of the baskets held about three pounds of candies and homemade popcorn in addition to the fruit. Some of the older girls had decorated the baskets with pink frangipani blossoms and large green leaves. The candy was almost the first the children had seen on this island without shops; most families had been hoarding their supplies for Christmas.

Before six the next morning, our young and the island children were up comparing the contents of their baskets. The *serious* gift-giving was to come later. This traditionally is a community ceremony on Pitcairn. No one, not even newlyweds, exchanges Christmas presents in private. Everyone knows exactly what his neighbor has given and got. The ceremony is normally held in the Square, but that morning and afternoon we had been having a lot of "grayway," and the entertainment committee decided to hold it in the roomy courthouse flanking one side of the public quadrangle. At dawn, the committee members had been up on the slopes cutting down the "family's" Christmas trees. The species chosen is the lush, densely leafed jessme tree which is possibly the arboreal antithesis of the traditional Christmas conifer. There are some Norfolk pines on the island, but they are too precious to cut for a single ceremony. The entertainment directors cut about a dozen jessmes and used them to turn the courthouse into a fairyland bower, the first example of something really artistic I had seen on the island.

The schedule called for the islanders to drop by during the afternoon to hang their presents on the trees and on clotheslines strung across the room for the overflow. The distribution of presents was to begin at 4:30. By that time, however, the first straw basketloads of gifts were just being toted up the hill. It took almost two hours for the families to hang up their presents. A few were gift-wrapped. Most were in brown paper and some were encased in newspaper. A lot were bare of any wrapping, particularly the imported items, naked in their factory plastic sheaths. The thought, and the gift itself, are what count on Pitcairn, not the element of surprise.

By 6:30, well over a thousand presents had been hung on the trees and on the lines. The ceremony was starting two hours late.

On the eve of Christmas gift-giving — delayed twenty-four hours so it would not fall on the Saturday Sabbath — the author's children fell in with the island tradition of hanging up pandanus baskets instead of stockings. During the night, the baskets became cornucopias of island fruit — pineapples, bananas, grapefruit, mangoes. At the bottom of each basket were homemade candies and cookies.

"Only two things start on time on Pitcairn, the church and the school," the retiring schoolteacher had told me.

The entire population of the island had assembled in the courthouse. The oldsters sat on the platform or on benches placed around the perimeter of the room. The children were running like demons among the trees, trying hard to respect the local Christmas rule that says no one may take a preview peek at the names on the presents. Pastor Webster called for silence, spoke a prayer of thanks to God for the things the islanders had been able to grow, make, or buy abroad, and gave a little homily on the subject of Christian giving. And then the bedlam began. It would take almost two hours to hand out the presents, and until the last one was cut down and presented, the courthouse would be filled with squealing, shouts, laughter, and general uproar.

Our ears were still ringing with the clangor of the ship's bell in the Square signaling the start of the ceremonies when Pervis in his stentorian voice bellowed out the first name: "Cla-a-a-rice." A man had been stationed by each tree and each line to cut down the gifts with his seamen's knife and boom out the names of the recipients. They all boomed. The carrying power of voices trained to make themselves heard over raging seas should not be underestimated.

In many cases, the homemade tags bore only one name. The recipient was left to guess whom it had come from. I had mentioned this to Millie as she was writing out her cards, and she had explained that it might seem boastful or conceited to claim credit for giving a gift on the anniversary of the Savior's birth. The most impressive presents were a gleaming two-wheeler English bicycle that had arrived many months earlier and had been hidden in a neighbor's home, and a rifle which Pervis was handing down to his burly, sixteen-year-old son, Daryl. He referred to it as his "musket."

Items of island handicraft — colored baskets with the words "Pitcairn Island" worked into the patterns, carvings of fish, birds, and wheelbarrows, and packets of bookmarks made from bleached and painted leaves (for what books, I wondered) — were hanging from every tree. I found it odd that a basketmaker in the Young family would give a basketmaking cousin in the Christian family a sample of her handiwork, particularly since both women turned out precisely the same basket. In a way, though, it made sense. If the present were not needed, the recipient could add it to her stock for trading aboard ships, in which case, in an almost cashless society, it was the equivalent of money. Others were giving long strings of pineapples to their relatives, watermelons, canteloupes, baskets of paw-paw (papaya), or small trays of wild strawberries. Among other gifts, our family received a total of thirty pineapples. It has already lodged in the family folklore as "The Pineapple Christmas."

The imported items were of impressive variety, considering the few ships that call at Pitcairn nowadays and the difficulties in off-loading cargo. There were wind-up cars, model speedboats, inflated turtles and canoes, toy tractors, baby sheets, plastic salad bowls, umbrellas against Pitcairn's sudden deluges, cans of English shortbread, loose tea in brown paper bags ("Pastor! It's *tea!*"), bundles of postcards, storybooks, cans of bully beef, single small bottles of English lemonade, and so on. The most pathetic present was a single lead pencil, handed out tagged but unwrapped. The most fatuous was a large, collapsible paper pineapple. The most pointed was a string-tied bundle of eight tubes of toothpaste presented, unwrapped, to an elderly woman. Old Morris was carrying around two brown-paper-wrapped bottles and telling everyone that the schoolteacher had remembered he had a wicked taste for beer. Actually, they were bottles of tomato ketchup.

The night ended with a hilarious concert in the courthouse, interrupted occasionally when a big, black mongrel, one of Super's sons, darted across the stage and through the bed-sheet curtain that skimpily concealed the backstage preparations. The men dressed up in old merchant marine uniforms to do skits about life at sea. Anderson led us in "Simon Says" and mathematical tricks. The young boys did a Wild West skit, and the Pastor next day chided the schoolteacher for not talking them out of a playlet that took place at a barroom rail and had simulated shooting; it was the wrong *tone*. The schoolchildren did a hula of sorts, a Maori poi-ball song, and chorused a lament entitled, "Why Don't the Parents Visit the School?" (The "tone" was getting better.) Brenda Christian, the curviest of the Christians, was Britannia wrapped in the Union Jack. There were some surprising cracks about the promiscuity of one of the island girls who has twice added to the population, usefully but illegitimately, after outsiders had come temporarily into Pitcairn's everyday life. (Here the tone was beginning to slip.) The *compere*, Island Secretary Ben Christian, in joke plastic nose and Groucho Marx glasses, brought down the house by making every mistake open to a master of ceremonies. The women plucked guitars and the men's glee club gave us a full-throated rendition of "Cling to the Bible, My Boy."

We all sang "God Save the Queen" in a room adorned with no fewer than three portraits of the Monarch and one of the Queen Mother. No one, I discovered later, had bothered to listen to the Queen's Christmas broadcast on short-wave radio.

CHAPTER FIFTEEN

FOUR PITCAIRNERS

Pervis Ferris Young

For the past eight years, the Lilliputian "political" arena in Pitcairn has been dominated by a Gulliver giant of a man, Pervis Young. (I have put quotation marks around the word "political" here because, as we shall see in a later chapter, politics simply are not found on Pitcairn, at least not in any form that would be familiar to an outsider.) He is a fifth-generation descendant of Midshipman Edward Young of the *Bounty*, whom Bligh, in the "wanted men" list he drew up in Batavia to help the Admiralty track down the mutineers, described as "22 years, 5 feet 8 inches. Dark complexion and rather a bad look. Dark-brown hair — strong made — has lost several of his fore teeth, those that remain are all rotten."

Over the years of mixed-blood breeding on Pitcairn, the Youngs have grown taller and become even more strongly made. Pervis — pronounced *Perwis* because of the trouble Pitcairners have with the "v," an inheritance presumably from Tahitian speech patterns — is an impressive eight inches taller than his forebear. He has trouble finding trousers that are long enough, with the result that they often stop well short of the large, bare feet. There has been some improvement in the dental department. He has a jutting chin and prominent ears. His hair is gray, in tight, wiry curls. In place of the "bad look," Midshipman Young's heir has the stern countenance of a simple and devout man doing his best with limited education to make honest and wise decisions for a society that

is beginning to know a few of the complexities of the outside world.

The hazel eyes and his Polynesian-brown face are the living record of the two bloodlines he inherited. The eyes, under heavy, bony eyebrows that are one of the stamps of the mutineer descendants, have a disturbing directness. At first meeting, they seem to have a chilly, interrogative cast. But the look is only part of Pervis' mien. I came to appreciate his friendliness and kindness, and left the island with a great measure of sympathy for him in the administrative job he is attempting in a community with special problems and limited resources.

He moved into the position of Island Magistrate from his chairmanship of the Internal Committee when the former Magistrate, John Christian, relinquished the post and moved to New Zealand for a spell. Pervis has since been elected to the Magistrate's office for two three-year terms. He has not yet made up his mind whether he will seek re-election. He has directed the affairs of the island during the period in which it has acquired the modest amount of mechanization it has today. The arrival of the Honda motorcycles and a Mini-Moke presented Pitcairn with a situation in which traffic regulation, albeit on a ludicrously small scale, became necessary. The Island Council decreed that the community should follow the British lead and drive on the left. In practice, the narrow dirt tracks allow only middle-of-the-road navigation. People with internal-combustion engines beneath the saddles had to be tested and licensed, and for this Pervis turned to the only man on the island with a lifetime of experience with automotive contraptions, the schoolmaster from New Zealand. In addition to his roles of government adviser, paymaster, financial overseer, and consultant on the entertainment committee, the teacher became the examiner, and sometimes the instructor, for driving tests. The combination motor-vehicle registration and driver's license fee was set at fifty cents annually. There were no silly quibbles about compulsory insurance.

The morning I spent with Pervis began with a visit to the island jailhouse, which is conveniently close to the Magistrate's house, a rather prickly walk of twenty yards through passion-fruit vines and high grass growing down one side of his land. I had asked seventy-

land Magistrate Pervis Young. In his hands, the "Bounty Bible." In the background, mounted on a plinth in the Square, one of the anchors from the *Bounty*, fished out of Bounty Bay in 1957 by American divers.

year-old Vernon ("Wernon") Young, who is the island policeman but enjoys the title Inspector of Police even though he has no force beneath him, to show me the jail. Vernon, however, felt the visit should be arranged by the Magistrate himself. Nevertheless, he did give me the stock joke about the jail after I had served up the requisite straight-man's line:

"How many people have been in the jailhouse?"

"Oh many, werry many."

"What were they in for?"

"Oh, they went there to clean it."

Side view, seen through the vines dense enough to bury any miscreant from the gaze of law-abiding society, the jail looks like a de luxe outhouse. The clapboard sides have been given a fresh coat of cream government paint, and the corrugated iron roof gleams in red public-works paint. There are two cells, one for the prisoner and one for the warder. They are identical in size, six feet by eight feet, and in decoration. Each has a barred gate inside the wooden outer door, a small barred window high in the wall facing the sea, but too high to afford any view of the free Pacific, two tiny shelves for the prisoner's personal effects, a bare light bulb hanging from the roof, and the prison regulations, covering visits, the duties of the prisoner in keeping his cell and the vicinity of the jail clean, thumbtacked to the wall. There are no toilet facilities. The prisoner either is let out to relieve himself or herself outside the jail or is escorted across to the Magistrate's house to use the facilities there.

All this tends to be rather theoretical. Neither Pervis, Vernon, nor anyone else could remember when the jail last was used. When Pervis and I tested the iron door of one cell, we found it was rusted rigidly into the half-open position. When I persevered in my attempt to close it, the doorframe to which the hinges were attached started coming loose from the wall. The cells were being used as storehouses for life jackets and government paint.

Rephrasing the question to avoid setting up the stock gag again, I asked Pervis what crime an islander would have to commit to wind up in the brig.

"We would use it only for something like serious violence or carnal knowledge," he said. He rolled his mouth around the "r" in "carnal" as if his tongue were trying to dislodge a piece of goat meat trapped between his back molars. "We would try those cases on the island. If someone commited a *murder*, or a *really* bad crime, then we would hold him in the cell just until a ship arrived to take him to New Zealand, where the Commissioner would arrange for him to be tried in a court there. But it would have to be a werry, werry bad thing." He seemed to feel that even this tiny house of detention was unnecessary. "It's too small a place, Pitcairn — where would a bad man hide?" he asked.

Pervis' rambling three-bedroom house is perched on sloping ground that ends suddenly in the unfenced lip of an escarpment that drops several hundred feet to the black rocks along the coast, just west of Bounty Bay. The veranda has a fine view of a vast sweep of the Pacific. Across a large porch table which his wife uses to store the baskets she has woven for trading, Pervis talked about the chores and responsibilities assigned to Pitcairn's chief executive. To refresh his memory on points that arose, he kept hauling from his plastic briefcase assorted documents. He is one of the few on the island to possess a complete folder of the laws and ordinances, and he carries this with him to all official meetings. The other papers in his portmanteau were the account sheets and estimates required by meticulous minds thousands of miles across the sea in Whitehall and Auckland.

"My job is to see that all the laws are carried out, to go through the secretary-treasurer's work, Ben's papers, when he's finished with them, and to register the births, deaths, and marriages," said Pervis. The registrar's role does not exactly plunge Pervis into a bureaucratic frenzy. The last wedding on Pitcairn had been four years ago, and the one before that took place in 1966. The year 1971 did produce, however, an unusually good crop of babies — two — and there were the deaths of Parkin Christian, Fred Christian, and his wife, Flora, to enter in the books.

Pervis is one of those who have become increasingly apprehensive about Pitcairn's ability to survive much longer. "When all the young people reach a stage, they up and go," he lamented. "There's no jobs for them here and no way of getting the money to provide those jobs. When the Commissioner was here recently from Auckland, that was his worry, finding some way of holding the people on the island. We could make it all right if we could attract back all the Pitcairners living in New Zealand; but finding what would draw them home is the thing we're always trying to find out."

The Island Magistrate himself would like to join the exodus. Would any other leader in any other society have the honesty, before an interviewer, to declare himself a would-be emigrant? "To tell you the plain truth, I like to go — to New Zealand," he confessed. "It's nothing I can plan because of *she* there." (He pointed toward the kitchen where the First Lady of Pitcairn, his wife, the plump Marona Estell, whom everyone calls "Pussy," was preparing the big "breakfast" that would be served just after midday. Before her marriage, "Pussy" was also a Young, Pervis' cousin.) "She doesn't want to leave, even though all her immediate relatives are already in New Zealand. It's the men, not the women, who are anxious to leave." (Others had told me the exact reverse.) "It's the lack of work here that drives the men away. There's nothing for them to do."

Pervis has lived in New Zealand for three brief periods. To support himself, he took factory jobs in Auckland and Wellington. "I liked it, oh, yes," he recalled. "I liked it because everything there was on time, because when you had work you stuck to one job. You knew what you were going to do each day, not like here where you do a bit of everything. I find it easier to live the New Zealand way. The first time we went it was *something* all right. It was going into a big city for the first time. The picture shows and magazines had given us an idea of what was there, but it was still something. Now, going there is just like coming home to Pitcairn. We don't go for the excitement — I think in the twenty months we spent in New Zealand altogether, Pussy and I only went out to restaurants three times. We go for the jobs. My boy Daryl wants to get there bad."

Finally, Pervis talked of the island's tourist potential, the obvious attraction it holds for the millions who have read the *Bounty* story in dozens of languages. "It all depends on the tourists who come here, I suppose, *if* they come, and the stories they carry back," he suggested. "The Island Council has set a figure of ten dollars a week per person for full board for those who wish to stay in island homes. It's werry cheap, really. We know that our homes are not furnished houses like the Outside. But the people you board with will be doing all your cooking, supplying all your food, doing your washing, providing all the things you need."

It is more than werry cheap. For those who want Spartan adventure, and can live without many of the things vacations are built around — restaurants, beaches, nightclubs, shopping, rented cars, the freedom to have a drink or buy cigarettes, access to a wide circle of new acquaintances, ease of moving on to new places; do I paint too austere a picture? — it is one of the world's greatest tourist bargains. But getting his client to and from Pitcairn and coping with the paperwork, the long delays, and the built-in uncertainties are tasks which no sane travel agent is likely to undertake.

Pervis again: "If someone wrote to me, Box 5, Pitcairn Island, South Pacific, and said they wanted to come as a tourist, I wouldn't say Yes automatically. It would go before the Council, and then we'd send him a form. If he could fill out the form, we'd look at it and maybe give him the OK, and then we'd send it off to the Governor in Auckland who issues the licenses. But some of the chaps who want to come here may do bad things here, may have done bad crimes and want to hide. Or they may want to come here and just lie around and do no work and be a botheration to the people. That's the sort of chap we have to watch out for.

"*If* the person is all right, it may take five months for him to receive his license back. It all depends on the shipping. And when they *do* get it, they sometimes don't come."

Each mail steamer, Pervis said, usually brings one or more applications from would-be tourists. Almost invariably, the applicants never go through the full rigmarole or are declared undesirable by either the Island Council or the Governor's office. As in more sophisticated tourist spots, desirability — "decency" in Pervis' book — is usually equated with the ability to pay.

"Many of these people can't prove they have the means to support themselves on the island and the money to pay their way off," said Pervis. "Then we would have to arrange the travel ourselves, get them off somehow, but so far we haven't had anyone stranded like that. If someone arrived on a yacht, without a license, we'd bang right on that fellow for his money — the landing fee and the money to keep him here. Just *enough* money to prove he was a decent chap. If you turn out to be a decent chap, the money is all refunded, after the board is taken out, at the end of the stay. If he doesn't want to board with a family, he could move into the new government hostel, and we'd charge him two dollars a day, or a dollar a day if he wanted to live in the older hostel."

Both these buildings are prefabricated bungalows from New Zealand, built, uncomfortably close by any town-planning standards, to the oldest house on the island, the sturdy, nail-less cabin built by Thursday October Christian. The white hostels are the only sign of residential modernity on Pitcairn. They have piped water, a hot-water system, terraces, trim kitchen cabinets, even shades on the ceiling lamps and not just bare bulbs. The newer one, a $10,000 two-bedroom house on concrete stilts, was erected in less than three weeks by islanders working under the direction of a Pitcairn exile, Robert Young, who had been seconded from his job with the New Zealand Ministry of Public Works. The building of the hostel provided some welcome excitement and some paid work, but the local labor had real doubts about the design. They told Robert that if some official or tourist walked through a picture window or one of the plate-glass doors, it could be months, perhaps a year, before a replacement could be obtained, and what sort of planning for Pitcairn was *that*.

"Pussy" is calling Pervis to his "breakfast," and as we part, the Island Magistrate acknowledges that the talk of tourism was all a bit academic. Nobody who could be regarded as a genuine tourist arrived in 1971. The previous year was also bare of tourists. In 1969, a single hardy vacationer stepped ashore. When I left Pitcairn, 1972 was looming as another zero year for tourism.

Thomas Coleman Christian

"This is VR6TC. Pitcairn Island. South Pacific . . . The handle is Tom. T-O-M. Tired-old-man. Tango-Oscar-Mike . . ." Through the loudspeaker grill of the Hallicrafter equipment, which the manufacturers donated to the island a few years ago, comes an answering voice from the American Middle West: *"Hi, Tom. This*

is Bill. B-I-L-L. Boy-I-Love-Ladies. How are things on your desert island? How's the lotus-eating life? No more mutinies?"

The man behind the equipment in a small, unkempt room in a part of Adamstown which the mutineers, with touching English folksiness, named Shady Nook is neither tired nor old. He stands six feet two inches and has limbs that move under powerful muscle. His complexion is medium-brown and his strong, handsome features carry more of a Polynesian cast than is found in many of the island men. At thirty-six, he is a thoughtful, deeply religious man, yet, at the same time, probably the most worldly and sophisticated native Pitcairner. He is Tom Christian, Fletcher's sixth-generation descendant, Pitcairn's radio officer, and the recipient of an annual salary of $1,534 that is dazzling by island standards. With a gratuity of $500 awarded under his contract, his public salary last year amounted to five times that of the Island Magistrate, seven times that of the postmaster, and twenty-four times that of the librarian. An island entrepreneur, he has modest supplementary income from such things as postcards and mail-order filmstrips about Pitcairn. He also carves and trades aboard ships. His financial resources have elevated him to the rarefied strata of the Pitcairn upper middle class. He can afford mail-order items from the United States — the ham shack is littered with old Sears, Roebuck & Company catalogues — and gadgets from New Zealand. His home is as unpretentious as the general run of Adamstown shanties, but it has an electric hot-water heater in the kitchen and his wife, Betty, uses electric beaters and an electric kettle. There is a Sony stereo tape machine as well as a console record player and a good library of religious and pop tapes and records. While most of the islanders pay about $1.50 a month as their share of operating the small community power generator, Tom's contribution comes to around $8 or $9, and he can pay it easily. He also has his own generator and a storage-battery power supply that gives him electricity throughout the day, not simply for a few hours at night, as well as a choice of 110 volts or the island standard of 240 volts. They have some social concern over status symbols on the island. Tom has every one of them.

His salary as radio officer is a reflection of the value, even the preciousness, the islanders attach to their link with the outside world. To keep him on Pitcairn — for how much longer is a moot point — they have voted him steadily increased income. If he leaves, and this is foremost in his thoughts at the moment, there will be no one left to keep the transmitters operating. The Island Council will have to pay several times even his current inflated salary to hire an operator from New Zealand. His contract in the job, an obligation he assumed when the islanders paid for his training in communications abroad, has a year to run. Before it expires, he probably will have accepted an offer to work for a Seventh-Day Adventist radio station, the Voice of Prophecy, in Glendale, California. Fletcher's heir will become one more immigrant to Southern California, and the island community Fletcher founded will face a crisis that very well could crystallize the talk about whether Pitcairn will have to be evacuated.

If Tom is a man in demand on the island, he is also in demand on the international airwaves. His QSL, the acknowledgment card ham radio operators send to one another when they make a contact, is the most sought after one that exists among hams. His radio shack is wallpapered with them. They are an impressive and cosmopolitan collection, but Tom dismisses them with a wave of an arm. "These are only the very early ones, the QSL's that came in over the first couple of months," he says. "Then I ran out of wall space. The rest are in crates, boxes on boxes of them, stored somewhere in Betty's parents' home. I tried once to work out how many different hams I'd talked with, and it came to well over ten thousand. Siberia, Persia, India, Africa, little places in South America, everywhere."

When Tom warms up his transmitter, they are waiting for him. There is a stampede to make contact that must make the ionosphere crackle both with radio activity and some testiness on the part of disappointed hams. "*Peet-cayn Eyerand, Peet-cayn Eyerand,*" comes a plaintive voice identified as Aki from Hokkaido; "*Please, please, whoever the breaker is, I've been trying to get Tom for two hours,*" says a Swede with perfect English. Tom leaves the equipment on when he breaks for a cup of Ovaltine — as a good Adventist he spurns tea, coffee, and all the stimulants — and the entreaties from faraway hams, from Melbourne to Moscow, go on interminably: "*Pitcairn Island, Pitcairn Island . . . Are you read-*

Tom Christian, "Tango-Oscar-Mike," a man in demand on the amateur airwaves, in his ham shack.

ing me? . . . Come in please . . ." A man in British Columbia is getting positively frantic.

"I have to stop sometime," Tom excuses himself over the drink. "I could be ten men and work that set for twenty-four hours a day and still they wouldn't be satisfied." There are some half a million licensed ham operators in the world who have yet to get Tom's QSL. Those who do make the contact are rewarded with a pat little speech about the island. Tom is usually too bored with the ritual to go much beyond the clichés.

VR6TC is more than Tom's hobby. It is the islanders' intimate bond with relatives who have moved off the island and are living abroad. Normally, ham operators are prohibited from conducting such third-party traffic. An exception is made for Pitcairn because it has no competing radio-telephone service. Once Tom has raised a ham in the desired country and location, the operator at the other end makes a "phone patch" connection with the relative's home telephone and the tenuous link is established. "Can you manage two pair of dungarees? You know the size," a Pitcairn exile in Arizona is asked. "And if you're putting together a parcel, are the sou'wester sets we talked about available?" When I was eavesdropping on such a conversation one night, the final request was for ten packages of pop-it-yourself popcorn for a child's birthday many months away.

As radio officer, Tom is paid not for such informal services but to operate the official radio station on Taro Ground, 870 feet above Bounty Bay. The station is a collection of trim little buildings, an island showplace and the neatest thing Pitcairn offers. It has impressive new equipment from Britain, its own generator and a rhombic antenna on 70-foot towers. The heavy transmitter units, including a 500-watt one, the large generator, and the steel sections for the antenna towers all had to be landed through the surf and then carried on men's backs up steep mountain tracks.

Tom sends weather reports from Taro Ground, daily except on the Sabbath, and handles about three or four cables a day over the link with Cable and Wireless Ltd. in Suva, Fiji. He also operates a marine radio, ZBP, which is both the community's vital link with passing ships and an important pick-up point for distress messages in a stretch of ocean where there are very few radio ears at shore stations.

Frequently, of course, the distress calls are *outgoing* ones. "Living on a doctorless island is one of the risks we take," says Tom. "In an emergency, we will try to call in a ship in the area that is carrying a doctor. If that's not possible, we try to solve the case by discussing it with a doctor whom the Commissioner in Auckland organizes for us and follow his instructions. There have been cases when we've had to stay on the radio for three days before we could get a ship. The fear — I suppose it's the island phobia — is appendicitis. That and fractures and uncontrolled bleeding."

Tom did not relate his own crisis with a ruptured appendix, but

I heard the story later from his wife. When he came down with excruciating abdominal pains, he had relayed the symptoms too many times to have any doubt about what it was. He asked for ice, and every tray, every scrap of frosting around the coils was rushed to his house by the owners of the few kerosene-operated iceboxes on the island. With the burners turned up as high as possible, new ice was made as fast as freezing coils could produce it. A freighter was three days' steaming away. Until it could reach Pitcairn, Tom's midsection was packed in ice. The ship arrived, but there was no doctor on board. The captain agreed to rush him to Auckland. Still packed in ice nine days later, he was carried off the freighter and sped to a hospital.

Almost every household has been through a similar crisis with appendicitis at some time. Many have seen loved ones die in agony, in their own bedrooms or in cabins of cargo ships which could not tackle the surgery. One man died in the longboat taking him out to a ship that *did* have a doctor. Yet at no time have the islanders given practical consideration to enabling one of their young men or women to earn a medical degree abroad. The community could certainly afford it with some outside help. But would a man with full medical training be content to remain long in a community of eighty-five? The islanders are aware that the answer is No.

Tom's radio duties also call on him to tap out in Morse some coded messages to the office of the Governor of Pitcairn. They go out in the familiar five-letter groupings. When I spent a morning with Tom in the radio station, the day after our entry into one of the world's most primitive little societies, I was astonished to find him transmitting an entire page of coded message. Who here, I wondered, could possibly have that much to relay in clandestine language? Perhaps the message was simply to advise the Governor that a family of five, aged from four to forty-three, had landed from New York with a camera crew.

There are, I discovered later, not one but two codes in use on the island. The Island Government has one, but its secrets are said to be of the rudimentary kind which a cryptographer could crack in about the time it takes to do a crossword puzzle. The other one is a top-secret code used by the New Zealand Armed Services. The members of the Pitcairn government are not privileged to know its mysteries. Only one man on the island, the schoolteacher, who also doubles as government adviser, has the codebooks and the formula. (I did extract the clue that it was a system based on literary classics, a different work each month with the encoder selecting the page number, but that is all.) Many things on Pitcairn were still mind-boggling to us at this early point in our stay. The discovery that the teacher had to be Mr. Chips by day and James Bond by night was not all that startling.

The location of the radio station high above Adamstown and Tom's relative affluence were factors directly responsible for the introduction of the Hondas to Pitcairn. Tom may be said to be the father of the motorbike era on the island. In 1966, weary of making a mile-and-a-half trip to the station on foot, up and down the mountain twice each day, he bought a Honda 90 from a distributor in Auckland and arranged a supply of gasoline in forty-four gallon drums. With no taxes or duties, it cost him $290. It took to the dirt tracks so well that the dealer soon had follow-up orders from Tom's cousins, who dipped into their savings and stepped up their output of curios to acquire powered wheels. By the beginning of 1972, there were thirty Hondas on the island, with nine more on order. Soon, there would be one motorbike for almost every two Pitcairners, an astonishing degree of mechanization in so short a space of time. Tom and his wife each have a Honda and he is talking of powering-up to a bigger model.

"Before the motorbikes, I used to arrive at the radio station sweating from the climb, but my health was a lot better," says Tom. "I'm chicken now. That's why I come down with the flu so badly when a ship brings in the germ. We all have softened up a bit, and we feel it whenever we exert ourselves, rowing, gardening, gathering firewood."

Like most of the Pitcairners, Tom has an ambivalent attitude toward the toys of civilization. They want the Hondas and the gasoline-powered chain saws, but they see also how they are changing the little society, changing it in ways that nibble away at the community spirit, the stirring sense of oneness that came from the time when many things could be accomplished only by everybody pulling together. The machines have made their lives a bit easier but also imposed fresh burdens on the community. Landing fuel on harborless Pitcairn has always been a problem and an expense, doubly so now that highly inflammable gasoline is involved. With the population declining, and ships growing fewer, new ways must be found to pay for the toys and the fuel they consume. The society has yet to come up with the answers; for the time being, it seems to be placing its faith in Pitcairn's historic ability to make do and survive. And all the while, the things that come in boxes from Osaka or Liverpool or Los Angeles constitute the hors d'oeuvres that tempt the young off the island to the seven-course meal they believe has been set for them in the outside world.

As a radio officer aboard merchant navy ships, as a trainee for eight months at the Adventist Voice of Prophecy in California, after which he made a public appearance tour in connection with the second *Mutiny on the Bounty* film, Tom has seen a good deal of the Outside. Certificates on the wall of his ham shack attest to the fact that he is an honorary citizen of New Orleans and St. Petersburg, Florida. The world now is luring him back.

Some time ago, Tom cut down coconut trees and leveled an area of ground behind his present house to build what I would guess is the first real "dream home" ever planned on Pitcairn. For personal and economic reasons, it probably will not progress beyond the planning stage. With much imported material, the house might cost Tom in the $10,000 to $11,000 range, with the owner providing all the labor. And once it was built, the investment virtually would be lost. Nobody, even if they had that sort of money, *buys* houses on Pitcairn, and nobody with the purchase price is likely to arrive with ideas of settling. If Tom were to migrate, his $10,000 house would be a white elephant. When as basic an operation as home-building is beclouded with doubt for a prospering family man in his prime, the true stultifying effect of life in a remote society, with no clear vision of its future, can be grasped.

Tom, his very Caucasian-featured wife, Betty, twenty-nine, and the pretty baby, Jacqueline Beth, who arrived after five years of marriage, go on living in a dunnage-timber house his grandfather built more than a century ago. It was erected on the site of Fletcher Christian's original house. (One day in Tom's pumpkin patch, I picked up a bent and stubby, inch-long bronze nail which,

I fancied absurdly, might have come from the *Bounty*. To my great surprise, after close examination and comparison with authenticated pieces of hardware from the ship, it turned out to be a genuine *Bounty* relic, one of the hundreds of nails that had been used on the hull sheathing and which the mutineers had frugally extracted. Generously, Tom let me keep it.) Close by Tom's house, depressing reminders of the drop in the colony's numbers, are the decaying shells of three other nineteenth-century houses, now abandoned. Their foundations have given way, and the moss-covered frames and walls tilt at wild angles. Tom's house is in an advanced stage of assault by termites. Alongside the electrical appliances are many makeshift touches. A pipe made from empty soft-drink cans carries away the drainage from the kitchen. A hawser stretched across the muddy backyard enables one to grope one's way with greater confidence at night from the back door to the outdoor privy.

Tom is a fine host, and one has the strong impression that he wishes his home were more impressive. "I wouldn't say we have a good house," he says. "We have lived in more comfortable houses abroad. But then it's not always the building that matters."

I asked Tom whether, having seen something of the world, he ever felt claustrophic on Pitcairn, whether he sometimes might not feel as if a giant saucepan lid had been placed on his life here. He disagreed at first, but his later remarks suggested there *was* an element of claustrophia. He pointed out that in his general age group, only two or three men were left on the island. "There have been times, of course, when I felt I wanted to get away for a break," he said. "When a component breaks down and you can't get a part, you do feel down and out, that you'd like to get away. It calls for patience to wait for a few months for something you could walk round the corner and buy in most other places." Each time he returned to Pitcairn from trips abroad, Tom found that he missed the stores, the supermarkets, and the nights before a television set. As compensation, he would walk down to the cliffs behind his house early each morning and spend an hour or two just watching the sea breaking wildly against the rocks.

Every morning for a year now, Tom has walked down to those same cliffs in the interests of science, carrying a small black suitcase about the size of an electrician's tool kit. The case, which contains gauges, dials, and a hand pump, was supplied by the Atmospheric Sciences Research Center of the State University of New York at Albany. The Center has enlisted Tom's help in testing the atmosphere over Pitcairn to determine whether continental pollution is invading the Pacific Ocean.

The day I watched Tom take an atmospheric sample on the cliffs, pumping through the machine air that had been windborne for some three thousand miles without passing over even a tiny land mass, the needle flicked up to three on a scale of one hundred. According to the folder of documentation Tom received with the kit from Albany, this meant that Pitcairners were breathing the cleanest possible air to be found anywhere, air quality of a purity ecologists expect to find only in mid-ocean regions, on remote mountaintops, or in the Antarctic. Out of curiosity, Tom tested the machine in the living room of his house. The needle went up to thirty, which is about what it would record in a medium-sized city with some industry. About an hour later, he repeated the test in his living room. By this time, the community had lit a fire in a barbecue pit on the lawn behind the Pastor's house, a quarter of a mile away, in preparation for a New Year's Day Maori *hangi*. I had also lit up a few cigarettes as we chatted in Tom's living room. When he went back to his air-tester, Tom seemed taken aback. He repeated the sampling procedure several times to make sure the machine was working properly. The needle each time climbed to the same level — sixty. "Gosh," said Tom, consulting his instructions. "It's the same as New York City air on a bad day!"

An outsider who has spent some time living within the community looks upon Tom as very much Fletcher Christian's heir. "His father, Fred, reflected totally the Polynesian part of his origin — his contentment with the life here, his oneness with nature, his ability to find simple solutions," this observer remarked. "But in Tom I see the characteristics I imagine Fletcher must have had — the ambition, the vanity, the grand schemes."

Whether or not Tom takes after Fletcher rather than his Polynesian great-great-great-grandmother, he is one of the few Pitcairners who appear to have thought at all deeply and independently about the community's origins. His fellow islanders are content to accept as gospel the MGM version, the early Charles Laughton-Clark Gable one, that is, which reached the island half a generation after it had been seen by the rest of the world. Tom is in the privileged position of having seen the second version while he was in the United States. He was dismayed to watch Marlon Brando die on a nonexistent beach in Bounty Bay soon after the mutineers' arrival — "If that had been the case, I wouldn't be here today."

He believes that many of the island young today "have forgotten how we started here." If, logically enough, the story of the mutiny and Pitcairn's history were to be taught in the island school in place of an exclusive diet of British, American, and Australasian history, Tom would like the mutineers' descendants to be told not only of Bligh's temper but also of Fletcher's taste for the good life of Polynesia. "In taking over the ship," Fletcher's heir surmises, "I'm sure that one of their reasons was they wanted to get back to the easier living and the free women of Tahiti. Fletcher must have liked the life on Tahiti. He must have had some feeling for it or he wouldn't have rebelled to return to it. The books picture Fletcher as a good-natured fellow, but that was not always true. Why would he have cast Bligh adrift? Why would he have brought Tahitians to Pitcairn and then deprived them of land? That was asking for the trouble they got."

I asked this descendant whether he felt Fletcher Christian had found on Pitcairn the happiness, the life he was seeking. Tom had evidently pondered the question before. He answered without hesitation: "I don't think so."

Brenda Christian

In the life-style, the character, and the dreams of an eighteen-year-old Pitcairner, we can find a record both of the island's past and the social pressures of the present moment that are casting a shadow over its future.

Brenda Christian is Fletcher's loveliest descendant, and in her desires and frustrations, one of the more complex. She is nubile in a very Polynesian way. Her body is brown and lithe; her movements have the freedom of the trade winds that blow over Pitcairn and the ocean spray that crashes against the cliffs. She alone on the island carries on the Tahitian traits of flirtatiousness and lack of inhibitions. Her life on Pitcairn seems one endless vacation of sun and sea. She does whatever she pleases. What matter if Pastor's wife is shocked at a sports gathering by Brenda's tiny bloomer outfit? She saw a picture of the outfit in a New Zealand fashion magazine, and lacking a local boutique, made it and the skimpy top that went with it, at home. She will go dutifully to prayer meeting but do so as a sweater girl in leather micro-mini and thigh boots. For a swim in Bounty Bay, she wears an exiguous print bikini. She has impressive cleavage and no wish to conceal it from the dour little commune; it must drive the young men, the cousin youths, into storms of desire. She is a pocket Venus, a nymphet of the sort that gave Humbert Humbert such a bad time. She doesn't smoke, swear, or drink, but is nonetheless a hell-raiser. One has the feeling she would like to shake up the island in ways comprehensible only to a teen-age girl who has been summoned home to an Iowa hamlet after a fling in Manhattan.

Shining chestnut tresses. Limpid brown eyes. A waist to be seized. A smile of mischief and allure. Shapely legs that flash in the surf or are seen propelling a bikinied body down deep in search of a twelve-pound crayfish into the churning waters along the coastal rocks. Brenda Christian is a flamelet of the fire that burns — only occasionally nowadays, I grant, but remember there have been two centuries of missionaries, a World War, and jumboloads of packaged tourism for those seeking the Pacific paradise — in Polynesian maidens from Bora Bora to Oahu to Pago Pago. If one's thoughts are exclusively hedonistic, purely escapist, she is what the South Seas are all about. If one is thinking vaguely about history, the conclusion might be that she was what the mutiny was all about, too. It is possible to glimpse Brenda and decide impressionistically, there and then, that it was Tahiti that did in the *Bounty* mission and not the temper of the man directing it.

She is gay and spirited and adventurous, and not quite old enough to find the boundaries of Pitcairn life closing on her. But I doubt very much whether she is happy being one of eighty-five people living on a dollop of land in the remote subtropics. She shares with the few other young Pitcairners — and bear in mind that her dating circle is limited to four men, four cousins, with only three other girls in her age group — a fundamental discontent over what the present offers and the future holds. You watch her playing musical chairs and simple games with the nine- and twelve-year-olds at a rather desperate evening social organized by Pastor in the courthouse, and wonder what on earth must be going through her mind.

She thinks vaguely about a career. But what career is possible here? She toys with the idea of staying on to run her own dress shop — "a boutique on Pitcairn with things we design and make here, *and* items from outside, think of that!" But in a poorish community of thirty-nine females, seven of whom are in their seventies or eighties, who would be her customers?

Fletcher's great-great-great-great-great-granddaughter is ready to leave. She has seen the Outside, both as a young girl and as a teen-ager. At ten, she was taken to Auckland when her family, one of the more affluent on the island, moved there briefly. At sixteen, she returned for two years of secondary education in Dunedin in the South Island of New Zealand. She had just returned to Adamstown when we arrived there and already was gazing yearningly out to sea and to that crowded world beyond the horizon. Her parents, Ivan and Dobrey, had moved back to their native island earlier than they had planned out of fear that they might leave a child bride in the arms of a Dunedin boy. (A Pitcairner is considered a full adult at eighteen and does not require parental permission to marry.)

When the Ivan Christians came home to Pitcairn, the French nuclear test season was under way and a handsome young Welshman, Michael Randall, an RAF technician, had been put ashore to monitor the explosions. Before too many days and nights had passed, Brenda and Michael were engaged and Brenda was thinking about a wedding, "a white wedding, here on the island, in Wales, anywhere" — *and* a home abroad. Michael went back to Wales when a Royal Navy vessel came to collect him and his instruments. He has discovered since that having a fiancée on Pitcairn and living in Wales is a very special, and quite expensive, circumstance. The lovers exchange cables every two weeks. Letters, said Brenda, could take four or five months. (I wanted to inquire,

Brenda Christian, Fletcher's great-great-great-great-great-granddaughter, on a rock Bounty Bay.

but didn't, about what one said in a fortnightly cable to one's sweetheart.)

I was chatting with Brenda and some of her friends on the grassy lip of a cliff looking down on a dramatic stretch of coast the islanders call Bitey Bitey. Her long hair was whipping back in the freshening breeze from the sea, like the closing shot in a shampoo commercial. I could see Brenda making a successful transposition to any Western society; yet there was a poignancy, an element of sadness in reflecting on such a transfer: she would be losing in the process her unique Pitcairn qualities, the things that made her Brenda Christian, island beauty, island tomboy; was even now on her way to becoming simply a pretty housewife tending a home in a suburban row.

The talk of engagement and marriage made me realize for the first time that newlyweds here face a unique dilemma. When you live on a tiny island, within a few hundred yards' walk of every single resident, with no established way of leaving the place, where and how do you spend your honeymoon? "It *is* a problem," Brenda giggled. "Where can you go here. What is there to get away *to?* But this is something we live with all our lives, *every day*, not only at honeymoon time." The honeymoon custom, in fact, does not exist on the island. Newlyweds usually move in with one or the other's parents. When a parent or grandparent dies, the house is taken over by the young. No one has built a new home on the island, Brenda tells me, since Pervis finished his in 1953. There are twenty-two inhabited dwellings today, and twenty-three abandoned ones. To young people like Brenda, the total lack of interest in structural renewal, in planning anew, presents gloomy daily reminders of the cousin-family's ability, or desire, to make a go of it for much longer.

And these young people are not the ones to revive and remake this society. Given their upbringing and their constricted opportunities, it would be wrong to expect it of them. What is uppermost in their thoughts is marriage — marriage off the island. (Brenda's sister Ruth fell in love with a New Zealander who arrived with a team of archaeologists and surveyors in 1964 and has been living away from her home island ever since.) These young have no interest in politics — island "politics," world politics. They are not even attracted, as are apolitical youth in most places, by the political celebrities, the dashing wielders of power, the charismatic ones.

When the French began their atmospheric nuclear testing in the area and Pitcairn found itself on the boundary of the danger zone, the youth contributed nothing to what turned out to be a touching, but gentle and ineffectual island protest. It was left to the visiting schoolmaster and a few older Pitcairners to frame. I ask Brenda about her political interests, and she shrugs a pair of pretty shoulders.

She is interested in little more than her hobbies. She learned to swim at three in the black rock pools at a place called Isaac's Rocks and is an impressive swimmer today. In New Zealand, she was appalled to find that the water was "smelly." And worse, "You had to *pay* to use the pool." The clear, free water was what she seemed to miss most about Pitcairn. Her brother, Steve, has an underwater gun and she borrows it for a day's spearfishing in crashing waters that would test the skill of a lifeguard. She collects *bladders* — fish bladders, which have to be blown up to make them look like anything, and goat bladders that have some sort of natural inflation. "They make a collection," says Brenda. "I have a boxful of them. It's something I've been collecting for years. You can't do anything *with* them. Just look at them occasionally and show them to friends."

Being the descendant of a celebrated mutineer, Brenda was something of a celebrity in New Zealand. She tried acting, but it came to nothing. Her other hobby is fashion, and at this she succeeds superbly. Brenda can show up for an evening affair in the village square, having negotiated the red mud of the main track, wash her legs and feet with water from the church well, and appear *soignée* in black pants, black sandals, silk top, elaborate coiffure, silver necklace, drop earrings, the lot. She was the only Pitcairner I saw wearing jewelry. She runs into some criticism: "When I wear my skirts too short, they complain. When the maxi comes in and I make them long like what the older women have been wearing all their lives, like what Aunt Lily the midwife wore when she delivered me, they say, Brenda, how old-fashioned you look. What can you do?"

When she is not sewing or swimming or looking for new bladders, she passes the time carving. Her curios, particularly leaping island fish, are the match of anything turned out by the men. She is addicted to Country-Western music which the teen-agers hear on records or, through freak reception, from local stations in the United States. On nights when there is no electrical activity in the atmosphere, a station in Sacramento and another in Oklahoma City are picked up with booming strength on the medium-wave band; and the C & W music, and all those tantalizing commercials about driving out for chicken so good you'll want to lick the fingers, come strangely to receptive young ears.

In New Zealand, she had the chance to go to dances; but either her church instruction or her lack of knowledge of the steps stopped her from doing so. "I spent most of my spare time there going to the pictures," she recalls. "The pictures were better than the television. Just occasionally I watched television. But I would stay home, of course, if Johnny Cash was on the telly."

I asked her what constituted a teen-age night out on Pitcairn. "Oh, we might spend the afternoon getting some crayfish — don't tell Pastor this, mind you — and go for a burn-up on the Hondas, up to the highest point on the island," she replied. "We'll cook the crayfish up there in buckets, and eat them while they're hot, and we might stay up there all night in one of the huts. It's cozy."

In short, then, Miss Brenda Christian, beauty, tomboy, bladder-collector, designer, frustrated actress, skin-diver, motorcyclist, fiancée of an absent Welshman, Adamstown resident for however brief a time remaining, is as unexpected as a snowfall in Bounty Bay. If ever the island enters the Miss Universe contest, she is the logical choice for "Miss Pitcairn." For the time being, the island beauty is not unappreciated. On the big coconut tree at the foot of the Pastor's lawn, someone has carved, in two-inch-high letters, the emphatic statement: I LOVE BRENDA. The author of this public cry of affection preferred to remain anonymous.

Norris Joseph Young

"Noggie" Young, twenty-two, is one fifth of the landed gentry of Pitcairn. With his brother, Donald, sixteen, and sisters Glenda, eighteen, Allison, five, and Pamela, three, Noggie is co-owner of precisely one-half of the island land, a circumstance which causes a certain amount of envy and ill feeling in Adamstown society. (One of the very conservative leaders of that society even suggested to me that all island land should be appropriated by the Island Government and then leased back to those needing it for agriculture or other purposes. Land tenure had got into such a hopeless mess over the years, what with laws being unclear in the old days and people leaving and not making proper arrangements' for the inheritance of their plots, that a bit of extreme socialism seemed the only remedy.)

Noggie's branch of the Young family took title to scores of acres of abandoned land after the first small group of Pitcairners moved back from Norfolk Island. His grandfather, Norris Henry Young, now eighty-four and the oldest man on the island, had many brothers and sisters who all died childless. Their land holdings passed to him exclusively, and, in turn, old Norris has left the land to Noggie's father, Henry Hugh. The father, now sixty-two, has already made the arrangements to transfer the land to his five children. There are some large tracts involved, but most of the landholding is an aggregation of odd-shaped scraps scattered around the coast and on the high ground. Some, in the Pitcairn manner, are just big enough to plant a few trees and erect a shed. The Young family land, *this* particular Young family, that is, is far too much for them to use themselves, so they permit the community to raise *miro* trees on some tracts and take one tenth of the wood in payment.

With this potential wealth behind him, Noggie works for the government as driver of the public tractor for a wage of about $35 a month. If ships arrive, he can make several times that amount from his carvings; but like all the young men on the island, he would far rather go spearfishing or zooming about on his motorcycle than squat in a workshop whittling wood into sharks or walking sticks or glueing together models of the *Bounty*. When trading days arrive, the stockpiles of curios which the middle-aged and old men and women take out to the ships put the young men to shame. Considering that the older generations also do most of the planting, weeding, and harvesting in the gardens and the cooking, clean-

"Noggie" Young continues his sanding of a carved gull on a cliffside perch high above the little village of Adamstown.

ing, and laundry at home, the productivity of Noggie's generation is markedly low.

Since Victorian days, the old folks on Pitcairn have been fretting about the younger generation and wondering whatever would become of them. Noggie's generation, however, seems to have been the first that brought real juvenile delinquency problems to the community.

"Ten years ago when I was at school here, they were wild and woolly days," Noggie recalls. "There were actually teen-age gangs formed. One group supported the teacher, who was a real strict one, and another group hated him, hated him because he liked the strap. [Corporal punishment, a strap about two feet in length is the instrument, is still allowed in the Pitcairn school, even for girls.] The ones who hated him would even get together arsenals of sticks and stones and talk about bombarding him on the way home. The prefects had to escort the children home from school in groups to stop the fighting. People used to go indoors when they heard us coming. Talk about tar sailors' swearing. They used worse. It's not like that today. The ruffians are all gone from the school."

The ruffians of that time are now the young adults. Noggie swears and so do most of the young unmarried men. Perhaps because of the power his family wields with its real estate, perhaps because he knows he will leave the island soon, Noggie says and does what he likes. He knows all the church ritual, and can sing hymns in a pleasant, ringing voice as well as any islander, but he rarely attends services. When he does take his seat in a pew, it is either because he wants to meet someone there or has nothing better to do. To Noggie, and to many of the young and middle-aged men, Sabbath service is often the only "excitement" Adamstown can provide. He often speaks of the missionary presence as simply "bloody Pastor there."

Noggie is Midshipman Edward Young's sixth-generation descendant. He is a burly six-footer who wears size 13 shoes whenever there is need to shod the lower extremities. He has an enormous chest and has been a powerful swimmer since early childhood. The huge rib cage, however, sits on a cushion of paunch. Noggie's love of *taro*, sweet potatoes, boiled bananas, *pillhai*, and all the other starchy things the island grows has left him with a potbelly that is unusual to find in an otherwise muscular man in his early twenties.

In skin color, he is about in the middle range of light-to-dark for the islanders. Disconcertingly, his sister Glenda is a pink-cheeked blond. Noggie is distinctly a brown man but several shades lighter than the darkest Tahitians. The other Polynesian aspects are full lips and snowy-white teeth. His nose is finer than most, more English than Tahitian. He has sight in only one eye. A glass eye in the left socket is his lifetime reminder of a childhood accident. The community was returning from trading aboard a passenger ship when horseplay among the boys turned into stick throwing. A stray shot hit Noggie in the eye. The liner was summoned back by radio, and the ship's doctor told Noggie's parents that he would lose the eye. In searing pain, Noggie was rowed out to the ship and arrangements were hurriedly made for him to travel with his father to hospital in New Zealand.

After some secondary school on the island, Noggie spent nine months in Fiji and a year and a half in New Zealand learning about machines. The money came from an Island Government grant that covered travel, boarding, and pocket money. He estimates that his education abroad cost about $2,000 in public funds. He returned with a Junior Certificate in engineering. He was under a contract obligation to remain on the island for two years in a government job.

For the same money he gets now as tractor driver, he came home to be the island's maintenance engineer, a post with heavy responsibilities for so young a man and so meager a pay packet. He was required to keep the lighting plant in working order, grease and operate the "flying fox" lift, check the Lister diesels in the longboats, maintain the derrick winch, and do any welding needed on publicly owned equipment or installations. No dedicated civil servant, Noggie grumbles that a Pitcairn public engineer's monthly pay is less than people used to make with a single receptive customer on a liner. From time to time he hatches other money-making schemes, but they all seem to come to naught. When we were there, he was wondering whether the community might lend Steve Christian and him a longboat, so they could offer to take venturesome tourists off the next ship to arrive. At five dollars a head, sightseers would be able to land on Pitcairn and see more of the society than carved birds and colored baskets. But there are regulations covering disembarking at Pitcairn. The ships never seem to wait long enough these days for escorted tours ashore. And the final deciding factor is always the condition of the sea. There are obstacles in the path of those who set out to be businessmen on Pitcairn.

Noggie's big frame is transported almost everywhere these days by Honda saddle rather than by his still powerful legs. The tank of his red motorcycle holds only a bit over a gallon, but this is sufficient for about 140 miles of hilly travel. He came of age simultaneously with the arrival of the Pitcairn automotive age. Yet he looks back on the days before mini-mechanization with some fondness.

"It was more exciting before the machines came," Noggie told me one day as we sat on the steps of the now hooligan-free schoolhouse. "There were more people here then, and we had to do things by manpower which seemed *impossible* — getting the boats out and back through the surf with just oars, getting loads up the hill on our shoulders, manhandling things everywhere in ways you wouldn't dream that men and boys could do.

"I started going out on the boats when I was twelve. If a ship was sighted and it looked like it was stopping, I was excused from school. At thirteen, I was appointed a member of the crew of one of the boats. The Hondas and the tractor have changed things in good ways and bad ways. Now we are Pitcairners as we always were, but we are starting to sit around watching machinery work."

Yet Noggie was preparing to leave for shores that have so many machines that new machines must be invented to deal with the harm the old ones cause to the environment.

"In six months, maybe sooner, I'll be going to Australia or New Zealand," he said. "I'll probably work in an auto garage. In New Zealand, for a time, I was earning $75 a week, $90 with overtime, and that's with Sundays free, which you don't get here. There's just not much going on here. The same thing over and over and over again. I'll probably marry off the island. What's the choice here? — three or four girls, and that's it."

Noggie left the island soon after we did.

CHAPTER SIXTEEN

THE PITCAIRN EXCHEQUER

I N A STUDY of any distinctive society, it would be customary to take up such areas as the economic structure, the political arrangements, and the system of law far earlier than I am doing here. I have left the examination of these matters until now for the good reason that Pitcairn does not lend itself to conventional methods of investigation. Although there is an annual budget, there is no real "economy." There is a political structure, but no politics. While the island laws make fascinating reading, they have to be applied so rarely nowadays — once, sometimes twice a year — that they are of interest more as museum pieces than as a gauge of present social conditions.

I was able to establish — by the valid, if unorthodox method of determining probable earnings through an examination of the tithes paid to the church, a procedure outlined later in a discussion of religion — that the per capita annual income on the island amounts to roughly $282. But basically, this is a moneyless society. Apart from the Coop merchandise two hours a week, what is there to spend it on? It was not until about halfway through the stay that I got out of the habit of slipping my wallet into my hip pocket when I dressed each morning. It was about this time also that it dawned on me that there was something missing in the accouterments of the womenfolk — even on the dressiest of occasions, they rarely carried any sort of handbag. They don't use cosmetics, they don't take pills, and they don't need money. Collectively, the islanders' annual income is about what a union plumber in New York or San Francisco takes in over a year by working a little overtime.

What little money is in circulation on the island has arrived in one of two ways — from a novel subsidy arrangement devised by the British government or from informal trading aboard ships; steadily more of the former, steadily less of the latter.

In the wartime year of 1940, the British government conceived a way of keeping the island functioning at no cost to the British taxpayer. It was decided to issue Pitcairn Islands stamps. (The plural is applied here because the Pitcairn administrative unit embraces three uninhabited and virtually uninhabitable atolls — Henderson and Oeno, each a good day's sail from Pitcairn, and Ducie Island, 293 miles to the east, which is not visited by the islanders.) For the previous fourteen years, the Pitcairners had been using New Zealand stamps; before 1926, letters sent from the island were simply franked: "Posted on Pitcairn Island; no stamps available." New Zealand, Australia, Britain, and a number of other countries delivered them as a courtesy.

Since October 15, 1940, when the island stamps were introduced, philatelists around the world have been responsible, unknowingly, for keeping Pitcairn in business, underwriting the cost of what little public construction has been undertaken. The stamps are beautifully designed, extremely colorful, and more imaginative often than Britain's own issues. Over the years, they must have given many a deceptive impression of the place, making it seem that Pitcairn is much more conscious of its image in the world, more go-ahead and more in the mainstream of modern life than is actually the case.

In helping out her smallest dependency, Britain assumes all the responsibility — the design work, which involves dispatching an artist to Pitcairn every few years, the printing of the stamps, even their distribution to stamp dealers. Only a very small percentage of Pitcairn stamps actually reach the island and are sold over the counter of the little post office. The stamps, evidently, are not a bad investment. On September 18, 1971, Urch, Harris & Co. Ltd., an investment concern in Bristol, England, ran a display advertise-

Recent issues of Pitcairn Island stamps

ment in British newspapers headed "200% Profit in Two Months." The ad had an illustration of the latest Pitcairn stamp novelty, a ten-cent stamp overprinted with the words "Royal Visit 1971," to commemorate Prince Philip's call there. Messrs. Urch and Harris told this "absolutely true" story of how well they had served their clients in urging them to buy block upon block of this particular issue: "Every month we distribute to our customers stamps which in our judgment represent sound investment potential. In April of this year the stamp illustrated above seemed so outstanding that we devoted all our attention to it and we distributed the stamp in quantity to everyone on the basis of 15p [newpence] per copy. Just two months later 'collector demand' was such that we were able to offer to buy back every copy at 45p each, giving all of our clients the chance of a 200% profit in just two months. As it has turned out, those clients who decided to hold on to the stamps have done even better for the stamp has now climbed to a retail price of 75p."

In such ways as this, Pitcairn makes profits for investment consultants and collectors on a scale the islanders would probably find mind-boggling. The reverse side of the coin is that the philatelic money enables a society which has never known taxation or customs duties to have an annual budget always in surplus.

The British government subtracts the cost of producing and distributing the stamps and remits the profits to Pitcairn to keep the island economy rolling along. New definitive issues are introduced from time to time, and there are special issues to spur sales. The best year was 1967, when there was an overprinting to mark the island's conversion to decimal currency, and two anniversaries to celebrate: the bicentenary of Pitcairn's discovery by Carteret, and the one-hundred-and-fiftieth anniversary of the death of William Bligh. Yes, William Bligh. (Would Fletcher Christian ever have dreamed that his descendants would be selling Pitcairn stamps honoring Bligh?)

Stamp income added $210,799 to Pitcairn's coffers in the fiscal year 1967–1968. In the same period there was an additional $21,660 flowing in from interest on money Britain has invested for the Pitcairners from past surpluses, and from development grants awarded by London.

The 1969–1970 fiscal year was more typical. The stamps and

interest brought in $87,852. The Island Council, or administrators abroad acting on Pitcairn's behalf, spent $73,169 of this, leaving them with a budget surplus of $14,683. Estimated revenue for 1971–1972 was $84,202, and the islanders were planning to spend $80,572 on public works and public administration, including the usual off-island expenditures, which take a good bite out of the total. This means that their budget surplus will have plummeted to $3,360 from the spectacular but unnatural high of $141,155 in 1967–1968. Like everyone else, the Pitcairners are feeling the pinch of inflation in their public affairs.

Their investment fund, however, is in good shape. It now exceeds a quarter of a million dollars, invested in gilt-edged official securities. For the fiscal year 1971–1972, interest was expected to swell the total by $18,020. In a community whose members have a very real interest in money, although they see not too much of it, the sum put away for them in distant official bank accounts does not, as one might expect, hold great fascination. Some of the older islanders are not even aware of its existence. None of the officials I talked with suggested that the fund should be raided and applied to much-needed public projects: paved roads, for example, so bare feet could travel down the main track without acquiring a thick sole of mud. "We like to know the money's there in case times get werry bad on Pitcairn," said one.

Until that day arrives, the stamp revenue should be sufficient to cover the salary and wages paid to those in civil employment. The Magistrate's job carries a stipend of $37 a month. The same salary is paid to the medical officer, the Pastor's wife. The island engineer gets $35 a month, the postmaster $26, and there are equally modest salaries for the public electrician, the two men who drive the tractor, the works supervisor, and the man who has charge of the boats and other equipment at the Landing. The inspector of police receives $17.60 a month, which puts the entire expenditure on police work at $211.20 for the year. The librarian is paid $7. The two salaried councilors get $105.60 apiece each year. The "dental officer," a member of the Christian family who took a limited course in dentistry at a clinic in Fiji, receives in *annual* remuneration the sum of $132. The "dentist," strangely enough, receives precisely the same annual salary as the assistant nurse. The

nurse herself is paid well over three times as much! Considering
the respective states of the islanders' bodily health — well above
average — and their teeth — well below average — I found this
imbalance especially curious. No one was able to explain it to my
satisfaction.

The Pitcairn pension, which one gets automatically at sixty-five,
amounts to $7 a month. The annual pension bill for 1970–1971
came to $1,848. Other public money is spent to enable the young
to complete secondary education abroad. When I was there, the
sum of $1,560 had been budgeted to send two students to schools
in Fiji and New Zealand. The budget also provides for modest
expenditures on such things as school supplies, building materials,
replacement parts for publicly owned machinery, medical supplies,
and so on. There is a cash reserve of a few thousand dollars which
Ben, the Island Secretary keeps in an old safe at the back of his
office.

The accounts contain numerous entries reflecting Pitcairn's seafaring connections:

New pintles and gudgeons for the long boats — $100.

Clearing rocks in Bounty Bay — $150.

There are also entries that bring out touchingly the Pitcairners'
concern for one of their number who is less able than most to fend
for himself: *Maintenance of Morris Warren* — $103.

This appeared in the estimates for 1971–1972. The previous year,
Morris' maintenance had cost the community $11 less. Another
item in the same estimates caught my eye: *Occupational therapy,
Morris Warren* — $12. This was an annual budgetary sum, and a
footnote was added to explain the entry to auditors in New
Zealand: "Pocket money for topping up fuel tanks." I have already
introduced old Morris as the only islander who smokes. His $12
from "occupational therapy" could be turned into six cartons of
cigarettes if a chief steward of a passing ship were willing to sell
him duty-free smokes. In return for the public money the community lays out for his maintenance, Morris carries out some weeding along the road and does what he can to keep the graveyard
tidy.

In addition, there are government handouts for the islanders
who keep public buildings clean, tend the two graveyards, and so

on. Payday is the last day of the month, provided this does not fall on the Saturday Sabbath, and the wages are paid in New Zealand or Australian dollars. If someone particularly wants United States dollars or Sterling, he can arrange to draw his wages in the equivalents in those currencies.

"We try to arrange jobs so that everyone on the island is getting a little something in public money," Pervis explained. "Without that money from the government, then it's werry, werry hard to live on Pitcairn today. But when the passenger boats were coming here regularly, it was better to keep *out* of government jobs. You could get more money out of the ships in those days than in the best public job." The good times return very occasionally. "On a good ship, like the *Sagafjord*, with three or four hundred passengers, the people come off with maybe three or four thousand dollars altogether from trading," Pervis estimated. "Some of the men, the good carvers, will come off with five hundred dollars each. When the big ones used to come, they would stay all day and we could trade from eight in the morning until late afternoon." Pervis himself was trying to build up a stock of twenty carved fish, ten vases, twelve birds, and some walking sticks, with handles of carved bird's heads, for the next liner to call, the *President Wilson*.

I had heard about the takings from the *Sagafjord* from Charles Christian, born in San Francisco forty-one years ago and one of nine Pitcairners who started life in the Outside. "She came in when I had *two hundred* carved turtles at home," he said. "I took 'em out and every one sold. They wanted turtles that day, and I could've sold more maybe. Two hundred turtles to ah Norwegian ship!"

Some were two-dollar pieces, some five dollars. For retired couples from California or the Middle West, these stiff, wooden turtles were the perfect present to bring back from a South Seas cruise for grandchildren's toy chests. At an average price of three dollars a turtle, Charles's takings that day constituted stupendous income for a participant in a threadbare economy, particularly one in which people pay no rent, no taxes, and have most of the food they need at their doorstep. In an hour or two of trading that day, Charles had stuffed into the front pockets of his jeans enough money to buy *two* Honda motorcycles. Two hundred turtles! And

Pitcairn transportation — a simulated traffic jam. The island Mini-Moke, the motorcycles and the traditional low-slung Pitcairn wheelbarrow. (Courtesy of Tom Christian)

would a Pitcairner tell a lie? . . . Only the day before, Pastor Webster had been telling me: "These are not poor people. They have the means." He was right, even though the hit Charles's turtles made aboard the Norwegian cruise ship was exceptional.

My chat with Charles took place on the Landing in Bounty Bay. All around us — it was a Thursday, the day the men traditionally have set aside for fishing for as long as any on the island can remember — was evidence of how a bountiful, unfished sea might transform the island economy, provided, of course, there was capital available, some training, and commercial organization. With the most primitive of gear, the men and boys had soon fished enough to make grand feasts possible in every home that night. Two Warren youths were using a natural basin of sea water in one of the rocks to clean a good haul of "dream fish." They looked like a chubby version of the flounder. "They got ah name 'dream fish' 'cos if you eat 'em late a' night, gosh, do you *dream*," the boys told me. A dugout fishing canoe manned by two generations of

men from one of the "Christian" families, had in its salt-rimed well
a mess of crayfish, reaching in size up to one I guessed would be a
ten-pounder, that would fetch real money in an American or European fish market. They were casually ripping out the snowy tail
meat and tossing it into a palm-frond basket. It would be used for
bait — bait! — to catch the biblically acceptable fish, the rock cod,
gray mullet, kingfish, barracuda, snapper, and a variety of small fish
with stripes and dots and abstract squiggles in every color of the
spectrum. Many have local names, some Tahitian inspired, others
invented on Pitcairn — *pickpick, faafaia, manuia, dottah,* and
upapa.

While I was well aware that the dietary rules of the Adventist
Church forbid the Pitcairners to eat crayfish, crabmeat, and any
of the shellfish found along the rocky shores, returning tender
crayfish meat to the sea struck me as gustatory sacrilege of the top
order. There *are* occasions, however, when the big crayfish end up
in Pitcairn bellies. "Oooh, I eat crayfish *sometimes,*" Charles confessed. "I like it. I shouldn't, but it's werry gud." Charles had
finished his fishing for the day — sinfully thinking, presumably, of
the forbidden crayfish — and had returned to a favorite rock by
the Landing to complete the hand-sanding of six turtles he had
carved from selected pieces of *miro* mottled in pink, cocoa brown,
and cream colors. The *President Wilson,* on one of her now rare
calls, was due any day. Six large turtles would fetch a total of $20
from the tourists; but six large crayfish, ten-pounders, the tail meat
frozen for a world market, would fetch close to that sum with just
a fraction of the effort.

The only solution Island Magistrate Pervis sees to the island's
dilemma lies in steady government subsidies or an investment
program: "I'd like to see them giving us the finance. It's werry hard
to build when you haven't anything back of you. You need machinery, equipment in Bounty Bay to make the work a bit easier.
I'd like to find some way of getting some income for the island. If
the stamps go down the drain, we have almost nothing. We talk
about a cannery business, for fruit or fish. We have the pineapples,
the oranges, lemons, and limes. They come here by the thousands.
They fall to the ground, and there's nothing we can do about it.

There's copra here, and plenty, plenty coconuts over on Oeno Island, but there's werry little being made of copra in the world today."

So it comes back to tiny rectangles of gummed paper, stamps intended not for the corners of envelopes but for collectors' albums and investment advisers. Stamps showing the *Bounty* anchor, Bligh's chronometer, the cave of Fletcher Christian, the *Bounty* Bible, Thursday October Christian's house, and all sorts of quaint echoes of the past. Even the nonpoliticians of Pitcairn are aware that if world philatelists ever were to lose their interest in Pitcairn issues, the island "economy" would crumble, and with it, almost certainly, the society itself.

CHAPTER SEVENTEEN

VOTE FOR JACK OR JILL

FROM THE COLONY'S EARLIEST DAYS, election time has coincided with Yuletime. The balloting usually has been held on Christmas Day itself, a choice of dates that seems positively loony to most outsiders. But, as with Christmas and all other events in the Pitcairn calendar, the annual election is conducted by the islanders in their own autonomous, one-big-family way, in clear disdain for the way matters are arranged in the big world. Put into the context of Western politics, the campaign reaches its crescendo on Christmas Eve. But any such comparison is nonsense. There is no electioneering on Pitcairn, no apogee in the campaign; in fact, no politicking at all in any recognizable form. Having chosen to go there over the Christmas–New Year period, we had the bonus of witnessing this noncampaign in a land without either hustings or the political factions to give them the fire of debate.

What we saw was the democratic system working at its most rudimentary level, probably not much differently from the way leaders were chosen and decisions made in New England hamlets two centuries ago.

Balloting on Christmas Day this year was out of the question since it fell on the Adventist Saturday Sabbath. The voting was postponed until the following Monday, the twenty-seventh. Apart from the lists of candidates posted on the community notice boards, there was no evidence of any kind, written or spoken, that an election was in the air.

On the eve of election day, I called on one of the candidates. Christy Warren had put his name down for the position of Island Councilor because, among other reasons, he wasn't happy over the fact that the Council had bought a small piece of land from him for $240, saying they needed it for a children's playground, and then proceeded to use it as the site for the new government hostel. "That wasn't right," said Christy, "to say you're going to do *one* thing and then do *another*." I imagined that Christy's thoughts would be preoccupied with the next morning's balloting but I was totally wrong. He had problems other than seeking a public position carrying a stipend of just over one hundred dollars a year.

"Glad you've come," said the candidate. "I'll put on the kettle, we'll have a nice big cup of my tea, and I'd like you to take a look at the fridge. You might know about these things." Christy's kerosene-powered, British-made refrigerator, for which, with a few spares, he had paid £94 only a year earlier, was no longer chilling his goat meat and his eggs.

"It heats up all right," said Christy. "The flame goes good there in the back, but it doesn't *freeze*. It must be something in the pipes. It could be werry clogged up there where the black pipes go around. I thought if we could tip it upside-down a few times — stir up the ammonia gas a bit — we might get it going again." Christy had lost the book of instructions, so I went along with this informal procedure. We tumbled the big fridge a few times across the floor, shook it once or twice, and then put it back on the special thronelike stand Christy had made for it. With a spirit level to test the alignment, tomorrow's candidate fiddled with a set of wedge-shaped chocks around the base to make sure he had the appliance in a precise vertical position. He lit the wick again, turned it up werry high, and we had one of Christy's mammoth afternoon teas. Three big cups later, we opened the door and felt the freezing coil. Nothing had happened. With fumes pouring from the flue, Christy's fridge was working better as oven than refrigerator.

"Tomorrow I'll look for that book of instructions again," he said. "I think I'll *die* if that thing doesn't work. You know, we're starting to get these machines on Pitcairn, like the ice-fridge that's clogged up there, but they break down, and there's no one here who knows how to *fix* them. And we can't put them right ourselves even *with* the book of instructions. Next time there's a ship with a real engineer aboard, I'll try to get him to come ashore if he can and take a look at my fridge."

I tried to reassure Christy by saying that the machines we use in an apartment in mid-Manhattan got clogged up, too, from time to time and getting them unclogged by experts was no easy matter. I said in parting that I hoped the election next day would go better for him, the oldest of the candidates, than this attempt at repairing the island's youngest refrigerator. Unhappily, it didn't.

Christy had waged a noncampaign along the lines of the noncampaigns of his five rivals for the position on the Council. He told me he may have nudged along his candidacy in chatting with two or three friends, but nothing more than that. Electioneering, I was to discover, was not only unnecessary and unwarranted on Pitcairn; many considered it downright arrogant, impudent even.

"You see the names on the board, and all you need to know is who's been nominated," said the candidate. "You don't go around saying, 'Vote for me, I'm a good man for the job.' That's cheating a bit, that's not the right way to run for public office. At least it's not the right way *here*."

The electorate had gathered in the Square before seven o'clock on the morning of polling day. There were sixty-one registered voters. Twenty-three of the voters, a good third of the electorate, were members of one family, the various generations of Christians old enough to be enfranchised.

One is eligible to vote on Pitcairn after turning eighteen. The island has had teen-age voters since November 30, 1838, when the Pitcairners persuaded Captain Elliott of a visiting British warship, H.M.S. *Fly*, to draw up a short constitution and a code of laws adapted from the informal ones already in force. This first constitution, like others that succeeded it, was penned, voted upon, and sealed in the great cabin of a man-of-war, one of the many romantic touches in the island's past. The earliest constitution provided for the annual election of a Magistrate, who must be island-born, "by the free votes of every native born on the island, *male or female,* who shall have attained the age of eighteen years; or of persons who shall have resided five years on the island." (Italics added.)

In addition to enabling islanders in their late teens to participate in local government, this constitution gave Pitcairn another important "first." Generations before their sisters in Britain or the United States won the right to vote, Pitcairn women were equal and full members of the electorate. The arrangements drawn up by the captain of the *Fly* in conference with the islanders represented the first time female suffrage had been written into a British constitution. Unfortunately, I can find no record of how this radical innovation was received in London when Captain Elliott sailed home. It did, appropriately enough, soon reach the ears of the teen-age Queen Victoria who had ascended to the throne a year earlier and who subsequently was to form close and sentimental bonds with Pitcairn Island. In the same report from H.M.S. *Fly,* she and the British government also learned that on this faraway dot of land, the inhabitants had adopted a community code that provided for yet another outlandish social idea. For the first time in any British legislation, compulsory schooling was written into this 1838 Pitcairn constitution. Not only was education compulsory; the islanders had to pay for it — a shilling per child per month. For times when ships were scarce and there was no cash income from the sale of provisions, the island legislature drew up a list of equivalents which could be accepted by the schoolmaster in lieu of the Queen's shillings: "Three good bunches of plantains, four shillings; one barrel of Irish potatoes, twelve shillings; one barrel of yams, eight shillings; one day's labour two shillings"; and so on.

The Pitcairners participating in this latest annual election did so mainly out of a sense of social responsibility but also because they knew they would incur a penalty if they didn't fill out a ballot slip. The island law provides that a fine shall be imposed on any registered voter who fails to turn out for an election. The regulations, printed before the Antipodes went in for decimalization and dollars, set the automatic fine for failure to vote at ten shillings, New Zealand.

' Island Magistrate Pervis Young and Island Secretary Ben Christian asked the voters to move into the courthouse for a short primer on the electoral procedure. Once everyone was inside, Ben went to the platform, called the meeting to order, and held up a small scrap of blackboard on which he had written in chalk three words: *Jack and Jill.* Waving the blackboard so all in the town meeting could see it, Ben, a most earnest holder of public office, began his patient and supersimplified explanation: "This is the way the committee wishes you to vote. [He meant procedurally, of course; it was not a case of a political Establishmentarian throwing his weight behind a specific candidate.] The names will be on the ballot like this." He pointed at the blackboard. "Jack and Jill. If you don't want Jill to be chairman of the Internal Committee, you put a line through her name, and if enough do the same, Jack is elected. The one you *don't* want in office, you just put a line through it. Does that make everything clear to you who are older?" The octogenarians and the septuagenarians at the back of the hall nodded gray or white heads. Before the actual voting got under way, Pervis used the occasion to remind "those of you with Hondas — be sure to take out the fifty-cent license the following Sunday, which is the second. And no driving on New Year's Day, which is the Sabbath." This was evidently a huge local joke, and everyone went to the polls in a jovial mood.

They were handed slips of paper about the size of a theater ticket and on which Olive, the Island Government typist, a job that pays her just under $16 a month, had typed the names of the candidates. The islanders formed a line along the porch of the courthouse. At the head of the line was a letterbox-type slot cut into the wall of the Island Secretary's little office at one end of the building. For those who had not come along with a writing instrument, a stub of a pencil dangled from a piece of string attached to a nail above the slot. Vernon Young, the island policeman, in civvies as usual since the regulations don't call for a uniform, had positioned himself beside the hole in the wall to see that the balloting went off fair and square. The voters chatted about their crops and the Christmas they had just observed as they waited their turn to mark their ballots and post them through the slot into a collection box that had been placed on the floor on the

Election day. The enfranchised members of the Pitcairn cousin-family line up on the porch of the Courthouse to slip their ballots through a letterbox-type slot cut into the wall of the Island Secretary's office.

other side of the wall. As he scribbled away at his ballot, old Morris muttered something which I couldn't quite catch but which I guessed amounted to a reproachful comment concerning one, several, or all the candidates.

Less than ten minutes after the last ballot had been dropped through the slot and Vernon had checked his list to make sure every eligible Pitcairner had put in an appearance, the Island Magistrate was ready to announce the results. Pervis' office, the top job, had not been at stake this year since this election was the Pitcairn equivalent of an off-year election in U.S. national politics. Pervis now took up a position at the head of the courthouse steps to tell us which Cousin Jacks had been voted into office. It had not been a day for the feminists. The sole Cousin Jill in the contention, Miss Marie Christian, twenty-five, failed by a single vote, sixteen to seventeen, to win one of the two elective positions on the Island Council.

In his attention-getting voice, Pervis announced that it had been a clean sweep by members of the Christian family. In the contest for chairman of the Internal Committee, Cairn Melvin Christian, fifty-four, had overwhelmed Henry Young, sixty-one, who owns one-half of the local land. (The committee's name, incidentally, dates from the early days when the islanders ambitiously established both an *internal* and an *external* committee. The latter was soon abolished when it was realized that Pitcairn actually had no business at all to conduct in the field of foreign affairs.) After the islanders gave a cheer for Cairn and he modestly acknowledged it, Pervis went on to announce that nine of the sixty-one registered voters had cast invalid ballots. (Millie told me that the practice is to leave the ballot blank, or alternatively to scratch out all the names, if a voter disapproves of the entire slate of candidates.)

Pervis went on to announce that Ivan Christian and Gifford Christian would be councilors for 1972. The next day, a radio message was received from Auckland naming Tom Christian as the Governor's appointed member of the Council, further reinforcing the Christian family's customary dominant position in island government.

A little confusingly, there is both a "council" and an "internal committee" involved in the direction of Pitcairn's affairs. The Council has two elected members, the Governor's nominee, and two more voting but unsalaried members named by the elected members. The chair at the monthly Council meeting is taken by the Island Magistrate, in whom are vested executive as well as judicial powers. The Internal Committee, under an elected chairman and with members appointed annually by the Council is responsible for arranging and supervising the public work for which all able-bodied males between fifteen and sixty-five are liable.

The Pitcairn Commissioner's office explains in these careful words the limitations, largely theoretical, which have been imposed on Pitcairn self-government: "The Council has authority to enact rules of the nature of bylaws which must be notified to the Governor, in whom resides the power of revocation and alteration. In practice, it is rarely that the Council exercises its legislative functions without consulting the Governor beforehand, and when it does, alteration is usually confined to textual amendment to make the meaning and intention of the rules legally exact." This means that the islanders can order their own affairs provided they allow British civil servants in Auckland to dress up the language of their statutes.

The "rules of the nature of bylaws" are drawn up by *men* and always have been. Surprisingly, in a community that has had female suffrage for one hundred and thirty-four years, no Pitcairn woman has ever held elective office. Marie Christian was the third woman to run for office. The first, in 1968, was Millie Christian. She tried again the following year and lost by a margin as small as Marie's in the latest election.

When I learned of our Millie's short and unsuccessful political career I thought I had stumbled on the genesis of Women's Lib on Pitcairn. I was also intrigued that gentle Millie in her mid-sixties, and not one of the livelier girls like Betty or Brenda or "Pussy," had been the first to raise the standard on behalf of the ladies. I asked Millie if she had run in the spirit of Women's Liberation.

Millie didn't answer for a few seconds, and the pause was given over to guffaws.

"Women's Lib? . . . Me? . . . No! I put my name in ah election because you get a *wage* every month for sitting on Council."

She didn't think Pitcairn needed a Women's Lib movement because the members of her sex had no real social grievances to put right. Her husband, Warren, was a good provider who helped around the house, kept their vegetable garden and the pineapple patch in order, and had regular income from his carving.

Millie was a trifle disappointed, however, that the members of her sex had not displayed much solidarity when she put her name down for Councilor. "You can guess on Pitcairn who has voted for you," she said. "You can guess that close relatives will vote for you, and when I was a candidate I though ah women would support me as well. But here I was, ah first woman to try, and they didn't vote for me!"

I asked Millie whether possession of the surname Christian carries unbeatable political clout. "Not really," she replied. "A Christian in an election can't count on ah support of *all* ah Christians on island because most years several *different* Christian families are among the candidates."

Pitcairn politics, by force of circumstances, of course, and in the most unsophisticated manner, are dynastic to the nth degree. Study the register of those who have held elective office in recent years and you come upon such entries as these:

1956: Island Magistrate, Parkin *Christian*; chairman of the Internal Committee, Arnold *Christian*; Councilors, Fred *Christian* and Warren *Christian*.

1963: Island Magistrate, John *Christian*; chairman of the Internal Committee, Radley *Christian*; Councilors, Ivan *Christian* and Elwyn *Christian*.

In this period, the Island Secretary was Ben *Christian*, and the radio officer Tom *Christian*.

In all, counting those appointed to clean public buildings and tend the graveyard, there are thirty-one islanders in public posts, or just over half the total adult population. This is an extraordinary proportion considering the size of the community and the very small amount of administrative work required to keep it functioning. But it has descended naturally from the family type of government John Adams gave the island. It meets the island's traditional needs and can cope with new problems as they arise.

The political structure of the island was once far more complicated than it is today. In October, 1892, the island elders held a conference aboard H.M.S. *Champion* with Captain Rooke and sought his views on how Pitcairn should be run. The official Pitcairn *Guide* records that the islanders at that time had begun to question their "social inertia" and attributed it to "weakness in their leaders." Captain Rooke felt that what was needed was a formal Parliament, not operating like the one at Westminster, of course, or the Congress of the United States, but an elected body, large enough to be representative of island views, that could decide what was in the public interest and what wasn't. A parliament of seven appeared to Captain Rooke to be the right number "to legislate, to plan for the public good, to execute all decisions of the court, and to see that all public demands are attended to without unnecessary delay." He suggested that they elect also a President, a Vice President, and a Secretary.

The islanders put this arrangement into effect on New Year's

315 VOTE FOR JACK OR JILL

Day, 1893, and coped with a parliamentary system of government for ten years. In 1904, the British Consul in Tahiti paid his first visit to Adamstown and discovered that the islanders were getting themselves into a political mess. The parliamentary arrangement was simply too cumbersome for such a small society. He persuaded the islanders to abolish it and return to the time-tested system of electing a Chief Magistrate to run things with the help of a small council of elected and appointed members. During the parliamentary experiment, for the first and only time in Pitcairn's history, executive and judicial functions were separated.

Either the Consul who drew up this new arrangement, R. T. Simons, or some learned soul in the community who transcribed his instructions indulged in some didacticism before an audience of roughly educated islanders. In the island records of the 1904 code and the new laws acquired with it, one comes across explanations in parentheses after many of the long or unusual words, a simple word or phrase to make the meaning clear to everyone:

The committee will deliberate (weigh in the mind) . . .
In this capacity he will be responsible for the disbursement (pay out) of Public Funds . . .
Remuneration (reward & recompense) . . .
All fines and penalties levied (collected) . . .
Rape (violation by force) . . .
Any householder or other person conniving (to wink at) at the offense . . .
In cases of a gross or serious character, recourse (application as for help) . . .
According to the gravity (seriousness) of the offence . . .

It is a document of special museum value, perhaps history's only example of an operation in which the author of a constitution felt he should also assume the role of lexicographer. Codification and dictionary in one package! One is left to wonder, though, why he didn't use the basic words in the first place in drawing up his new social order for a simple people.

With slight modifications, and a tightening-up in the area of legalities, the system introduced in 1904 is the one that operates today. The Pitcairners manage their affairs with decorum and with fine attention to detail. There have been no political scandals since the brief period of tragicomic dictatorship in the middle of the nineteenth century. The books are kept meticulously, and Olive types up the accounts beautifully.

A community without any real politicians or politics has managed to make a go of self-government and the democratic process. It could be faulted, perhaps, in one major area. In interviews with the community's leaders, I detected an appalling lack of interest in long-term planning.

CHAPTER EIGHTEEN

A LAW FOR AN ANVIL,
AND LATER FOR ADULTERY

We MAY JUDGE a society by the laws its makes, provided, of course, those laws are written exclusively by members of the tribe. The exercise is of dubious value when, as is usually the case in dependent communities, the written statutes are not a natural outgrowth of the local common law but are enactments drawn up by an external colonizing or exploiting authority.

Pitcairn falls largely into the first category, a place of homespun law. Although this is somewhat less true than it once was, the laws have always represented the sort of code by which the Pitcairners themselves wished to live. While the phraseology of the island statutes today is not dissimilar to that found in laws in force in many countries within the British sphere, the laws basically were either inspired by the islanders or selected by them after reviewing the established codes of others.

In the very early days, the laws were so totally the work of indigenous hands and minds that they have about them an ingenuousness and a quaintness one might expect to find in the rules drawn up by a group of schoolboys founding a tree-house secret society. They were simple and to the point. They reflected the society's uncomplicated problems. Vast areas of human evil could safely be omitted by the lawmakers until at least the early 1830's since no expression of that evil was to be found on Pitcairn during

John Adams' patriarchate. This was common law in its purest form, a growing volume of regulations based on island custom, usage, and the decisions of the wisest in their midst, predominantly Adams himself.

The island archives for the period in which written law first appeared contain some magnificent examples of what constituted "crime" in Pitcairn's Golden Age, the period before the whaling ships began to stop there fairly regularly in the 1940's. There was even a special law for that precious hunk of English iron that came off the *Bounty*, the ship's anvil, which had permitted the Anglo-Tahitians to repair the tools they used on land and sea and also fashion new ones. It was known then as the "public anvil" rather than the *Bounty* anvil. Law for the Public Anvil read as follows: "Any person taking the public anvil and public sledge-hammer from the blacksmith's shop, is to take it back after he has done with it; and in case the anvil and sledge-hammer should get lost by his neglecting to take it back, he is to get another anvil and sledge-hammer, and pay a fine of four shillings."

Crops and livestock were of crucial importance, and there were laws to deal with the guilty, the four-legged as well as the two-legged guilty:

If a fowl is found destroying the yams or potatoes, the owner of the plantation, after giving due warning, may shoot the fowl, and retain it for his use, and may demand of the owner of such fowl the amount of powder and shot so expended, as well as the fowl. The fowls are all toe-marked.

If a cat is killed without being positively detected in killing fowls, however strong the suspicion may be, the person killing such cat is obliged, as a penalty, to destroy 300 rats, whose tails must be submitted for the inspection of the magistrate, by way of proof that the penalty has been paid.

Goats, and other quadrupeds, must be earmarked.

If a pig gets loose from its sty and commits any depredation, the owner is obliged to make good the damage, according to the decision of the magistrate, whose duty it is to survey the injury alleged to be done, and from whose decision a reference, if necessary, may be made to a jury; but the final appeal is to the captain of the next man-of-war touching at the island.

Adams, and perhaps the older ones among the children he had raised, knew what mayhem had followed the invention by McCoy of *ti*-root whiskey, and there were specific laws prohibiting strong drink on the island:

No person or persons shall be allowed to get spirits of any sort, from any vessel, or sell it to strangers, or any person on the island. Any one found guilty of so doing shall be punished by fine, or such other punishment as a jury shall determine on. No intoxicating liquor whatever shall be allowed to be taken on shore, unless it be for medicinal purposes. Any person found guilty of transgressing this law shall be severely punished by a jury.

The law continued, in the same paragraph:

No females are allowed to go on board a foreign vessel of any size or description, without the permission of the magistrate; and in case the magistrate does not go on board himself, he is to appoint four men to look after the females.

Both these decrees have their equivalents in contemporary Pitcairn law. It is still illegal to land liquor, although I was pleased to discover, in that phrase ". . . unless it be for medicinal purposes," some juridical justification for that heel of a bottle of Johnnie Walker Red Label which Christy showed me one night. Women today are allowed to go on board only cruise ships or passenger liners, and in these situations there are always at least four Pitcairn males to "look after the females."

But gradually, after the two migrations, after the island innocents had come into contact with the strangers from the whalers and warships, the men picking up bad habits, the women worse things, the society began to change and the laws changed with it. There developed a need for a broad new set of statutes with harsh penalties for wrongdoing. They were still only monetary penalties; the idea of incarcerating men had yet to be written in the law books. Nevertheless, it was a society far removed from the simple order of John Adams' time.

Where once the colony had only to worry about an unreturned

anvil and sledgehammer, or a straying fowl with a taste for someone else's yams, it now had to take into account such matters as adultery, fornication in general outside wedlock, "scandal," peeping toms, bastard children, the carrying of concealed weapons, assault, theft, even contempt of court and malicious gossip. In itself, the Pitcairn legal code that evolved during the middle and later years of the nineteenth century is an object lesson in how rapidly the civilized world can contaminate, tempt, and degrade a once-pure tribe.

Yet as late as 1884 there was still no mention of murder in the Pitcairn statutes. The act of taking another human life, slaying a kinsman or kinswoman, was so unthinkable that they deemed unnecessary even the inscription of the crime in their code. It was, after all, in the Lord's Commandments, a fundamental clause of His Moral Law. The closest the island lawmakers came to the question of homicide was in Law 22 of a basic thirty-one-law code drawn up when the colony was nearing the end of its first one hundred years of existence: "Threatening the life of any person or persons will be regarded as a great crime. Any such threats will be punishable by the decision of the court."

Even murderous *talk* was considered such a heinous sin that the statutemakers could not bring themselves to define a suitable punishment. Were such a "great crime" to come to their notice, the Island Magistrate and the two-man jury he could enlist to help him decide a case would always be able to fall back on the laws of the mother country.

It is so even today. "In instances where there is no local law, the law of England is applied so far as circumstances permit," explains the Pitcairn Governor's office.

The basic code that was in force at the time of Pitcairn's centenary was an aggregation of laws which had been drawn up in the years after Adams' death in 1829. It is a fascinating document, and it is worth quoting fairly fully from it. The fines here are given in pounds sterling and shillings although at one time during the middle years of the nineteenth century, when shipping touching at Pitcairn was predominantly American vessels from New Bedford, Salem, and Nantucket, the island ordinances stipulated payment of fines in American dollars. A selection of the early laws:

Law 1.   No one shall be allowed to assemble the court without a good evidence or satisfactory proof against an opposing party or parties, without laying himself open to punishment. Anyone so offending shall be fined sixpence an hour for that time.

Law 2.   Refusal to obey any of the lawful orders of the court shall be punishable by a fine of from one to five pounds sterling. Insulting the court will be regarded as a grave offence. . . .

Law 4.   Any two persons convicted of the crime of fornication shall pay a fine of within £4 to £20. Should said crime result in offspring, the father shall support the child as long as it lives. Further, anything coming from the father to support his illegitimate child, as long as it lives with the mother, shall be sent to the mother through the hands of the Parliament.

Law 5.   Any persons convicted of the crime of adultery, shall be punished by paying a fine within £10 to £25.

Law 6.   If two persons of the opposite sex, one, or both of whom, at the time shall be legally married, shall associate together in secluded places or otherwise, on terms of intimacy not consistent with his, or her, marriage vows, or in a manner to cause separation from his, or her, husband or wife, they shall on conviction be fined within £2 to £10. Any person or persons aiding or abetting them in this crime shall pay the same amount. It shall be lawful for the court to punish the crime of adultery by banishment from the island as well as fining the parties.

Law 7.   It shall be unlawful for two persons of the opposite sex to associate together at such times and in such places as shall tend to create scandal, or to endanger the morals of the rising generation by their evil example. Further, it shall be unlawful for any householder to allow any such persons who may have thus offended, to meet at his, or her, house, or premises, to further their evil designs without fear of discovery. Fine from £1 to £3 sterling.

Law 8.   It shall be unlawful for anyone of the opposite sex to intentionally remain near the place where the women and girls do their washing. Anyone so offending, shall pay a fine of from £2 to £4. [This had nothing to do with laundry. The interpretation I was given on the island of this particular decree was that it referred to bodily washing and reflected a peeping-tom problem that had arisen at some point.]

Law 9.   It shall be unlawful for any persons to raise a fake report against his neighbour out of malice or revenge. Whoever is convicted of such offence, shall pay a fine of from 10 to 20 shillings.

Law 10.   Whoever is convicted of stealing, shall be fined within £1 to £10. The stolen property also shall be made good.

Law 11.   Parents shall be responsible for property stolen by their children (for the purpose of supporting their families, or otherwise), from the age of 16 years and under. . . .

Law 13.   Any man who shall beat, or in any way abuse his wife, shall pay a fine of within £1 to £15.

Law 14.   Any person, in a quarrel, striking his opponent with the fist, or with any kind of weapon, shall pay a fine of from £1 to £6. Should the blow be returned, save in a case of self-defence, both parties shall pay the same fine. Any one is at liberty to defend himself. [I find the wording of this law a trifle puzzling; perhaps it is just as well Her Majesty's Government has brought in its own wordsmiths.]

Law 15.   It shall be unlawful for any person to carry concealed weapons, or to appear before the court or parliament with deadly weapons on their person. The fine for this law is £1 to £10.

Law 16.   Any person or persons after this date, 24, September, 1884, maliciously wounding, or causing the death of a cat without permission, will be liable to such punishment as the court will inflict. Further, any person, or persons aiding, or abetting in the aforesaid misdemeanour, will also be convicted under the same indictment. Should any dog, going out with his master, fall in with a cat, and chase him, and no effort be made to save the cat, the dog must be killed for the first offence. Fine 10 shillings. Cats in any part of the island doing anyone damage must be killed in the presence of one of the members of parliament. [The island was having serious problems with rats, and the cats were valued as exterminators rather than pets.]

Law 17.   It shall be unlawful for any person or persons to treat cruelly, or to beat in an unmerciful manner, their fellow beings, or animals of whatever kind, to injure them or in any way to inflict pain. First violation of the law punishable by reprimand of the court. Subsequent violations by fine of from 12 to 40 shillings. . . .

Law 19.   Any person or persons going after fowls in any part of the island, must call one or more of the other parties who have chickens in the same direction. Should any of the parties refuse to go, they must bear whatever damage may be done. Anyone found going without consulting any of the said parties, is amenable to a fine of from 4 to 20 shillings.

Law 20.   Should any dog be found killing fowls or eating eggs, he is to be killed for the first offence.

Law 21.   Shooting goats from the bend of the ridge at White Cow's
Pen inland toward Aute Valley, and following the same line up to
William's Block, and across to the head of McCoy's Valley, Taro
Ground and so on throughout the entire boundary line for goats, is
strictly prohibited. Fowls may be killed with bullets if found in the
place allotted to goats. Discharging of bullets from firearms anywhere within the village, is not allowed, except it be into the air, or
into the sea. First offence reprimand. Second offence eight shillings. . . .

Law 23.   It shall be unlawful for any one to land from ships, drugs
of any kind without first getting permission from the President.
[This was inscribed during Pitcairn's short-lived and ill-fated parliamentary era.] Anyone found doing so shall be punished. Further,
it may be lawful for parents to treat their own children in case of
sickness with any kind of medicine that may alleviate their pain,
or give relief. But no one will understand that he is at liberty to
treat, or give any dose of medicine, unless it be one of his own family, without first getting licence from the President. If anyone be
found so doing, he shall be severely punished, as the court shall decide.

Law 24.   Any person or persons going to the sugar mill, and eating
the sugar cane which belongs to another after it has been cut and
brought there, and that without the permission of the owner of said
sugar cane, shall be submitted to whatever punishment or fine the
judge may see fit to impose upon him.

Law 25.   From henceforth, no person or persons are allowed to bring
cocoanut or cocoanuts from T'Otherside unless accompanied by one
or more of the members of parliament, on the first week of every
month, on Sundays, unless otherwise arranged through unforeseen
circumstances, and further, no one, while at the above named place
will be permitted to use cocoanuts from other persons trees, without first obtaining permission from the owner or owners thereof. All
cocoanuts needed for cooking while stopping at T'Otherside must be
gathered in the presence of one of the members of parliament.

Law 26.   All the men, and the boys from the age of 14 years and up-
ward, to whatever age the parliament may think proper to limit, are
to be employed in the public work on the island, whenever their
services are required.

Law 27.   Any person, or persons, calling at, or passing by, places
where public work is being done, or where persons are filling ap-
pointments made by the judge, President or parliament, staying

around, meddling, or interfering with them in their business, and thus hindering work, or in any way causing trouble, must be submitted to whatever penalty the judge may think fit to impose. . . .

Law 29.   Whoever shall do any action which, though it has not been mentioned above, is contrary to the decency, peace and good order of the Island, shall be punished by a fine not exceeding —— [This was a nice catch-all ordinance. After concocting it, the lawmakers perhaps were so entranced by the novelty of such an all-encompassing decree that they were unable to set the appropriate penalty range.]

Law 30.   Reports from children under the age of 14, will be noticed. Also, offenders under that age, when found guilty of glaring misdemeanours, will have punishment meted out to them by the parliament.

Law 31.   The use of bows and arrows, rifles, revolvers, or firearms of any description, by children under the age of 14 years, is strictly prohibited.

In 1904, after the British Consul in Tahiti arrived and abolished the parliamentary system of government, the laws were broadened further. The language became a good deal more sophisticated than the plain phrases the islanders had worked out aboard the Queen's warships with the well-educated captains from English public schools — well-educated, that is, as Victorian gentlemen who nevertheless lacked the one specialty, legal training, that was needed here. By the beginning of the twentieth century, the crimes, too, were becoming a bit more worldly.

The prison was built and the statutes were rewritten to provide for referral of cases involving "great crimes" to the High Commissioner's Court for the Western Pacific. Jail terms for serious offenses were to be served off the island in a prison under the High Commissioner's control.

The law of this small, no-longer-pure land now had to be expanded to cope with such matters as seduction of a minor ("a fine of £20, with or without imprisonment, not to exceed one month"); rape (the case to be tried by the High Commissioner's Court off the island); slander (a fine of from 10 to 20 shillings); and even abortion ("a serious crime, punishable by a lengthy term of imprisonment. Any such cases occurring on Pitcairn Island must be brought to the notice of the Deputy Commissioner who will deal with them under the provisions of His Majesty's Order in Council. The Chief Magistrate will not fail to keep himself informed of any such cases or suspected cases, and will immediately act as directed above").

And at last the specter of sinister death had come to Pitcairn, death by man's hand rather than God's. Even so, the language was euphemistic; the words "murder" or "manslaughter" were not used: "In the event of the death of a person under suspicious circumstances, the Chief Magistrate assisted by his council, will enquire into the matter, examine witnesses and take down evidences and submit the same, together with his covering report, for the consideration of the Deputy Commissioner."

Nine years earlier, there *had* been a murder, a double slaying in fact, which sickened and horrified even those Pitcairners who had glimpsed some of the outside world's sins and enormities. A member of the Young family, in love with another woman, threw his wife and baby girl off the black cliffs to their deaths on the rocks below. A British warship carried him off to Suva, Fiji, where he was tried. The noose of a colonial gallows snapped his neck.

His direct descendant is a frail, stooped man in his declining days, his hands palsied, his hearing ebbing away in senility. Several times I chatted with him in the Square after Sabbath service or a public gathering. It would have been inhumane to question him about the family shame.

It is part of the cynicism of the age that when confronted with an individual, family, or community with an exceptional reputation for virtue and "goodness," most of us, I think, immediately begin searching for secret vices, the flaws and deficiencies we are certain must be concealed behind the pious panoply. The human reflex, in itself, is sad enough. Even sadder is the fact that most of us are not unhappy when we uncover the hidden or latent imperfections. We trot them out as exhibits to justify our own shortcomings or in an attempt to demonstrate the universality of the human condition.

The darkest contemporary feature of that condition quite clearly is an increase, worldwide, in human violence and aggression. I per-

sonally saw no act of even slight violence during the stay on
Pitcairn, nothing in word or deed that would qualify as aggression
in any real form. Were the Pitcairners simply on their best behavior with strangers in their midst? I doubt this very much. The
court records, at least, suggest that this is a most peaceable community. In one recent three-year period — 1966, 1967, 1968 — only
one case, a misdemeanor, which resulted in a conviction and fine,
was tried before the Island Court.

But we must remember that we are dealing here with an unusual community, an assembly of interrelated families. The outsider may never glean the full and true picture. In a conventional
family, it would be a perverted member who prattled willingly to
a stranger about the secret vices and nastiness of his kin. The
tendency is to hush up the wrongdoing of a family member that
society at large has not detected. This, too, I believe happens on
this island. Squabbles and human imperfections are resolved quietly within the family.

In some instances, these squabbles obviously lead to physical
violence, although the official court record does not reflect such
outbursts. The Pitcairners, after all, are human, and I find it hard
to believe that there is *never* resort to ferocity and brute force, that
no one on the island is ever guilty of raising his hand against a
kinsman or kinswoman. Since the court record was unenlightening
on the subject, I raised the matter with the "inspector of police,"
Vernon Young. He said he handled on the average one or two
"police" matters a month but in honesty could not recall when he
last investigated a case involving violence. What were the "one or
two" monthly police alerts? "Lost and found property," said Vernon. "That's the only reason people call on the policeman."

In pursuing the subject with those men and women who were
more willing than others to speak objectively about the community's good and bad sides, I came to the conclusion that on the
adverse side of the ledger, wrongdoing on Pitcairn is limited very
largely to two categories — wife-beating and juvenile mischief.
Each reveals interesting things about the society, and both, perhaps, stem from a common cause which might be identified
roughly as boredom. There had been a severe case of wife-beating
shortly before we landed on Pitcairn. In earlier accounts of Pitcairn

life, there are occasional references to wives getting unusually ferocious thrashings at the hands of their men.*

The most recent Pitcairn case of wife-beating did not come before the Island Magistrate. What happened was that the offender was roundly lectured by his neighbors, he promised not to strike his lady again, the beaten wife did not bring charges, and there the matter rested.

Did this husband, like other Pitcairn men in other years, assault his wife from sheer ennui, from the tedium of his daily rounds in a community of limited excitement? In a recent essay, Dr. Erich Fromm, the author and psychoanalyst, reported that boredom as serious pathology was slowly finding proper recognition. "Man is a passionate being, in need of stimulation," Dr. Fromm wrote, "he tolerates boredom and monotony badly, and if he cannot take a genuine interest in life, his boredom will force him to seek it in the perverted way of destruction and violence."

With greater certainty, we can attribute to boredom and monotony the acts of juvenile delinquency the island has experienced in recent years. The delinquency is limited and minor, but it has taken a strange form — arson, wanton burning of scrub and young trees in an area the Island Council has set aside for reforestation. There were several such instances, and one was bad enough to bring to the attention of the Court.

The Court consists of the Island Magistrate and two Councilors. Jurisdiction is limited to felonies and misdemeanors committed by Pitcairn residents, or simple civil actions brought by one islander against another. In criminal cases, the maximum punishment is a fine of $50 or imprisonment on the island for one hundred days in that insecure little brig by Pervis' house. In civil cases, jurisdiction exists only if the sum in dispute does not exceed $200, or $400 with the consent of the parties. The Island Magistrate passes sen-

---

* I had already encountered an analogous situation on another small island, Anguilla in the Lesser Antilles in the Caribbean, the place Britain was obliged to "invade" in March, 1969, to unseat an *opéra bouffe* revolutionary regime that had declared the island independent. Anguilla has greater numbers than Pitcairn; but life there proceeds at a similarly slow pace and, with seven denominations competing for attention on a small island, the Anguillans are as preoccupied as the Pitcairners with matters of faith and godliness. On Anguilla, the most bothersome matter for law-enforcement officials is wife-beating.

tence or judgment. He has powers of summary jurisdiction in criminal cases where the penalty does not exceed a $10 fine, and in civil cases where the amount in dispute does not exceed $10. Appeals are lodged through, and serious cases handled by, the Commissioner in Auckland.

As Magistrate, Pervis Young had to assemble the Court only once in 1971. Some lads had been playing with fire on a slope where the community was trying to raise a stand of *miro* trees. The ringleader alone was charged. Sadly, the defendant who stood before Pervis and the Councilors at the table set up in the white courthouse was the Magistrate's own son, Daryl, then aged fifteen. He was convicted and fined $25.

CHAPTER NINETEEN

A TENTH FOR THE LORD

P ITCAIRN POSSESSES two hundred and forty-seven Bibles, or nearly three for every man, woman, and child. The islanders actually counted them during a survey in August and September of 1971. The check list of the Scriptures revealed that one family owned nineteen Bibles and three New Testaments, another fifteen Bibles and three New Testaments. The Bible, says Pastor L. A. J. Webster, is the best-read book on the island, and from my study of the islanders' reading habits, I have no grounds for disagreeing with him. "The word of God increases in importance on Pitcairn," says the Pastor. "As strife and chaos increase in the world, the ageless wisdom of the Scriptures becomes an increasingly important factor in Pitcairn life, for we here are affected by those forces just as others are, even though we are separated from any continent by more than three thousand miles of ocean. No, the word of God will never 'go out of style.' Especially not on Pitcairn Island, where its influence turned bloodshed to order, and sorrow to joy."

Pastor Webster is fifty-five, a short, lean man with eyes that can penetrate the unrighteous one moment and switch quickly to friendliness and encouragement for the believer the next. In the missionary service of the Lord, he has shifted his household twenty-three times across the South Pacific since 1944 — to Papua, to the Solomons, to communities in his native Australia, to New Zealand — to Pitcairn. Pitcairn appears twice in the list of moves. He says he did not volunteer to come back to Adamstown, the most remote pastorate of his Church, but when a second posting was offered to him in 1971, he deemed it his Christian duty to accept. Although the islanders refer to him frequently as "the Missionary," he concedes there is very little missionary work for him to do in a place where all are adherents to Adventism, at least nominally. He regards Pitcairn as a relatively easy post, "without the pressures and activities of other areas I've been in." But he quickly modified this remark by saying that he thought humanity was "pretty much the same wherever you find it — the problems are the same."

So far as Pitcairn is concerned, Pastor Webster's present problems include an occasional demonstration by a member of his flock of one or more of the well-established human shortcomings — wife-beating perhaps, or cursing; a lack of respect for the dietary principles of Adventism; a certain inattention to the homework he gives his congregation each Tuesday night prayer meeting on the lessons of the Scriptures; the laziness of overindulged, Honda-wheeled young; and the introduction of some nasty habits by callers from the outside world. He has not a shred of inner doubt that Seventh-Day Adventism is right for our time and right for his island flock. "I think it becomes more and more relevant as we look out at the world and its mess," says Pastor.

Adventists basically are evangelical Protestants who believe that the Bible must be interpreted literally and all who tamper with it in the slightest manner are damned. As a result, they observe, or rather are urged to observe, the Mosaic dietary laws. They set aside Saturday as their Sabbath because the Old and New Testaments are replete with references to the Seventh Day having been specially blessed and hallowed by the Lord, an infinite blessing that is to be associated not with a principle or an institution but with a specific "day." They expect sons, daughters, and strangers within their gates to observe it with them. The other elements mentioned in the Fourth Commandment of the Decalogue handed to Moses on the mountain — manservants, maidservants, cattle — do not exist on Pitcairn and are not involved here in the application of Moral Law. Adventists believe in the visible return of Christ at some indefinite date in the future. The founder of their faith, a Massachusetts Baptist minister named William Miller, actually

Pastor L. A. J. Webster, or "the Missionary" as some of the older members of the community refer to him, on a gray day at the Landing. He returned for a second two-year posting in Seventh-Day Adventism's most remote pastorate.

predicted the end of the world for 1843, then changed the Day of Judgment to 1844 when nothing untoward happened in 1843.* Subsequently, he went back to his study of the prophecies of Daniel and Revelation and decided that Christ would return at some later, unchartable time, the hell fires would burn on earth, the wicked would perish forever, and there would be redemption for the righteous living, resurrection for the righteous dead, and the Millennium would have its beginning. Modern Seventh-Day Adventism does not set a date for the Second Coming — it has been shown to be a hazardous business — but does acknowledge its emergence from a group which did establish such a date. From time to time, there have been fanciful news stories that the Pitcairners were following in William Miller's theological tracks, had made their own prediction about the end of the world, and in the

* For those who are interested, William Miller's prediction was based on a study of Daniel 8, Verse 14.

light of this, had abandoned their crop planting. I found no evidence that there had been any such Doomsday watches, and the islanders dismissed the stories with great laughs.

Nevertheless, the more devout read eagerly the articles in the popular literature published by the Adventists — bundles of the well-produced magazines arrive from Sydney and Los Angeles in every consignment of mail — which deal with hair-raising matters: "The Day the Earth Burns Up," "When Will He Come?" "Apocalyptic Voices Warn Our Fragile Planet," "He is Almost Here." The stories are printed alongside suitably horrific illustrations: pictures of nuclear clouds, simulated hell fires, and so on. A major current in Adventist belief is that the world is getting worse and worse and that the Scriptures long ago predicted that this would happen. In borrowing copies of these magazines from the islanders, I was intrigued by the passages they had underlined and, presumably, committed to memory: "Aspirin causes 5 per cent of all deaths in general hospitals throughout Australia," and "America is rapidly sinking into idolatry. . . . We are serving the god of pleasure, money and sex, while we are outwardly still religious" (Billy Graham in Shea Stadium, New York City, June 24, 1970). A favorite quotation that came up in a church context on Pitcairn was a line from novelist Jess Moody: "Someone called our time an elephant hanging from a cliff with its tail tied to a daisy." They had not read the book, simply heard the quote in a sermon.

I mention these matters because they throw light on facets of the Pitcairners' Adventism. They have, it struck me, a morbid fascination with evidence from any quarter that the Apocalypse might be forming up in the wings, that world famine, the Bomb, cataclysmic earthquakes, a new ice age perhaps, will hasten both the destruction of the planet and the Day of Judgment. The environment of their everyday life, the shanty homes, the disorder, may be a reflection of such thinking. Why bother to pretty things up if it may all, in an earthly sense at least, be ending soon?

Their House of God, however, is trim and well maintained as a mark of respect for the Maker. Like churches in many other communities, it is far too big now for the congregation it serves. When fifty or sixty of the islanders turn out for the Sabbath service, there is still plenty of room left on the twenty-four rows of long pews, handmade and stiff-backed at the correct Victorian angle. The church, inside and out, has only two touches that might be described as decorative. Over the pulpit are inscribed the words: "Holiness Unto the Lord." Behind the pulpit is an oil painting from a deliberate, amateur hand, showing Christian's Cave and the Gibraltar-like rock it was etched from. The artist has painted his own message into the picture, a line from the Psalms: "The Lord is My Rock and My Fortress."

We were well "churched" that first Sabbath in Adamstown. We attended Sabbath school, which is held in the courthouse, infants' Sabbath classes, which are held in a small storeroom at the back of the Church, and finally Sabbath service itself. All told, about four hours of religious instruction.

While the under-fives, including the two babies under one year of age, went to the lessons for infants, crayoned religious pictures, and sang such verses as, "I have a doggie, God made the doggie," the boys, girls, teen-agers, and a number of their parents assembled for Sabbath school instruction. The youths, in T-shirts, jeans, and shoeless as usual, took the back row of seats. They made a good deal of noise and seemed to have turned out simply because there was nothing much else doing in Adamstown on a Saturday morning. Tom Christian, in slacks and neat white shirt, who had arrived to take the Sabbath school with a straw basket full of Adventist literature, several Bibles, and hymnals, decided to aim his instruction at a lower age level:

"How can you shine for Jesus, Michael?" Michael wasn't really sure, and Tom gave some examples: "If your mother tells you to go out and feed the chooks and you do it, would that be shining for Jesus? . . . It's helping mummy and daddy. It's being kind and good to everyone. Now if I had two peaches on this table, Michael, and one was bigger than the other, and I asked you and Anne to come up, which one would you take? Well, you'd take the bigger one, wouldn't you? Well shining for Jesus is sacrifice, sacrifice in little things. When someone throws a stone at you, you'd like to throw it back. But not doing so is sacrifice." Tom scowled here in the direction of the back row where some of the boys were teasing the curvaceous Brenda. "Shining for Jesus is also reverence in church and not playing the fool!" he said solemnly. The boys were quieted.

He then challenged the irreverent young at the back of the room to give him one of the Ten Commandments. He was offered the Eighth. "Right," said Tom, "Thou shalt not steal. Now what is stealing? If you see a garden of big, luscious juicy pineapples, and if you stay long enough, you may be tempted to steal one. So perhaps best to move on and then temptation will pass." Whether Tom's technique is in keeping with the prescribed Adventist methods for Sabbath instruction of the young, I had no way of knowing. But it gave me fascinating insight into the simple manner in which moral character, ideas of right and wrong, the cooperative spirit, are instilled into Pitcairn minds from generation to generation. Less successfully, I felt, in the case of the present young generation.

Next we sang a hymn, to the tune of "Tell it Again," intended to draw attention to the fund-raising for a medical missionary launch which Pitcairn and other Adventist flocks in the Pacific were hoping to send into "the Jungles of Borneo-land."

> *They need a boat, they need a boat,*
> *To ply the rivers where roads cannot go.*
> *Into the jungles we'll send our new boat,*
> *Carry them medicines, help heal their woe.*

The young of doctorless Pitcairn that day contributed $12 to help buy a launch to send some "missionary bold" to where "children are covered with sores, sickness and death are the lot of just scores." Since it was Christmas, we concluded with four verses of "Silent Night."

The Sabbath school program was well meshed with the Church service itself. When we moved over to the church hall, the medical launch for the jungles of Borneo-land was the theme of a playlet two of the men were performing beside the pulpit. The playlet also was intended to draw attention to two other fund-raising drives, one to build "lamb shelters" in the Philippines for "poor lambs of the flock," the other to pay for the building of a new Adventist hospital in Hong Kong. The projects receiving special attention that year were those in the Church's Far Eastern division where, Anderson Warren told us in his play lines, there were "238,000 Adventists, and more being baptized every day," out of a potential congregation of 390 million. The play took place in front of a large display board explaining these drives in maps and diagrams. The large heading read: "Three S.S. Objectives." There were huge arrows pointing at the three target areas. Anyone recalling the "objectives" of another organization with the same monogram might have been momentarily taken aback. Here, "S.S." stood for Sabbath School.

Anderson demonstrated how easily money could be raised for the Church and deserving foreign charity: "One of us who set aside ten cents from every carving he sold on the ships has given us thirty New Zealand dollars for the investment fund. And Ronnie has given us the thirty-two cents he got for his second birthday. The Lord has promised to bless those who give like that."

Pervis, who, since he was retiring that week as Elder, gave the sermon the Pastor normally would deliver, spoke of other rewards: "Can you walk anywhere on our old earth and go into someone's mansion and live in it? No, folks, of course you can't. Well, Jesus is preparing His mansion for you, preparing it for the life evermore you will live with Jesus in His kingdom."

While Pervis was sermonizing about the living arrangements in the Hereafter, my thoughts, I confess, were on another subject, the fact that the principle of separation of Church and State was not, and never had been, applied on the island. Island Magistrate Pervis and Island Secretary Ben Christian, the No. 1 and No. 2 men in the Island Government, were also the Church's two Elders. The big Pitcairners conducted most of the service. The little Pastor sat on a seat behind the pulpit for a good deal of the time. There was nothing Machiavellian about it, of course, but it was interesting nonetheless. A British-inspired, turn-of-the-century rule that the Island Magistrate could not also serve as Church Elder has evidently been dropped.

We sang four hymns. The older ones carried the singing, filling the too-big wooden hall with their beautiful voices. Few of the young lent their throats to the hymnody. Some had drifted out of the hall to chat on a bench in the church entrance. They were not dodging the collection plate. Unlike the Sabbath school practice, none is passed around in the Sabbath service itself. The Church's principal funds are contributed under the tithe system, "a tenth for the Lord."

One evening at the Pastor's house, a pleasant cottage with an attractive garden, a lawn running down to the cliffs, and, right by the cliffs, a flagpole for raising the Union Jack when ships are sighted, the Pastor went over with me the workings of the tithe system on the island. All tithes are paid now in cash. As recently as 1965, however, a tithe house stood just off the main track down from the church. In this building, Pitcairners who had no money for their tithe would deposit under the Pastor's supervision one tenth of the produce from their plots — pineapples, bananas, potatoes, corn, melons, tomatoes, and so on — for possible community trading aboard ships. What money was collected would go to the Church. In practice, however, most of the food rotted in the tithe house. Either the ships didn't come, or those that did call were often not interested in wasting time to take on a small quantity of fresh supplies. The tithe house was pulled down to make way for the little generator Adamstown acquired in 1968. Thus another priceless museum piece was lost to Adamstown, even if it was merely a shed the islanders were accustomed to skirting with a wide berth because of the stench from the putrefying food inside.

I asked Pastor Webster whether his congregation paid an honest cash tithe today. He said he assumed they did but had not bothered to investigate the matter. "But it should be possible to work it out," he added. "In my experience, the islanders spend whatever money they get, although one or two may be savers. The tithes this past year [1971] came to about $2,400, plus another $900 for special appeals, distress calls, giving for missionary work, and so on. If that represents a tenth of what all the families took in in cash over the year, the total money available to the community *should* amount to $24,000. Vi says the Coop does about $800 in business a month, which makes $9,600 over the year. Certain families get together and place orders in bulk for things from New Zealand.

A pause in the Square after Sabbath Meeting. In their declining years, the old have seen the coming to Pitcairn of the internal combustion engine.

This spending [and here Pastor leafed through some adding machine slips] comes to a total for everybody of about $10,000 over the year. The islanders altogether also spend a few hundred dollars a year in mail-order things or big items from abroad. If you put all those items together you get a grand total of about $24,000 for the island, which makes the $2,400 tithe income just right. Exact!"

Pastor seemed pleased with the outcome of the arithmetic. His guest was also happy to get for the first time a fairly accurate picture of the island economy in, to use an overgrand phrase, the "private sector." The Pitcairn GNP then, if one excludes the fish they take from the sea, the things they grow in their gardens, and their subsidy funds from abroad, amounts to about $24,000. Divided among eighty-five islanders, this gives a per capita annual income of $282.

"The point is that Pitcairners *pay* their tithes," the Pastor continued. "I don't have to go around inquiring whether people are actually giving their 'tenth.' They know there are other kinds of 'abundance.' It's interesting here to look at what happens to Pitcairners who come back after being abroad in New Zealand or Australia or Tahiti. It takes them about six months to settle back into a Pitcairn routine. I think they then realize they gained nothing abroad. They appreciate the Bible's words that a man's life consists *not* of the abundance he possesses . . . The consumer goods they are getting now — stoves, fridges — these things are good provided physical output is kept up and fidelity to the Church remains."

The talk about tithes had taken place after a pleasant dinner at the Pastor's residence. *During* dinner, we talked, fittingly enough, about the Adventist rules covering eating and drinking. Pastor's wife had prepared a spread which, while sumptuous, was fully in accord with these strictures. There were two meatlike meatless dishes on a dainty well doilied table. The centerpiece was a platter of glutenburger "steaks" smothered with a gravy prepared with a yeast extract to give it some zest. "We are having vegetarian 'goat' tonight," said Pastor. The other "meat" dish was a plate of cold cuts, baloneylike slices cut from a loaf of soybean sausage. "A protein molecule is a protein molecule, whether it's in a piece of steak or a soybean," said Pastor. "A butcher couldn't tell the difference."

It was the first completely vegetarian meal I had ever eaten, and I am ready to concede that it was exceptionally tasty. With the glutenburgers and the soybean baloney, we had home-baked rolls, several vegetables, three salads, including a delicious combination of grated carrot and grated coconut, a choice of three fruit juices, and cakes and fruit salad for dessert. The finale, served in our honor, was coffee. As he poured it, Pastor Webster assured us that it was a nonstimulating, non-habit-forming coffee made from grain. "Ecco" was the brand name, and the Pastor got it, curiously, from a place where people eat and drink whatever they please, even strong, stimulating, addictive *espresso*. "I was surprised," said our host, "to find it is made in Italy."

Pastor told us of one occasion when, feeling a sudden malarial attack coming on, he felt he simply had to have a cup of strong real coffee. He went into a restaurant — not on Pitcairn, of course — and ordered coffee. It immediately provided the mental and physical pick-up he was looking for. "Tea and coffee are all right if taken *medicinally* at times when you need them," Pastor explained. "The trouble is they become a crutch, a habit that people lean on. The Bible tells us that we must keep that part of the brain that exercises moral control uninhibited by such things. Jesus on the cross, you recall, refused the gall and vinegar that was offered to him in his hour of pain."

Tea-drinking, he continued, was something that had grown up on Pitcairn in the last few years "with the imports." He then ticked off a list of Known Tea Drinkers on the island, with devout Christy at the top. "These people now must have their tea as a mental starter at various times of the day," Pastor commented. (There may be more Known Tea Drinkers on Pitcairn than Pastor realizes. Warren Christian, earlier that same day, had said that many of the islanders indulged in a little harmless deception by serving, whenever Pastor dropped in, not the tea they usually drink, but Ovaltine or fruit juice. In the old days, the pastors were given bran tea, which is nonstimulating and considered acceptable, because things like Ovaltine and Milo could not be imported. Christy later was to suggest to me that the *non*-tea-drinkers, his rule-book cousins who went in for various substitutes for the good stuff from Ceylon, might be the ones hurting their insides: "I've seen them pound and soak the orange leaves they pick to make something they drink and call 'orange tea.' You should look at the stain that's left in the cup. It's *blue!* Now what *that* does to their stomachs is not for me to say. Tell me where in the Bible it says that Christy shouldn't drink tea. Or eat a good piece of red meat that you can get from the ships occasionally.")

Pastor that night told us there were varying degrees of vegetarianism among his Adventist friends. He seemed to be undermining his own case at one point when he told a story of a friend who had stuck to a diet consisting largely of grain and had made himself very ill. It turned out to be ergot poisoning. Pastor's own experience with vegetarianism had been a far happier one: "I was raised on three meat meals a day in Australia until I became a Seventh-Day Adventist as a young man. I stopped it then, and I have noticed an improvement in physical output as a result of vegetarianism. Our children haven't had a bit of meat in their lives, and they're bigger and healthier than I am. (As evidence, he pointed to the wedding-day pictures placed around the room of his four sons and a daughter.)

"We are *ovo-lacto*-vegetarians," Pastor informed us as he poured another cup of Ecco and offered condensed milk to go with it. "That means we eat eggs and dairy products, although there are some stricter vegetarians who won't touch them." I asked him to enlighten us on Adventism's stand on food and drink.

"They are dietary *principles* really, not dietary *laws*," he said. "We don't regard meat-eating as a sin, particularly in a place like this where food supplies are short. It becomes a personal matter. You eat first the best things, then the second best, and so on. If you were on a desert island and there was a barrel of salt pork, which is 'unclean,' you'd eat it to live. . . . Am I upset to see the Pitcairners eating crayfish? I think it should upset *them* more than me. Crayfish is one of the things forbidden by God's word.

"We make a distinction, as the Bible does, between 'clean' and 'unclean' foods." He then launched into a quotation from the Book of Leviticus:

And the Lord spake unto Moses and to Aaron, saying unto them,
Speak unto the children of Israel, saying, These are the beasts
which ye shall eat among all the beasts that are on the earth.

We then got down to specifics — whether ducks, geese, even
swans, might be acceptable if chicken-eating did no harm — and
here the conversation got considerably more complicated. To make
sure of his facts, Pastor walked over to his desk and returned with
a well-thumbed, home-indexed little black Bible. The dinner continued with Pastor intoning from his chair at the head of the table,
the words of Leviticus 11:

Whatsoever parteth the hoof, and is clovenfooted, and cheweth the
cud, among the beasts, that shall ye eat,
Nevertheless these shall ye not eat of them that chew the cud, or of
them that divide the hoof: as the camel because he cheweth the cud,
but divideth not the hoof; he is unclean unto you.
And the coney, because he cheweth the cud, but divideth not the
hoof; he is unclean unto you.
And the hare, because he cheweth the cud, but divideth not the
hoof; he is unclean unto you.
And the swine, though he divide the hoof, and be clovenfooted, yet
he cheweth not the cud; he is unclean to you.
Of their flesh shall ye not eat, and their carcase shall ye not touch;
they are unclean to you.
These shall ye eat of all that are in the waters: whatsoever hath fins
and scales in the waters, in the seas, and in the rivers, them shall ye
eat.
And all that have not fins and scales in the seas, and in the rivers,
of all that move in the waters, and of any living thing which is in the
waters, they shall be an abomination unto you.
They shall be even an abomination unto you; ye shall not eat of
their flesh, but ye shall have their carcases in abomination.
Whatsoever hath no fins nor scales in the waters, that shall be an
abomination unto you.
And these are they which ye shall have in abomination among the
fowls; they shall not be eaten, they are an abomination: the eagle and
the ossifrage, and the ospray.

And the vulture, and the kite after his kind;
Every raven after his kind;
And the owl, and the night hawk, and the cuckow, and the hawk after his kind.
And the little owl, and the cormorant, and the great owl.
And the swan, and the pelican, and the gier eagle.
And the stork, the heron after her kind, and the lapwing, and the bat.
All fowls that creep, going upon all four, shall be an abomination unto you . . .

And so on, through two pages of Leviticus, taking in the prohibitions on weasels and mice and ferrets and lizards and snails and moles. Pastor pointed out here that swans definitely had been mentioned as unclean food. We debated what "fowls that creep, going upon all four" might be. My wife suggested the platypus, which creeps on only one continent, and that four thousand miles from Pitcairn. The Pastor wasn't sure. He had been sure a few days earlier when the entertainment committee, arranging the Maori *hangi* feast we were to have on New Year's Day, put up a notice in the Square asking "*yawley* bring along shark and crayfish for the supper." (*Yawley* is the Pitcairnese equivalent of the Deep South's "you-all.") Pastor strode up to the Square and crossed out "shark and crayfish." He explained to the schoolmaster that in an underground oven, the flavor of biblically unacceptable things from the sea would permeate the acceptable items and thus possibly give offense to the purer religionists attending the *hangi*. The young men, however, thought they *would* be putting shark and crayfish into the dirt oven until the very last minute, "You'll see," they told me. "Pastor'll let us have shark and crayfish at the *hangi*." They didn't have them. At the time of the dispute, I had asked Pastor about sharks. Might not they have *very small* scales? "Perhaps under a microscope scales might be apparent on sharks," he said, "but none that can be seen by the naked eye." Then, and again at the dinner of glutenburgers and Leviticus at Pastor's, my mind was prodded into reflecting on the complexities of the religion John Adams had taught his little mixed-breed flock from the Bible of Fletcher Christian.

In one of his best epigrams, G. K. Chesterton concluded: "Christianity has *not* been tried and found wanting; it has been found difficult and so not tried."

To many of the older Pitcairners, Christianity, and belief based on literal interpretation of the Scriptures, are not, in any way, considered "difficult." When she has finished at the Church organ accompanying a hymn at Sabbath service, Irma Christian drops to her knees in prayer in an ecstasy of devotion. Before church, Millie Christian has been singing out in the kitchen, gleeful in preliminary work in the service of the Lord. There is to be communion that Sabbath day, and it is Millie's turn to make the communion wine.

She has taken half a box of Sunmaid raisins from California and is stewing them in a pan of water. When the juice has been extracted after about an hour's boiling, the "wine" is poured into a container, minus the exhausted raisins, allowed to cool, and taken to Sabbath meeting. Millie let me take a sip. She will make the communion wafers from the same dough she rolls between her chubby hands to make the Pitcairn equivalent of breadsticks. For the wafers, she will take small dollops of the dough and flatten them with her thumb into a baking disc about the size of a Ritz cracker. Millie and the others will be attaining union with their Jesus later that day, and be mystically united again as a community, with a Eucharist sacrament of endearing plainness. There were no "difficulties," no churchly hocus-pocus for the islanders in repeating the words uttered at the Last Supper. "This is my body," they said, and knew they were nibbling leftover breadstick dough. "This is my blood," and it was the juice of raisins from the Golden West.

With solemnity, but the same disdain for frilly ritual, the ceremony of the Washing of the Feet was carried out by all the adults. For this symbol of humility, the community separated, the women going into the rear room of the church, the men crossing the Square to the courthouse. Each group was provided with metal basins, pitchers of water, and towels. Those men who had worn shoes took them off; the others simply rolled up their trousers. They paired off, one man washing and drying the feet of the man sitting across from him, then having his feet washed and dried by his pair-mate when the positions were reversed.

As part of their Eucharist sacrament, the islanders were displaying humility before God and in the presence of strangers. I thought, too, at this moment of the community's strange sense of shame from the past, a guilt-sickness over what a small group of their forebears did almost two centuries ago, but one which has proved astonishingly enduring in a remote colony. I have dealt with this sense of guilt in Part I. I shall return to it here since I discovered on Pitcairn that my views on this point were shared by the man who has twice been the spiritual leader of the community.

Pastor Webster edged into the subject one day by remarking that there were "clearly factors in the Pitcairners' past that colored their religious consciousness." I asked him to expand on that. He said that during both his stays on Pitcairn he had detected vestigial traces of guilt over a mutiny that took place in 1789. "I'm quite sure that Fletcher Christian leading that mutiny and bringing the men and women here had a guilt complex," the Pastor added. "The leader soon took to the deepest recesses of the island. And today, something of it is borne out in the personality of the people, the descendants. They may not admit it, but guilt has colored the people's thinking and conduct. There has been no firsthand information passed down from father to son. The local historians, the people who have looked into this past, have all been people from the Outside, Amelia Young, Roy Clark today, not the island-born."

The island-born today are far more interested in the heavenly future than their *Bounty* past. From this, there has evolved an attitude toward and an acceptance of death that is astonishingly matter-of-fact. The plots in the cemetery are lost to weeds, and even the most recent graves are left untended for the most part. The day after the passing, at the age of eighty-seven, of a well-loved father, Tom Christian, the pious son, was able to be the life of a party with his guitar-playing. He could even make a mild joke about it the next night when he was talking with a ham radio friend in America: "That flu hit me hard. It was a real

beast. For a time I didn't know who would make it to the box
first, Dad or me."

Happy deaths? The Pitcairners believe in the "happiness of
death" and evidently have done so over the years.

In the late 1840's, at a time of intense religious preoccupation
with such matters, a group of Americans inquired of George
Nobbs, the as-yet-unordained spiritual leader of Pitcairn, whether
there had been any instances of "extraordinary conversion" on the
island. They seemed to be fishing here for evidence of miracles in
a community whose reputation for piety was already beginning to
spread to the pulpits and sermon-writers of England, America, Europe, and Australia.

The Reverend Mr. Nobbs — he became a priest in 1852, or-
dained by the Bishop of London in Fulham Church with orders
naming him "Chaplain of Pitcairn's Islands" — penned a sermon
in answer to the American group. Its theme was "Happy Deaths":

Had inquiry been made for examples of HAPPY DEATHS, I could have
replied with unmitigated satisfaction; for I have seen many depart this
life, not only happy, but triumphant. And herein is, I think, the test
of the Christian character; for when we see a person, who for a number
of years has not only in word but in deed adorned the doctrine of God
our Savior in all things, brought by sickness or casualty to the confines
of the eternal world, about to enter the precincts of the silent grave,
yet with unabated energy and fervor proclaim his hope of a glorious
resurrection; when we see a person, suffering the most acute pain, ex-
horting and encouraging others to pursue the same path he had trod;
telling the love of God to his soul, and of his desire to depart, that he
may enter into the presence of his Redeemer; when we witness such
unwavering confidence, amid such intense sufferings; and when the
sanity of the patient is undoubted, — can we hesitate to say at the
demise of such a one, 'Let me die the death of the righteous, and let
my last end be like his!' It has been my felicity to witness several departures of this description within a few years: two from accidents, one
from a cancer in the breast, one shortly after child-birth, and one from
disease of the heart. All these died in faith.

The old among those living Pitcairners who trace their descent from Mr. Nobbs's flock have no embarrassment about tell-

ing an outsider that they are awaiting a happy and triumphant death.

I am sure the elderly islanders, as they sit and meditate on the benches in the Square after Sabbath service, are inwardly untroubled about the meaning of their life and what follows its closing. I am sure that dear Millie, as she answers the Sabbath summons of the bell in the Square and trudges alone up the hill to church through a torrential downpour, has a very practical idea of heaven, of a life in an eternal Hereafter where there is no hauling of buckets from stone well to rusty bathtub, where there are no "chooks" wandering fifty times a day into her dining room and leaving their droppings on the rough floorboards for her to scrape up, where the mud and dust and long days of toil on Pitcairn are finally behind her.

CHAPTER TWENTY

A PAST TO BE FORGOTTEN

I F THERE WERE frustrations in my research gathering on the island, they were solely in the historical area, in my probing for handed-down legends or documents from the last century that might throw some light on the mutiny itself and on the mental attitude toward it of those generations of Pitcairners closest to the event.

So far as historical facts are concerned, I came away with few more than I had carried to Pitcairn in my head and in a box of books and photostated historical documents. There are occasions, though, when a *lack* of folk legends, a *lack* of those community records that go beyond simple statistics, are significant clues in examining something controversial that happened long ago; certainly not as valuable as hearing the father-to-son tales or perusing the written record in old papers, but useful nonetheless in their very negative contribution.

Pitcairn today offers the outside researcher no real folk legends from its earliest days and very little in the way of physical relics and mementos of its origin. The islanders are hiding nothing. Apart from a few pieces of iron, copper, or bronze, they simply don't exist. Might father-to-son storytelling once have been the custom, only to be obliterated by the descending ones in a society growing away from its past? The evidence suggests not.

The situation is that there is an appalling gap between the amount of knowledge about the mutiny, about Bligh and Christian, that would have arrived on the island in the heads of nine mutineers in 1790 and the amount that was circulating by the time the first sons born on the island came of age. Remember here that one mutineer lived in their midst until the children of mutiny were almost forty.

The earliest British and American visitors to the colony discovered this gap. I had felt at one point that these men simply may have been poor interrogators, poor probers, whose feelings of sympathy for the struggling little community suppressed the questions they should have been asking. Some might have been, but most were not; Captain Beechey in 1825 was a particularly thorough investigator. Although they were dealing with bright young men and women who had been raised in an intimate society, who had lived all their lives in close association with a survivor of the mutiny party, the first visitors learned virtually nothing new or hard about the revolt itself. Once the decision was taken to allow him to remain on Pitcairn, John Adams was in the comfortable position of telling his callers only as much as he wished to disclose. Those first visitors came away with colorful accounts of the progress that had been achieved by a strange band of devoutly Christian mixed-breeds seeking the goal of human perfection. The grown children, the visitors found, knew the name William Bligh, knew there had been a row over some "cocknuts" aboard a ship called the *Bounty* and that the vessel had been brought in some irregular fashion to Pitcairn, but that is about all.

John Adams had provided his flock with none of the details. Nor did Midshipman Edward Young, whose children would have reached the age at which they could appreciate stories of their heritage well before his death in 1800.

One theory I heard on the island was that Adams' silence was a reflection of the fact that he had no one to talk to; no one, that is, of his own age group and background. But in his prime years, Adams was dealing with twenty- and thirty-year-olds. They were mentally alert and would have a natural curiosity about the past of a Patriarch who was obviously different from the lot of them. There was no language barrier — they spoke a dialect with their darker-skinned mothers or grandmothers, but with Adams they spoke English on a par with his own, the English he had taught them.

My belief is that Adams, from deep-seated guilt, told them very little and no more. If any written records had been left in addition to Young's sketchy diary, Adams saw that they were destroyed before they could reach the hands either of the Royal Navy or the members of his own flock. The old Patriarch imparted to them too little knowledge to form a pool for folk legends and, in the course of his intense religious instruction, just enough transmitted guilt to make the acquisition of those legends seem unattractive. There was no substantial Pitcairn folklore then about the *Bounty*, the mutiny, and Fletcher Christian, and consequently there is none today.

Inherited guilt remains an important element in the Pitcairn psyche. After all these years, the people living on Pitcairn now are still a bit ashamed of the men they are descended from and the circumstances in which the colony was founded. This sense of shame is marked in the older ones, less apparent in the young men and women who have been educated by teachers from outside the island. That any shame or guilt exists at all, in any age group, I find most curious. English families who have proof that one of their forebears was a pirate on the Spanish Main take some pleasure in seeing that this fact is entered faithfully on the family tree. An American would make no bones about the fact that he is descended from Jesse James; the chances are that he would do whatever he could to cash in on the blood link. Contemporary Australians who trace their origins back four or five generations are quite forthright in acknowledging that a forebear or two probably arrived in Botany Bay or Port Phillip in convict chains from England.

Isolation, and the smallness of their community, have kept the inhabitants' guilt alive on Pitcairn. The outside world's interest in them has nourished it from time to time. And certainly intense religious instruction has done nothing to lighten the unjustified burden of shame.

The present Pastor is satisfied that most members of his congregation regard their origins as "dishonorable history." He suggested that anyone who doubted this might inspect John Adams' grave, the only known burial site of any of the mutineers who died on the island. (The surviving mutineers did not bother to erect even simple markers to their sailmates as, one by one, they came to brutal ends on Pitcairn. Was this further evidence of the initial guilt?) But Adams' place of burial is recorded because he held a special place in a colony of innocents he raised to manhood. Although this grave is only a short walk from Warren's and Millie's house, it was several days before I found where it was. The grave is at the end of an overgrown trail that starts behind one of the houses at a small pen made of tree branches for the householder's domesticated goats. The trail is not marked in any way, but this is hardly surprising since tourists very rarely come ashore. There are actually three graves here, the resting places of Adams, his wife, and one of their daughters, but only the Patriarch's has a headstone:

Sacred
To the Memory of
MR. JOHN ADAMS
Who Died March 5th 1829
Aged 65 Years.
IN HOPE

The lettering is still decipherable because photographers from time to time have rubbed chalk into the chiseled inscription to bring out the wording. I appreciated the "Mr." that Adams — "Reckless Jack" as he was once known — had been given on his marker. In the founding years, there had been only two "Mr.'s" on the island, *Mr.* Christian and *Mr.* Young, the only two "gentlemen" members of the mutiny party. The others were called by surname without social rank — "Quintal" or "Brown." Posthumously, John Adams became a "Mr." His tombstone was broken in two at some period but has been roughly cemented together. Grass is growing over the grave, and there are only wild flowers. This is certainly not an island shrine. The Pastor suggested that the unkempt condition of Adams' grave was significant.

"If it could be forgotten, they wouldn't mind," he told me.

John Adams' grave marker. In death, he became a "Mr."

"And as for a museum, you can't find hardly a relic from the *Bounty*."

All outsiders who spend any time with the Pitcairners are astonished to find that the story of the *Bounty* and the mutiny is not taught in the course of history classes at the island school. The most relevant bit of history in the world for these people is intentionally left out of the curriculum. It was not taught when the islanders were educating their young themselves, and the community does not feel it should be taught by others, now that education is in the hands of nonislanders. It is not a case of the visiting teachers being told, "Don't include the *Bounty* story when you're talking history." Rather they acquire this sense of what the community wants by an osmotic process. "Several of them [the older Pitcairners] came to me in my early days and made it clear that the children were already 'bored by the *Bounty* yarn,'" said one of these outsiders who had taught on the island. Hollywood's efforts at explaining the mutiny were good enough for the Pitcairners.

The anniversary of the mutiny, April 28, is ignored on Pitcairn. Once, in a radio talk with Tom, I reminded him that we had just passed the anniversary of Fletcher's revolt. "Oh, was it?" he replied. "No, we didn't celebrate it. In fact, no one mentioned it. It was quite overlooked. But I'll mention it around."

Also ignored is the anniversary of the mutineers' landing on Pitcairn, January 15. The day they *do* celebrate, with enthusiasm that varies by degree from year to year, is January 23, the anniversary of the *burning* of the *Bounty*. The Pitcairners have selected for the "Bounty Day" not the date on which their community got its start, but the calendar day on which the founding fathers destroyed the vessel which had carried them there.

And they celebrate this anniversary today in a way which, psychologically, may be interesting. They burn a replica of the *Bounty*. The *Bounty* model, about six feet long, is a rough affair made by lashing together the dried trunks of banana palms, fashioning sails out of the large leaves, and filling the hull with dried pandanus so it will burn well. It is floated in Bounty Bay and set afire by members of the entertainment committee to the cheers of the islanders. We left Pitcairn just before January 23, 1972, and so missed Bounty Day in Bounty Bay. But Tom Christian provided a report in his weekly contact with the Adventist radio station in Glendale, California: "Sunday was filled with water sports — boat races using oars and outboard motors, swimming events, and other games. And much food. 'Bounty Day' is the only day of the year when we take a backward look at what happened to our fore-fathers. We don't look back on those times much."

When you ask the islanders to look back on these times and give their own interpretation of why their forefathers mutinied, the answers do not suggest that any deep thought has been given to the whole subject. Three fairly typical answers I got from the descendants, each a man of some standing in the community, were these:

— "It was all in that Charles Laughton film. It was the cruelty of Bligh. He liked to see blood on the men. All that whipping in the film! If I'd been Fletcher, I couldn't have put up with it. It went too far. I would've done the same thing as Fletcher did. . . . But that's not to say we have any *grudge* against Bligh."

— "Oh, it was the row over the coconuts. Our Fletcher was a good man, well, a fairly good man, and Bligh said he had been stealing more coconuts than he was entitled to."

— "It was all in the book* by those two American fellows. What were their names again? Of course, I don't know if it's *true* or not. No one here really has strong feelings on it."

The astonishing conclusion is that an American or British high school student who has been assigned to read as part of a summer study course the celebrated book by "those two American fellows" knows more about the story and the protagonists than the very ones who trace their descent from the whole adventure.

Long ago, visiting officials of the British government detected

---

* *The Mutiny on the Bounty*, by Charles Nordhoff and James Norman Hall (Boston: Little, Brown, 1932). Also, by the same authors, *Men Against the Sea* (1934), and *Pitcairn's Island* (1934). These books must be read with the knowledge that they are fictionalized treatments — among the finest we have in romances of the sea — within the historical framework. As the reader who is familiar with the Nordhoff and Hall *Mutiny* will realize, Part I of this book takes issue on many points with their interpretation of the events and the respective characters of the men who brought them about.

John Christian and one of his $20 models of the square-rigger his great-great-grandfather pirated. His model in re-creating the *Bounty* — a plastic toy from a Chicago factory.

in the islanders both an ignorance of their own past and a total lack of interest in its tangible relics. As a result, all of the precious documents of Pitcairn's past, including the *Register of Pitcairn's Island* and the Pitcairn *Book of Records,* have been moved for safekeeping to archives elsewhere. The *Bounty* Bible is the only major exception. Some photostatic copies of early records exist on the island, and these were made available to me for my study. What few records are left in the hands of the Island Government are all photostats of the originals in vaults abroad.

The islanders are left with the *Bounty* anchor, which is too heavy to be carried away as a souvenir, the ship's anvil, one of her axes, some rudder pintles, ballast bars, and sheathing nails. Virtually all the artifacts of Pitcairn's earlier civilization, the Polynesians who had departed mysteriously long before the mutineers came, have also left the island in one way or another. One item had a narrow reprieve. An islander who hacked free one of the three carved Polynesian idols in a coastal cave, thinking it might fetch a good sum on a ship, was obliged to cement it back in place.

A move was made some years ago to start a small "museum" in Adamstown. It ended in disaster and left the island with actually *fewer* relics than it possessed before the idea was suggested. With the inspirational push being provided by an outsider, the community set up a large glass case in the church and invited families to contribute pieces of *Bounty*ana. For a month or two, the glass case contained an impressive collection. But the odd visitor, including some who should have known better, approached the glass case as a show window of historic merchandise that could be bought wholesale. If an outsider were interested in a piece, he could track down the owner from the information on its tag and make a private deal to acquire it. Vi McCoy, who was entrusted with the *Bounty*'s anvil and ax at the death of her husband, Floyd, told me she saw how the case was being emptied and decided to rescue her pieces. The ax and the anvil, the latter minus its point after a century and a half of constant use, are now in safekeeping in Vi's home.

Their *Bounty* past interests them really only when it has a contribution to make to the curio trade.

The most prolific, if not the best island carver of models of the *Bounty* is seventy-six-year-old John Christian, a former Island Magistrate. He turns out nine-inch-high models for $20, foot-high ones for $25, and super versions that run as much as $50. He mails them to dealers and private collectors in the United States, adding $5 apiece for the postage. One collector in New Jersey has bought eight of John's copies of the ship. They are attractive, if rather primitive examples of the art of model ship building. He bends and paints scraps of tin for the sails, uses tiny shells as the blocks for the running rigging, and encases each model in a display box painted a curious shade of powder blue.

The night I interviewed John amidst a litter of wood, rasps, knives, glue, brushes, and paint, he had seventeen completed models of the *Bounty* on hand and three more were nearing completion. I bought one of the $20 models and complimented him on his productivity. "It's not bad really for an old man who has lost the sight of one eye and has a cataract on the other," he said. With this knowledge, I was even more impressed by his output. If need be, this frail old man, almost blind, could turn out two or three models of the *Bounty* in a week.

We talked about the mutiny, and John said he was ashamed to say it but actually he knew not too much about the revolt or even about the ship his ancestors had landed from. He acknowledged that he had acquired his own history from Charles Laughton and Metro-Goldwyn-Mayer. In any event, he did not feel the historical background was all that important. "Just because we come from Fletcher Christian and them, doesn't mean we have to *be* like them. If you make up your mind to be the *best* people, you can be the *best*," he said. It was rather well put.

The most prolific carver of *Bounty* models was working on the rigging of a $25 model as we chatted. With a charming smile, he admitted that in all the years he had been carving the ship, he didn't know where the great cabin was, how the small boats were stowed on deck, where the events of the mutiny had taken place, or where the breadfruit trees were kept. He did, however, have the right number of sails on each mast — three, rather than the four MGM gave its expensive replica to make it more photogenic.

I asked John what design he worked from in developing his *Bounty* replicas, hoping he might produce a yellowing sketch or a painting done from memory by one of his predecessors, or, lacking those, perhaps some shred of folklore.

"You'll laugh probably when you hear this," said John, "but my design was taken from a plastic '*Bounty*' toy that came here, oh, quite a few years ago. It was made by some toymaker in America. Chicago? Yes, Chicago, I think."

CHAPTER TWENTY-ONE

OVER THE HORIZON, GROUND ZERO

T HE FRENCH CLAIM their possession of nuclear bombs and other weapons of mass destruction will greatly assist in maintaining liberty in the world, and that therefore it is essential for them to carry out the proposed tests. . . . The people of Pitcairn are living in fear of what the future holds for their island. Why should we, a helpless handful of people, be swept aside like straws in the wind?

At about the same time Pitcairn was being settled by Fletcher Christian and his party, in France, a woman, Mme. Roland, was being led to be executed. As she approached the guillotine she cried out, "O Liberty! What crimes are committed in thy name!" This could easily be the cry of Pitcairn today.

Those editorial words appeared in the June, 1963, issue of the *Pitcairn Miscellany*, the mimeographed sheet of island happenings that is produced once a month at the schoolhouse, written by the schoolmaster or his wife, and is the closest thing Pitcairn has to a newspaper. The threat anticipated in the editorial became a reality three years later when France detonated her first nuclear device in the Pacific and General de Gaulle expensively gave his nation the *force de frappe* he had promised.

The test site selected, the island of Mururoa, is 530 miles to the northwest of Pitcairn, which places the residents of Adamstown on the fringe of the danger zone. Also in this category are several hundred inhabitants of Mangaréva and the southern islands of the Tuamotu Archipelago. All these latter islands belong to France and contain no indigenous protest industries to challenge the right of men in Paris to let off thermonuclear devices in the atmosphere. Pitcairn is the sole non-French community in the area, and French politicians and nuclear scientists had to take this into account in selecting Mururoa as their Ground Zero. It was not to prove a stumbling block of any consequence.

The editorial bleat in the *Pitcairn Miscellany*, some letters written to London and Auckland, and concern expressed to the occasional visitor have been the only protests to emanate from Adamstown over the fact that, for four months of each year, the air they breathe, the land they till, and the seas they fish are poisoned to an unknown degree by the worst contaminants known to man. Pitcairners have learned to live with the Bomb in their backyard. "We are not happy about the tests," says Tom Christian. "But what can we do. We are so small, only a handful of people. I believe Australia and New Zealand have made protests against the French decision to go on testing in the air, but we on Pitcairn have not submitted any official complaint. Would they pay any attention if we did? What would our protest mean?"

John Christian, seventy-six, who was Island Magistrate when the French started their nuclear tests, had the major responsibility of deciding whether Pitcairn should fire off a diplomatic protest to Paris by way of London. The decision was to do nothing, that a resolution expressing the will of ninety-odd souls would be ignored on the conference tables of the mighty. It might even be regarded as a trifle impertinent or fatuous. "By why should we, a helpless handful, be swept aside," said John one day as he paused in his serial production of $20 and $25 models of the good, non-nuclear ship *Bounty*. "Surely somewhere in the hearts of the French authorities, there must be a feeling of guilt that through their actions people are having their freedom to live as they wish taken from them."

The protests that are voiced now during each test season — the months from June to September — are addressed in prayer to the Almighty. Sometimes, almost as if by divine arrangement, the explosions occur at particularly dramatic, particularly apposite moments for those more serious-minded ones on the island who have pondered their grim message.

In June, 1971, I was in radio touch with the island three days after the Pitcairners had heard and felt what they guessed was the mightiest bomb France had detonated in five years of testing. The blast came on a Saturday, and most of the islanders were gathered in the little white church when the reverberating sound wave rolled over Pitcairn. The fabric of the church shook, the plain window glass rattled, the very pews they were sitting in trembled. "It was at twenty-two minutes until the noon hour, right in the middle of our Sabbath service, when the sound of the explosion swept over Pitcairn," said Tom over his ham radio transmitter. It was perhaps the loudest sound ever heard on an island where violent, man-made noises are few and far between. "It seems to take about forty-five minutes for the sound wave to reach us from Mururoa. Heads turned 'round in the church because we don't often *hear* that kind of sound on Pitcairn. But the service continued, and we simply put our trust in the good Lord, as we have in the past when other tests were conducted, that He would watch over our people."

While there is resignation today, there was some panic that first year Pitcairn heard the atomic bangs. Several of the old people had their bags packed, their most precious items of furniture crated, ready to leave. Their neighbors urged them to stay, to take their chances with the other members of the cousin-family. And, as so often happens, the wish of the community prevailed.

There was one bad moment in 1970 when the islanders thought there may have been a nuclear miscalculation and the French Navy had been sent to carry off the population temporarily to a safer spot. "As the fallout cloud was drifting toward Pitcairn," the schoolteacher recalled, "a French frigate arrived to join a Royal Navy ship that was standing off Bounty Bay. We were right in the line of fire — the French no longer seem to wait for the perfect [weather] conditions. We were uncertain for a time whether the French ship was there to take us off if something serious had gone wrong. Both ships eventually sailed off and we stayed."

On another occasion, the Royal Navy thought it might have an evacuation mission to perform. A day after the French had exploded a bomb suspended beneath a balloon released from Mururoa, a Norwegian ship was passing by Pitcairn. As it came abeam of Adamstown, the captain decided to salute the islanders by setting off some flares. The pyrotechnics were seen by a British frigate steaming on a fallout-monitoring run some thirty miles from Pitcairn. Thinking that the flares might be distress signals from the islanders, the captain swung off his course and headed at flank speed for Bounty Bay. He was relieved to find there was no emergency. For their part, the islanders were happy to be offered an unexpected opportunity to peddle some more curios.

Both Britain and the United States use Pitcairn as a shore base from which to monitor the French tests in addition to the monitoring carried out aboard warships and by patrolling aircraft. Two RAF technicians arrive each June with boxes and instruments, and the Royal Navy comes back to collect them and their data when a test season is over. Two or more American monitors, with larger boxes of instruments and unnecessary quantities of C rations, arrive and leave on much the same schedule. The RAF men's findings are sent back to Whitehall, and the results of the American monitoring go to the Department of Defense and the Atomic Energy Commission in Washington. There they remain, as the secret garnerings of allies who eavesdrop on each other's nuclear business. The Pitcairners, who understandably would like to know what has been injected into their atmosphere, are never given a look at the formal results of the monitoring. They do, however, get an occasional informal peek as the monitoring proceeds, and what they see is less than reassuring.

With the casualness of manner that the British military services have been known to display in approaching matters of some technical complexity — casual, that is, in comparison with American military methodology — the RAF monitors set up their Geiger counters and other instruments in the small woodworking room attached to the schoolhouse. The American monitors carry their instruments up to the highest point of the island, the ridge above Palva Walley, establish a small base there, and operate in conditions of far greater secrecy than do the RAF pair. The islanders speak of the large and mysterious mirrors the "Yanks" erect on the Palva ridge and point at Mururoa, as if they were under orders from Washington to attempt to bounce back to the Pentagon each flash of nuclear light from each French fireball. One time, an officer came ashore in civvies from a French warship and wanted to climb up to Palva Walley to see what the Americans were doing there with their mirrors. The Island Council said No, sorry, he couldn't. It didn't seem right. "But the Frenchie *did* succeed in going up the Walley to take a look at the Yanks and their big mirrors," an islander confided to me.

Since the British instruments are set up on school premises, the schoolteachers are in a position to get a sneak look at the monitoring procedure. As laymen, however, they are not capable of interpreting the findings, deducing their radioactive implications. Nor, for that matter, are the monitors themselves. The RAF men are simply technicians operating instruments and keeping a log of how high the needles move on various scales. Yet schoolteacher Russell Henry saw and understood enough to convince him that the islanders should be showing greater concern than they do about living on the edge of an atomic danger zone.

"There is concern on the island already that the tests are not being monitored properly," he told me, "not properly at least in the sense that we are always kept in the dark about the results. After each round of tests, you hear complaints here about skin diseases. Vula had a particularly bad rash after last year's tests, and I had some skin trouble on the top of my head. Whether this is seasonal or has something to do with atmospheric testing, I don't know. But we should be told more than we are about what the monitoring detects. As a father, I worry about the effects this will have on my children."

The RAF technicians had told Henry when they were setting up their fallout-measuring gear that "if we get a reading of twenty on this one, we could be in trouble; that's the time we'll have to get out and do something." The teacher was with them in the woodworking room one day when the Geiger gauges began recording in an area which Henry felt was uncomfortably close to the twenty mark. He doesn't recall the exact level.

"It had rained all night and all day after this test, and the rain was coming from the direction of Mururoa," he said. "I was watching one of the instruments that the RAF monitor said should have been clicking once every nine seconds. It was really rattling away. It must have been clicking thirty or forty times a minute.

The monitor came in and said to me, 'Things are not too good. We should do something.' What we *should've* done was to tell people to wash their fruit, to wash down the public square where the children play, to start wearing shoes, to use only water that was collected before the rain came with the radioactivity, and take other sensible precautions. I had got into the routine of taking out the downpipe from the school tank whenever we knew that a test was about to be conducted. Some of the islanders do the same with their own wells and also see they have bottled water on hand so they don't have to rely on rainwater after a test. Some keep their bags packed in case they have to leave in a hurry. Roy was packed. Vi had her bags ready. But they are the exceptions. On that day, the day the instrument was clicking away thirty or forty a minute, we talked about what we should do, whether the Island Council should make some sort of announcement, but we decided there was really nothing we *could* do. Only a few had bottled water. Any water the island in general would be using to wash food, or wash down the square, would be water that had fallen through the fallout. No solution. What was the point of alarming the people?

"The French say that any radioactivity from the rain will have decayed after four days. But the American monitor who came here talked about strontium 90 having a 'life' of a hundred years. We are the ones it concerns most and we are kept in the dark."

Was the agitation among the islanders on that occasion such that a squeak of protest might eventually be heard from Pitcairn? The schoolteacher doubted it: "The attitude of the people is to do nothing. They don't want to say anything that might offend the French. They don't want to do anything that might stop the ships coming to Pitcairn."

Tom had said he doubted whether the French Government would pay any heed to a complaint from the Pitcairners. He went on to remark that "anyway, the folks quite like to see the ships around. The French ships come on goodwill visits and there are Royal Navy ships and American vessels around for the tests. It gets quite busy here. The men from the ships purchase carvings and that always pleases the folks here."

Since the annual French test season had ended three months before our arrival on the island, I did not have an opportunity to observe firsthand the way the islanders react to the explosions. There were seven in 1971. An eighth blast was scheduled but called off, the explanation being that the big seventh bang provided enough information to make the eighth redundant. The impression I got from the islanders was that the June-to-September test period brings a much-needed note of worldly festivity to Adamstown. There are young strangers, the monitors, boarding in several homes, the men have new trading outlets, the boys can swap something for an exotic French T-shirt, and while ordinary shipping bypasses that area of the Pacific during the test months, there are military vessels dropping by, even, once, a chopper landing next to the Adamstown burying-ground from one of the modern French Navy helicopter-carriers. It was sad, though, to realize that the island came by this festivity bonus for the worst possible reasons, that a few of the island young actually looked forward to the arrival of June and the start of another round of atmospheric testing. Sad, too, to think that the health and child-bearing of some of these young conceivably might be impaired by the very same governmental action that was bringing a little outside excitement temporarily into their lives. But what was particularly distressing was the discovery that the community hesitated to raise its little voice in the matter, that it effectively had become a victim of self-intimidation. To draw unnecessary additional attention to the Mururoa tests might scare away shipping that would otherwise call at Bounty Bay.

As I was completing these pages, a letter arrived from our island host. The envelope bore the jaunty Pitcairn eight-cent stamp — a painting of a longboat braving the surf, with the Queen's crowned head in profile in the upper-right corner. The mail had taken the usual unconscionable length of time. I recognized Warren's deliberate hand and the black ink. The major piece of island news was that the community was getting ready to receive the RAF monitors for another test season. "We hope that everything will be OK," Warren remarked of the coming thermonucleonics. "We will only have to wait and see what will happen."

ACKNOWLEDGMENTS

M Y MAJOR DEBT is to the people of Pitcairn, both for their kindnesses and for their cooperation in practical ways which permitted me to carry out this study. I am indebted also to my newspaper, to Lord Hartwell, editor in chief of the Daily Telegraph of London, and to the editors of the publications in the Telegraph group, for granting me a sabbatical to undertake the journey to the island. I must acknowledge, too, the additional chores my colleagues handled while I was away from my New York desk for three months.

I wish to thank the officers and staff of the Seventh-Day Adventist radio station, the Voice of Prophecy, in Glendale, California, for the short-wave radio facilities they put at my disposal before, during, and after the Pitcairn stay; M. Jacques Briquet, an airline executive in Papeete, Tahiti, who assisted me greatly in overcoming logistical and bureaucratic hurdles; Captain Gildas Le Guen, M. Bernard Moitessier, and the crew of the ketch Maylis for getting us to Bounty Bay through a nasty sea; Qantas Airways for travel assistance over more conventional stretches of the Pacific; Dr. Joseph Owen of New York City, who took on for me the tricky assignment of posthumously psychoanalyzing William Bligh and Fletcher Christian; Mr. Paul Peralta-Ramos of New York City, who made available to me the rich resources of his private library; and Mr. Philip Jones Griffiths of Magnum

Photos and Tom Christian, who made available the photographs of contemporary Pitcairn.

Finally, I wish to thank my wife for her research assistance and for sparing me some of the transcribing work on the island; and our three children for obediently carrying out parental orders. Just before we landed on doctorless Pitcairn, we instructed them not to come down with appendicitis, contract exotic diseases, or break any bones during the weeks ahead. They didn't.

INDEX

Elphinston, Mr., 34
Endeavour, 10, 42, 61, 72
Endeavour Straits, 55, 91
Esmeralda, 166
Evans, John, 120, 206

Falconer's Marine Dictionary, 60
Fat's House, 250
Fiji, 165, 294, 300, 301
Five-Month Starve, 168, 195
Flattie, 150
Flogging. *See* Corporal punishment
Fly, H.M.S., 308, 309
Folger, Mayhew, 113, 117–119, 136
Food: on *Bounty*, 27–28, 70–73; and
    Pitcairners' religion, 124, 125, 132,
    167–168, 225, 260, 304, 338–342;
    abundance of, 139–140; for party,
    176–177, 249; attitude toward, 181,
    230–232; Christmas, 259–260
France, 42, 89; and England, 13, 118;
    and Haiti, 41; and Pitcairn, 144;
    nuclear tests, 155, 188, 217, 286,
    289, 357–363
Fremantle, Capt., 144
French Revolution, 9, 73, 118
Friendly Islands. *See* Tonga
Fromm, Erich, 327
Fryer, John, 17, 27, 69, 70
Fulham Church, London, 345

Gable, Clark, 46, 56, 284
Gambier Islands, 8, 120, 149
Games, 249–255
Gates, Elder and Mrs., 128
George III, King, 5, 17, 23, 64, 155
Gibraltar, 18
Gibson, Dr. David, 232
Gibson, Sam, 61
Glendale, Calif., 151, 276, 353
Government, Pitcairn, 312–313, 314–316
Graham, Billy, 332
Great Barrier Reef, 38
Great Britain, 52, 214, 250; impor-
    tance of breadfruit project, 41, 42;
    and Spain, 69; war with France,
    118; and Pitcairners' religion, 125;
    moves Pitcairners to Norfolk Is-
    land, 144; and Pitcairn stamps,
    164, 297–299; sex ratio, 184; life

expectancy, 200; and French nu-
    clear tests, 360
Guayaquil, Ecuador, 238, 240

Haiti, 41
Hallet, Mr., 35
Harwood, Edward, 53
Hawaii, 5, 41, 228
Hawkesworth, Dr. John, 10; *Hawkes-
    worth Voyages*, 102
Hayden, Levi, 165
Hayes, Charlotte, 10
Hayward, Thomas, 35, 61
Headache, 150
Health: of sailors, 72; of evacuated
    Pitcairners at Tahiti, 142, 143; of
    Pitcairners, 200, 232, 301
Hefner, Hugh, 215
Henderson Island, 178, 259, 297
Henry, Russell, 183; comments on
    Pitcairn, 195–197, 225–227; leaves
    Pitcairn, 238–239, 244; traffic reg-
    ulation, 269; and nuclear tests, 359,
    361–362
Heywood, Peter, 31, 39, 54, 55, 112
Hill, Joshua, 119–122
Hill of Difficulty, 159, 240
Historical Society of Connecticut, 165
Holland, 13
Homosexuality, 57–58
Hong Kong, 334
Hood, Lord, 38
Hough, Richard, 57
Howard, Trevor, 48
Howe, Lord, 18
Huggan, Thomas ("Old Bacchus"),
    27, 53, 73, 94
Hull, England, 13

Iddeeah, 58
Illegitimacy, 207, 216–217, 321
Imogene, H.M.S., 123
Inbreeding, 199, 202, 203, 204–210
Indian Ocean, 60
Infant mortality, 201
Internal Committee, 269, 312
Isaac's Rocks, 289
Island Council, 269, 272, 273, 276,
    300, 307, 312, 327, 361, 362
Island Court, 326, 327–328

Voice of Prophecy, 276, 281
Voters, Pitcairn, 308–309

Waldegrave, Capt. W., 132, 136, 216
Wallis, Samuel, 9, 29, 78
Wapping, England, 87
Warren, Agnes Christian, 188, 205
Warren, Anderson, 163, 229, 265, 335
Warren, Christy, 169, 193–194, 195, 203, 219–220, 229, 245, 319, 339, 340; as candidate, 307–308
Warren, Mima, 159, 170, 194
Warren, Morris, 220, 224, 257, 265, 301, 311
Warren, Samuel, 188, 206
Warren family, 188, 258
Washington, George, 9
Webb, Clement, 61
Webster, Pastor L. A. J., 167, 168, 183, 217, 220, 229, 253, 258, 264, 303; on dancing, 222–223; described, 329–330; on tithe system, 336–338; dinner and diet, 338–342; on Pitcairners' guilt, 344, 349–350
Wellington, N.Z., 196, 272
West Indies, 12, 17, 19, 22, 32, 41, 42, 60, 75, 89, 123
Where Freddie Fall, 4, 153
White, James, 124
White Cow's Pen, 323
Wilkinson, C. S., The Wake of the Bounty, 112
William's Block, 323
Williams, John, 37, 102, 105, 106, 188
Wolf, Archibald, 61
Women: of Tahiti, 30–31, 45, 46, 79–80, 84–85, 86–88, 93, 285; of Pitcairn, 127, 159, 207, 184, 185, 309

Wood, Lt., observations of Pitcairners, 199–200
Wordsworth, William, 139
World War I, 194
World War II, 94, 97, 158
Wrongdoing, 270–271, 325–328, 330

Yankee, 164
Young, Allison, 291
Young, Amelia, 344
Young, Daryl, 264, 272, 328
Young, Donald, 290
Young, Edward, 37, 51, 54, 55, 73, 99, 101, 111, 150, 205, 206, 267, 348, 350; diary accounts, 105, 109, 113; wife, 108; and Tahitians' uprising, 108, 109; education of Adams, 131; silence about mutiny, 139; descendants, 293
Young, Glenda, 290, 293
Young, Henry Hugh, 291, 312
Young, Hilda, 179
Young, Marona Estell ("Pussy"), 272, 274, 313
Young, Moses, 205
Young, Norris Henry, 185, 211, 291
Young, Norris Joseph ("Noggie"), 169, 235; described, 290–295
Young, Pamela, 291
Young, Pervis, 189, 225, 235, 258, 264, 288, 327, 328, 335; and author's landing, 152, 153, 155, 157; and the AE (EA), 240, 241, 243–245; cricket game, 250, 252, 253; described, 267–274; on economy, 302, 304; and elections, 310–312
Young, Robert, 274
Young, Rosalind Amelia, 152, 247
Young, Theodore, 159, 185
Young, Vernon, 270, 310, 311, 326
Young family, 187, 188, 205, 258
Young's Rocks, 150

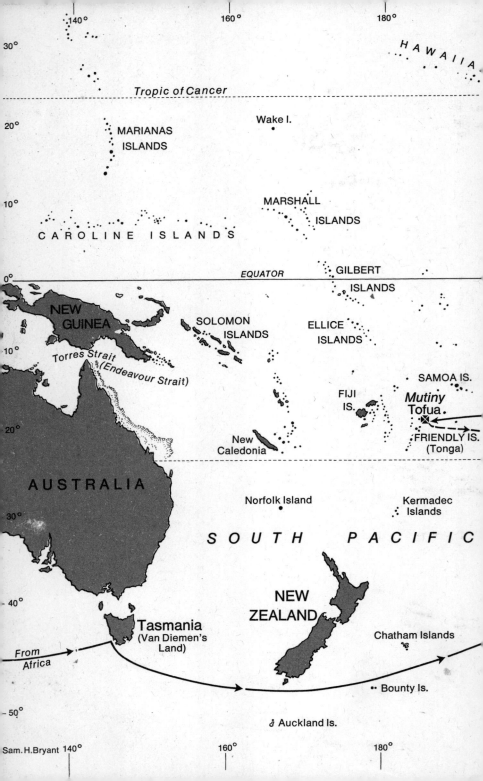